Richard Kuntschke

Network-Aware Optimization in Distributed Data Stream Systems

Richard Kuntschke

Network-Aware Optimization in Distributed Data Stream Systems

Sharing Data Stream Contents and Processing Results in Distributed Environments

VDM Verlag Dr. Müller

Impressum/Imprint (nur für Deutschland/ only for Germany)

Bibliografische Information der Deutschen Nationalbibliothek: Die Deutsche Nationalbibliothek verzeichnet diese Publikation in der Deutschen Nationalbibliografie; detaillierte bibliografische Daten sind im Internet über http://dnb.d-nb.de abrufbar.
Alle in diesem Buch genannten Marken und Produktnamen unterliegen warenzeichen-, marken- oder patentrechtlichem Schutz bzw. sind Warenzeichen oder eingetragene Warenzeichen der jeweiligen Inhaber. Die Wiedergabe von Marken, Produktnamen, Gebrauchsnamen, Handelsnamen, Warenbezeichnungen u.s.w. in diesem Werk berechtigt auch ohne besondere Kennzeichnung nicht zu der Annahme, dass solche Namen im Sinne der Warenzeichen- und Markenschutzgesetzgebung als frei zu betrachten wären und daher von jedermann benutzt werden dürften.

Coverbild: www.purestockx.com

Verlag: VDM Verlag Dr. Müller Aktiengesellschaft & Co. KG
Dudweiler Landstr. 99, 66123 Saarbrücken, Deutschland
Telefon +49 681 9100-698, Telefax +49 681 9100-988, Email: info@vdm-verlag.de
Zugl.: München, TU, Diss., 2008

Herstellung in Deutschland:
Schaltungsdienst Lange o.H.G., Berlin
Books on Demand GmbH, Norderstedt
Reha GmbH, Saarbrücken
Amazon Distribution GmbH, Leipzig
ISBN: 978-3-639-10262-8

Imprint (only for USA, GB)

Bibliographic information published by the Deutsche Nationalbibliothek: The Deutsche Nationalbibliothek lists this publication in the Deutsche Nationalbibliografie; detailed bibliographic data are available in the Internet at http://dnb.d-nb.de.
Any brand names and product names mentioned in this book are subject to trademark, brand or patent protection and are trademarks or registered trademarks of their respective holders. The use of brand names, product names, common names, trade names, product descriptions etc. even without a particular marking in this works is in no way to be construed to mean that such names may be regarded as unrestricted in respect of trademark and brand protection legislation and could thus be used by anyone.

Cover image: www.purestockx.com

Publisher:
VDM Verlag Dr. Müller Aktiengesellschaft & Co. KG
Dudweiler Landstr. 99, 66123 Saarbrücken, Germany
Phone +49 681 9100-698, Fax +49 681 9100-988, Email: info@vdm-publishing.com
Copyright © 2008 VDM Verlag Dr. Müller Aktiengesellschaft & Co. KG and licensors
All rights reserved. Saarbrücken 2008

Printed in the U.S.A.
Printed in the U.K. by (see last page)
ISBN: 978-3-639-10262-8

Abstract

The management of streaming data in distributed environments is gaining importance in many application areas such as sensor networks and e-science. This is mainly due to both, the need for immediate reactions to important events in input streams as well as the requirement to efficiently handle enormous data volumes that are generated, for example, by modern scientific experiments and observations. At the same time, data needs to be accessible by various collaborative, often geographically distributed communities and sciences. In this thesis, we address the above issues by introducing a model and a prototype implementation of a distributed data stream management system (DSMS), and by devising network-aware optimization techniques for efficient resource usage in terms of computational load and network traffic in such a system. We use the term StreamGlobe to denote both, the theoretical model of our DSMS as well as its actual prototype implementation. The prototype serves as a research platform for evaluating our optimization approaches which are at the core of this thesis. We further use an application-specific astrophysical flavor of StreamGlobe called StarGlobe to demonstrate the applicability and effectiveness of distributed stream processing in an actual astrophysical e-science scenario.

Scarce resources such as computational power and network bandwidth limit the number of continuous queries a DSMS can handle concurrently. Making intelligent and efficient use of these valuable resources is thus mandatory in order to offer the best service possible to users. We achieve this goal by introducing data stream sharing, an optimization technique based on in-network query processing and multi-subscription optimization. In-network query processing enables us to distribute continuous query processing in the network while multi-subscription optimization allows us to share data streams for satisfying multiple similar queries. Thus, data stream sharing allows for efficient resource usage and provides a potential increase in the number of queries a distributed DSMS can process concurrently with the available resources.

The effectiveness of data stream sharing depends on the existence of streams in the network that are suitable for sharing. If the available preprocessed result streams of previously registered queries do not contain all the necessary data required by a new query, sharing must resort to using the corresponding original streams to satisfy the new query. To alleviate this problem, we develop data stream widening, a technique that is able to alter existing streams to additionally contain all the necessary data for a new query. We introduce an abstract property tree (APT) and its extension, an abstract property forest (APF), for representing, matching, and merging queries and data in a distributed DSMS to enable the combination of data stream sharing and data stream widening. The improved representation of queries and streams allows for a more effective optimization and additionally supports a larger class of queries.

Data stream widening requires the treatment of disjunctive predicates. However, traditional query optimization largely neglects the handling of such predicates. We therefore devise, compare, and discuss methods for matching and evaluating disjunctive predicates in the context of data stream sharing and data stream widening. The presented approaches are generic and thus applicable to other domains as well. Altogether, data stream sharing, data stream widening, and the methods for handling disjunctive predicates add up to a powerful optimization approach for continuous queries over data streams in a distributed DSMS such as StreamGlobe.

Contents

List of Figures

List of Tables

List of Algorithms

CHAPTER 1

Introduction

In recent years, data management systems increasingly face new challenges that call for a paradigm shift from processing persistent data to processing data streams. Evolving data management applications, e. g., in e-science, e-health, and e-business, increasingly require support for stream-based processing of experimental, observational, and monitoring data. On the one hand, the reason for this demand lies in the requirement to analyze the most up-to-date information as soon as it arrives in order to be able to take immediate action if necessary. On the other hand, certain application domains are confronted with the problem of handling data volumes that are growing at exponential rates. The sheer masses of data and their quick growth have started to make traditional data analysis approaches increasingly useless in the respective communities. Instead of collecting, storing, and subsequently analyzing the data, stream-based data processing can help to perform processing and analysis tasks on-the-fly while data is being collected or generated.

Examples for the requirement of immediately processing most current data on arrival are alerter services in e-science, e. g., in astrophysics. These alert researchers of interesting events such as gamma ray bursts[1] or other kinds of energy fluctuations during experiments and observations. In e-health, examples comprise bedside patient monitoring as well as the newly evolving field of mobile home-based patient monitoring, which alert physicians to initiate rescue measures if a patient's vital signs reach critical values. Radio frequency identification (RFID)[2] is an example from the e-business domain that recently sparked great interest in both, research and economy. RFID is of special importance for supply chain management as it allows the automated monitoring of supply chains on various granularity levels—from containers to pallets to single product items—during each step of the chain, from manufacturers to suppliers to vendors and customers. The data delivered by RFID readers forms continuous data streams that require efficient handling and processing.

The problem of large and exponentially increasing data volumes is especially crucial for

---

[1]See, for example, the Gamma Ray Burst Coordinate Network (GCN) at http://gcn.gsfc.nasa.gov.
[2]See, for example, [Bornhövd et al. (2005)].

astrophysics[1], as Alex Szalay, an astrophysicist from Johns Hopkins University, emphasized in a talk given at TUM in summer 2005. Focusing on e-science in general, it can be observed that scientific experiments and observations in many fields, e. g., in physics and astronomy, create huge volumes of data which have to be interchanged and processed. With experimental and observational data coming in particular from sensors and online simulations, the data has an inherently streaming nature. Furthermore, continuing advances will result in even higher data volumes which makes storing all of the delivered data prior to processing increasingly impractical. Hence, in such e-science scenarios, processing and sharing data streams will play a decisive role. It will enable new possibilities for researchers, since they will be able to subscribe to interesting data streams of various sources without having to set up their own devices or experiments. This results in much better utilization of expensive equipment such as telescopes and satellites. Further, processing and sharing data streams on-the-fly in the network helps to reduce network traffic and to avoid network congestion. Thus, even huge streams of data can be handled efficiently by removing unnecessary parts early on, e. g., by early filtering and early aggregation, and by sharing previously generated data streams and processing results.

The challenges described in the previous paragraphs fuel the need for *data stream* management systems (DSMSs) for processing streaming data. DSMSs complement traditional *database* management systems (DBMSs) used for handling persistent data. The striking difference between DBMSs and DSMSs consists in the fact that in DBMSs, data is persistent and queries are volatile, i. e., one-time queries arriving in the system are processed over a persistent set of data and disappear after processing has finished. In DSMSs, however, persistent queries are executed over volatile, i. e., streaming, data. Persistent queries are also called standing or continuous queries in the literature.[2] In this thesis, we use the term *continuous queries* throughout. We propose a model and a prototype implementation of a distributed DSMS called *StreamGlobe*. The system architecture is based on aspects known from Grid computing and Peer-to-Peer (P2P) networking. StreamGlobe serves as the basis for investigating network-aware optimization techniques for enabling efficient resource usage in such an environment.

Efficiency is a very important aspect in the design of a DSMS. Since data streams usually require real-time or near real-time processing, any DSMS must be concerned with efficient algorithms for stream processing and with optimization techniques for making the best use of potentially scarce resources such as memory and processing power. Furthermore, since data and queries often emerge at various places, many actual DSMSs are inherently distributed, e. g., for managing a distributed supply chain or for enabling e-science collaborations among various research institutions that are spread across the globe. This thesis puts the focus on logical network-aware optimization of continuous queries in a distributed DSMS. Similar to traditional logical optimization, e. g., reordering operators in a logical algebra operator tree, we are concerned with the appropriate placement of stream-based query processing operators on distributed network nodes. However, our optimizations take place at the query level rather than at the algebra operator level. Our guideline is to reduce computational load and network traffic on network nodes and network connections in a distributed DSMS by means of *data stream sharing*. We thus aim at sharing data streams and processing results among multiple similar queries in a network whenever this is possible and seems reasonable. Physical optimization on the intra-operator level such as choosing an appropriate evaluation algorithm for a certain logical operator focuses on optimizing actual query processing at a single node. Previous work in this direction by Stegmaier (2006) forms the basis of local query processing in our setting.

---

[1]See, for example, [Szalay et al. (2000)].
[2]See, for example, [Terry et al. (1992)] and [Golab and Özsu (2003a,b)].

The data stream sharing approach is based on multi-query optimization (MQO) as introduced by Sellis (1988). While, due to its complexity, multi-query optimization has not gained too much importance in the area of DBMSs for which it was originally conceived, it has been identified as an important optimization technique for DSMSs. Babcock et al. (2002), for example, state that

> *"In data stream applications, where most queries are long-lived continuous queries rather than ephemeral one-time queries, the gains that can be achieved by multi-query optimization can be significantly greater than what is possible in traditional database systems."*

Referring to the adaptive Eddy query execution framework [Avnur and Hellerstein (2000)] they go on to say that

> *"[...] to adapt the joint plan for a set of continuous queries as new queries are added and old ones are removed remains an open research area."*

Investigating a similar issue in the context of StreamGlobe is one of the primary objectives of this thesis.

Golab and Özsu (2003a,b) identify two approaches for executing similar continuous queries together: sharing query plans and indexing query predicates. In this thesis, we adopt the former approach. However, we also consider query predicate indexing in the context of predicate matching and predicate evaluation for data stream sharing in Chapter 6.

As mentioned before, the shift from persistent data to streaming data also brings about changes in the notion of queries. We take a closer look at the differences in the next section.

1.1 System and Query Type Classification

DSMSs have very special demands with respect to query processing and optimization. To better understand what these demands are and to compare them to those of other data management systems, we introduce a generic system and query type classification in Figure 1.1. This classification is inspired by a talk given by M. Tamer Özsu at the EDBT 2006 conference.

We classify data management systems with regard to the two dimensions query complexity and throughput. Query complexity denotes the expressiveness of the employed query language. Query languages at the high end of the spectrum allow for complex nested queries with user-defined functions and predicates while languages at the low end only allow for rather simplistic queries, e. g., containing only simple built-in predicate filters. In terms of throughput, we differentiate between systems and query types enabling high data throughput in query processing, i. e., many data items per time unit can be evaluated against a query, and those inducing a comparatively slower evaluation.

We distinguish between three different types of data management systems. These comprise traditional DBMSs, stream-based DSMSs, and publish&subscribe (pub&sub) systems. Each of these systems is based on its own typical type of queries. In traditional DBMSs, queries are usually short-lived one-time queries that may enter the system at any time and disappear after they have been completely processed over the persistent data of the current database state. Query languages like SQL[1] for relational databases and XQuery[2] for XML[3] databases allow users

---

[1] See, for example, [Melton and Simon (2002)].
[2] See [W3C (2007d)].
[3] See [W3C (2006a,b)].

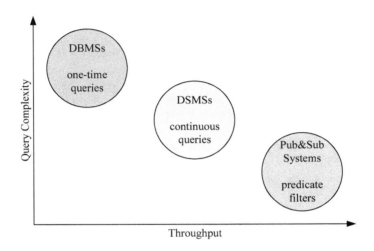

Figure 1.1: System and query type classification

to formulate very complex queries and provide extensive support for user-defined application logic. XQuery, for example, basically constitutes a turing-complete functional programming language that also incorporates some non-functional concepts such as explicit iteration using `for` loops. On the other hand, publish&subscribe systems optimize for excessive throughput of data items, processing event streams with high data rates against large sets of simple, usually predicate-based subscriptions using sophisticated index structures. Compared to traditional DBMSs, publish&subscribe systems clearly trade query complexity for increased throughput.

As we can see from Figure 1.1, DSMSs are situated between traditional DBMSs and publish&subscribe systems in our classification in terms of both, query complexity and throughput. Query complexity tends to be lower in DSMSs compared to DBMSs since certain types of queries would be too slow or not meaningful over streaming data. Consider a nested-loops algorithm over infinite input streams for example. But DSMSs still have higher demands in terms of query complexity than mere predicate or event filtering as employed in publish&subscribe systems. Considering the other dimension of our classification, throughput requirements in DSMSs tend to be higher than in traditional DBMSs since stream processing must be able to keep up with reasonably high input stream rates. However, the increased query complexity in DSMSs limits their throughput compared to publish&subscribe systems.

Summarizing, we may say that DSMSs try to find a compromise between sufficiently expressive and flexible query languages on the one hand and reasonably high data stream processing rates on the other hand.

1.2   Contributions and Outline

In this thesis, we present methods for network-aware optimization of continuous query processing over data streams in a distributed DSMS. We focus on optimizing resource usage in terms of computational load and network traffic. Our investigations are based on a theoretical DSMS model named StreamGlobe which we have also put into practice as a prototype implementation. We have further augmented this implementation with domain specific application logic from the field of astrophysics to demonstrate its effectiveness in an actual e-science environment. Based on the StreamGlobe model and prototype, we develop and evaluate *data stream sharing* as a valuable optimization approach to reduce computational load and network traffic in a distributed DSMS. We go on to augment this optimization technique with *data stream widening* and its complement *data stream narrowing* to achieve even better results and applicability. Finally, we take an in-depth look at efficient predicate handling in the context of the above solutions. Altogether, the techniques introduced in this thesis form a solid optimization framework for efficient resource usage in a distributed DSMS such as StreamGlobe.

In detail, the contributions of this thesis and its outline are as follows:

Chapter 2 – The StreamGlobe Distributed Data Stream Management System

introduces the architecture of the StreamGlobe system. StreamGlobe is a model as well as a prototype implementation of a distributed DSMS that serves as our research platform. We describe the architectural basics of StreamGlobe, the peer architecture, and the network organization. StreamGlobe forms the basis and defines the setting for the optimization techniques developed and presented in this thesis. We have implemented the basic StreamGlobe architecture and all our optimization techniques in the prototype implementation. The prototype serves as a proof of concept and as a basis for empirical performance evaluation studies.

We have previously presented parts of this chapter at the *1st International Workshop on Data Management for Sensor Networks (DMSN 2004)* [Stegmaier et al. (2004)], at the *GI Workshop Dynamische Informationsfusion (Informatik 2004)* [Stegmaier and Kuntschke (2004)], and in an article in the *Datenbank Spektrum* [Kuntschke et al. (2004)].

Chapter 3 – The StarGlobe System: An Astrophysical Flavor of StreamGlobe

presents a domain- and application-specific extension of StreamGlobe focused specifically on supporting certain common data-intensive tasks in astrophysics. We introduce the astrophysical challenge, describe the deficiencies of current solutions, and subsequently explain how StarGlobe helps to overcome them. A performance evaluation substantiates the impressive performance gain achieved by StarGlobe as compared to conventional solutions and emphasizes that the StarGlobe approach provides a valuable computing platform for e-science applications.

We have previously presented parts of this chapter at the *2nd IEEE International Conference on e-Science and Grid Computing (eScience 2006)* [Kuntschke et al. (2006)].

Chapter 4 – Data Stream Sharing

introduces the *data stream sharing* optimization technique. We start this chapter with an illustrative example, a high-level description of the general problem, and our idea for solving it. We then continue with the formalization of data streams and data windows in the context of this thesis. Next, we introduce *WXQuery*, our XQuery-based subscription language for continuous queries over XML data streams which constitutes an augmented fragment of XQuery. The core of the chapter subsequently introduces our approach for enabling data stream sharing based on query and stream properties, a cost function for evaluating query plans, and the actual data stream sharing algorithms dealing with selection, projection, and aggregate queries. Finally, a performance evaluation shows the benefits of data stream sharing compared to the traditional approaches of data shipping and query shipping.

We have previously presented parts of this chapter at the *2nd International Workshop on Pervasive Information Management (PIM 2006)* [Kuntschke and Kemper (2006a)] and have given a system demonstration at the *31st International Conference on Very Large Data Bases (VLDB 2005)* [Kuntschke et al. (2005b)]. Further, parts of this chapter have appeared in *Lecture Notes in Computer Science, Vol. 4254 (LNCS)* [Kuntschke and Kemper (2006b)] and as *Technical Report TUM-I0504* [Kuntschke et al. (2005a)].

Chapter 5 – Advanced Data Stream Sharing: Matching and Merging Queries and Data

describes a formal model for translating WXQueries into an abstract property tree representation used for matching and merging queries and data streams. Matching the property tree of a newly arriving query with that of an existing stream determines whether the stream is reusable as input to the query. If the query and the stream do not match, merging their property trees results in a new property tree. The new tree describes the unified stream that covers all the contents of the original stream as well as the data additionally needed by the new query. Query templates allow the translation of abstract property trees back into corresponding queries. These can be installed in StreamGlobe to create a widened data stream that additionally satisfies the demands of the new query. We introduce this *data stream widening* approach for selection, projection, and aggregate queries. Subsequently, we extend our solution to support window-based join queries over data streams. After describing the necessary extensions to the StreamGlobe model and implementation for supporting data stream widening and its complement data stream narrowing, we assess the effectiveness of widening by means of some performance experiments using our StreamGlobe prototype implementation.

Chapter 6 – Matching and Evaluation Strategies for Disjunctive Predicates

addresses the issue of efficiently handling disjunctive predicates in the context of data stream sharing and data stream widening. Disjunctive predicates can be created as a result of data stream widening and need to be dealt with during the further matching of queries and data streams as well as during query evaluation. In this chapter, we start by introducing our notion of disjunctive predicates and by describing the problems of predicate matching and predicate evaluation. We then continue to introduce several algorithms for solving the predicate matching problem for disjunctive predicates. We describe two efficient heuristics and an exact solution. After dealing with predicate matching, we turn our attention to the problem of efficiently evaluating disjunctive predicates in a DSMS. We describe a simple iteration-based algorithm as well as an index-based evaluation approach that provides for increased evaluation performance. The introduction of the algorithms concludes with a detailed complexity analysis and a comparison of the presented matching and evaluation algorithms. Finally, an extensive performance evaluation empirically confirms the findings of this analysis.

We have previously presented parts of this chapter at the *15th ACM Conference on Information and Knowledge Management (CIKM 2006)* [Kuntschke and Kemper (2006c)] and as *Technical Report TUM-I0615* [Kuntschke and Kemper (2006d)].

Chapter 7 – Conclusion and Outlook

summarizes the thesis and provides an outlook on further interesting research challenges in the area of network-aware optimization in distributed DSMSs.

CHAPTER 2

The StreamGlobe
Distributed Data Stream Management System

The StreamGlobe distributed DSMS constitutes the foundation on which we build our network-aware optimizations presented in later chapters of this thesis. We use the term StreamGlobe to denote both, the theoretical model of the DSMS as well as its actual prototype implementation which serves as a research platform for evaluating our optimization approaches.

2.1 Introduction

To enable the data stream sharing optimizations which are at the core of this thesis, we use a combination of *Peer-to-Peer (P2P) networking* and *Grid computing*[1] techniques. P2P has gained lots of attention in the context of exchanging persistent data—in particular for *file sharing*. In contrast, we apply P2P networks for the dissemination of individually subscribed and transformed data streams, allowing for *data stream sharing*. By using the computational capabilities of peers in the P2P network, we can push data stream transforming operators into the network, thus enabling efficient *in-network query processing*. This yields a reduction of network traffic, enables load balancing among peers, and improves flexibility since any peer can register arbitrarily complex queries by delegating query processing to other peers in the network. At the same time, *multi-subscription optimization* allows the sharing of data streams and the reuse of computational results among various peers. This provides for both, reduced network traffic and decreased computational load on peers. Ultimately, more subscriptions can be processed concurrently with the available resources. We propose StreamGlobe as a DSMS model and prototype to meet these challenges. The StreamGlobe implementation adheres to established Grid computing standards and thus fits seamlessly into existing e-science platforms. To ensure interoperability, StreamGlobe is built on top of standards such as XML and XQuery for representing data streams and specifying subscriptions.[2]

---

[1] See [Foster and Kesselman (2004)].
[2] The terms *query*, *continuous query*, and *subscription* are treated as synonyms throughout this thesis.

In detail, we present the following contributions in this chapter:

- We introduce an example application scenario from the astrophysics domain which serves as an illustrative example for our solutions throughout the thesis (Section 2.2). The scenario consists of a simple example network topology and an actual astrophysical example data set which we use as input data stream in the system. Chapters 4 and 5 introduce some example queries over this data.

- We describe the architecture of StreamGlobe concerning network architecture, super-peer architecture, thin-peer architecture, optimizer integration, external operator integration, and network organization. We further briefly introduce the StreamGlobe prototype implementation.

2.2   Example Application Scenario

The following astrophysical e-science scenario serves as an illustrative example for the application of StreamGlobe throughout the thesis. Consider Figure 2.1 which illustrates an exemplary StreamGlobe network. We classify peers in a StreamGlobe network as *super-peers*[1] and *thin-peers*, also simply called *peers* in the following. Super-peers usually are powerful stationary servers providing extensive query processing capabilities and forming a stable *super-peer backbone* network. In contrast, thin-peers are less powerful, possibly mobile devices used to register queries and data streams in the system. In the example network of Figure 2.1, SP_0 to SP_7 are super-peers constituting the super-peer backbone network and P_0 to P_4 are thin-peers. P_0 is a satellite-bound telescope that detects photons and registers a data stream called photons at super-peer SP_4. This data stream contains real astrophysical data collected during the ROSAT[2] All-Sky Survey (RASS) [Voges et al. (1999)] which we obtained through our cooperation partners from the Max-Planck-Institut für extraterrestrische Physik[3].

StreamGlobe deals with streams of XML data. The example stream photons complies to the DTD shown in Figure 2.2. As its name implies, the data stream delivers a stream of photons detected by a satellite's photon detector. Each photon in the data stream is represented by an XML element photon that incorporates the coordinates of the corresponding photon (coord), the pulse height channel, i. e., the detector pulse caused by the photon when hitting the detector (phc), the photon's energy in keV (en), and the time of its detection in seconds since the start of the observation (det_time). The coordinates consist of the celestial coordinates of the position in the sky where the photon was detected (cel) and the coordinates of the detector pixel where the photon actually hit the detector (det). Celestial coordinates comprise the right ascension (ra) and declination (dec) of a point in the sky, measured in degrees. Detector pixel coordinates contain the two-dimensional coordinates of the respective pixel on the detector plain (dx, dy).

Figure 2.3 visualizes the astrophysical example data set. The data set contains an extract of the RASS data collected by the ROSAT satellite during its mission in the 1990s. Figure 2.3(a) illustrates the data distribution in terms of the celestial coordinates right ascension (ra) from $0°$ to $360°$ and declination (dec) from -90° to +90°. The band of data in the figure reflects the flight path of the ROSAT satellite in earth orbit during data collection. Figure 2.3(b) shows the same data in terms of the detector pixel coordinates dx and dy. The data distribution in this

---

[1] See [Yang and Garcia-Molina (2003)].
[2] http://wave.xray.mpe.mpg.de/rosat
[3] http://www.mpe.mpg.de

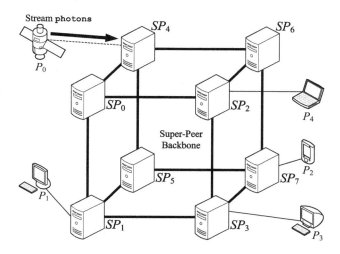

Figure 2.1: Example DSMS scenario

figure reflects the shape of the photon detector. Figures 2.3(c) and 2.3(d) visualize the energy of the detected photons in terms of their celestial coordinates and their detector pixel coordinates, respectively. From Figures 2.3(a) and 2.3(c), we can clearly see an increased concentration of highly energetic photons in an area around a right ascension of 135° and a declination of -45°. These are photons from the Vela supernova remnant. Figure 2.4 takes a closer look at a small subset of the Vela region. The upper part of the figure shows all the photons detected in this area on the right and their energy distribution on the left. The dense concentration of photons with relatively low energy values does not allow to recognize any further structures in this area. However, if we filter out all photons with energy values below 1.3 keV as shown in the lower part of the figure, a new egg-shaped structure becomes visible. This structure constitutes the RX J0852.0-4622 supernova remnant [Aschenbach (1998)] which was discovered only through this kind of selective data analysis. This simple example illustrates how the appropriate

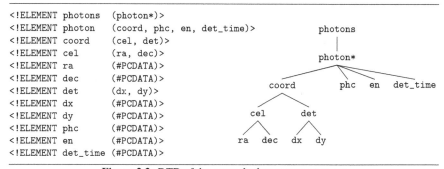

Figure 2.2: DTD of the example data stream photons

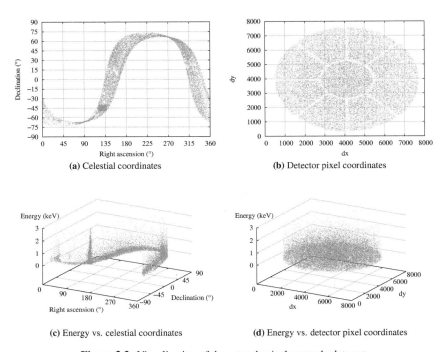

(a) Celestial coordinates

(b) Detector pixel coordinates

(c) Energy vs. celestial coordinates

(d) Energy vs. detector pixel coordinates

Figure 2.3: Visualization of the astrophysical example data set

processing and analysis of scientific data can help to gain new insight and research results.

For simplicity, we consider only one single data stream in our example. However, it is also possible to register multiple data streams at one or more super-peers in the network. Also, while each element in the example DTD except for the photon element occurs exactly once, more complex DTDs with varying element occurrences ("?", "+", "∗", "|") are also possible and can be handled accordingly.

Peers P_1 to P_4 in the example network of Figure 2.1 are devices of astrophysicists used to register subscriptions in the network referencing the available data stream as input. Subscriptions are registered using *WXQuery*, our XQuery-based subscription language that we introduce in detail in Chapter 4. Our example queries use the example data set introduced above and focus on the Vela and RX J0852.0-4622 areas of the data sample.

2.3   StreamGlobe Architecture

The following overview introduces the basic architecture of the StreamGlobe distributed DSMS including network architecture, super-peer architecture, and thin-peer architecture. Further, we describe the integration of the optimizer component and of the support for external operators within the StreamGlobe architecture and discuss three alternatives for organizing the network

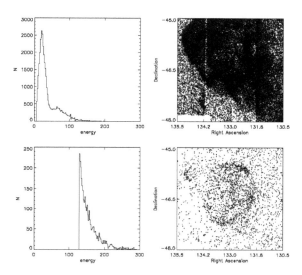

Figure 2.4: The RX J0852.0-4622 supernova remnant

of a distributed DSMS. Eventually, we briefly introduce our StreamGlobe prototype implementation. Figure 2.5 shows a generic overview of the StreamGlobe architecture.

2.3.1   Network Architecture

As described in the previous section, the StreamGlobe network architecture is based on the concept of *super-peer networks* as introduced by Yang and Garcia-Molina (2003). Consequently, we distinguish between super-peers and thin-peers in StreamGlobe. The P2P aspect of StreamGlobe consists in the fact that each peer in the network can act as a client and as a server at the same time. Super-peers, for example, may receive data streams from neighbor peers, process the received streams, and subsequently forward and therefore serve them to other neighbor peers. Likewise, thin-peers may act as servers by delivering data streams to the super-peer backbone network and as clients by registering subscriptions referencing available streams at a super-peer in the backbone. Further common aspects of P2P systems such as mobility of peers and churn play a subordinate role in StreamGlobe since we consider the backbone network and its super-peers to be stationary and stable. Due to the volatile characteristics of streaming data and the problem of imminent data loss, handling data streams in a P2P network with lots of churn is far more difficult than handling file exchange. Furthermore, dealing with node failure is beyond the scope of this thesis.

Super-peers in StreamGlobe are implemented as collaborating Grid services as described in Section 2.3.2 below. Since current Grid middleware platforms do not provide any means for data stream transfer, we implemented our own StreamGlobe Transfer Protocol (SGTP) for requesting and delivering streams across peer boundaries using TCP/IP socket connections. Thin-peers act as interfacing components for registering and subscribing to data streams in the super-peer backbone network. We take a closer look at the actual interface in Section 2.3.3.

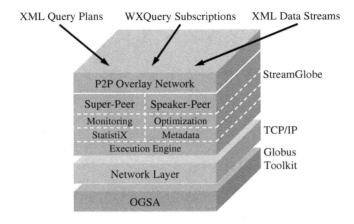

Figure 2.5: StreamGlobe architecture

The super-peers of the overlay backbone network are connected according to some topology. The contributions presented in this thesis are independent of the actual topology used. Therefore, we do not elaborate on this issue any further. For the validity of our approach it is, however, important that there is a reasonable relation between the P2P overlay network we consider and the underlying physical network. The optimization of network traffic and peer load in the overlay network must yield a corresponding optimization benefit in the physical network. This implies, for example, that topological neighbor peers should also be geographically close. An important question in this context is how to construct the overlay network on the basis of an existing physical network in order to achieve such a reasonable relation. Among others, Ratnasamy et al. (2002) have already examined similar problems. However, this issue is beyond the scope of this thesis.

2.3.2 Super-Peer Architecture

As already mentioned above, super-peers in StreamGlobe are implemented as collaborating Grid services running on top of a Grid middleware. We use the Globus Toolkit[1] implementation of the Open Grid Services Architecture (OGSA) introduced by Foster et al. (2005) for this purpose. As Figure 2.5 shows, the peers of the overlay network sit on top of the Globus OGSA implementation and the TCP/IP network layer used for data stream transfer between peers. Super-peers also communicate with each other via the remote procedure call mechanisms of the Globus Toolkit to exchange control messages and metadata. This communication basically consists of web service calls using the Simple Object Access Protocol (SOAP)[2]. Each super-peer offers a facility for continuously monitoring its current computational load and the incoming and outgoing network traffic on all of its network connections in the P2P overlay network. Furthermore, the so-called StatistiX component of a super-peer is responsible for collecting statistical information about original XML input streams registered at the respective peer. The collected data comprises the average frequency of data items arriving on the stream

---

[1]http://www.globus.org
[2]See [W3C (2007a)].

and the average sizes and occurrences of all the XML elements contained in these data items. The optimizer needs this information for estimating the data rates of result data streams in generated plans. These constitute a vital cost function parameter for estimating the costs induced by a certain plan. We introduce the details of the StreamGlobe cost model in Chapter 4.

StreamGlobe allows multiple super-peer services to run in a simulated environment on a single physical machine. This is convenient for testing and for demonstration purposes. In normal operation, each super-peer service runs on its own physical machine. A hybrid mode of operation allows to mix super-peers running exlusively on a single machine with super-peers sharing their physical machine with other super-peers in a simulated environment.

2.3.3 Thin-Peer Architecture

Thin-peers can connect to a StreamGlobe super-peer backbone network and may join or leave the network at any time. When joining the network, a thin-peer registers itself at any super-peer in the backbone and subsequently forwards all of its requests, e. g., for registering a new data stream or a new subscription, to the super-peer it is associated with. The super-peer then initiates the appropriate handling of the request as described in the next section.

We use XML scenario files to build up the super-peer backbone network and to register streams and continuous queries in StreamGlobe. Scenario files describe the network topology and specify data streams, queries, and the super-peers where to register them. Appendix A.1 on page 177 shows a small example scenario file. Appendix A.2 on page 181 contains the XML Schema definition of scenario files.

2.3.4 Optimizer Integration

In the StreamGlobe super-peer backbone network, one of the super-peers takes the role of the so-called *speaker-peer*. In addition to its normal super-peer duties, the speaker-peer runs a metadata management and optimization component that is responsible for executing all of the optimization logic that we develop and introduce in this thesis. A super-peer receiving a stream or query registration request from an associated thin-peer forwards this request to the speaker-peer responsible for the backbone network. The speaker-peer subsequently updates its metadata repository to reflect the changes in registered streams and queries. When registering a new query, the optimizer component of the speaker-peer generates various alternative distributed XML query evaluation plans for the query and compares them according to a cost function. Evaluating the cost function requires current monitoring and statistics data that the speaker-peer requests and retrieves from the monitoring and statistics components of the affected peers via Globus Grid service calls. Finally, the execution engine distributes the best plan found to the affected peers in the backbone network and executes it. The execution engine is a local component of each super-peer.

Query evaluation plans have a recursively nested structure where each subplan contains the local plan of a certain super-peer as well as all the subplans the local plan depends on and that need to be installed at neighbor peers. The speaker-peer starts the plan distribution by sending the complete plan to the root peer of the plan hierarchy which is the peer that registered the corresponding query. The execution engine of this peer extracts and removes the local subplan from the overall plan and asynchronously sends the remaining subplans to the corresponding neighbor peers which proceed with their local plans in the same manner. When the installation of all subplans at neighbor peers returns successfully, the execution engine of the local peer synchronously installs and starts executing the operators specified in its own local plan, using the now available result streams of any neighboring subplans as inputs. Appendix A.3 on page 186 shows an example of a distributed query evaluation plan for installing query q_1 introduced in Figure 4.2 of Chapter 4 in the StreamGlobe network of Figure 2.1. Appendix A.4 on page 190 contains the XML Schema definition for distributed query evaluation plans in StreamGlobe.

Due to the human-readable XML format of query evaluation plans, it is also possible to write such plans manually. The StreamGlobe client interface offers a component that allows to install manually written plans directly in the system, thus bypassing the query interface and the optimizer component. This is useful for being able to execute plans with special operators and logic that are not yet supported by the query language or the optimizer component. This feature also allows full control over the structure of the plans to be installed and executed in the system. We use this facility in Chapter 3 to enable the execution of highly domain-specific astrophysical application scenarios in a special astrophysical flavor of StreamGlobe called StarGlobe.

2.3.5   External Operator Integration

In addition to the interface for manually written query plans, StreamGlobe also offers a convenient interface for easily integrating arbitrary user-defined operators to provide maximum flexibility. The interface consists of a special stream processor implementation that entirely encapsulates streaming XML serialization and deserialization and offers a simple push-based iterator interface to implementers of user-defined application-specific operators. The iterator interface provides the common `open`, `next`, and `close` methods. The `open` and `close` methods serve for initializing and cleaning up the iterator before and after the iteration as in a usual pull-based iterator. The `next` method of the push-based iterator differs from the `next` method of a conventional pull-based iterator in that it has a single parameter that represents the next element in the iteration. Stream sources push the next element arriving in the stream into the operator by calling the operator's `next` method with the corresponding element as a parameter.

Figure 2.6 shows a schematic view of the StreamGlobe external operator integration. The stream processor receives and appropriately preprocesses the XML input streams via stream handlers. It also serializes the operator result to the XML output stream via an appropriate stream writer. The stream processor is an internal component of StreamGlobe. The stream iterator is the only part that a developer of external functionality must implement to integrate an external operator. Each stream iterator is required to implement the push-based iterator interface described above. Thus, the implementation of a simple three method interface allows for the addition of powerful user-defined application logic to StreamGlobe. At the same time, the details of XML stream serialization and deserialization are hidden from the implementers of such domain-specific operators. This makes StreamGlobe easily extensible even for non-experts with respect to StreamGlobe internals such as users from the e-science and astrophysics application domains. StreamGlobe loads user-defined operators as mobile code from a code archive which can be located either in the local file system or on a remote web server which we denote as a *function provider*. Loading and executing user-defined mobile code raises security issues which are beyond the scope of this thesis. Braumandl et al. (2001) have already addressed security issues concerning mobile code in distributed environments in the context of the *ObjectGlobe* system. ObjectGlobe is a precursor of StreamGlobe dealing with distributed query processing over persistent relational data on the Internet.

We have used the StreamGlobe external operator interface to create the domain-specific StarGlobe system for astrophysical applications introduced in Chapter 3. The StarGlobe sys-

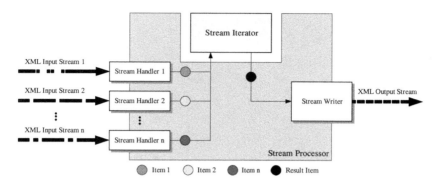

Figure 2.6: StreamGlobe external operator integration

tem differs from StreamGlobe solely through the addition of various user-defined astrophysical operators that can be used for building and executing actual astrophysical workflows.

2.3.6 Network Organization

Since the speaker-peer is a centralized component in the StreamGlobe super-peer backbone network, the question of scalability arises. In principle, there are three possibilities for organizing the network with the necessary speaker-peer functionality:

- The simplest solution is a *centralized* approach where one super-peer takes the role of the speaker-peer for the entire backbone network. In this case, the speaker-peer has a global view on the network. The speaker-peer therefore has access to all the necessary metadata information about streams, queries, monitoring data, and statistics needed for managing the system and for optimizing newly registered queries. However, this approach obviously does not scale since the speaker-peer would become a bottleneck in a growing network with an increasing number of peers, streams, and queries.

- At the other end of the spectrum, a *fully distributed* implementation of the speaker-peer functionality would solve the scalability problem. In this solution, each super-peer adopts a part of the speaker-peer functionality and communicates with other, usually neighboring super-peers to obtain necessary metadata from remote sources. While this approach eliminates the central bottleneck, it causes a lot of communication overhead between super-peers which is counterproductive when optimizing for resource usage.

- Due to the shortcomings of the first two approaches, a *hierarchical* network organization is the most promising solution in practice. Figure 2.7 shows an abstract illustration of such a hierarchical network organization for an arbitrary network topology. The network organization is divided into several hierarchy levels. The lowest level (Level 0 in Figure 2.7) represents the entire P2P overlay backbone network. This network is divided into subnets indicated by circles around sets of peers in Figure 2.7. The number of levels in the hierarchy depends on the actual size of the overall network and on the subnet sizes. The filled black super-peers in Figure 2.7 are speaker-peers having a global view on their respective subnets, i. e., each subnet chooses one of its super-peers as its speaker-peer.

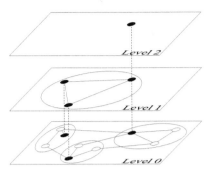

Figure 2.7: Hierarchical network organization

Each speaker-peer is responsible for performing local optimizations within its subnet. On the next level of the hierarchy (Level 1 in Figure 2.7), only the speaker-peers of the level directly below are visible. These form a reduced network that is again divided into subnets. In the example of Figure 2.7, Level 0 consists of three subnets with three super-peers each, while Level 1 consists of a single subnet containing the three speaker-peers of Level 0. The subnets of Level 1 are handled just as those of Level 0, i. e., they again choose one of their super-peers as the speaker-peer responsible for optimizing that subnet. In the next hierarchy level above, again only these speaker-peers remain visible. Finally, the top-level in the hierarchy (Level 2 in Figure 2.7) contains only one super-peer which is the root of the entire network hierarchy.

As long as the speaker-peer of a subnet discovers shareable versions of requested data streams in its own subnet, it can make local optimization decisions. In this case, the complete optimization can be performed on an intra-subnet level and no inter-subnet communication is necessary. Otherwise, i. e., if the speaker-peer cannot find a shareable local version of a data stream requested by a new subscription, the speaker-peer contacts the speaker-peers of the neighboring subnets via the virtual neighborhood relationships of the next hierarchy level above. The speaker-peers of the neighboring subnets can in turn search their local subnets for shareable streams. If they find any suitable streams, they can route them to the requesting speaker-peer via a route that needs to be mapped onto the network connections in the original P2P overlay network. The stream discovery might propagate all the way up to the root of the hierarchy in the worst case. The root may be replicated among several super-peers to avoid that it becomes a bottleneck.

The hierarchical approach constitutes a compromise between the centralized approach and the fully distributed approach. It therefore combines the strengths of both solutions. This allows efficient local optimization decisions due to the global view of the optimizer component on the respective subnet and further enables a scalable distribution of the optimization logic in the potentially large overall network. At the same time, the hierarchical approach avoids the disadvantages of the individual approaches by enabling scalability and reducing metadata communication.

In this thesis, we focus on network-aware optimization in a single subnet with a single speaker-peer. Note that this corresponds to the centralized approach introduced above but is

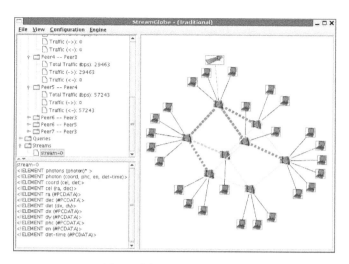

Figure 2.8: StreamGlobe GUI

also an integral part of the hierarchical approach. Implementing the hierarchical network organization in our StreamGlobe prototype is a matter of future work.

It is the task of the network designer setting up a StreamGlobe backbone network to choose
a reasonable subnet size. Empirical tests can help to determine which number of peers, streams,
and queries can be handled efficiently within a single subnet. Since the backbone network is
assumed to be stable, subnets and speaker-peers can be determined and set up in advance. Thus,
there is no need for algorithms that handle the case of super-peers joining or leaving the network
by dynamically partitioning or merging subnets. Further, there is no necessity for algorithms
that perform an automatic speaker-peer selection.

2.3.7 Implementation

We have implemented a Java prototype of the StreamGlobe distributed DSMS including our
optimization techniques presented in later chapters of this thesis. We used Java 5 and based
the original version of the prototype on the Globus Toolkit 3.2.1 middleware implementation
of OGSA. The Globus Toolkit 3.2.1 constitutes a reference implementation of the Open Grid
Services Infrastructure (OGSI) specified by Tuecke et al. (2003). The evaluation presented in
Chapter 5 was conducted after we switched the StreamGlobe implementation to Java 6 and to
the new Globus Toolkit 4.0.3 OGSA implementation which is now based on the Web Services
Resource Framework (WSRF) specified by Czajkowski et al. (2004).

For the experiments presented in later chapters of the thesis, we installed the StreamGlobe
prototype on a blade server. We used one blade for each super-peer. The blades each were
equipped with at least one Intel Xeon processor at 2.8 GHz and with at least 1 GB of RAM.
Some of the blades used the SuSE Linux Enterprise Server operating system in version 8. The
remaining blades used the same operating system in version 9.

Figure 2.8 shows a screenshot of the StreamGlobe GUI. The GUI is used to continuously monitor and visualize the current network state. The network shown in the figure is that of Figure 2.1 after the registration of the example data stream of Figure 2.2 and 25 randomly generated queries. The screenshot shows a network state that occurred without using our data stream sharing optimization technique introduced in Chapter 4. The dotted lines represent busy network connections. The lack of any optimization leads to overloaded network connections indicated by orange and red colors in the network graph. Using data stream sharing in this scenario actually causes all network connections to stay green, i. e., no overload situations occur.

The StreamGlobe execution engine uses the FluX query engine developed by Koch et al. (2004a,b) for processing WXQueries over XML data streams. FluX is an event-based query engine that efficiently processes queries over XML data streams. It minimizes buffer consumption through optimizations exploiting the data stream schema. Extensions made by Stegmaier (2006) enable FluX to support our augmented WXQuery subscription language employed in StreamGlobe and introduced in Chapter 4. Since the focus of this thesis is on network-aware optimization in distributed DSMSs rather than on stream-based query processing, we refer to the literature for more information on FluX and on the actual processing of WXQueries.

2.4 Related Work

StreamGlobe is a successor of the ObjectGlobe system described by Braumandl et al. (2001). While ObjectGlobe focuses on distributed query processing over persistent relational data on the Internet, StreamGlobe constitutes a distributed DSMS based on XML data streams. Kossmann (2000) surveys techniques for distributed query processing over persistent data. StreamGlobe is related to work in the fields of data stream management, P2P data management, Grid computing, and network architecture.

2.4.1 Data Stream Management

With StreamGlobe being a system that handles and processes data streams, it is worthwhile to take a look at other approaches to building data stream management systems.

Numerous DSMSs have been proposed in recent years. One of the most prominent among them is the Stanford Stream Data Manager (STREAM) [Arasu et al. (2003a); Babu and Widom (2001); Motwani et al. (2003)] developed at Stanford University. STREAM constitutes a comprehensive prototype DSMS incorporating its own declarative query language CQL [Arasu et al. (2002, 2003b,c, 2006); Arasu and Widom (2004a,b)] for continuous queries over data streams and relations. CQL is based on SQL and introduces additional syntax for the specification of data windows over streams just as WXQuery does with respect to XQuery. STREAM processes data streams by transforming them into relations using special windowing operators and by converting the query results back into streams again if necessary. In contrast, StreamGlobe directly processes XML data streams.

Telegraph is a major project of the Berkeley Database Research group embracing various subprojects. PSoup [Chandrasekaran and Franklin (2002)] builds on Telegraph and combines the processing of one-time and continuous queries by treating data and queries symmetrically. This allows new queries to be applied to old data and new data to be applied to old queries. TelegraphCQ [Chandrasekaran et al. (2003); Krishnamurthy et al. (2003)] is a system for managing and for adaptively processing continuous queries over data streams using, among other things, the Eddy [Avnur and Hellerstein (2000)] approach for adaptive tuple routing. The query language StreaQuel was developed in the context of TelegraphCQ. Like CQL, StreaQuel is based on SQL and introduces a construct for specifying data windows. The language further uses a special for loop construct for iterating over time. Lerner and Shasha (2003) propose AQuery, another SQL-based query language and query algebra. AQuery is a language for ordered relational data. The language treats table columns as arrays and allows navigation in the columns via order-dependent operators such as next, previous, first, and last.

Sullivan and Heybey (1998) introduce Tribeca as a stream-oriented DBMS designed for network traffic analysis. They claim that, due to performance concerns and a semantic mismatch between operations used in network traffic analysis and those provided by standard DBMSs, conventional DBMSs are not suitable in their application domain. Instead of focusing on fast random access, transactional updates, or relational joins, Tribeca aims at enabling fast sequential access to a stream of traffic records and at offering the ability to filter, aggregate, define windows on, demultiplex, and remultiplex large streams of network traffic data.

Gigascope [Cranor et al. (2002, 2003a,b)] is a stream database for network applications such as network monitoring, traffic analysis, and intrusion detection. It is developed as an industrial project at AT&T Labs-Research. Gigascope introduces GSQL as an SQL-like stream database language that is essentially a restriction of SQL with some stream database extensions. This is similar to the WXQuery subscription language offered by StreamGlobe which constitutes an augmented fragment of the XQuery language with additional support for window-based queries over infinite data streams. Newer developments aim at distributing Gigascope in a—however still centrally coordinated and scheduled—cluster to be used in applications such as network security monitoring. Johnson et al. (2005) describe a mechanism for generating heartbeats in Gigascope. These carry punctuations used for unblocking streaming operators with multiple inputs over slow or bursty input streams.

PIPES [Krämer and Seeger (2004)] constitutes a flexible and extensible infrastructure providing fundamental building blocks for implementing DSMSs that focus on continuous query processing over autonomous data sources. PIPES also contains separate frameworks that establish a basis for essential DSMS runtime components such as the scheduler [Cammert et al. (2007a)], the memory manager [Cammert et al. (2006)], and the query optimizer. Further, Cammert et al. (2007b) address the issue of dynamic metadata management in PIPES. The constituents of PIPES are implemented as part of the XXL library[1], which is a comprehensive Java library described by van den Bercken et al. (2001).

All of the above systems are centralized and tuple-based whereas StreamGlobe constitutes a distributed DSMS for managing XML data streams. Aurora [Carney et al. (2002)] is a system for monitoring applications that also implements a centralized tuple-based stream processor. Basically, Aurora constitutes a data flow system that uses the boxes and arrows paradigm known from workflow systems to specify operators (boxes) and their interconnections (arrows) for processing tuple streams. Cherniack et al. (2003) describe two complementary large-scale distributed stream processing systems, Aurora* and Medusa. Aurora* is a distributed version of Aurora with nodes belonging to a common administrative domain. Medusa, on the other hand, supports the federated operation of several Aurora nodes across administrative boundaries. Further development aiming at enabling new DSMS functionality such as dynamic revision of query results, dynamic query modification, and flexible optimization led to the Borealis system [Abadi et al. (2005)]. Borealis is a distributed multi-processor version of Aurora built upon the techniques of Aurora* and Medusa. Its current focus is on quality-of-service management, load distribution, high availability, and fault tolerance in data stream processing. The

---

[1] http://www.xxl-library.de

commercial DSMS StreamBase[1] is a descendant of these academic projects.

Implemented in the context of Telegraph, the continuously adaptive continuous query approach (CACQ) of Madden et al. (2002b) supports the sharing of physical operators among queries in a centralized, tuple-based environment. Chen et al. (2000) describe NiagaraCQ, a continuous query extension of the XML-based Niagara distributed database system. NiagaraCQ intends to achieve a high level of scalability in continuous query processing by grouping continuous queries according to similar structures. In StreamGlobe, we employ a similar multi-query optimization approach to reduce network traffic and peer load in a distributed DSMS. In contrast to NiagaraCQ, our approach explicitly deals with and exploits the aspect of queries and data streams being distributed over peers in a network. Further, our solutions allow more flexible sharing of data streams, e. g., by sharing query result streams anywhere in the network and by dynamically altering the characteristics of a stream to fit the needs of a larger set of queries.

Shah et al. (2003) propose Flux, an adaptive partitioning operator for continuous query systems. Flux operators are placed between producers and consumers in a data flow and adaptively partition the state of pipelined operators across a shared-nothing architecture while the pipeline continues processing. This allows for parallel execution and thus for improved scalability. In StreamGlobe, we use a different approach that builds on sharing common work and data among multiple queries to increase scalability. Shah et al. (2004) have extended Flux with a technique for masking failures to achieve high availability and fault tolerance for long-running data flows. OSIRIS-SE [Brettlecker and Schuldt (2007); Brettlecker et al. (2004, 2005)] focuses on reliable, fault-tolerant data stream management in distributed environments, especially in the context of healthcare applications. The OSIRIS-SE system is based on the OSIRIS [Schuler et al. (2003, 2004)] prototype of a hyperdatabase [Schek et al. (2002)] infrastructure. Dealing with fault tolerance in StreamGlobe is an issue of future work.

Naturally, data streams play an important role in the area of sensor networks. The Cougar project [Bonnet et al. (2001); Demers et al. (2003); Fung et al. (2002); Yao and Gehrke (2002, 2003)] is a sensor database that allows users to query sensor networks using declarative queries. A query optimizer transforms these queries into query plans for in-network query processing which reduces resource usage and thus extends the lifetime of sensor network nodes. A similar system constituting a distributed query processor is TinyDB [Madden et al. (2005)]. Like Cougar, TinyDB allows declarative querying of distributed sensors using in-network processing for reducing sensor power consumption. In contrast to DSMSs where data is pushed into the network by the data sources, systems such as Cougar and TinyDB usually trigger periodic updates of sensor data via corresponding update intervals specified in queries. As part of the Telegraph project, the Fjords architecture for queries over streaming sensor data introduced by Madden and Franklin (2002) aims at managing multiple queries over many sensors. The main optimization goal in Fjords is to limit sensor resource demands such as power consumption while maintaining high query throughput. Apart from power consumption, which is the main target of query optimization in distributed battery-powered sensor networks, robustness in potentially hostile environments is another important issue. In contrast, StreamGlobe focuses on different optimization goals such as network traffic and computational load on peers in a stable, stationary backbone network.

Apart from DSMSs and sensor networks, document routing is also related to our setting. Like StreamGlobe, many document routing systems use XML together with XPath or XQuery to provide support for flexible generic data exchange. XFilter and YFilter are two approaches for efficient XML message filtering [Diao et al. (2003)]. While XFilter [Altinel and Franklin

---

[1]http://www.streambase.com

(2000)] concentrates on indexing techniques for enabling high throughput filtering, its successor YFilter [Diao et al. (2002); Diao and Franklin (2003b)] builds on the experience of XFilter and combines filter predicates into one single non-deterministic finite automaton to enable the shared processing of common prefixes in query paths to increase performance. XTrie by Chan et al. (2002a,b) is an index structure based on tries that supports the efficient filtering of streaming XML documents using XPath expressions. In contrast to StreamGlobe, where subscriptions are "real" queries enabling the transformation of input data, content-based document filtering and routing treats subscriptions as boolean queries, i.e., it only checks whether a document matches a certain subscription or not. ONYX [Diao et al. (2004)] comprises an architecture and techniques for the content-based dissemination of XML data in large-scale distributed publish&subscribe systems based on the filtering techniques of XFilter and YFilter. Like StreamGlobe, this system is based on an overlay network. Diao and Franklin (2003a) explicitly deal with XML message brokering.

Cayuga [Demers et al. (2006)] is a centralized publish&subscribe system based on non-deterministic finite automata that introduces many extensions compared to traditional publish&subscribe systems. These extensions comprise, among others, support for stateful subscriptions and a subscription language with increased expressiveness including parameterization and aggregation. Cayuga also employs multi-query optimization for increasing subscription evaluation performance. SASE [Wu et al. (2006)] constitutes a centralized event processing system that executes complex subscriptions over streams of RFID data. Subscriptions are specified in a declarative event language that supports time-based sliding windows. In contrast to ordinary publish&subscribe systems, SASE is also able to correlate events. Finally, the HiFi approach introduced by Franklin et al. (2005) addresses the requirements of high fan-in systems, i.e., systems that need to handle many incoming data streams at a single node.

StreamGlobe uses a histogram-based approach for enabling selectivity estimations over data streams as described in Section 4.4.4. These are necessary for estimating the costs of query evaluation plans generated by the StreamGlobe optimizer. The literature provides many sophisticated approaches for analyzing data streams and for collecting appropriate data stream statistics. Among them are, for example, solutions that rely on kernel [Heinz and Seeger (2006)] or wavelet density estimators [Heinz and Seeger (2007)].

2.4.2 P2P Data Management

Over the years, P2P data management has inspired the development of a number of relevant techniques and prototype systems.

The first generation of P2P systems primarily featured file sharing applications such as Napster and Gnutella. Napster has been the first successful P2P system for exchanging files in a global scale. It uses central directory servers to locate files. However, this centralism constitutes a potential bottleneck and thus limits scalability. Gnutella works without any centralized metadata repository using a scoped broadcast service that propagates queries to neighboring peers. Subsequently, the peers send their results back to the requester. The drawback of this approach is that it floods the network with queries and query results which again limits scalability.

The second generation of P2P systems consists of structured overlay networks. Research in this area mainly focuses on indexing techniques for scalable and efficient data retrieval. Many of these indexing techniques are based on distributed hash tables (DHTs). Among the approaches developed in this context are content-addressable networks (CANs) [Ratnasamy et al. (2001)]. In a CAN, the logical address space is organized as a multi-dimensional torus. Data is mapped onto the torus using a hash function and peers in the system are responsible for holding the data of a certain region in the torus. Regions are disjoint and their union covers the entire data space. CANs handle joining or leaving peers by dynamically splitting and assigning regions to peers and by handing over regions to neighbor peers and merging them with the local region of the neighbor peer if possible. Chord [Stoica et al. (2001, 2003)] takes another approach by introducing a virtual key ring as address space, mapping data onto the ring according to a hash function. Peers are responsible for a certain section of the ring and manage all the data mapped onto that section. Since data and peers are mapped arbitrarily onto the ring, Chord does not preserve any neigborhood relationships between data or peers. Pastry [Rowstron and Druschel (2001)] improves this situation by introducing the notion of physical neighborhood. While also using a virtual key ring as address space, the mapping of peers onto the ring can additionally take into account physical neigborhood relationships, i. e., peers that are close to each other in the physical network are also close to each other in the P2P overlay network. The question of how close peers are in the physical network can be answered by arbitrary metrics, e. g., geographical distance or bandwidth of existing network connections. Tapestry [Zhao et al. (2004)] is similar to Pastry and puts a special focus on fault-tolerant routing. P-Grid, described by Aberer et al. (2003a), provides a scalable access structure specifically designed for P2P information systems. All hash-based techniques have in common that they only support point queries, i. e., the retrieval of data objects—usually files—matching a certain query. They are therefore not suitable for more complex tasks such as distributed query processing and data stream management as applied in StreamGlobe.

Beyond DHT-based indexing techniques, various other topologies for P2P networks have been developed. Yang and Garcia-Molina (2003) introduce the concept of super-peer networks. These networks are meant to improve the scalability of P2P networks by using a super-peer backbone network. The super-peers usually are powerful servers. Less powerful, possibly mobile thin-peers can register and deregister themselves in the network via the super-peers. We employ the super-peer concept as an integral part of the StreamGlobe architecture. HyperCuP, described by Schlosser et al. (2002), uses hypercubes as P2P network topologies. It thereby achieves a logarithmic upper bound for the number of hops needed to get from one super-peer in the network to any other super-peer. Content-based construction of the overlay network might lead to neighboring peers in the overlay network being far apart in the physical network. Ratnasamy et al. (2002) propose solutions for the problem of constructing overlay networks that preserve the topology of the underlying physical network.

DHT-based P2P networks rely on a global schema describing the data objects to be handled. In contrast, schema-based P2P networks [Aberer et al. (2003b); Brunkhorst et al. (2003)] are able to deal with various existing schemas in one P2P system. Research efforts in the area of peer data management systems (PDMSs) aim at building a distributed peer-based data management system to enable the transparent querying of a P2P system in the form of a traditional distributed DBMS. PDMSs such as Piazza [Halevy et al. (2003); Tatarinov et al. (2003)] reformulate queries[1] to fit the different schemas at various peers. Mutant query plans [Papadimos et al. (2003)] implement distributed query processing at peers close to the data. PIER [Huebsch et al. (2005, 2003)] is a distributed query engine based on structured overlay networks intended to bring database query processing facilities to widely distributed P2P environments. However, PIER destroys data locality by using a hashing scheme that arbitrarily distributes data over peers. Newer approaches such as HiSbase [Scholl et al. (2007)] remedy this problem by using a locality-preserving distribution scheme.

---

[1] See [Tatarinov and Halevy (2004)].

2.4.3 Grid Computing

StreamGlobe builds on and extends the Open Grid Services Architecture (OGSA) and its reference implementation, the Globus Toolkit, by adding data stream management and data stream processing capabilities to the Grid computing domain.

GATES [Chen et al. (2004)] is a related approach that also builds on Globus and tries to introduce data stream processing into Grid computing. While GATES mainly concentrates on data stream analysis and quality-of-service aspects in Grid-based data stream delivery, StreamGlobe primarily focuses on network-aware query processing and optimization in a distributed DSMS.

Another system building on OGSA is OGSA-DAI[1] (Open Grid Services Architecture Data Access and Integration). As the name suggests, this project is concerned with developing a middleware to enable the access and integration of data from various distributed data sources via the Grid. It also contains a distributed query processor called OGSA-DQP. In contrast to StreamGlobe, OGSA-DAI has no special focus on data streams.

Recent efforts in applying database and Grid computing techniques to support data-intensive e-science applications, e. g., in astrophysics, high-energy physics, or biology and medicine, have gained much attention. Nieto-Santisteban et al. (2005) devise efficient solutions for the astronomical problem of finding galaxy clusters using conventional database techniques. GridDB introduced by Liu and Franklin (2004) is a software overlay that provides data-centric services for scientific Grid computing. These examples prove the demand for efficient data management systems for huge data volumes in current and future e-science applications. We demonstrate the effectiveness of StreamGlobe in a real astrophysical application in Chapter 3.

2.4.4 Network Architecture

Multicast techniques route data towards receiving ends in a way that reduces network traffic by transmitting the same message or document only once for multiple recipients. Multicast is mainly used in local area networks. Deering and Cheriton (1990) introduce extensions to TCP/IP routing capabilities to enable multicast over wide area networks. Huang et al. (2003) investigate multicast in the context of ad-hoc and sensor networks to support efficient multicast in evolving networks. Castro et al. (2002) introduce Scribe, a scalable, decentralized multicast infrastructure based on the Pastry P2P system.

It is important to point out that our work in StreamGlobe differs from multicast in a major way. Multicast techniques as mentioned above mainly operate on the network level, i. e., they prevent the redundant transmission of equal data packets of a data stream. This is sufficient for, e. g., video streams, since such streams always have the same content for each recipient. In the context of StreamGlobe, this assumption does not hold since an original data stream may exist in various preprocessed and transformed instances. Hence, techniques working on the network level do not achieve satisfying improvements with respect to network traffic. In contrast, StreamGlobe provides multicast techniques on an application or content-based level by means of data stream sharing. Instead of merely reusing existing messages or documents needed in identical versions at various network sites, StreamGlobe is able to perform extensive in-network transformations of data streams. Therefore, it can dynamically create appropriate data streams for data stream sharing that best fit the queries to be answered while at the same time reducing resource usage in the overall network.

---

[1]http://www.ogsadai.org.uk

2.5 Summary

In this chapter, we have described our StreamGlobe model and prototype implementation of a distributed DSMS. The presented architecture serves as the basis for the optimization techniques which are at the core of this thesis. We have further introduced an example scenario using an astrophysical e-science setting which serves as a running example throughout the thesis.

StreamGlobe offers possibilities for future work in many directions. First and foremost, an extension of the prototype implementation to support multiple subnets in a hierarchical network organization would be beneficial. Apart from that, StreamGlobe can be extended by additional client interfaces for supporting data streams and subscriptions in various domain-specific formats and subscription languages. We have exemplarily realized such extensions for the VOTable format[1] and the Astronomical Data Query Language (ADQL)[2].

---

[1]See [IVOA (2004)].
[2]See [IVOA (2005)].

CHAPTER 3

The StarGlobe System:
An Astrophysical Flavor of StreamGlobe

Two of the most important challenges currently faced by the field of e-science are the analysis of huge volumes of scientific data and the connection of various sciences and communities. While the former is necessary to cope with the increasing complexity of scientific experiments and observations, the latter enables scientists to share scientific interests, data, and research results. An astrophysical flavor of StreamGlobe called *StarGlobe* addresses these issues by processing large volumes of data on-the-fly in the form of data streams and by combining multiple data sources and making the results available in a network. By means of parallelization, pipelining, and early filtering, StarGlobe drastically reduces the execution time of scientific workflows and at the same time returns first results early on while the processing of the remaining inputs is still proceeding. This increases efficiency and convenience for the scientific user.

3.1 Introduction

Information fusion across various data sources is an important task in many e-science applications. In this regard, transmitting all the necessary data from the data sources to the data sink for processing (data shipping) is problematic and does not scale with the expected large and increasing data volumes of the near future. Executing operators at or close to the data sources (query shipping) if the operators reduce the data volume or distributing query processing operators in a network (in-network query processing) are promising solutions to this problem. In-network query processing as employed in the StarGlobe system can also be combined with parallel and pipelined processing of data streams. This enables further improvements of performance and of response times in e-science workflows.

Throughout this chapter, we use *spatial matching*, which is a current issue in astrophysics, as an example e-science scenario to describe and to evaluate our approach. Spatial matching is an important step in the process of determining *spectral energy distributions (SEDs)* of celestial objects. SED assembly and subsequent classification as described by Adorf et al. (2004) are rather complex problems. In order to discover and to classify new astronomical objects such as active galactic nuclei, brown dwarfs, or neutron stars, it is not sufficient to just survey the sky using one specific observation method. Rather, photometric data from various wave bands and catalogs, i. e., data archives, have to be combined to gain ideally seamless SEDs of celestial objects. This scenario poses a real challenge due to several reasons such as the distribution of catalogs over various locations, the potentially large data volumes, and the need for often complex data transformations. One of the greatest difficulties is the lack of a unique (database) key for the identification of astronomical objects. Instead, the only way of identifying these objects is by using *uncertain* sky positions.

There exist only few tools, such as the GAVO (German Astrophysical Virtual Observatory) *crossmatcher* developed by Adorf et al. (2005), that are able to perform the crossmatching of catalogs which serves as a basis for subsequent SED assembly and classification. During the process, the GAVO crossmatcher acquires astrometric and photometric data from catalogs covering different wavelength ranges and loads them into a main memory database. Afterwards, the crossmatcher applies various transformations to spatially match astrometric data using statistical methods. Due to the combinatorial explosion during a multi-catalog join, the amount of data can grow so rapidly that it exceeds main memory and cannot be handled anymore.

In this chapter, we present a solution to this problem using our StarGlobe system. StarGlobe is an astrophysical flavor of StreamGlobe that augments StreamGlobe with functionality specifically tailored to the needs of the astrophysics community. In StarGlobe, data from multiple catalogs is streamed into a StreamGlobe network and processed in a pipelined fashion. We integrated the astrophysical application logic using the external operator interface of StreamGlobe introduced in Section 2.3.5 of Chapter 2. StarGlobe is able to transform and to spatially match large volumes of astrometric data. In addition, the system dramatically reduces the time needed to produce and to return the first result data item. Therefore, first results are available after a relatively short period of time due to pipelined stream processing. This is much more convenient for astronomers than having to wait for the entire process to complete before receiving any results as in the straightforward approach.

Using DSMSs and exploiting their benefits is an important step in coping with the challenges of the near future. The amount of data in astronomy is growing at an exponential rate. Soon, observational data collected by satellites and telescopes during certain sky observations, e. g., in the LOFAR[1] project, will exceed available storage capacities. Also, the traditional way of collecting and storing all observational data first and of subsequently analyzing it may not be appropriate for future applications. Therefore, alternative ways of processing and analyzing data *on-the-fly* as in StarGlobe are necessary.

In detail, we make the following contributions in this chapter:

- We introduce SED assembly and classification as an actual astrophysical e-science application that can benefit from research results in computer science in general and from data stream management in particular.

- We describe our StarGlobe implementation of spatial matching using the StreamGlobe external operator interface introduced in Chapter 2. Spatial matching is an important prerequisite for SED assembly and classification.

- An evaluation of our solution proves that *StarGlobe* constitutes a valuable computing platform for solving the task of spatial matching in an astrophysical application.

---

[1] http://www.lofar.org

3.2 Problem Statement

SED assembly and subsequent *classification* [Adorf et al. (2004)] is a common problem in astrophysics. The basic idea is to construct an approximate SED for a celestial object by combining photometry from various catalogs covering different wavelength ranges and to classify the object on the basis of its SED. A major problem in this context is the fact that observational data usually are (in some cases also geographically) distributed over many large database tables called *catalogs*. Also, since the data are obtained through various sky observations conducted using different measurement instruments, they contain individual variances due to a variety of reasons, including measurement uncertainties of the instruments used. These uncertainties concern the celestial coordinates, i. e., the positions (astrometry), as well as the photometric data, i. e., the intensities (photometry), of the object under investigation. Therefore, it is very likely that the coordinates of the same object slightly differ from each other in different catalogs. This makes it non-trivial to perform *spatial matching*, i. e., to combine (crossmatch) corresponding objects or even entire catalogs, which is a prerequisite for SED assembly.

Solutions such as the GAVO crossmatcher [Adorf et al. (2005)] load the results of each queried catalog into a main memory database. These so-called *primary match results (PMRs)* are then combined[1] and filtered in memory (in-memory matching). A major disadvantage of this data shipping approach is the fact that it can easily lead to a memory overflow when matching too many sources, particularly when many catalogs are involved. Besides, scientists initiating a spatial matching process for SED assembly have to wait for the crossmatcher to finish completely before receiving any results. Thus, they are unable to gain immediate feedback concerning the correctness of the specified parameters. We address these issues with an alternative approach using and enhancing the stream processing capabilities of a Grid-based DSMS.

3.3 The SED Scenario

This section gives an explanation and a summary of the mechanisms of SED assembly and classification to the extent necessary for understanding the approach we describe in this chapter.

3.3.1 Overview

As motivated in an astrophysical publication by Adorf et al. (2004), SED assembly and classification are essential exploratory techniques to discover new astronomical objects such as obscured active galactic nuclei, brown dwarfs, isolated neutron stars, or planetary nebulae. The key principle is the combination of multi-wavelength photometric data from different catalogs to assemble an ideally seamless SED of a celestial object. The workflow of SED classification consists of the following five steps (see Figure 3.1):

1. catalog query

2. spatial (or astrometric) matching

3. assembly of raw photometry

4. photometric transformation

---

[1]A left outer join is computed over the input list of objects and all primary match results. The input list can be a complete catalog by itself.

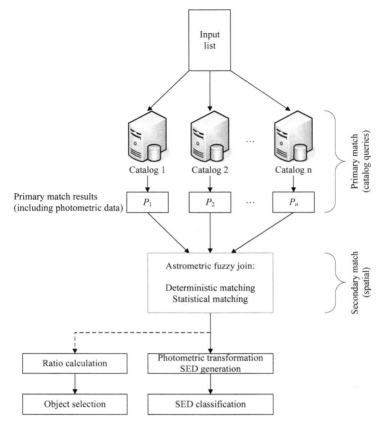

Figure 3.1: SED assembly and classification workflow

5. actual SED classification

In the first step, astronomers usually create an input list of astronomical objects they are interested in. The celestial coordinates of the objects could be derived, e. g., from a catalog which the astronomer wants to use as a starting point. Besides the coordinates, the list also contains an identifier for each object. The input list is then used to query various catalogs covering as many wavelength ranges as needed. For each object in the input list, a domain-specific selection called *cone search* is conducted on each catalog. For each catalog, the results of the search, the associated photometric data, and the *id*s of the corresponding objects from the input list are returned in a primary match result (PMR). The PMRs are the basis for the astrometric matching performed in the second step which we explain in detail in Section 3.3.2.

When the astrometric matching is complete, photometric data has to be assembled and transformed into an SED in the third and fourth step. Photometric transformation (the actual SED assembly) is a non-trivial process which we do not explicitly address here. Figure 3.2 illus-

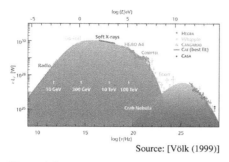

Source: [Völk (1999)]

Source: [Völk (1999)]

Figure 3.2: Spectral energy distribution of the emissions from the Crab Nebula

Figure 3.3: The Crab Nebula in the constellation Taurus

trates what the results of a photometric transformation could look like by the example of the emissions from the Crab Nebula in the constellation Taurus. Figure 3.3 shows the Crab Nebula in optical light. The dashed line in Figure 3.1 indicates that, alternatively to the photometric transformation, so-called *ratios* of photometric values can be calculated to filter characteristic objects (e. g., radio-loud objects: $F_{radio}/F_{optical} > ratio_{threshold}$).

After photometric transformation, the resulting SED can be fed into a statistical classifier for supervised classification. This final step performs photometric matching with precomputed *template SEDs* which may be synthesized based on a library of template spectra [Adorf et al. (2004)]. Subsequently, astronomers can review and evaluate the results of the classification.

The emphasis of our work lies on the spatial matching in the second step.

3.3.2 Spatial (Astrometric) Matching

After having completed the first step of the SED assembly and classification workflow, i. e., all PMRs of each queried catalog have been collected, the secondary match can be performed (see Figure 3.1). This match is fuzzy since a statistical method of result filtering is applied (*fuzzy match*). The fuzzy match itself consists of a deterministic and a statistical part. The deterministic part is basically a left outer equi-join over the *id* attribute (indicated by $\bowtie_{id}$) of all PMRs $P_1, \ldots, P_n$ including the input list I on the very left side:

$$(((I \bowtie_{id} P_1) \bowtie_{id} P_2) \bowtie_{id} \ldots) \bowtie_{id} P_n$$

Here, *id* is an attribute introduced in I to identify objects in all PMRs related to one *id* in I.

The fuzzy part takes the result of the join and calculates a statistical metric, hypothetically assuming that all objects within one join result item, also denoted as *counterparts*, belong to the same physical source. This metric is subsequently referred to as the *reduced χ^2-metric* [Adorf et al. (2005)]. Figure 3.4 illustrates two join results or *spiders*, each consisting of three counterparts from three different catalogs that obviously fit together forming two *match candidates*. Match candidates with a χ^2-value above a certain user-defined threshold are discriminated because they are statistically unreasonable match combinations. In Figure 3.5, one counterpart is associated with both match candidates. The spider on the lower left seems to be quite reasonable. But the spider on the upper right connecting the stray counterpart with a dashed line probably does not make sense and can be dropped because its reduced χ^2 is too high. One can view the $\chi^2_{reduced}$-metric as a measure of *compactness* of a spider or match candidate.

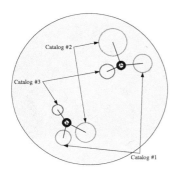
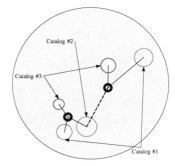

Figure 3.4: Two spiders   **Figure 3.5:** Stray counterpart

We calculate the χ^2_{reduced}-value for each match candidate as follows:

1. Calculate the weighted mean (Euclidean) coordinates of all n counterparts within one match candidate (assuming that the two-dimensional spherical coordinates of each object have already been transformed into three-dimensional Euclidean coordinates on the unit sphere):

$$\vec{m} = \frac{1}{w} \cdot \sum_{i=1}^{n}(w_i \vec{v}_i) \, , \qquad (3.1)$$

where $w_i = 1/\sigma_i^2$ is the statistical weight factor for each counterpart $i \in [1..n]$, $w = \sum_{i=1}^{n} w_i$ is the sum of all weight factors, σ_i is the astrometric uncertainty associated with each counterpart i, and $\vec{v}_i = (x_i, y_i, z_i)^T$ are the Euclidean coordinates of a counterpart i.

2. Normalize the Euclidean coordinates of the weighted vector $\vec{m}$ to the unit sphere:

$$\vec{\overline{m}} = \frac{\vec{m}}{\sqrt{x_m^2 + y_m^2 + z_m^2}} \, , \qquad (3.2)$$

with $\vec{m} = (x_m, y_m, z_m)^T$.

3. With $\vec{\overline{m}}$ as *optimum center* (see small thick black circles in Figures 3.4 and 3.5 which represent the formal astrometric uncertainty) now calculate arc distances between each counterpart i and the optimum center $\vec{\overline{m}}$:

$$\varphi_i = \arccos(\vec{v}_i \cdot \vec{\overline{m}}) = \arccos(x_i x_{\overline{m}} + y_i y_{\overline{m}} + z_i z_{\overline{m}}) \, , \qquad (3.3)$$

with $\vec{\overline{m}} = (x_{\overline{m}}, y_{\overline{m}}, z_{\overline{m}})^T$.

4. The *Mahalanobis distance* r_i between each counterpart i and the center $\vec{\overline{m}}$ then is:

$$r_i = \frac{\varphi_i}{\sigma_i} \, . \qquad (3.4)$$

5. χ^2 is calculated from:

$$\chi^2 = \sum_{i=1}^{n} r_i^2 \, . \qquad (3.5)$$

6. Finally, the reduced χ^2-value is calculated by dividing χ^2 by the *degrees of freedom* (per spider):

$$\chi^2_{\text{reduced}} = \frac{\chi^2}{2n - 2} .$$

(3.6)

This sketch of the calculation steps provides the background for the distributed spatial matching scenario presented in this chapter.

3.4 Astrometric Matching in StarGlobe

This section presents the spatial matching scenario that we have implemented and executed in StarGlobe. We also report on the results observed when executing the scenario workflow.

3.4.1 Preliminaries

Spatial matching is an important step in the process of SED assembly and classification. PMRs from various catalogs are combined which can lead to an enormous growth of data volumes. The challenge is to remove combinations that do not fit together and to select only valid match candidates for further processing and classification. Straightforward approaches such as the GAVO crossmatcher calculate all possible combinations of PMRs en bloc in main memory and subsequently filter only good match candidates using the χ^2_{reduced}-metric. As already mentioned in Section 3.1, this approach will run out of main memory when matching too many catalogs.

Exploiting the fact that StarGlobe is a distributed system, we take a different and very promising approach. By distributing the combination phase of the spatial matching process over multiple peers, StarGlobe allows us to parallelize processing. We can thus join many more PMRs at the same time. This enables us to include more catalogs to produce match candidates containing even richer information.

In addition, we split up χ^2_{reduced}-filtering, which is usually done *after* the deterministic matching in the workflow of SED assembly (see Figure 3.1), and relocate it at the join operators of the deterministic matching process as shown in Figure 3.6. This results in a tight integration of the deterministic as well as the statistical process, thereby improving selectivity and preventing bad match candidates from yielding unnecessary combinations at a very early stage. Also, network traffic is reduced and throughput of valid match candidates at single peers is increased. Yet, we need to be careful not to filter out match candidates too early if their χ^2_{reduced}-value lies slightly above the threshold. At first glance, these are bad match candidates. But as long as further counterparts could join a match candidate, the match candidate's χ^2_{reduced}-value could drop below the threshold. This may happen when an existing match candidate is joined by another counterpart whose coordinates lie near or exactly on the optimal center of the spider. This would contribute to the compactness of the spider such that its χ^2_{reduced}-value decreases. Therefore, we need to specify thresholds on filter operators placed at inner nodes more generously. To assure that no valid match candidate is accidentally dropped, we divide the local χ^2 by the maximum degree of freedom a match candidate can reach throughout the assembly process. This degree depends on the number of catalogs being spatially matched.

Another feature of the distributed approach is that first results are returned rather quickly during processing in contrast to the straightforward approach where no results are returned as long as the calculation proceeds. This is due to the fact that StarGlobe constitutes a DSMS using non-blocking query operators that process data streams on-the-fly in a pipelined fashion.

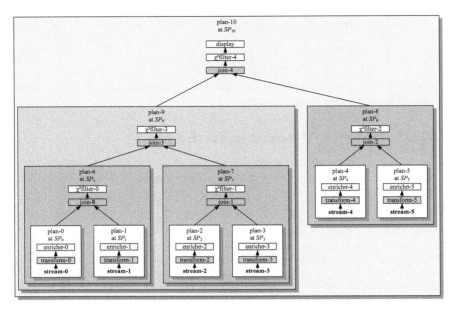

Figure 3.6: Schematic illustration of the distributed query evaluation plan

In order to support astrophysical scenarios like the following, we have augmented StarGlobe with additional stream iterator implementations using the StreamGlobe external operator interface. Stream iterators in StarGlobe are basically non-blocking operators for processing data streams. The additional operators comprise a *sigma enricher* for attaching necessary uncertainty information to data stream items, a generic, non-blocking, progressive *merge join* operator used for matching data items, and a χ^2_{reduced}-*filter* operator for performing the filtering as described in Section 3.3. To realize real-life spatial matching scenarios for SED assembly, we have acquired PMRs from different astrophysical data catalogs shown in Table 3.1.

3.4.2 Spatial Matching Scenario

In our spatial matching scenario for SED assembly, we use an input list of 50 sources from RASS-BSC [Voges et al. (1999)]. Since there does not yet exist a module to directly query the VizieR catalog service[1] from Centre de Données astronomiques de Strasbourg (CDS)[2] and to stream the results automatically into StarGlobe, we currently retrieve the PMRs manually and convert them to XML. Table 3.2 shows the queried catalogs. The search radii used for querying the catalogs are quite large, yielding a comparatively large number of PMRs. This is due to the fact that the coordinates of the source objects taken from RASS-BSC have rather large uncertainties. The density of a catalog also has an impact on the size of the result set. The higher the density, the more objects are returned within the search radius.

---

[1] http://vizier.u-strasbg.fr
[2] http://cdsweb.u-strasbg.fr

CATALOG	SPECTRAL BAND	# OBJECTS	FULL NAME
2MASS	near-infrared	470,992,970	Two Micron All Sky Survey
FIRST	radio	811,117	Faint Images of the Radio Sky at Twenty centimeters
GSC-2	optical	455,851,237	The Guide Star Catalog Version 2.2
NVSS	radio	1,773,484	1.4 GHz National Radio Astronomy Observatory Very Large Array Sky Survey
RASS-BSC	X-ray	18,806	ROSAT All-Sky Survey Bright Source Catalog 1RXS (1st ROSAT X Survey)
USNO B1.0	optical	1,045,913,669	Whole-Sky United States Naval Observatory B1.0 Catalog

Table 3.1: Catalogs used in the spatial matching scenario

CATALOG	SEARCH RADIUS	TABLE	# PMRS	STREAM SIZE
2MASS	90 arcsec	II/246/out	611	229 KB
FIRST	90 arcsec	VIII/71/first	60	27 KB
GSC-2	90 arcsec	I/271/out	722	350 KB
NVSS	90 arcsec	VIII/65/nvss	32	14 KB
USNO B1.0	90 arcsec	I/284/out	666	260 KB

Table 3.2: Catalogs queried using an input list of RASS-BSC sources

Figure 3.7 shows the Grid-based network topology that we use for this spatial matching scenario. The PMRs are streamed into the network at SP_1 to SP_5. The input list is injected at SP_0. In this scenario, the input list itself is included in the matching process, which is possible in SED assembly. We split up the left outer join of Section 3.3.2 and distribute it over several peers within the network. Thus, a transformation of the n-way left outer join becomes necessary to make sure no tuple (or match candidate) is accidentally dropped. The basic principle of the transformation is that some left outer joins on certain inner nodes need to be replaced by full outer joins. The transformation is based on the following theorem.

Theorem 3.1 *Let $A := \{[a_1, \ldots, a_l]\}$, $B := \{[b_1, \ldots, b_m]\}$, and $C := \{[c_1, \ldots, c_n]\}$ be relations and let $A.id \in \{a_1, \ldots, a_l\}$, $B.id \in \{b_1, \ldots, b_m\}$, and $C.id \in \{c_1, \ldots, c_n\}$ be their corresponding join attributes, respectively. Then the following applies:*

$$(A \bowtie_{A.id=B.id} B) \bowtie_{A.id=C.id} C \equiv A \bowtie_{A.id=B.id \vee A.id=C.id} (B \bowtie_{B.id=C.id} C) \qquad \square$$

PROOF: We present the proof in Appendix B on page 195. ∎

In our example, the join

$$((((I_{RASS-BSC} \bowtie_{id} P_{2MASS}) \bowtie_{id} P_{FIRST}) \bowtie_{id} P_{USNOB1}) \bowtie_{id} P_{NVSS}) \bowtie_{id} P_{GSC-2}$$

is transformed to

$$((I_{RASS-BSC} \bowtie_{id} P_{2MASS}) \bowtie_{id} (P_{FIRST} \bowtie_{id} P_{USNOB1})) \bowtie_{id} (P_{NVSS} \bowtie_{id} P_{GSC-2}).$$

The network topology of Figure 3.7 reflects the transformed join order.

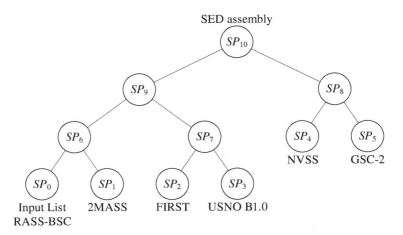

Figure 3.7: Network topology

To illustrate the effectiveness of early filtering during spatial matching, Table 3.3 shows the results of two different workflow executions. The first execution employs early χ^2_{reduced}-filtering while the second does not. The stream size in the table represents the intermediate size of an output stream directly after each join operator (see Figure 3.6), i.e., after the join but before the following filter operator in case of early filtering. The table also shows the corresponding number of match candidates that are under consideration at each step. Early filtering keeps the number of match candidates considerably lower after *join-3* and *join-4* compared to the approach without early filtering. Since intermediate result sets are much smaller, performance with early filtering is much better. Without early χ^2_{reduced}-filtering, the workflow generates large intermediate results with many irrelevant match candidates. Remember that, without early filtering, the χ^2_{reduced}-filter is only applied once after the complete join has been computed. Consequently, in this case, no irrelevant match candidates are filtered until after *join-4*. Therefore, 99.9% of all match candidates in the result of *join-4* are dropped at *filter-4* when no early filtering is employed. This can be seen from comparing stream sizes after *join-4* and after *filter-4* in Table 3.3. The loss of performance is obvious when comparing the durations of both workflow

	WITH EARLY FILTERING		WITHOUT EARLY FILTERING	
	Stream size	# Match candidates	Stream size	# Match candidates
After join-0	808 KB	611	808 KB	611
After join-1	1,874 KB	1,138	1,874 KB	1,138
After join-2	1,387 KB	826	1,387 KB	826
After join-3	6,355 KB	2,522	46,525 KB	15,489
After join-4	14,356 KB	3,815	1,838,648 KB	364,299
After filter-4	1,364 KB	318	1,364 KB	318
Duration hh:mm:ss	00:02:58		02:46:00	

Table 3.3: Workflow execution results

| | # MATCH CANDIDATES | | FILTER RATIO |
	Before filtering	After filtering	
At join-0	611	289	47.3%
At join-1	1,138	452	39.7%
At join-2	826	458	55.4%
At join-3	2,522	400	15.9%
At join-4	3,815	318	8.3%

Table 3.4: Filter ratios with early filtering

executions.[1] With early $\chi^2_{reduced}$-filtering, this astrometric matching scenario runs more than 50 times faster than without.

Table 3.4 shows the number of match candidates before and after each $\chi^2_{reduced}$-filter operator at the various join nodes in the network when using early filtering. Additionally, the table shows the resulting filter ratio (selectivity) at each $\chi^2_{reduced}$-filter.

Summarizing, our approach has proven to be highly beneficial in the presented scenario. Executing the spatial matching workflow in StarGlobe vastly reduces the negative effects of input coordinates with high uncertainties on overall performance by means of early filtering of intermediate results. Also, even for high quality input coordinates with small uncertainties, the parallel and pipelined streaming execution of workflow operators further improves performance and increases convenience by delivering first results early on during processing.

3.5   Related Work

The functionality presented in this chapter is also provided by the GAVO crossmatcher which was developed by Adorf et al. (2005). However, as we have pointed out before, the approach pursued in the crossmatcher does not use early filtering, parallelization, or pipelined stream processing. It thus imposes strict limitations on the sizes of computable problems due to excessive resource consumption. If main memory size is insufficient to hold all the necessary data, the approach taken by the crossmatcher becomes infeasible. Also, the crossmatcher delivers the entire result to the user at the very end of the processing which can take a considerable amount of time to complete. Our StarGlobe approach drastically reduces processing time and memory consumption by means of parallel and pipelined stream processing. Further, StarGlobe instantly delivers generated result items in a pipelined fashion.

The SkyQuery system [Budavári et al. (2002); Malik et al. (2003)] and its redesigned version OpenSkyQuery [Budavári et al. (2003); O'Mullane et al. (2004)] are federated databases which are based on web service technology. These systems enable users to query distributed catalogs called (Open)SkyNodes and to perform crossmatching of various catalogs in a similar way as presented in this chapter. However, OpenSkyQuery currently has some limitations, e. g., in the number of rows that can be returned in an answer to a query. This is due to performance issues since, in contrast to StarGlobe, OpenSkyQuery does not yet employ optimization techniques such as parallelization and pipelined stream processing. In an ongoing cooperation with the group of Alex Szalay at Johns Hopkins University, we continue to investigate possibilities of integrating our work with theirs.

---

[1] For the evaluation, we executed the workflows on a blade server using 11 blades, each equipped with an Intel Xeon processor at 2.8 GHz and 1 GB of RAM.

As already pointed out in the previous chapter, many different data stream management systems have been proposed in recent years. However, none of these systems has been used to specifically support real-life e-science applications. This is the first work to investigate the impact of employing a Grid-based distributed data stream management system for supporting and improving an actual (astrophysical) e-science workflow.

3.6 Summary

This work demonstrates the possible benefits for the scientific community of combining research efforts in computer science with those of other scientific disciplines such as astrophysics. Recent research efforts in computer science in the field of data stream management provide new solutions for existing scientific problems. StarGlobe is a new platform for efficiently executing actual astrophysical e-science scenarios using data streams. We have shown the successful execution of an astrometric matching scenario in StarGlobe. In this scenario, we combined the extensive processing of multiple data streams with the application of possibly complex transformations and statistical methods in order to efficiently crossmatch astrophysical data catalogs. The result data stream can be subscribed at any peer connected to the StarGlobe network. Subscribed streams may be further processed, e. g., through supervised classification used to discover new astronomical objects such as obscured neutron stars or hidden galaxies.

The research community benefits from our approach in many ways. First, larger problem sizes can be handled without running into problems concerning available computing resources, especially in terms of main memory. With early filtering and parallelization reducing memory consumption and processing time, StarGlobe is prepared for the challenges of the anticipated data explosion of the next decade. Second, using pipelined stream processing, e-science workflows can deliver first results early on in a pipelined fashion while the computation of the remaining results is still running. This enables scientists to check the correctness of their parameter settings and to start working on the results early on. Of course, our approach is also applicable to many other matching scenarios in all fields of science, business, and engineering.

As far as future work is concerned, automatic retrieval of PMRs would eliminate the need to query astronomical catalogs like VizieR/CDS manually. Within the scope of the development of the GAVO crossmatcher, our astrophysical cooperation partners from the Max-Planck-Institut für extraterrestrische Physik (MPE) have developed a component which performs the PMR acquisition. They intend to make the component available for integration into StarGlobe in the future. As an intelligent content provider, the adapted component could then be used to query various remote catalogs in parallel and to stream the results into the StarGlobe network. Furthermore, scientific workflows are currently specified in the form of manually written XML documents in StarGlobe. This workflow description corresponds to a distributed query evaluation plan in StreamGlobe as introduced in Chapter 2 and contains specifications of operators, operator placement on peers, and the data flow that has to be established between operators and peers. An optimizer for automatic plan generation would relieve researchers from having to write their own query plans which is desirable especially for complex scenarios. In the remainder of the thesis, we investigate optimization techniques within StreamGlobe for automatically generating optimized distributed query evaluation plans for queries specified using our XQuery-based WXQuery subscription language.

CHAPTER 4

Data Stream Sharing

Scarce resources such as computational power and network bandwidth limit the number of continuous queries a DSMS can handle concurrently. Making intelligent and efficient use of these valuable resources is thus mandatory in order to offer the best service possible to users. We achieve this goal by introducing *data stream sharing*, an optimization technique based on *in-network query processing* and *multi-subscription optimization* that enables us to distribute continuous query processing in the network and to share data streams for satisfying multiple similar queries. Thus, distributed DSMSs using this optimization can satisfy more continuous queries concurrently with their available resources.

4.1 Introduction

As already motivated in Chapter 1, data stream processing is a valuable means for coping with the requirements of novel applications in e-science, e-health, and e-business. The aim in e-science, for example, is to enable various researchers and research institutes to share their research data, e. g., sensor measurements of complex experiments in physics or telescope observation data in astronomy. This allows for resource sharing as well as multiple evaluation and analysis of data. Furthermore, continuing technological advances will result in even higher data volumes which makes storing all of the delivered data prior to processing increasingly impractical. Also, transmitting all the data over physically limited and therefore potentially congested network connections is a problem. This is especially true if only small subsets of the data or some processing results—which usually constitute a much smaller data volume than the input data—are actually needed. To enable efficient data sharing and processing, it is imperative to reduce the huge amounts of data generated by scientific experiments and observations as early as possible and to reuse computational results if appropriate. Thus, the transmission of unnecessary data, the redundant transmission of data streams, the redundant execution of operators, and therefore network and peer overload can be prevented.

We propose *data stream sharing* as a new optimization technique addressing these issues. Data stream sharing is based on two main optimization approaches. These are (1) *in-network*

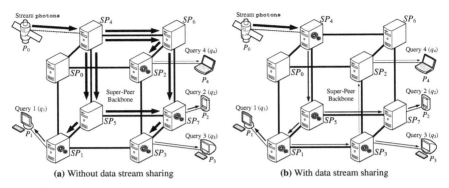

(a) Without data stream sharing   (b) With data stream sharing

Figure 4.1: Example DSMS scenario

query processing for distributing and executing newly registered continuous queries in the network and (2) *multi-subscription optimization* for enabling the reuse and sharing of existing (parts of) data streams that were generated to satisfy previously registered subscriptions. These optimizations are an integral part of our StreamGlobe system. To enable them, we use *Peer-to-Peer (P2P) networking* and *Grid computing* techniques as introduced in Chapter 2.

As a motivating example for the application of StreamGlobe, we introduce an astrophysical e-science application. Consider Figure 4.1 which illustrates an instance of the exemplary network of Figure 2.1 once without and once with data stream sharing. Peers P_1 to P_4 in the example network are devices of astrophysicists used to register subscriptions in the network. Subscriptions are registered using *WXQuery*, our XQuery-based subscription language that we introduce in detail in Section 4.3. We only consider Queries 1 (q_1) and 2 (q_2) of Figure 4.1 here. Queries 3 (q_3) and 4 (q_4) are presented in Section 4.3. All queries reference data stream photons introduced in Section 2.1 as their single input. Figure 4.2 below shows Query 1 (q_1).

```
<photons>
  { for $p in stream("photons")/photons/photon
    where $p/coord/cel/ra >= 120.0
      and $p/coord/cel/ra <= 138.0
      and $p/coord/cel/dec >= -49.0
      and $p/coord/cel/dec <= -40.0
    return
    <vela>
      { $p/coord/cel/ra } { $p/coord/cel/dec }
      { $p/phc } { $p/en } { $p/det_time }
    </vela> }
</photons>
```

Figure 4.2: Query 1 (q_1)

This query selects an area in the sky that contains the Vela supernova remnant and delivers the celestial coordinates, the pulse height channel, the energy, and the detection time of all the photons detected in that area. The `stream` function was newly introduced by us and indicates a possibly infinite data stream used as input to the query. Query 2 (q_2) is shown in Figure 4.3 below and filters a smaller section of the sky.

```
<photons>
  { for $p in stream("photons")/photons/photon
    where $p/en >= 1.3
      and $p/coord/cel/ra >= 130.5
      and $p/coord/cel/ra <= 135.5
      and $p/coord/cel/dec >= -48.0
      and $p/coord/cel/dec <= -45.0
    return
      <rxj>
        { $p/coord/cel/ra } { $p/coord/cel/dec }
        { $p/en } { $p/det_time }
      </rxj> }
</photons>
```

Figure 4.3: Query 2 (q_2)

This query selects the area of the RX J0852.0-4622 supernova remnant which is situated within the area of Vela. Note that the section of the sky selected by q_2 is completely contained in the section selected by q_1. Also, q_2 is only interested in photons having an energy value of at least 1.3 keV.

We first consider Figure 4.1(a) which shows the traditional scenario of answering queries in the network. The thickness of the arrows associated with the various network connections indicates the size of the data streams transmitted over these connections. Each of the four queries in the system only needs a certain part of the original data stream. However, in each case, the entire stream gets transmitted from the data source to the peer that registered the query, leading to the transmission of unnecessary data. Since query execution for each subscription takes place at the super-peer that the subscribing peer is connected to, queries that perform the same operations on the same input data streams cause redundant execution of operators. Note that this scenario already performs a basic form of data stream sharing since it transmits stream photons from P_0 to SP_4 only once and then forwards multiple copies to various other peers.

Figure 4.1(b) shows the situation when using our stream sharing approach which answers newly registered subscriptions using (parts of) data streams already present in the network. These data streams have been generated for satisfying previously registered continuous queries. We assume that queries q_1 to q_4 have been registered one after another in ascending order in our example. Obviously, we can significantly reduce network traffic and processing overhead by avoiding redundant transmissions and computations through sharing previously generated data streams. For example, when q_1 is registered, its execution can be pushed into the network and the query can be processed at SP_4 instead of at SP_1. The result is then routed to P_1 via SP_5 and SP_1. When q_2 is registered afterwards, it can reuse the stream constituting the answer for q_1 at SP_5 because the result of q_2 is completely contained in the answer for q_1. The result data stream of q_1 is duplicated at SP_5, yielding two identical streams. One is used to answer q_1, the other is filtered using the selection and projection of q_2. This results in a new stream that constitutes the result of q_2 which is subsequently routed to P_2 via SP_7. We present more details on this and on the registration of queries q_3 and q_4 in Section 4.4.

The contributions presented in this chapter comprise the following:

- First, we describe the problems of matching subscriptions and data streams and of suitably placing query operators in the network. Furthermore, we establish a formal notion of data streams and data windows (Section 4.2).

- Then, we introduce *Windowed XQuery (WXQuery)*, our XQuery-based subscription language for continuous queries over XML data streams enabling the formulation of queries including window-based operators (Section 4.3).

- We develop a properties representation for data streams and subscriptions in the network. This representation forms the basis for finding reusable streams enabling data stream sharing (Section 4.4.2).

- We give a formal definition of shareability among properties representations of subscriptions and streams (Section 4.4.3).

- We devise a cost model for estimating the costs of distributed query evaluation plans generated by the optimizer (Section 4.4.4).

- We introduce algorithms for optimizing the evaluation of newly registered continuous queries in a distributed DSMS by sharing possibly preprocessed data streams available in the system (Section 4.4.5).

- Finally, Section 4.5 shows some evaluation results obtained using our StreamGlobe prototype implementation that demonstrate the benefits of data stream sharing in a distributed DSMS.

4.2   Preliminaries

We start by introducing and describing the problems of matching subscriptions and data streams and of placing query operators in the network. We further establish our notion of data streams and data windows in the context of this thesis.

4.2.1   Problem Statement

Our goal is to efficiently integrate, distribute, and execute newly registered continuous queries over data streams in a StreamGlobe network. We thus reduce network traffic and peer load, avoid network congestion and peer overload, enable load balancing among peers and network connections, and increase flexibility in terms of the kinds of subscriptions a peer can register. We employ a local optimization approach to incrementally include new subscriptions in an existing network. Note that static multi-query optimization on a set of subscriptions is a different problem. However, if appropriate, it could be used for periodic or event-based global reoptimization to complement our approach. The core problem that has to be solved in order to achieve our goal is the discovery of reusable (parts of) data streams. Solving this problem requires taking into account schema- or structure-based information (e. g., projections) as well as content-based information (e. g., selections) about subscriptions and data streams. In order to enable the efficient comparison of subscriptions and data streams, we abstract from the textual representation of the subscription and the data stream schema. Instead, we use a properties approach introduced in Section 4.4.2 to gather the relevant properties of subscriptions and data streams. On this basis, it is possible to compare the properties of a new subscription with those of existing data streams in the network. In our approach, the contents of a data stream are represented by the properties of the subscription generating the respective stream. Therefore, a subscription corresponds to a data stream, i.e., the result data stream of that subscription, and vice versa. This implies that a subscription and its corresponding result data stream are represented by the same properties.

In general, the above mentioned comparison of subscriptions and data streams will identify more than one shareable stream for a given subscription. This leads to multiple possible evaluation plans. The choice for one of those plans is made according to a cost function taking into account additional network traffic and peer load caused by the new operators. Section 4.4.4 introduces the details of the cost model.

4.2.2 Data Streams

Before dealing with data stream sharing, we first introduce our notion of data streams in the context of this thesis.

Definition 4.1 (Data stream) A data stream S is a possibly infinite sequence (s_i) of data items s_i with $i \in \mathbb{N}^+$. Only the next data item arriving on the stream can be read from the stream at any time. After reading a data item s_i from the stream, access to any data item s_j with $j \in \mathbb{N}^+$ and $j \leq i$ is not possible any more.   □

Data streams in our context are possibly infinite streams of XML data. Each stream consists of a sequence of XML elements called *data stream items*. The sequence of data stream items is enclosed in a *data stream root element*. The data stream root element can only have a single subelement in the schema or DTD of the stream, namely the root element of the data stream items. Since the stream consists of a sequence of data stream items, the root element of the data stream items can and generally will have multiple occurrence in the data stream schema. The structure of a data stream item is arbitrary. In the DTD of our example data stream photons shown in Figure 2.2, the data stream root element is photons and the data stream items are the XML subtrees rooted at the photon elements. Note that the opening photons tag marks the beginning of the corresponding data stream while the closing photons tag marks its ending. The stream contains a possibly infinite sequence of photon elements. A data stream can be referenced via a *stream node*, corresponding to a document node in standard XML.

The order of the data objects in a data stream depends on the sort order of the stream. A data stream can deliver its data stream elements either sorted according to a certain sort order or unsorted.

Definition 4.2 (Sort order) A data stream $S = (s_i)$ is called sorted according to an order $\lhd$, if and only if:

$$\forall i, j \in \mathbb{N}^+ : i < j \Leftrightarrow s_i \lhd s_j$$ □

Note that the order of data stream items as they are produced and sent out on the stream by the data source implies a *stream order* corresponding to the document order of persistent XML documents.

4.2.3 Data Windows

For being able to execute stateful operators such as aggregations over possibly infinite data streams, we employ a window-based approach. The contents of a data stream are partitioned

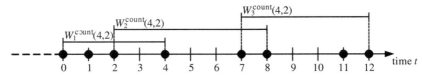

Figure 4.4: Example of a count-based data window with window size 4 and step size 2

into a sequence of data windows and the contents of each data window can subsequently be processed, e. g., by computing an aggregate value over the window contents. In accordance with the literature [Golab and Özsu (2003a,b)], we distinguish *count-based* data windows and *time-based* data windows.

Count-based Data Windows

Count-based data windows have a fixed size in terms of the number of items contained in the window. Items are inserted into the window as they arrive on the corresponding data stream. As soon as the window is completely filled, the processing of the window contents starts. Processing can be as simple as writing the window contents to the output stream which basically corresponds to a grouping of the data stream. However, it can also involve a more complex computation such as an aggregation. The window is updated each time after the processing of the current window contents has finished. The update is performed by sliding the window, leading to the removal of some items from the window contents and to the addition of some new items arriving on the data stream. In a count-based data window, the step size of the window, i. e., the amount by which the window slides along, is given in terms of the number of items that need to be removed from the window contents and to be replaced by new items read from the data stream during each update. Data items are removed from the window contents according to a FIFO strategy. Figure 4.4 shows an example of a count-based data window with window size 4 and step size 2. The bullets in the figure indicate data items arriving on the stream.

Definition 4.3 (Count-based data window) Formally, the definition of the k-th count-based data window $W_k^{count}(\Delta, \mu)$ with window size Δ and step size μ on a data stream S is as follows:

$$W_k^{count}(\Delta, \mu) := \{s_i \in S \mid 1 + (k-1) \cdot \mu \leq i \leq \Delta + (k-1) \cdot \mu\} \qquad \square$$

Time-based Data Windows

Time-based data windows are not organized by the number of items contained in the window but by the value of a certain subelement which is called the *reference element* of the window. A data item is contained in the window if and only if its reference element value is greater than or equal to the lower bound and less than the upper bound of the window. This implies that there must be a total order defined on the values of the reference element and that the lower bound and the upper bound of the window must be defined in terms of the data type of the reference element. In this thesis, we will always assume integer values for the window bounds and the reference element value. Note that the reference element value does not necessarily need to be a real time value. Rather, it suffices if it is an abstract logical time value which basically can be any value of a totally ordered domain. Also note that, for time-based windows to work properly

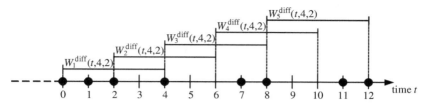

Figure 4.5: Example of a time-based data window with window size 4 and step size 2

on data streams, the reference element values of subsequent data stream items in a data stream must be monotonically increasing. The step size of a time-based data window then indicates the amount by which the lower bound and the upper bound of the window need to be increased during a window update. All elements with reference element values less than the new lower bound are subsequently removed from the window while all new elements arriving on the data stream with reference element values greater than or equal to the new lower bound and less than the new upper bound are inserted into the window. When the data window is completely filled, i.e., all data items with reference element values satisfying the above condition have been inserted, the window contents can be processed and the window can be updated again. Figure 4.5 shows an example of a time-based data window with window size 4 and step size 2. Again, the bullets in the figure indicate data items arriving on the stream.

Definition 4.4 (Time-based data window) Formally, the definition of the k-th time-based data window $W_k^{\mathrm{diff}}(r,\Delta,\mu)$ with reference element r, window size Δ, and step size μ on a data stream S is as follows:

$$W_k^{\mathrm{diff}}(r,\Delta,\mu) := \{s_i \in S \mid s_1.r + (k-1) \cdot \mu \le s_i.r < s_1.r + \Delta + (k-1) \cdot \mu\}$$

Reference element values r are monotonically increasing:

$$\forall s_i, s_j \in S : i < j \Rightarrow s_i.r \le s_j.r \qquad \qquad \square$$

4.3 The WXQuery Subscription Language

In StreamGlobe, we use our *Windowed XQuery (WXQuery)* subscription language for registering subscriptions over XML data streams. WXQuery is an augmented fragment of the XML query language XQuery [W3C (2007d)] with added support for window-based operators.

In Definition 4.5 below, α is a WXQuery expression and χ denotes a condition. A tag name is denoted by t. Further, \$x and \$y are variables representing XML trees, where \$y can also start with a function call to reference a document node or the stream node of a data stream such as stream("photons") in the example subscriptions. A variable representing an aggregate result is denoted by \$a. The variable \$z can represent any of the three kinds of variables \$x, \$y, or \$a as described above. We use $\overline{\pi}$ to denote a relative path that only employs the child axis ("/"). It does not include wildcards ("*"), conditions ("[p]"), or other axes (e.g., "//"). A relative path π differs from $\overline{\pi}$ in that it can also contain conditions. An aggregate function is denoted by Φ, i.e., $\Phi \in \{\mathtt{min}, \mathtt{max}, \mathtt{sum}, \mathtt{count}, \mathtt{avg}\}$. In an actual query, each occurrence of the patterns introduced above must be instantiated to an actual object, e.g., each α needs to be instantiated to an actual WXQuery expression and each π needs to be instantiated to an actual relative path. Patterns are treated like non-terminals in grammar productions, i. e., multiple occurrences of the same pattern in an expression can and generally will be instantiated to different actual objects. For example, the two occurrences of α in the conditional expression (Expression 4 in Definition 4.5 below) will in general be instantiated to different expressions, one for the if-then part and one for the else part.

We use a syntax resembling regular expressions to mark optional or recurring parts of a query. Expressions enclosed in $[\![\ ]\!]^?$, $[\![\ ]\!]^*$, or $[\![\ ]\!]^+$ in the definition are optional, can occur zero or more times, or can occur one or more times, respectively. A vertical bar ($|$) indicates an alternation. An expression of the form $\alpha_{i_1,\ldots,i_n}$ represents a WXQuery expression from a restricted set of expressions. For example, $\alpha_{1,2}$ stands for any one of the two element constructor expressions numbered 1 and 2 in the definition below and $\alpha_{3,4,5,6,7}$ stands for any one of the remaining expressions numbered 3 to 7.

Definition 4.5 (WXQuery) The WXQuery subscription language comprises all subscriptions that consist only of the following expressions:

1. $<t/>$
   (empty direct element constructor)

2. $<t>\ [\![\alpha_{1,2}\ |\ \{\alpha_{3,4,5,6,7}\}]\!]^*\ </t>$
   (direct element constructor)

3. $[\![\text{for }\$x\text{ in }\$y[\![/\pi]\!]^?[\![|\text{count }\Delta\ [\![\text{step }\mu]\!]^?|\ |\ |[\![/]\!]^2\overline{\pi}\text{ diff }\Delta\ [\![\text{step }\mu]\!]^?|]\!]^?\ |$
   $\text{let }\$a := \Phi(\$y[\![/\pi]\!]^?)]\!]^+$
   $[\![\text{where }\chi]\!]^?$
   $\text{return }\alpha$
   (FLWR expression)

4. if χ then α else α
   (conditional expression)

5. $\$y/\pi$
   (output of subtrees reachable from node $\$y$ through path π)

6. $\$z$
   (output of subtree rooted at node $\$z$)

7. $([\![\alpha[\![,\alpha]\!]^*]\!]^?)$
   (sequence)   □

Appendix D on page 201 contains the full WXQuery EBNF grammar. The FLWR expression in the WXQuery definition introduces our new syntax for expressing data windows, e. g., for use with window-based aggregates. Query 3 (q_3) in the network of Figure 4.1 is an example for the use of such an aggregate. Figure 4.6 below shows the query.

```
<photons>
  { for $w in stream("photons")/photons/photon
      [coord/cel/ra >= 120.0 and
       coord/cel/ra <= 138.0 and
       coord/cel/dec >= -49.0 and
       coord/cel/dec <= -40.0]
      |det_time diff 20 step 10|
    let $a := avg($w/en)
    return <avg_en> { $a } </avg_en> }
</photons>
```

Figure 4.6: Query 3 (q_3)

Query 4 (q_4) employs a different window and is shown in Figure 4.7 below.

```
<photons>
  { for $w in stream("photons")/photons/photon
      [coord/cel/ra >= 120.0 and
       coord/cel/ra <= 138.0 and
       coord/cel/dec >= -49.0 and
       coord/cel/dec <= -40.0]
      |det_time diff 60 step 40|
    let $a := avg($w/en)
    where $a >= 1.3
    return <avg_en> { $a } </avg_en> }
</photons>
```

Figure 4.7: Query 4 (q_4)

The definition of a data window is enclosed in "|" characters. Count-based windows—indicated by the keyword count—contain a fixed number of items given by the numeric value of Δ. Optionally, a step size μ determining the update interval of the data window can be specified. For example, the window |count 20 step 10| defines a data window that always contains 20 data items and removes the 10 oldest entries from the window while adding the next 10 new data items arriving on the stream during each update. If omitted, the step size defaults to the value of Δ, meaning the contents of the window are completely replaced by new ones during each update.

The situation is analogous for time-based windows, except that Δ indicates the size of the window in time units and the step size indicates the time interval between two successive data windows. Again, the step size defaults to Δ if omitted. Time-based windows can only be applied on data streams that are sorted according to the values of a particular *reference element* that is used to control the window. This premise could be somewhat relaxed to a fuzzy order by requiring that a fixed sized buffer is sufficient to derive the total order. An example for a time-based window is |det_time diff 60 step 40| in query q_4. Note that the path inside the window is not meant to be evaluated yielding a sequence as defined by the conventional XQuery semantics. Rather, it specifies the reference element controlling the window. The path to the reference element is either absolute starting at the data stream root element (photons in our example data stream) or relative to the context node of the data window (photon in the example queries). Note that an absolute path may specify a reference element that is not a descendant of the window context node. In this case, the implementation must implicitly add the reference element to each item in the window since the reference element value is needed for evicting items from the window during subsequent window updates. Also, if the window context node may occur multiple times within a single data stream item, one reference element value may be valid for multiple items in the data window at the same time. We expect each data stream item to contain a unique reference element in practice, e.g., a timestamp. If the reference element is missing, we completely ignore the corresponding data stream item and all of its subelements and do not insert them into the window. If the reference element occurs multiple times within a data stream item, we use the first occurrence in stream order.

Basically, the WXQuery window syntax constitutes an XPath extension that allows the addition of a window definition to the end of a path. The semantics of the window extension is such that the result of an XPath expression is a sequence of windows instead of a sequence of items. The contents of each window in turn form a sequence of items. The window extension also brings about changes in the semantics of for loops in WXQuery as compared to XQuery. In addition to iterating over a sequence of items, a for loop in WXQuery can also iterate over a sequence of sequences, i.e., a sequence of windows. Therefore, in contrast to standard XQuery, a for loop in WXQuery can also bind a sequence, i.e., the contents of a window, to a variable. The WXQuery window syntax allows the definition of sliding and tumbling windows as described in the literature [Golab and Özsu (2003a,b); Patroumpas and Sellis (2006)]. For tumbling windows, the window step size μ is larger than the window size Δ, resulting in a sequence of windows that does not necessarily cover each data item in the input stream. In this thesis, we restrict the discussion to sliding windows with $\mu \leq \Delta$ and to queries with at most one data window per input data stream. In addition to sliding windows, which have two sliding endpoints, the literature further describes fixed windows, which have two fixed endpoints, and landmark windows, which have one fixed and one sliding endpoint.

It is worth pointing out that WXQuery data windows as introduced above could also be expressed using conventional XQuery syntax. Compare, for example, the WXQuery specifying a count-based data window in Figure 4.8 with a possible equivalent formulation in standard XQuery in Figure 4.9. We handle window construction in standard XQuery using a recursive function *cwin* that returns the next window each time the function is called. Figures 4.10 and 4.11 show an according example for a query with a time-based data window. Again, we use a recursive function *dwin* for window construction in XQuery. The reasons why we introduced a new window syntax in WXQuery are threefold.

- First, as can be seen from the examples, the new syntax is much less verbose and easier to read than the standard syntax.

- Second, the semantics of the recursive function in standard XQuery requires reading the entire input data before starting to build the first window. This blocking behavior is not applicable when dealing with possibly infinite data streams. Therefore, the new window syntax in WXQuery is also meant to express the streaming nature of the query and of query processing.

- Third, the dedicated window syntax can be implemented easier and more efficiently through special-purpose built-in operators.

Note that in the standard XQuery syntax, an explicit root element for each data window is introduced. It shows up as a direct element constructor in the recursive functions of Figures 4.9 and 4.11, constructing an element cw or dw enclosing the window contents, respectively.

```
for $w in doc("data.xml")/a/b|count 4 step 2|
return
  <result>
    <win> { $w } </win>
  </result>
```

Figure 4.8: WXQuery with count-based data window

```
declare function local:cwin($count as xs:integer,
                            $step as xs:integer,
                            $data as node()*) as node()*
{
  let $cwin := fn:subsequence($data, 1, $count)
  let $tail := fn:subsequence($data, $step + 1)
  return
    if (fn:count($data) < $count) then
      ()
    else
      if (fn:count($data) = $count) then
        (<cw> { $cwin } </cw>)
      else
        (<cw> { $cwin } </cw>, local:cwin($count, $step, $tail))
};

for $x in doc("data.xml")/a
return
  <result>
    { for $w in local:cwin(4, 2, $x/b)
      return
        <win> { $w/* } </win> }
  </result>
```

Figure 4.9: XQuery with count-based data window

The query formulations in standard XQuery also explicitly reveal the behavior when reaching the end of a finite input stream. The end of a stream is indicated by an end of stream marker, i. e., a closing data stream root element tag. Three different semantics are possible when reaching the end of an input stream:

Cut The *cut* semantics only returns data windows that are guaranteed to contain all the relevant data. For count-based windows, this means that the final data window is not returned if it contains less data elements than specified by the window size. For time-based windows, processing terminates whenever the final data item arriving in the input stream enters the current data window. The corresponding data window is not returned. This implies that the cut semantics can lead to some items at the end of the data stream never being returned as the contents of a window. The XQueries of Figures 4.9 and 4.11 yield this semantics.

Gather The *gather* semantics gathers all remaining data items at the end of a data stream in one final window and returns this window before terminating. For count-based windows, this can cause the final window to contain less elements than specified by the window size. For time-based windows, the final window returned is the first window containing

```
for $w in doc("data.xml")/a/b|c diff 4 step 2|
return
  <result>
    <win> { $w } </win>
  </result>
```

Figure 4.10: WXQuery with time-based data window

the final data item of the input data stream. The XQueries of Figures C.1 on page 198 and C.3 on page 199 in Appendix C yield this semantics.

Run The *run* semantics continues to construct and to return data windows until the final data item of the input stream leaves the current window during the window update process. All non-empty windows up to that point are returned before processing terminates. This causes the windows to run empty when reaching the end of the input stream. Therefore, when using count-based data windows, the run semantics can cause the final $\lceil (\Delta - 1)/\mu \rceil$ windows to contain less data items than specified by the window size. The XQueries of Figures C.2 on page 198 and C.4 on page 200 in Appendix C yield this semantics.

We use the cut semantics for count-based data windows and the run semantics for time-based data windows in our StreamGlobe implementation. Note that the handling of the end of a finite data stream is an issue that is dealt with here for the sake of completeness. It does, however, not affect the processing of a running stream before reaching the end of the stream.

The let construct of WXQuery is restricted compared to ordinary XQuery as it is only used to assign to a variable a singleton aggregate result value. Conditions in our context, whether they appear in a where clause ("χ") or within a path ("[*p*]"), are *predicates* that consist of *atomic predicates*. A predicate is either a single atomic predicate or a conjunction of atomic predicates. We deal extensively with disjunctive predicates in Chapter 6. Atomic predicates can be of the form $\$v \, \theta \, c$ or $\$v \, \theta \, \$w + c$, where $\$v$ and $\$w$ represent either aggregate values or paths of the form $\overline{\pi}$, c represents a constant value, and $\theta \in \{=, <, \leq, >, \geq\}$. Constant values can be negative and are either integer values or decimal values with a finite number of decimal places.

We concentrate on filtering operators, i.e., on selection and projection operators, as well as on window-based aggregate operators in this chapter. Thus, the subscriptions we consider always have one single input data stream. Furthermore, we restrict ourselves to queries with a single for loop in the context of this chapter. We introduce support for more complex queries including join queries with multiple input streams in Chapter 5.

During in-network query processing, we postpone any restructuring of the query result to a postprocessing step at the super-peer that is connected to the peer that registered the original subscription. Restructuring comprises the construction of new elements in the result returned by a query as well as the reordering and renaming of input stream elements in the query result. The result of the postprocessing is delivered to its final destination and is not considered for further reuse in the network. Therefore, in the case of subscriptions employing only selection and projection operators, the schema of a data stream generated during in-network query processing can differ from the schema of the corresponding original data stream only by some missing elements that have been removed by a projection operator. Selection operators do not affect the data stream schema at all. We denote queries whose result streams have a schema that is a subset of the corresponding input stream schema as *structure-preserving* queries.

Definition 4.6 (Structure-preserving query) A *structure-preserving query* denotes a query that employs only selection and projection operators, i.e., a query for which the schema of

```
declare function local:dwin($start as xs:integer,
                            $diff as xs:integer,
                            $step as xs:integer,
                            $data as node()*,
                            $refs as node()*) as node()*
{
  let $dwin := for $i in $data
               let $ds := for $d in $i/descendant-or-self::node()
                          where some $r in $refs satisfies $r is $d
                          return $d
               where $ds[1] >= $start and $ds[1] < $start + $diff
               return $i
  let $tail := for $i in $data
               let $ds := for $d in $i/descendant-or-self::node()
                          where some $r in $refs satisfies $r is $d
                          return $d
               where $ds[1] >= $start + $step
               return $i
  return
    if (fn:count($dwin) = fn:count($data)) then
      ()
    else
      (<dw> { $dwin } </dw>, local:dwin($start + $step, $diff, $step,
                                        $tail, $refs))
};

for $x in doc("data.xml")/a
return
  <result>
    { for $w in local:dwin(0, 4, 2, $x/b, $x/b/c)
      return
        <win> { $w/* } </win> }
  </result>
```

Figure 4.11: XQuery with time-based data window

---

the query result may differ from the schema of the query input only by one or more missing elements that have been removed by a projection operator. □

Example 4.1 (Structure-preserving queries) Queries q_1 and q_2 of Figures 4.2 and 4.3 are examples of structure-preserving queries. □

We postpone any other more complex data stream schema transformations to the postprocessing step. The only exception are subscriptions containing aggregate or join operators. In this case, a result data stream with a generic schema is produced by in-network query processing. The generic schema consists of a generic enclosing element for each data stream item in the result data stream and one generic subelement for each aggregate or join result value computed in the subscription. We denote queries that generate a completely new result schema as *structure-mutating* queries.

Definition 4.7 (Structure-mutating query) A *structure-mutating query* is a query that contains data windows, aggregate function calls, or joins, i. e., a query for which the schema of the query result may be completely different from the schema of the query input.   □

Example 4.2 (Structure-mutating queries) Queries q_3 and q_4 of Figures 4.6 and 4.7 are examples of structure-mutating queries.   □

We require each result item returned by a query to contain at least one element of the query input or an aggregate value based on elements of the query input. Thus, we can guarantee that the result of in-network query processing contains all the necessary information for postprocessing. An example for an invalid query would be a query that returns an empty tag for each photon with an energy value above a certain threshold. Since attributes in XML data can always be converted into corresponding elements, we restrict ourselves to dealing with elements. Remember that we defer the introduction of support for join queries with multiple input streams and the handling of disjunctive predicates to later chapters.

4.4   Data Stream Sharing

The data stream sharing optimization technique comprises a properties approach for representing subscriptions and data streams, shareability and dependency relations between the properties of subscriptions and data streams, a cost model, and the algorithms for finding, comparing, and choosing an appropriate stream for satisfying a new subscription. Furthermore, this section presents the handling of window-based aggregate operators as well as some optimizations and extensions that further improve the effectiveness and the applicability of data stream sharing.

4.4.1   Overview

Figure 4.12 gives a schematic overview of the data stream sharing optimization process in StreamGlobe. The WXQuery parser is part of the optimizer component within the speaker-peer of a StreamGlobe network as described in Section 2.3.4. The parser transforms a newly arriving WXQuery obeying the language syntax presented in Section 4.3 into an internal abstract properties representation introduced in Section 4.4.2. The properties representation serves as input to the actual data stream sharing optimization algorithm. The main part of the algorithm is the discovery component introduced in Algorithm 4.1 of Section 4.4.5. The data stream discovery algorithm is responsible for searching the StreamGlobe backbone network for shareable streams suitable for satisfying a new query. The discovery algorithm retrieves the current network state, including network topology and properties of available data streams, from a metadata repository maintained by the speaker-peer. The algorithm employs the property matcher to determine whether there are possibly preprocessed data streams available in the network which satisfy the requirements of the new query. The property matcher matches the properties of found data streams with those of the new query using Algorithm 4.2 of Section 4.4.5. If sharing a stream is possible, the plan generator creates a corresponding distributed query evaluation plan such as the one shown in Appendix A.3 on page 186. The optimizer chooses the best plan among all generated plans according to a cost model introduced in Section 4.4.4. Finally, the execution engines of the affected super-peers in the StreamGlobe backbone network deploy and execute the chosen distributed query evaluation plan as described in Section 2.3.4.

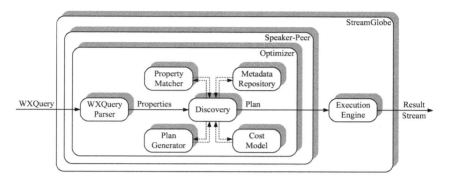

Figure 4.12: Schematic illustration of the optimization process

4.4.2 Query and Data Stream Properties

We represent both, subscriptions and data streams using the same kind of properties representation. This is possible since a subscription can always be regarded as producing a result data stream and a data stream can in turn always be regarded as being the result of a subscription.

The properties of subscriptions and data streams consist of three parts and describe how the associated (result) data stream is generated. Figures 4.13 to 4.16 show simplified schematic illustrations of the properties of Queries q_1 to q_4 from Sections 4.1 and 4.3. Properties describe a subscription or a data stream as a set of original input data streams, a set of operators for each input data stream and, for each operator, a set of conditions specifying the operator. The operators reflect how the respective input data stream is transformed into the represented (result) data stream. Operator conditions comprise selection predicates, projection elements, data window specifications, or aggregate operators in combination with the identifier of the corresponding aggregated element. Predicates, e. g., selection predicates, are stored using a graph representation as shown in Figures 4.13 to 4.16. We introduce this representation in more detail in Section 4.4.5. Data windows for window-based aggregate operators are also stored in a specific format containing the ordered reference element (only for time-based windows), the window type (count or diff), the window size (Δ) and the step size (μ).

We obtain the properties of a newly registered subscription by parsing the (W)XQuery subscription and translating it into its corresponding (W)XQueryX [W3C (2007c)] representation. From this representation, which is a standard XML file, we extract the necessary information to be stored in the properties data structure using XPath [W3C (2007b)]. The properties approach

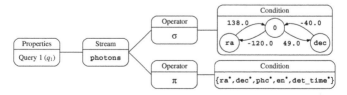

Figure 4.13: Abstract properties of q_1

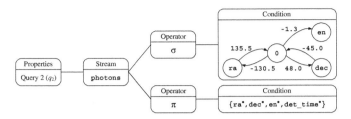

Figure 4.14: Abstract properties of q_2

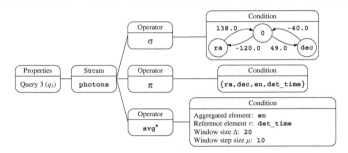

Figure 4.15: Abstract properties of q_3

described here supports queries with multiple input data streams and without nesting. In Chapter 5, we introduce an extended, more flexible properties structure which supports a larger class of queries including nested queries and joins. Furthermore, the extended properties structure enables advanced and even more effective data stream sharing.

Note that the properties structure as described above serves two purposes. First, it represents the parts of the originally queried input data streams that are required for satisfying the corresponding subscription. Second, it describes the contents of a subscription's result data stream relative to the contents of the subscription's input data streams. Also note that properties abstract from transformation details such as the exact structuring of query results as specified in the corresponding original queries.

4.4.3   Shareability and Dependency Relations

In order for a subscription to be able to reuse an existing data stream in the network, the data stream to be reused must contain all the necessary information for satisfying the subscription.

Definition 4.8 (Shareability relation) The *shareability relation* $\sqsubseteq_{\mathrm{sr}}$ is defined on the set of subscription and data stream properties. For two subscription or data stream properties p and p', $p' \sqsubseteq_{\mathrm{sr}} p$ indicates that the data stream represented by p can be used as input to satisfy the subscription represented by p'. For the shareability relation to be valid, both properties must reference the same original input data streams. Furthermore, for selection operators, the selection predicate $\sigma_{p'}$ of p' must imply the selection predicate σ_p of p, i.e., $\sigma_{p'} \Rightarrow \sigma_p$. For projection operators, the set R' of elements *referenced* in p' must be a subset of the set $\overline{R}$ of *returned*

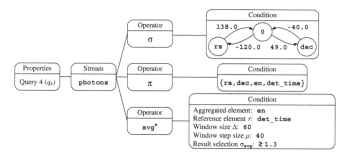

Figure 4.16: Abstract properties of q_4

elements in p, i.e., $R' \subseteq \overline{R}$. An exception from the requirements concerning selection and projection operators occurs when reusing the results of window-based aggregate operators. In this case, the aggregate operator, the aggregated element, and any selection predicates filtering the input data prior to aggregation must be equivalent. Furthermore, any selection on the aggregate result must fulfill the same condition as described for selection operators above. Eventually, the data windows defined in p and p' must be compatible. Let W be the data window defined in p with a window size of Δ and a step size of μ. Let W' be the data window defined in p' with a window size of Δ' and a step size of μ'. Then, W and W' are compatible according to our definition if they have the same window type (count-based or time-based), are defined on the same element, use the same reference element (only for time-based windows), and the following three conditions which are detailed in Section 4.4.6 hold:

- $\Delta' \bmod \Delta = 0$

- $\Delta \bmod \mu = 0$

- $\mu' \bmod \mu = 0$ $\qquad\qquad\qquad\qquad\qquad\qquad\qquad\qquad\qquad\qquad\qquad\qquad$ □

Theorem 4.1 *The shareability relation defines an antisymmetric, transitive partial relation.* □

PROOF: Let p, p', and p'' be the properties of three subscriptions or data streams.

Antisymmetry $(p \sqsubseteq_{\mathrm{sr}} p' \wedge p' \sqsubseteq_{\mathrm{sr}} p \Rightarrow p = p')$:
First, $p \sqsubseteq_{\mathrm{sr}} p' \wedge p' \sqsubseteq_{\mathrm{sr}} p$ implies that p and p' reference the same input data streams. For selection operators, it yields that $\sigma_p \Rightarrow \sigma_{p'} \wedge \sigma_{p'} \Rightarrow \sigma_p$, i.e., $\sigma_p \Leftrightarrow \sigma_{p'}$. For projection operators and in the absence of any aggregate values, $R \subseteq \overline{R'} \wedge R' \subseteq \overline{R}$ holds. Here, R and R' denote the sets of elements referenced in p and p' while $\overline{R}$ and $\overline{R'}$ denote the sets of elements returned as output elements by p and p', respectively. Further, from $\overline{R} \subseteq R \wedge \overline{R'} \subseteq R'$ follows $R \subseteq \overline{R'} \subseteq R' \subseteq \overline{R} \subseteq R$ and therefore $R = \overline{R} = \overline{R'} = R'$. Finally, if p contains a data window W and p' contains a data window W', it remains to be shown that $W = W'$. From $\Delta \bmod \Delta' = 0 \wedge \Delta' \bmod \Delta = 0$ follows $\Delta = \Delta'$. Similarly, from $\mu \bmod \mu' = 0 \wedge \mu' \bmod \mu = 0$ follows $\mu = \mu'$. Therefore, $W = W'$ since the remaining properties of both windows are equal due to $p \sqsubseteq_{\mathrm{sr}} p' \wedge p' \sqsubseteq_{\mathrm{sr}} p$. For the same reason, the remaining properties of any aggregation are also equal.

Transitivity $(p \sqsubseteq_{\mathrm{sr}} p' \wedge p' \sqsubseteq_{\mathrm{sr}} p'' \Rightarrow p \sqsubseteq_{\mathrm{sr}} p'')$:
From $p \sqsubseteq_{\mathrm{sr}} p' \wedge p' \sqsubseteq_{\mathrm{sr}} p''$ follows that p, p', and p'' all reference the same input data streams. For

selection operators, the transitivity of predicate implication yields $(\sigma_p \Rightarrow \sigma_{p'} \wedge \sigma_{p'} \Rightarrow \sigma_{p''}) \Rightarrow$ $(\sigma_p \Rightarrow \sigma_{p''})$. For projection operators, $R \subseteq \overline{R'} \wedge R' \subseteq \overline{R''}$ holds in the absence of any aggregate values. Because of $\overline{R'} \subseteq R'$, the transitivity of the subset relation yields $R \subseteq \overline{R''}$. Finally, it remains to be shown that a data window W in p with window size Δ and step size μ can reuse a data window W'' in p'' with window size Δ'' and step size μ''. Because of $p \sqsubset_{sr} p' \wedge$ $p' \sqsubset_{sr} p''$, we know that $\Delta \bmod \Delta' = 0 \wedge \Delta' \bmod \Delta'' = 0$. This yields $\Delta \bmod \Delta'' = 0$. Similarly, $\mu \bmod \mu' = 0 \wedge \mu' \bmod \mu'' = 0$ yields $\mu \bmod \mu'' = 0$. Furthermore, because of $p' \sqsubset_{sr} p''$, the condition $\Delta'' \bmod \mu'' = 0$ holds for the data window defined in p''. The remaining properties of any aggregation are equal in p and p'' due to $p \sqsubset_{sr} p' \wedge p' \sqsubset_{sr} p''$.

The shareability relation $\sqsubset_{sr}$ is not a total relation. As a counter-example, consider queries q_2 and q_3 of Sections 4.1 and 4.3, respectively. Their properties are incomparable according to $\sqsubset_{sr}$, i.e., $\neg(p_{q_2} \sqsubset_{sr} p_{q_3}) \wedge \neg(p_{q_3} \sqsubset_{sr} p_{q_2})$. This is due to the fact that q_3 is an aggregating query that returns an aggregate value which cannot be shared by the non-aggregating query q_2. Furthermore, the selection predicates of the selection operators in q_2 are more restrictive than those in q_3. Thus, the result data stream of q_2 does not contain all the necessary data for satisfying q_3. An even simpler counter-example are two queries referencing different input data streams. Such queries obviously are incomparable according to $\sqsubset_{sr}$.

The shareability relation is neither reflexive nor irreflexive. The fact that the set R of elements referenced in p can be a proper superset of the set $\overline{R}$ of returned elements in p contradicts the reflexivity of the shareability relation. Furthermore, the window condition $\Delta \bmod \mu = 0$ does not necessarily hold for an arbitrary p. On the other hand, the possibility of queries with $R = \overline{R}$ and, for each data window defined in the subscription, $\Delta \bmod \mu = 0$ contradicts the irreflexivity of the shareability relation. Note that the shareability relation can be made reflexive by treating semantically equivalent properties as a special case that always allows result sharing among such properties. For the sake of clarity and a shorter presentation, we omit this special case in the algorithms presented in this chapter.   ∎

The shareability relation can be visualized as a *shareability graph*.

Definition 4.9 (Shareability graph) A shareability graph $G_{sg} = (V_{sg}, E_{sg})$ is defined as a directed graph with a set of vertices V_{sg} and a set of edges E_{sg}. A vertex in the graph represents the properties of a subscription or a data stream, respectively. A directed edge from a vertex p to a vertex p' indicates that the (result) data stream represented by p can be shared to satisfy the query represented by p', i.e., $p' \sqsubset_{sr} p$.   □

Figure 4.17(a) shows the shareability graph for queries q_1 to q_4 in the example network of Figure 4.1. Queries q_2, q_3, and q_4 can share the result of query q_1. Furthermore, query q_4 can additionally share the result of query q_3. Note that, due to the transitivity of the shareability relation, the edges from p_{q_1} to p_{q_3} and from p_{q_3} to p_{q_4} imply the edge from p_{q_1} to p_{q_4} in the graph. Also, q_1, q_2, and q_3 could theoretically share their own result streams as input streams. This is not possible for q_4 since $\Delta \bmod \mu = 60 \bmod 40 = 20 \neq 0$ holds for this query. However, when handling the special case of semantically equivalent properties described above, sharing would theoretically also be possible in this case.

Definition 4.10 (Dependency relation) The *dependency relation* $\sqsubset_{dr}$ is a restriction of the shareability relation including only those pairs of properties that depend on each other in an actual system state. For two subscription or data stream properties p and p', $p' \sqsubset_{dr} p$ indicates that the data stream represented by p is actually used as input to satisfy the subscription represented by p'.   □

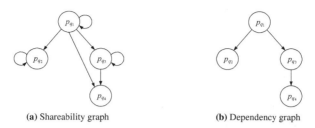

(a) Shareability graph   (b) Dependency graph

Figure 4.17: Shareability and dependency graphs for queries q_1 to q_4

Theorem 4.2 *The dependency relation defines an irreflexive, asymmetric partial relation.* □

PROOF: The irreflexivity follows from the fact that a query cannot use its own result data stream as input in an actual system state. The asymmetry follows from the fact that two queries cannot mutually use their result data streams as inputs in an actual system state. The rest of the theorem follows directly from the definition of the dependency relation and from Theorem 4.1. ■

The dependency relation can be visualized as a *dependency graph*.

Definition 4.11 (Dependency graph) A dependency graph $G_{dg} = (V_{dg}, E_{dg})$ is defined as a directed graph with a set of vertices V_{dg} and a set of edges E_{dg}. A vertex in the graph represents the properties of a subscription or a data stream, respectively. A directed edge from a vertex p to a vertex p' indicates that the (result) data stream represented by p is actually being shared to satisfy the query represented by p', i. e., $p' \sqsubset_{dr} p$. □

The set of vertices of a dependency graph is identical to the set of vertices of the corresponding shareability graph. The set of edges of a dependency graph is a subset of the set of edges of the corresponding shareability graph. Figure 4.17(b) shows the dependency graph for the example network state of Figure 4.1(b).

4.4.4   Cost Model

The cost function f_{cost} used in our cost model focuses on the amount of additional network traffic and peer load caused by answering a new subscription. Other parameters such as latency of network connections and memory usage of stream processing operators could also be added. To define f_{cost}, we need to introduce some notation. Let p be the properties of a new continuous query q that is to be registered in the network. Then $\overline{size}(p)$ denotes the average size of one data stream item (e. g., one photon) of the stream represented by p. Let P_q be the set of properties of all input data streams of q, $\overline{occ}(n_s)$ the average occurrence and $\overline{size}(n_s)$ the average size of element n_s in the input stream represented by properties s, and Π_{p_s} the set of projection elements of p concerning the input stream represented by s. Then, for a subscription that only contains selection and projection operators, $\overline{size}(p)$ is calculated using the following formula:

$$\overline{size}(p) := \sum_{s \in P_q} \left(\overline{size}(s) - \sum_{n_s \notin \Pi_{p_s}} \left(\overline{occ}(n_s) \cdot \overline{size}(n_s) \right) \right) \tag{4.1}$$

Note that in the above formula, $\overline{\text{size}}(p)$ denotes the average size of one data stream item in the stream represented by p, e. g., one photon element in stream photons, whereas $\overline{\text{size}}(n_s)$ denotes the average size of one subelement n_s, e. g., of the phc subelement of a photon. For aggregate queries, the result data stream is a stream of aggregate result values. The average result data stream size is therefore independent of the input stream size in this case and is computed as the size of the computed aggregate values and their surrounding element tags. For queries returning the contents of data windows, the average size of a data window needs to be determined. For count-based data windows, this can be done by multiplying the window size with the average size of the items contained in the window and by adding the sizes of the enclosing window tags. This works analogously for time-based data windows except that the average number of data items contained in a window must be estimated as the product of the input stream frequency and the window size.

The average frequency of data items in the stream represented by p is denoted by $\overline{\text{freq}}(p)$. With $\text{sel}(\sigma_p)$ denoting the selectivity of the subscription represented by p, $\overline{\text{freq}}(p)$ can be computed as follows:

$$\overline{\text{freq}}(p) := \text{sel}(\sigma_p) \cdot \sum_{s \in P_q} \overline{\text{freq}}(s) \tag{4.2}$$

Note that the expression $\sum_{s \in P_q} \overline{\text{freq}}(s)$ in this formula depends on the semantics of the employed operators in q. The above formula is valid for selection operators. Projection operators do not influence $\overline{\text{freq}}(p)$. For window-based queries, $\overline{\text{freq}}(p)$ depends on the step size defined for the data window and the average frequency of the input data stream. For count-based data windows, $\overline{\text{freq}}(p)$ corresponds to the frequency of the corresponding input data stream divided by the step size μ of the data window. For time-based data windows, $\overline{\text{freq}}(p)$ depends on the distribution of the values of the reference element in the data stream items arriving on the input stream. To be able to estimate the frequency of the result data stream in such a case, we keep track of the average increment of the reference element value between two successive data items arriving on the stream. Dividing the step size μ of the time-based data window by this average increment yields the average number of data items that need to be read from the stream before the window update is complete. Then, as with count-based data windows, we divide the frequency of the input data stream by this estimated number of data items to obtain the estimated average frequency of the result data stream.

Introducing b_e as the maximum bandwidth of a network connection e, we can characterize the relative amount u_e^b of bandwidth of e used by the additional data streams routed over e for answering q using the following formula:

$$u_e^b := \frac{\sum_{p \in P_e} \left(\overline{\text{size}}(p) \cdot \overline{\text{freq}}(p) \right)}{b_e} \tag{4.3}$$

Here, P_e denotes the set of properties of all additional data streams added over e to answer q.

The average computational load caused by an operator o on a peer v with a set of input stream properties P_o is denoted by $\overline{\text{load}}(o, v, P_o)$. The maximum load of a peer v is represented by l_v. The relative amount u_v^l of computational load on a peer v caused by the additional operators in O_v installed at v for answering a new subscription can be computed as follows:

$$u_v^l := \frac{\sum_{o \in O_v} \overline{\text{load}}(o, v, P_o)}{l_v} \tag{4.4}$$

Cost function inputs such as average frequencies of data stream items, average sizes and occurrences of elements, and selectivities of operators are obtained from statistics and selectivity estimations. Collecting statistics over XML data has already been investigated in the literature before. For example, Freire et al. (2002) propose an XML statistics model and framework for collecting statistics over persistent XML documents. In StreamGlobe, the StatistiX component introduced in Section 2.3.2 is responsible for collecting the necessary statistics for each original input stream registered in the network. The statistics of the original stream, e. g., the average frequency of data stream items arriving on the stream, can then be used to compute the corresponding statistics for transformed versions of the stream. An example for this is the multiplication of the selectivity of a selection operator with the original stream frequency to obtain the average frequency of the transformed stream as in Equation 4.2 above. The StatistiX component also maintains histograms of element values. The optimizer uses these histograms for selectivity estimations. We use equi-width histograms in StreamGlobe since these can easily be updated continuously with new values arriving on input streams. To avoid that histograms grow indefinitely over infinite streaming inputs, we proceed as follows. Whenever the size of a histogram, i. e., the number of values contained in the histogram, exceeds a certain threshold, we initialize a second histogram and subsequently add each newly arriving value to both histograms. Selectivity estimations continue to use the first histogram during this phase since the new histogram does not yet contain enough values to allow meaningful estimations. After the size of the first histogram reaches another threshold, we switch to the new histogram for subsequent selectivity estimations and deallocate the old histogram. The difference between the second and the first threshold thus yields the minimum amount of values a histogram must contain before it is considered to deliver sufficiently meaningful selectivity estimations.

The average load $\overline{\text{load}}(o, v, P_o)$ of an operator o on a peer v with a set of input stream properties P_o depends on the performance of the executing peer, expressed by a performance index (perfindex(v)), and the characteristics of the operator itself. For example, assuming a linear dependency of the load caused by a selection operator σ from the frequency $\overline{\text{freq}}(s)$ of its only input stream s, the average load caused by σ on a peer v can be defined as $\overline{\text{load}}(\sigma, v, \{s\}) :=$ baseload(σ) $\cdot$ perfindex(v) $\cdot \overline{\text{freq}}(s)$. Here, baseload($\sigma$) represents a base load factor for the selection operator. Factors like base loads of operators and performance indices of peers as well as formulas for combining these factors yielding realistic load estimations have to be determined, e. g., on the basis of reference values.

The cost function f_{cost} is then defined as follows:

$$f_{\text{cost}}(\mathscr{P}) := \gamma \cdot \left(\sum_{e \in E_{\mathscr{P}}} \left(u_e^b + \max(0, (u_e^b - a_e^b)) \cdot \exp(u_e^b - a_e^b) \right) \right) + \\ (1 - \gamma) \cdot \left(\sum_{v \in V_{\mathscr{P}}} \left(u_v^l + \max(0, (u_v^l - a_v^l)) \cdot \exp(u_v^l - a_v^l) \right) \right) \tag{4.5}$$

In this function, $\mathscr{P}$ denotes the evaluation plan of the new subscription. The plan describes which operators have to be installed on which peers and how the generated data streams have to be routed through the network. Furthermore, $E_{\mathscr{P}}$ is the set of network connections and $V_{\mathscr{P}}$ is the set of peers affected by plan $\mathscr{P}$. A weighting factor $\gamma \in [0, 1]$ determines which part of the cost function should be more dominant—network traffic or peer load. We add an exponential penalty for overload situations on peers and network connections. The relative amount of available bandwidth on network connection e and of available computational load on peer v is represented by a_e^b and a_v^l, respectively. A plan $\mathscr{P}$ is better than another plan $\mathscr{P}'$ according to cost function f_{cost}, expressed by $\mathscr{P} \prec_{f_{\text{cost}}} \mathscr{P}'$, if and only if $f_{\text{cost}}(\mathscr{P}) < f_{\text{cost}}(\mathscr{P}')$.

4.4.5   Stream Sharing Algorithms

We now describe our stream sharing algorithms for registering and efficiently satisfying new continuous queries in a distributed DSMS. The algorithms search for shareable data streams in the network, compare the properties of new subscriptions to those of existing data streams, and decide which streams to reuse at which peers.

Query Registration

The query registration algorithm searches for shareable data streams in the network and decides for each available data stream whether that stream can actually be shared for answering the new query. This decision is made by comparing the query properties with the corresponding data stream properties. Further, the algorithm decides whether a newly found evaluation plan for the new query is better than the previously best plan.

The algorithm is divided into four parts. The REGISTERQUERY algorithm shown in Algorithm 4.1 describes the discovery of shareable data streams and the generation of corresponding query evaluation plans. The MATCHPROPERTIES and MATCHPREDICATES algorithms which are detailed in Algorithms 4.2 and 4.3 handle the matching of properties and of predicates, respectively. Finally, the MATCHAGGREGATIONS algorithm deals with the matching of aggregate operators. Beginning with Algorithm 4.1, the inputs p_q and v_q are the properties of the new subscription q and the network node where q is registered, respectively. The output of the algorithm is the evaluation plan $\mathscr{P}$, describing how the network has to be changed in terms of installed operators and routed data streams in order to satisfy q. Note that there will always be at least one plan that is suitable for answering q—provided that q refers to existing inputs— namely the plan using the originally registered versions of q's input streams. The goal of our approach is to find possibly transformed versions of these streams that can be used for satisfying q, potentially by applying some further transformations. The available transformed versions of streams result from in-network query processing of previously registered continuous queries.

Algorithm 4.1 starts with an empty plan $\mathscr{P}$ (line 1) and iterates over all input data streams of q (line 2). The getInputStreams function retrieves from p_q the stream identifiers of the original input streams referenced in the query. It then uses these identifiers to obtain from the speaker-peer metadata repository the set of properties representing these original input streams. For each such input data stream, the algorithm performs some initialization tasks (lines 3–6). Since we restrict the discussion to queries with a single input stream in this chapter, the for loop in line 2 of Algorithm 4.1 is iterated only once for our example queries. First, the algorithm initializes a FIFO queue L_V for network nodes (peers) and another queue L_P for properties. Then, the algorithm stores the properties p_s of the currently considered input data stream s and the network node where this input data stream is registered in p_b and v_b, respectively. The getSource function retrieves the data stream source node from the speaker-peer metadata repository. The variables p_b and v_b represent the properties of the current best solution for the data stream chosen as input for satisfying q and the network node where to find and reuse that stream. Installing the new subscription at the super-peer at which the corresponding original input stream is registered and routing the result to the subscribing peer via a shortest path in the network is set as the initial evaluation plan. This plan is generated by means of the generatePlan function that takes as inputs the properties p_b of the data stream chosen for reuse, the node v_b where to reuse that stream, and the node v_q where the query to be answered is registered and where the query result is needed. At each time during the remaining execution of the algorithm, the current best plan for input data stream s is represented by $\mathscr{P}_s$. Note that the initial plan does

---

Algorithm 4.1 REGISTERQUERY

Input: The properties p_q of the subscription q to be registered and the node v_q where q is to be
     registered.
Output: A distributed query evaluation plan $\mathscr{P}$.

```
 1:  𝒫 ← ∅;
 2:  for all pₛ ∈ getInputStreams(p_q) do
 3:     L_V ← ∅; L_P ← ∅;
 4:     p_b ← pₛ; v_b ← getSource(p_b);
 5:     𝒫ₛ ← generatePlan(p_b, v_b, v_q);
 6:     add(L_V, v_b);
 7:     while L_V ≠ ∅ do
 8:        v ← dequeue(L_V); mark(v);
 9:        for all data streams available at v that are variants of pₛ do
10:           enqueue all associated properties in L_P;
11:        end for
12:        while L_P ≠ ∅ do
13:           p ← dequeue(L_P);
14:           if MATCHPROPERTIES(p, p_q) then
15:              for n ∈ getTargets(v, p) do
16:                 if (¬(isMarked(n)) ∧ (n ∉ L_V)) then
17:                    add(L_V, n);
18:                 end if
19:              end for
20:              𝒫ₛ′ ← generatePlan(p, v, v_q);
21:              if 𝒫ₛ′ ≺_{f_cost} 𝒫ₛ then
22:                 p_b ← p; v_b ← v; 𝒫ₛ ← 𝒫ₛ′;
23:              end if
24:           end if
25:        end while
26:     end while
27:     unmark all nodes;
28:     add(𝒫, 𝒫ₛ);
29:  end for
30:  return 𝒫;
```

---

not reuse any existing preprocessed data streams in the network. Finally, the algorithm adds the
start node v_b of the search in the network as first node to L_V.

If a subscription references more than one input stream, the subscription algorithm handles
each stream individually. The algorithm assures that at least the relevant parts of each input
stream are delivered to the super-peer connected to the peer that registered q. Any combination
of input data streams as demanded by the subscription is performed at this peer during the final
postprocessing step and the result of this combination is not considered for reuse in the network.
This is the same as with any restructuring of the query result as described in Section 4.3. We
investigate possibilities for reusing join result streams in Chapter 5.

After the initialization, the algorithm performs a breadth-first search in the network graph for
each input stream, starting at the super-peer at which the corresponding original input stream of

q is registered. Using a LIFO queue for L_V instead of a FIFO queue would cause the algorithm to perform depth-first search which would be equally possible. We chose breadth-first search because we expect this search strategy to find a good plan earlier than depth-first search. This assumption is based on the fact that breadth-first search takes all potentially shareable branches of a stream into account in turn, instead of examining one branch to the end before switching to the next one. This is, however, only relevant if the optimization is stopped early, e. g., because the optimization time should not exceed a certain threshold. If the optimization is carried out to the end, both search strategies yield the same result. The peers in L_V are dequeued one after another (line 8). Each peer in L_V is marked in order to handle circles in the network graph, i. e., to consider each node at most once. For each dequeued peer, all properties of data streams that are available at the currently handled peer and that are variants of p_s are subsequently inserted into L_P (lines 9–11). These properties are then consecutively taken out of the queue and matched against the properties p_q of q using Algorithm 4.2 (lines 12–14). We describe this process in detail further below. Network connections that do not have any associated properties because they do not carry any data streams are ignored during the breadth-first search. Also, non-matching properties do not add any peers to L_V since following these paths cannot yield a reusable data stream. Pruning the search in this way leads to the breadth-first search traversing only the relevant part of the network instead of the entire network.

If a property p has been successfully matched, its corresponding stream can be reused for answering q. Any unmarked peer to which the stream corresponding to p is delivered is added to L_V to be processed later on (lines 15–19). The getTargets function retrieves the corresponding set of target peers from the speaker-peer metadata repository. For any found solution, the generatePlan function generates a new plan $\mathscr{P}'_s$ (line 20). Then, the algorithm computes the value of the cost function f_{cost} for the plan reusing the found data stream and compares the obtained cost value against the cost value of the current best solution (line 21). Only if the new solution is better according to f_{cost}, we replace the current best solution and store the new best solution along with its cost function value for future comparisons (lines 21–23). When there are no properties left in queue L_P, the next node in L_V is considered. If there are no more nodes left in L_V, the best plan $\mathscr{P}_s$ found for input stream s is added to the overall plan $\mathscr{P}$ for evaluating q (line 28). When all input streams of q have been considered, the algorithm terminates and returns the current best solution for plan $\mathscr{P}$ as the final result.

The termination of the algorithm is guaranteed since there is only a finite number of input data streams of q and of nodes and data streams in the network. For each input data stream, each node can be added to L_V at most once and each time through the while loop in line 7 of the algorithm, one node gets dequeued from L_V. Similar considerations apply to properties of data streams and L_P.

Matching Properties

Algorithm 4.2 is responsible for identifying shareable streams by matching the properties of subscriptions and data streams. For each input data stream of a subscription, the properties of the subscription reflect which operators and operator conditions the subscription employs to transform the respective input stream into the subscription result. These properties need to be matched with the properties of the data streams encountered during stream discovery to find shareable streams for each input stream of the new subscription. The inputs for the properties matching algorithm are the properties p of the data stream that is considered for reuse and the properties p' of the newly registered subscription. The algorithm returns true if these properties match and false otherwise. When restricting the discussion to queries with a single input stream,

---

Algorithm 4.2 MATCHPROPERTIES

Input: The properties p of a data stream to be reused and p' of a subscription to be registered.
Output: true if p and p' match; false otherwise.

```
 1: for all s′ ∈ getInputStreams(p′) do
 2:     smatch ← false;
 3:     for all s ∈ getInputStreams(p) do
 4:        if s = s′ then
 5:           smatch ← true; O ← getOperators(s); O′ ← getOperators(s′);
 6:           for all o ∈ O do
 7:              match ← false;
 8:              for all o′ ∈ O′ do
 9:                 if o = o′ then
10:                    C ← getConditions(o); C′ ← getConditions(o′);
11:                    if o = σ then
12:                       G ← getPredicateGraph(C); G′ ← getPredicateGraph(C′);
13:                       if MATCHPREDICATES(G, G′) then
14:                          match ← true; break;
15:                       end if
16:                    else if o = Π then
17:                       R̄ ← getReturnedElements(C); R′ ← getReferencedElements(C′);
18:                       if (R̄ ⊇ R′) ∨ isAggregated(s) then
19:                          match ← true; break;
20:                       end if
21:                    else if o ∈ {min,max,sum, count,avg} then
22:                       if MATCHAGGREGATIONS(C, C′) then
23:                          match ← true; break;
24:                       end if
25:                    else
26:                       i⃗ ← getParameters(C); i⃗′ ← getParameters(C′);
27:                       if i⃗ = i⃗′ then
28:                          match ← true; break;
29:                       end if
30:                    end if
31:                 end if
32:              end for
33:              if match = false then
34:                 return false;
35:              end if
36:           end for
37:           break;
38:        end if
39:     end for
40:     if smatch = false then
41:        return false;
42:     end if
43: end for
44: return true;
```

each of the `for` loops in lines 1 and 3 of Algorithm 4.2 is iterated only once.

If the input streams of both properties match—checked in lines 1–4 of Algorithm 4.2—the algorithm fetches the operators used to transform the inputs from the properties data structures (line 5) and assigns them to the operator sets O and O', respectively. For each operator in O, there must be a corresponding operator in O'. For example, if O contains a selection operator, the data stream represented by p is only considered for reuse if p' also contains a corresponding selection. Otherwise, the stream of p would not contain all the data needed by q. If a corresponding operator is found in O', we need to assure that the conditions of both operators are compatible. The conditions are fetched from the properties data structures in line 10 of the algorithm. We distinguish four cases (lines 11–30), i. e., selection, projection, window-based aggregate, and unknown operators. If the corresponding operators are selection operators (lines 11–15), the algorithm retrieves the graphs representing the selection predicates (line 12) and tries to match them using Algorithm 4.3. In case of a projection operator (lines 16–20) and in the absence of reused aggregate values, the set $\overline{R}$ of elements that are actually contained in the data stream represented by p has to be a superset of the set R' of all the elements referenced in the new query. Returned elements are marked with bullets in the sets of projection elements within the properties of the example queries of Figures 4.13 to 4.16. Elements that are referenced in a query but not returned as part of the query result appear as unmarked elements in the projection operator conditions of the respective properties. Note that we assume that a query either returns elements from the input stream or aggregate values based on elements from the input stream. The solutions presented in Chapter 5 also allow queries that return a mixture of input elements and aggregate values. However, processing such queries in the network close to the data sources is only beneficial if their result stream causes less network traffic than the input streams. If o and o' are one of the window-based aggregate operators min, max, sum, count, or avg, the MATCHAGGREGATIONS algorithm described further below needs to assure that the corresponding conditions and data windows are compatible (lines 21–24). Reusing aggregate values also induces changes in the handling of selection and projection operators as described in Section 4.4.3. All other operators are handled in the fourth and final case (lines 25–30). These are operators with unknown semantics, in particular user-defined functions. We only require their semantics to be deterministic, i. e., the same operators applied to the same inputs must always yield the same results. The algorithm then demands that not only the operators but also their input vectors as retrieved in line 26 of the algorithm are equal for reusability. More sophisticated techniques for identifying reusable user-defined operators involve the development of suitable operator descriptions which remains an issue for future work.

Matching Predicates

A predicate is represented by a weighted directed graph $G = (V, E)$ within the corresponding properties. The construction and representation of predicate graphs are an extension of earlier work by Rosenkrantz and Hunt (1980) on the processing of conjunctive predicates. In addition to integer valued variables and constants, we also allow decimal values with a finite number of decimal places. First, predicates are normalized to contain only comparisons of the form $\$x \geq c$, $\$x \leq c$ and $\$x \leq \$y + c$ where $\$x$ and $\$y$ represent paths and c represents a constant integer or decimal value. Each path in the predicate becomes a node in V. An atomic predicate of the form $\$x \leq \$y + c$ is represented by a weighted directed edge in E from node $\$x$ to node $\$y$ with weight c. Further, V contains a node for the constant zero. An atomic predicate of the form $\$x \leq c$ is represented by an edge from node $\$x$ to node zero with weight c. An atomic predicate of the form $\$x \geq c$, which can be expressed as $0 \leq \$x - c$, is represented by an edge from node

---

Algorithm 4.3 MATCHPREDICATES

Input: The predicate graphs G of a data stream considered for reuse and G' of a new subscription to be registered.

Output: true if the predicates of G match the predicates of G'; false otherwise.

```
 1: for all v ∈ V do
 2:    vmatch ← false;
 3:    for all v' ∈ V' do
 4:      if v ≡ v' then
 5:        vmatch ← true;
 6:        for all e ∈ {x ∈ E|x connected to v} do
 7:          ematch ← false;
 8:          for all e' ∈ {y ∈ E'|y connected to v'} do
 9:            if ζ(e) ⇐ ζ(e') then
10:              ematch ← true; break;
11:            end if
12:          end for
13:          if ematch = false then
14:            return false;
15:          end if
16:        end for
17:        break;
18:      end if
19:    end for
20:    if vmatch = false then
21:      return false;
22:    end if
23:  end for
24:  return true;
```

---

zero to node $\$x$ with weight $-c$. As illustrating examples consider Figures 4.13 to 4.16 which contain the predicate graphs of the selections in queries q_1 to q_4. After the construction of G, the predicate can be checked for satisfiability and is minimized using techniques introduced by Rosenkrantz and Hunt (1980). If an operator's predicate is unsatisfiable, the corresponding subscription can be rejected. A minimized predicate does not contain any redundant atomic predicates. Note that the construction of the properties together with all the steps described in this paragraph is performed only once for each new subscription during the registration process.

The MATCHPREDICATES algorithm shown in Algorithm 4.3 can match any predicates in the described graph representation, e. g., selection and join predicates. In this chapter, we use it to match the predicates of selection operators. The algorithm takes as inputs the data structures G and G' of the weighted directed graphs representing the selection predicates of the existing data stream and the new subscription. It compares these graphs and returns true if the predicates of G' imply those of G, i. e., reusability of the data stream is not prevented by the predicates. One prerequisite for the possibility of data stream sharing is that, for each node v in the node set V of G, there exists an equivalent node v' in the node set V' of G', denoted $v \equiv v'$ in line 4 of Algorithm 4.3. Nodes are equivalent if the variables represented by them refer to the same element. Furthermore, if two equivalent nodes v and v' have been found, for each edge e con-

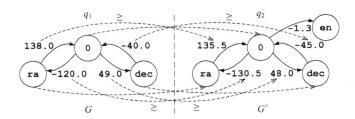

Figure 4.18: Matching predicates

nected to v there must be an edge e' connected to v' such that the atomic predicate represented by e, denoted $\zeta(e)$, is compatible with the atomic predicate represented by e', denoted $\zeta(e')$. In our algorithm, this is the case if $\zeta(e) \Leftarrow \zeta(e')$ in line 9. Figure 4.18 shows an example matching for the predicate graphs of queries q_1 and q_2. For brevity, only the variable names instead of the full paths are shown as node labels in the figure. The dashed arrows indicate the matching vertices and edge weights. All the edge weights of q_1 are greater than the corresponding edge weights of q_2 which indicates that the required predicate implications are true. The definition of $\zeta(e)$ for any edge e in a predicate graph G can be formally expressed as

$$\zeta(e) := (\text{sourcelabel}(e) \leq \text{targetlabel}(e) + \text{weight}(e))$$

where $\text{sourcelabel}(e)$ and $\text{targetlabel}(e)$ denote the absolute path to the variable represented by the source node and the target node of edge e, respectively, and $\text{weight}(e)$ denotes the weight that is associated with edge e.

Examples

We now consider queries q_1 and q_2 of Section 4.1 as illustrative examples for the algorithms described above. We start with the network topology of Figure 4.1. We further assume that stream photons has already been registered in the network and is available at super-peer SP_4. Note that it suffices to consider the super-peer backbone network in the algorithm since the thin-peers are only the start and end points of data streams but do not transform any streams.

Example 4.3 (Query 1 (q_1)) When q_1 is registered, the algorithm first constructs the corresponding properties of the query including the minimized weighted directed graphs representing the selection predicates. The only peer in the network that has a reusable stream is SP_4 and the only reusable stream is the originally registered stream photons. Consequently, the selection and projection operators of q_1 are installed at SP_4 and the result is routed to P_1 using a shortest path in the network, e. g., via SP_5 and SP_1.   □

Example 4.4 (Query 2 (q_2)) Query q_2 is registered at P_2 after q_1 has been registered. At this point in time, the original stream photons is available at SP_4 and the stream filtered by the selection and projection operators of q_1 is available at SP_1, at SP_5, and at SP_4, where it is generated. The algorithm determines that the filtered stream is suitable for answering q_2 because the atomic predicates of the minimized selection predicates in q_1 are all implied by corresponding atomic predicates of the minimized selection predicates in q_2, as can be seen from Figure 4.18. Further, the set of projection elements returned by q_1 is a superset of the set of elements referenced in q_2. Note that, in this example, the original predicates are already minimized since they do not contain any redundant atomic predicates. Altogether, the algorithm identifies four possible solutions for reusing a stream to answer q_2. These include the original stream photons at SP_4 as well as the filtered stream generated for answering q_1 at SP_4, at SP_5, and at SP_1. We assume that reusing the filtered stream at SP_5 yields the lowest value for cost function f_{cost}. Therefore, this stream is duplicated at SP_5. After installing the selection and projection operators of q_2 at SP_5 for performing the necessary additional filtering, the filtered copy of the stream is routed to P_2, again using a shortest path in the network which is via SP_7. □

4.4.6 Window-based Aggregation

Reusing the results of window-based aggregate operators has been studied in the literature before, e.g., by Arasu and Widom (2004c). Our approach differs from this specific previous solution in two ways. First, we introduce a step size in our windows which allows us to explicitly specify when a new aggregate value shall be computed. Second, we consider existing results of other subscriptions for reuse instead of precomputing aggregate results that might never be used. Following Gray et al. (1996), we categorize aggregate operators using three classes. These classes comprise distributive (e.g., min, max, sum, count), algebraic (e.g., avg), and holistic (e.g., median, quantile) aggregates. We concentrate on the distributive and algebraic aggregate operators mentioned above.

The MATCHAGGREGATIONS algorithm is used in Algorithm 4.2 to compare the conditions of window-based aggregate operators. The algorithm compares such operators by examining their input data, their results, and their data windows as follows. First, MATCHAGGREGATIONS checks whether the aggregate considered for reuse and the new aggregate employ the same aggregate operator, are based on the same input data, and aggregate the same element. Furthermore, we need to handle selections in aggregate subscriptions more restrictively than in other subscriptions. We need to assure that any selection performed on the aggregated data stream prior to the aggregation is equivalent in both the reused and the new aggregate subscription. Second, we check whether the aggregate result which is considered for reuse has been filtered in any way. As an example, consider query q_4 which filters its aggregate result $a using the predicate $a > 1.3. Reusing such aggregate values for computing more coarse-grained window aggregates is not possible in general since a part of the necessary data might have been removed. However, these aggregate values can still be reused for aggregates that apply the same or a more restrictive filter on the aggregate result as long as all other prerequisites for reusability are fulfilled.

Eventually, the algorithm examines the data windows of both operators. For time-based windows, reuse is only possible if both windows have the same ordered reference element, e.g., det_time in queries q_3 and q_4. For both, count-based and time-based windows, we require the window size and the step size of the windows to be compatible for being able to reuse existing aggregate values without any further complex optimizations or transformations. One requirement for this is that the window size of the new subscription is a multiple of the window size of the data stream considered for reuse. This guarantees that a fixed number of reused windows fits into one new window. Furthermore, the window size of a reused aggregate's data window must be a multiple of its step size. This assures that a sequence of non-overlapping windows, i.e., aggregate values, covering the entire input data can be obtained—possibly by ignoring some windows or aggregate values. Note that ignored aggregate values might have to be buffered temporarily to be reused for computing subsequent values of the new aggregate.

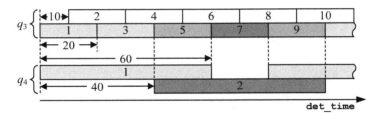

Figure 4.19: Reusing window-based aggregates

Finally, the step size of the window of the new subscription also needs to be a multiple of the step size of the window of the data stream considered for reuse. This guarantees that the reused aggregate delivers an aggregate value at least each time the new aggregate has to produce one. Formally, we can state these three conditions for data window reusability as follows:

- $\Delta' \bmod \Delta = 0$

- $\Delta \bmod \mu = 0$

- $\mu' \bmod \mu = 0$

Note that for the values of avg aggregates to be shareable, we internally represent such aggregates by their appropriate sum and count values. These values are actually transmitted in the super-peer network. The final aggregate value is computed at the super-peer at which the corresponding subscription is registered by evaluating (sum/count). The described internal representation of avg aggregates also enables their reuse for computing sum and count aggregates, i. e., the requirement of equal aggregate operators for shareability can be relaxed.

Example 4.5 (Queries 3 (q_3) and 4 (q_4)) As an example illustrating how our algorithm handles window-based aggregates, consider queries q_3 and q_4 as introduced in Section 4.3. We assume the network of Figure 4.1 with queries q_1 and q_2 already registered as described earlier. Query q_3, which can reuse the result data stream of q_1, is registered at peer P_3 in the network and computes the average energy of all photons detected in a certain area of the sky. The time-based data window has a size of 20 time units and requires the computation of a new aggregate value every 10 time units. Further, q_3 does not filter the aggregate result values in any way. Query q_4 is another aggregate query that employs the same aggregate operator, references the same input data stream, aggregates the same element, and uses the same selection predicate as q_3.

Obviously, in terms of cost function f_{cost}, reusing the result data stream of q_3 at SP_3 is the best solution for answering q_4, provided that reuse is possible. In order to determine shareability, the data windows of both subscriptions need to be compared. Figure 4.19 illustrates the situation. Windows of q_3 that are shaded in light or dark gray in the figure are shared by a correspondingly shaded window of q_4. Windows of q_3 that are shaded in medium gray are shared by two different windows of q_4. Unshaded windows are not shared at all between q_3 and q_4. We compute 60 mod 20 = 0 for the window sizes and 40 mod 10 = 0 for the step sizes of the windows as well as 20 mod 10 = 0 for the window size and the step size of the result data stream of q_3, meaning that reuse is possible. Since 60 div 20 = 3 holds, three consecutive non-overlapping windows of q_3 are needed to form a window of q_4. Because of 20 div 10 = 2, only every second aggregate value of q_3 is to be reused for q_4. Eventually, 40 div 10 = 4 indicates

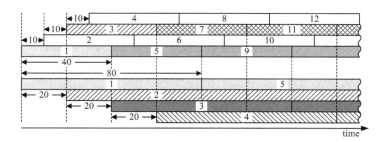

Figure 4.20: Window selection for reusing window-based aggregates

that each time four values of q_3 have been seen, only two of which have been reused, a new aggregate value of q_4 is computed.   □

For being able to reuse previously computed aggregate values of window-based aggregate operators to compute more coarse-grained aggregates, we have developed an operator for selecting the appropriate values during query evaluation in the FluX query engine. Note that we do not necessarily need every single aggregate value of an existing aggregate result stream and that we do not necessarily need the values in the same order as they appear in the reused stream. Therefore, the aggregate value selection operator employs Algorithm 4.4 to select the appropriate values and to buffer and to reorder these values if required.

Example 4.6 (Reusing aggregate values) We assume a stream data window with window size $\Delta = 40$ and step size $\mu = 10$. The query window has a window size of $\Delta' = 80$ and a step size of $\mu' = 20$. Figure 4.20 illustrates the two data windows. The shading and hatching of the windows in the figure indicates which stream windows are shared by which query windows. The stream window with number 5, for example, is shaded in medium gray since it is shared by both, the query window with number 1 shaded in light gray and the query window with number 3 shaded in dark gray. Similarly, the stream window with number 7 is cross-hatched since it is shared

---

Algorithm 4.4 SELECTAGGREGATEVALUES
___
Input: Window sizes Δ and Δ' as well as step sizes μ and μ' of the data window to be reused and the new data window, respectively.
Output: The correct sequence of aggregate values for reuse.

1: buffer first $((\Delta' - \Delta) \text{ div } \mu) + 1$ aggregate values arriving on the stream;
2: **repeat**
3:    $i \leftarrow 0$;
4:    **while** $i < (\Delta' \text{ div } \Delta)$ **do**
5:       send value at buffer position $i \cdot (\Delta \text{ div } \mu)$ to the query engine;
6:       $i \leftarrow i + 1$;
7:    **end while**
8:    remove first $(\mu' \text{ div } \mu)$ values from buffer and read next $(\mu' \text{ div } \mu)$ values from stream into buffer;
9: **until** the buffer contains no more values;

by the two hatched query windows with numbers 2 and 4. Algorithm 4.4 starts by buffering the first $((\Delta' - \Delta) \text{ div } \mu) + 1 = ((80 - 40) \text{ div } 10) + 1 = 5$ aggregate values arriving on the stream. It then sends the aggregate values at buffer positions $i \cdot (\Delta \text{ div } \mu)$ for $0 \leq i < (\Delta' \text{ div } \Delta)$ to FluX. Since $\Delta' \text{ div } \Delta = 80 \text{ div } 40 = 2$ and $\Delta \text{ div } \mu = 40 \text{ div } 10 = 4$, these are the values at buffer positions $0 \cdot 4 = 0$ and $1 \cdot 4 = 4$. Afterwards, the first $\mu' \text{ div } \mu = 20 \text{ div } 10 = 2$ values are removed from the buffer and the next two values are read from the stream and added to the buffer. After updating the buffer, the values needed for computing the next window aggregate value reusing the values in the buffer can be determined as above.   □

The reusing query that is executed in the FluX query engine uses the aggregate values delivered by Algorithm 4.4 as input. The query computes the corresponding final aggregate values over these input values using the appropriate aggregate function (e. g., sum for computing sum and count aggregates) and a count-based data window with equal window size and step size, both set to $(\Delta' \text{ div } \Delta)$.

Note that Algorithm 4.4 buffers all the aggregate values arriving on the input stream. This can be avoided by exactly identifying the aggregate values that need to be buffered and by immediately discarding all the others. Appendix E on page 205 shows the resulting alternative algorithm. Up to now, the StreamGlobe prototype uses an implementation of Algorithm 4.4.

4.4.7 Extensions and Optimizations

On the basis of the algorithms of Section 4.4.5, we now introduce some further extensions and general optimizations improving the quality and the efficiency of data stream sharing.

Bypassing

The result of any subscription evaluation in the network is routed towards the receiving peer via a shortest path in the network. In order to avoid congested network connections and overloaded peers, we introduce a simple bypassing mechanism, thus increasing the search space of our algorithm. Whenever a plan is discovered to cause an overload situation on any network connections or peers, a new internal network graph representing the original network without the overloaded connections and peers is constructed. Then the plan is modified to route its data over shortest paths within this reduced network. This can be repeated multiple times until no overload occurs or the reduced network does not contain any valid paths to the target peer any more. Each plan found during this procedure is compared against the current best plan as described earlier in this chapter.

A disadvantage of the above solution is that the shortest path algorithm needs to be executed multiple times if an overload situation is predicted. Furthermore, the approach can lead to network partitioning in the reduced network, making it impossible to find an overload-free evaluation plan although one might exist. This can be avoided by using an alternative bypassing scheme which computes appropriate weights for each network connection and then uses a shortest path algorithm to find the weighted shortest path between two peers in the network. In this case, the shortest path algorithm needs to be executed only once during the generation of a query evaluation plan. The weight of a network connection can be computed by determining weights based on the current amount of network traffic and peer load on the respective network connection and its two incident peers, and by adding the peer weights to the weight of the network connection. A disadvantage of this scheme is, however, that the weights of network connections and peers need to be updated each time the network state changes.

If the number of iterations needed to find an overload-free plan is low, we expect the first by-passing approach to be more efficient. Independent of the used bypassing solution, the system can reject a query if no plan without overloaded network connections or peers can be found. Irrespective of whether bypassing is used or not, rejecting queries currently is the default behavior in StreamGlobe for dealing with insufficient resources.

Optimized Loop Computation

The loops in the algorithms of Section 4.4.5 iterate over sets of streams, peers, vertices, edges, and properties. Some of these sets contain rather few items in practice, e. g., the operators in a query or the vertices and edges in a predicate graph. This leads to a small number of loop iterations. Additionally, many loops can be exited early, e. g., as soon as a match is found—indicated by the break statements in the algorithms. Some loop computations can be optimized by employing an execution similar to merge joins. For example, the first two loops in Algorithm 4.3 can be executed in a merge join fashion if the vertices in V and V' are sorted lexicographically according to their labels, i. e., according to the paths they represent.

Caching Matching Results

Routing a data stream through the network via several peers without transforming the stream leads to identical data streams and data stream properties being available at many different peers in the network. The basic algorithm of Section 4.4.5 does not take this into account when searching for shareable streams and matches each of the identical properties anew. Furthermore, the algorithms make no difference between incoming and outgoing data streams at a certain peer. This leads to each data stream property being matched twice, once at the source peer and once at the target peer of the corresponding stream. Both problems can be avoided by identifying identical versions of already matched properties and by reusing the corresponding cached matching result.

Exploiting Local Matches

A special case occurs when two or more subscriptions with identical properties are registered at peers that are connected to the same super-peer in the network. This might easily occur in a multi-user network where several users have the same interests and register continuous queries at the same point in the network. Using the basic algorithm, each of these queries would be optimized individually. Therefore, for each such query, the search for shareable streams would start at the super-peers where the input data streams of the query are registered and then traverse the network using breadth-first or depth-first search as described in Section 4.4.5. However, in each case, the result would be to reuse the already present answer to the subscription at the super-peer connected to the subscribing client as this will obviously yield the lowest value for cost function f_{cost}. The situation can easily be improved by checking a new subscription's super-peer for the presence of reusable streams prior to executing the actual query subscription algorithm. The approach could even be extended to checking the properties of data streams available at peers in the neighborhood of the subscribing peer. This could be done either by checking the neighboring peers or, for larger networks where a larger neighborhood should be considered, by flooding the network with a data stream request and using an adaptable horizon for the flooding depth.

4.5 Evaluation

This section presents the results of a performance evaluation that we conducted using our StreamGlobe prototype implementation. For the evaluation, we installed the system on a blade server. Each super-peer ran on one blade. The blades had a 2.8 GHz Intel Xeon processor and 1 GB of main memory each. They were interconnected by a 100 MBit/s LAN. We report on four scenarios here. The first one is the example scenario of Section 4.1 with 8 super-peers, 1 data stream, and 4 queries. The second scenario is based on the same network topology as the first but registers 25 queries in the system. The third scenario is a small scenario using 4 super-peers, 1 data stream, and 4 queries. Three of the super-peers form a triangle in the network topology of this scenario and the fourth, which is the super-peer where the data stream is registered, is connected to one of the three super-peers in the triangle. The fourth scenario uses a 4×4 grid topology with 16 super-peers, 2 data streams, and 100 queries. All data streams and queries are based on real astrophysical data. We generated the queries using a predefined set of query templates for selection, projection, and aggregate queries. For each generated query, the query generator randomly chose a template according to a uniform distribution. Constant values in the template, e. g., in selection predicates or data window definitions, were chosen uniformely from a predefined set of values to enable a certain degree of similarity and shareability between the generated queries. Table 4.1 summarizes the four evaluation scenarios.

For each scenario, we compare three strategies. *Data shipping* simply transmits the entire input data stream from the data source to the target super-peer for each query using a shortest path in the network. The entire query evaluation takes place at the target super-peer. *Query shipping* evaluates each query completely at the super-peer the data source is registered at. The query result is transmitted to the target peer again using a shortest path in the network. This obviously only works for queries that reference a single input data stream which is the case for all the queries used in the evaluation. Finally, *stream sharing* uses our previously described optimization algorithms. The evaluated algorithm implementations correspond to the algorithms as introduced in Sections 4.4.5 and 4.4.6. The extensions and optimizations of Section 4.4.7 were not used in the evaluation. Note that in the worst case, i. e., if no shareable streams can be found for any query, stream sharing degenerates to query shipping. In the evaluated scenarios, unless explicitly stated otherwise, all queries were registered successfully for all three strategies and no queries had to be rejected due to overload situations.

Figures 4.21 and 4.22 show evaluation results in terms of average CPU load in percent and average network traffic on network connections in kbps for the example and the extended example scenarios. As can be seen from the diagrams, query shipping leads to massive peaks of CPU load at data stream source peers (SP_4 in the diagrams) since all the computations on the respective stream are executed there. CPU load at source peers scales linearly with the number of corresponding queries registered, e. g., by a factor of 6 from about 7% in the scenario with 4 queries in Figure 4.21 to about 42% in the scenario with 25 queries in Figure 4.22. On the

SCENARIO	NETWORK TOPOLOGY	# PEERS	# DATA STREAMS	# QUERIES
Example	3-dimensional hypercube	8	1	4
Extended example	3-dimensional hypercube	8	1	25
Small	irregular	4	1	4
Grid	4×4 grid	16	2	100

Table 4.1: Evaluation scenarios

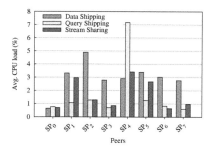 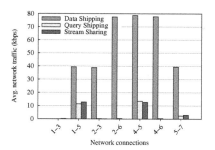

Figure 4.21: Example scenario: 8 super-peers, 1 data stream, 4 queries

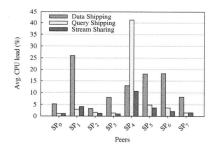 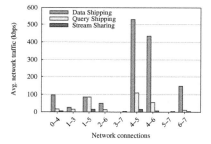

Figure 4.22: Extended example scenario: 8 super-peers, 1 data stream, 25 queries

other hand, the network traffic caused by query shipping is comparatively low. Data shipping, as expected, causes much more network traffic but also relatively high CPU load over the entire range of super-peers in the network since all the data needs to be forwarded over many peers and network connections, often even multiple times. Stream sharing distributes computational load much better over the peers in the network than query shipping and causes less overall CPU load than data shipping. Furthermore, network traffic is also greatly reduced compared to the other two strategies due to the effects of reusing streams for multiple queries.

Figures 4.23 and 4.24 show the results for the remaining two scenarios in terms of average CPU load in percent and accumulated network traffic in MBit including both, incoming and outgoing traffic for each super-peer. The results, especially for the larger grid scenario, show that our approach significantly reduces network traffic at single peers as well as overall in the network. Data shipping transmits the entire original data stream through the network multiple times, once for each subscription referencing the stream as input. Note that query shipping already significantly reduces network traffic by means of early filtering at the data stream source. However, like data shipping, query shipping still transmits one distinct data stream through the network for each query. Stream sharing is able to further reduce network traffic by using multi-subscription optimization, transmitting data streams through the network only once and sharing them for satisfying multiple similar or equal queries. The CPU load caused by stream sharing is comparable to the load caused by the other approaches on most peers in the shown scenarios except for the peak at the data stream source peers for query shipping. We expect our approach

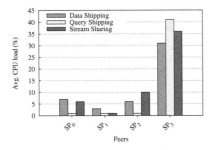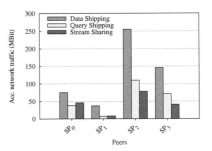

Figure 4.23: Small scenario: 4 super-peers, 1 data stream, 4 queries

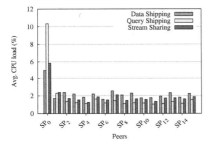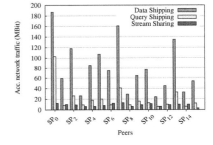

Figure 4.24: 4×4 grid scenario: 16 super-peers, 2 data streams, 100 queries

to distribute load better over peers in larger scenarios than the other two approaches. This expectation is confirmed by the results of an additional test where we limited the maximum CPU load of peers to 10% of their actual capacity and the maximum bandwidth of network connections between peers to 1 MBit/s. We then used the grid scenario and determined how many queries had to be rejected by the system because no query evaluation plan without causing overload on peers or network connections could be found. While query shipping had to reject 35 and data shipping had to reject 47 out of the 100 queries that we tried to register, our stream sharing approach only rejected 2 queries.

Inevitably, data stream sharing is associated with a certain optimization overhead. Tables 4.2 and 4.3 show the times a query took from the beginning of its registration until it was success-fully installed and executed in the network in the extended example scenario and in the 4×4 grid scenario, respectively. The stream sharing approach stays within a factor of three of the other two much simpler approaches. This is acceptable since we are dealing with continuous queries that usually remain registered over long periods of time. The difference between the query registration times of data stream sharing and the other two approaches is expected to grow for increasing network sizes and increasing numbers of queries. This is due to the larger effort invested in query optimization. The more queries have been installed in the system, the more alternatives for data stream sharing the query optimizer has to take into account when a new query is registered. However, many real application scenarios, e. g., e-science collabora-tion networks, are not expected to grow far beyond the dimensions of our largest evaluation

TIME (ms)	DATA SHIPPING	QUERY SHIPPING	STREAM SHARING
Average	931	890	2153
Minimum	390	284	509
Maximum	2078	2032	5025

Table 4.2: Query registration times in the extended example scenario

TIME (ms)	DATA SHIPPING	QUERY SHIPPING	STREAM SHARING
Average	1363	1287	3558
Minimum	265	250	672
Maximum	4953	4802	11855

Table 4.3: Query registration times in the 4×4 grid scenario

scenarios. Also, if query registration times should not exceed a certain threshold, we can stop the optimization process early and use the best query evaluation plan found so far.

4.6 Related Work

Data stream sharing is closely related to multi-query optimization (MQO) [Roy et al. (2000); Sellis (1988); Zhou et al. (2007)]. Traditional MQO mainly aims at optimizing the evaluation of a batch of queries over persistent data. Instead, data stream sharing incrementally optimizes queries one after another when they are registered in the network, based on the current network state. The streaming paradigm opens many new possibilities in our setting compared to traditional MQO. This is mainly due to the dynamic nature of streaming data and the persistent nature of continuous queries over data streams. For example, as we show in Chapter 5, we can dynamically widen data streams by relaxing predicates or window definitions in the system to make an initially unsuitable stream shareable. Furthermore, it is possible to narrow a data stream if some of its data is not needed any more due to the deletion of queries from the system.

Sharing of work between queries over streams has also been addressed in previous work by Krishnamurthy et al. (2004). Our solution mainly differs from this approach in that we consider distributed subscription evaluation among peers in a network. CACQ [Madden et al. (2002b)] is related to stream sharing in that it allows the sharing of physical operators. However, CACQ is centralized and tuple-based and does not consider the sharing of potentially preprocessed data streams in a network. NiagaraCQ [Chen et al. (2000)] groups continuous queries according to similar structures to share common computations, thus increasing scalability. As already mentioned in Section 2.4, the major difference between NiagaraCQ and our approach in StreamGlobe consists in the fact that StreamGlobe explicitly deals with and exploits the aspect of queries and data streams being distributed over peers in a network. This allows for more flexible sharing of data streams compared to NiagaraCQ, e. g., by sharing query result streams anywhere in the network. Also, Chapter 5 presents the details of our data stream widening optimization technique that further increases the flexibility of data stream sharing by dynamically altering the characteristics of a stream to fit the needs of a larger set of queries. Ayad and Naughton (2004) investigate static optimization techniques for continuous queries with sliding windows over infinite data streams. They also devise a cost model to assess the costs of query evaluation plans and aim at minimizing resource usage if available resources are sufficient while random load shedding is used to cope with insufficient resources. In contrast to stream sharing, this approach does not employ any multi-query optimization. Seshadri et al. (2007) propose a system that optimizes the execution of stream-based queries in a distributed DSMS using optimization techniques such as network-aware join ordering, operator reuse, and delayed filtering for increasing possibilities for reuse. The system integrates query planning and deployment planning in a single step and limits the search space by using hierarchical network partitions similar to the hierarchical network organization planned for StreamGlobe as introduced in Section 2.3.6. In each partition, one of the nodes contained in the partition takes the role of a coordinator. Reusable streams are discovered by means of stream advertisements. A coordinator knows about all stream advertisements in its partition. Stream advertisements and coordinators thus correspond to properties and speaker-peers in StreamGlobe. The main differences in StreamGlobe compared to the approach of Seshadri et al. (2007) are the use of XML data streams, the explicit development of a subscription language, the notion of data windows, and a closer look at reusability depending on operator types and properties. Gedik and Liu (2006) consider quality of service aspects for stream delivery in a distributed DSMS using the concept of stream delivery graphs. They compare several algorithms for constructing such delivery graphs and use load shedding to drop tuples in input streams if available resources are insufficient. Currently, StreamGlobe rejects queries for which no plan without a predicted overload situation on peers or network connections can be found. Introducing load shedding or explicit quality of service guarantees in StreamGlobe remains an issue for future work. While StreamGlobe processes continuous queries over data streams in an exact way, Dobra et al. (2004) address the issue of multi-query optimization in the context of sketch-based approximate query evaluation through sharing sketches among multiple concurrent queries. The concept of sketch-based approximate query processing has been introduced by Dobra et al. (2002).

Ahmad and Çetintemel (2004) consider network-aware operator placement in a distributed, DHT-based query processing system. Although generic, the proposed algorithms focus on push-based continuous queries and use a cost function that aims at minimizing bandwidth consumption in the overall network. The algorithms also allow to trade bandwidth usage for satisfying latency bounds on query results. In contrast to data stream sharing in StreamGlobe, this approach does not take into account the CPU load incurred by query processing operators on respective peers and it does not perform any multi-query optimization. Pietzuch et al. (2006) introduce a spring embedder approach to network-aware operator placement in distributed DSMSs. Their solution uses a stream-based overlay network (SBON) for managing operator placement and establishing the connection between the DSMS and the underlying physical network. Operator placement works by computing the cost-optimal operator coordinates in an abstract cost space according to the spring embedder model and by subsequently mapping the computed position onto an actual node in the physical network. The used cost metric takes into account the latency of network connections and the data rate transferred over these connections. Periodic reevaluation combined with operator migration enables an adaptation to changing network states. The SBON layer also performs basic multi-query optimization by combining operators with equal inputs that are placed close to each other in the cost space and by distributing the corresponding operator output to all recipients using a multicast operator. Therefore, multi-query optimization is a subordinate step that is performed after operator placement whereas in StreamGlobe the search for shareable data streams is the primary step that guides operator placement. Srivastava et al. (2005) describe an efficient optimal algorithm for operator placement in tree-shaped data acquisition networks as introduced, e. g., by Franklin et al. (2005). The leaves of the tree form the data sources and the root forms the data sink. The network model assumes that nodes towards the leaves of the tree have less bandwidth and less computational power. Therefore, the goal of the operator placement algorithm is to place operators in a way that minimizes the combined cost of query processing and data transfer. For example, placing a filter operator closer to the data sources reduces transfer costs but, due to the reduced resources of nodes close to the leaves of the network tree, may incur higher computational costs. The operator placement algorithm can handle uncorrelated filter operators and is subsequently extended to also support correlated filter operators and multi-way stream joins. Clearly, this approach depends on a particular network model and topology whereas data stream sharing in StreamGlobe does not require a specific network topology.

Further, the problem of query containment has a strong relation to data stream sharing. Query containment has already been studied for querying XML data, mainly in the context of optimizing query rewriting in peer data management systems (PDMSs) [Tatarinov and Halevy (2004)]. Dong et al. (2004) investigate support for nested queries in this context. Schwentick (2004) summarizes a selection of algorithms proposed for XPath query containment. However, as with MQO, the main difference to our work lies in the fact that we are dealing with persistent queries and volatile data instead of persistent data and volatile queries. Query containment, especially for XML queries, is a difficult problem. We were able to make it manageable by exploiting the properties of our distributed system architecture, i. e., by postponing complex restructuring until a data stream reaches its final destination in the super-peer backbone network.

Semantic caching [Chen and Rundensteiner (2002); Dar et al. (1996)], where reusable data consists of previously computed and cached results of one-time queries over persistent data, is one of the main application areas of query containment. Semantic caching differs from query subscription in streaming environments mainly by the difference between processing persistent data and processing data streams. In our setting, the cached data corresponds to the—albeit volatile—data streams flowing through the network.

The question of which previously generated data stream should be reused for answering a newly subscribed continuous query is similar to the problems of view materialization and view selection in the context of persistent data [Theodoratos and Sellis (1997, 1999)]. In view materialization, however, data is materialized before queries are posed whereas in our scenario, reusable data streams are generated by previously registered queries in the network.

Even closer related to our work are more recent approaches to materialized XML views that deal with using views in query processing [Balmin et al. (2004); Mandhani and Suciu (2005)], for speeding up routing decisions in XML content-based document routing [Gupta et al. (2002, 2003)], and for efficiently supporting queries over XML views of relational data for increased flexibility and interoperability [Shah and Chirkova (2003); Shanmugasundaram et al. (2001)]. The IBM XML Query Graph Model (XQGM) of Shanmugasundaram et al. (2001) is a graph-based internal query representation for XQueries over XML views of relational data used in the XPERANTO middleware system. An incoming XQuery is directly translated into an XQGM by the query parser and the internal query representation is used to employ query rewriting optimizations and to compose the query with the views it references. The XQGM is subsequently processed and decomposed into two parts. One part captures the memory and data intensive processing and is pushed down to the relational engine while the other part constitutes a tagger graph structure used to construct the XML query result. This approach is clearly related to ours since we also use an abstract internal query representation for optimizing (W)XQuery processing. The main differences are that StreamGlobe does not use a relational backend but directly processes XML data and that we deal with data stream processing in a distributed environment. While the XQGM approach mainly aims at exploiting the facilities of proven relational database backends for efficiently processing XQueries over a flexible and interoperable XML view interface, StreamGlobe targets efficient resource usage in a distributed DSMS by means of sharing common work and data among multiple long-running continuous queries. Some approaches combine materialized views with multi-query optimization to increase the performance of materialized view selection and maintenance [Mistry et al. (2001)] and to improve query processing performance for XQueries over XML views [Zhang et al. (2003b)]. Further approaches address the issues of query rewriting for XML queries using nested views [Onose et al. (2006)], semantic caching for XPath queries [Xu (2005)] and XML databases [Hristidis and Petropoulos (2002)], and a framework for handling XML data with incomplete information [Abiteboul et al. (2001, 2006)]. Abiteboul (1999) has also published some general thoughts on views and XML. Most of the above work on XML views exclusively supports XPath queries. Only few approaches support a usually heavily restricted subset of XQuery. Also, in contrast to StreamGlobe, these solutions work solely on XML documents and do not consider data streams. Consequently, there is no notion of data windows either.

Another subject related to data stream sharing is data integration. Instead of matching new subscriptions with existing data streams as is the case in our domain, data integration in the previously mentioned peer data management systems (PDMSs) [Tatarinov and Halevy (2004)] uses schema matchings in order to match a new query with various data sources that have different, yet similar schemas.

Schema matching is one possible approach for comparing newly registered subscriptions with existing data streams in the network. Many different solutions for this problem have been proposed [Dhamankar et al. (2004); Rahm and Bernstein (2001)], also in the context of XML data [Doan et al. (2001, 2000)]. However, generic schema matchers only match static schema information. This is sufficient for structural filters such as projection operators, but not for content-based filters such as selection operators. Supporting content-based filters requires an appropriate extension of the matcher. Furthermore, generic ontology-based schema matchers do not work without user interaction. Since we do not need the matching power of such ontology-based matchers in our context but we do need to match the results of structural and content-based filters alike, we have instead taken a different approach based on the abstract properties of subscriptions and data streams.

We employ the FluX query engine developed by Koch et al. (2004a,b) for processing continuous queries over XML data streams. The major contribution of FluX is the ability to process XQueries over streaming XML data while minimizing buffer consumption by exploiting schema information of processed XML streams. Stegmaier (2006) has provided the necessary extensions to FluX to support our WXQuery subscription language which constitutes an augmented fragment of XQuery. Other examples of streaming XQuery implementations besides FluX include Raindrop [Su et al. (2003)] and XQRL [Florescu et al. (2004, 2003)]. These can be used to process standard XQueries. For being able to execute window-based WXQueries, they need to be augmented with support for our WXQuery window extensions introduced in Section 4.3. Li and Agrawal (2005) propose a different approach for efficiently evaluating XQueries over streaming data. Instead of considering the schemas of the input streams, they concentrate on the properties of the queries to be evaluated. Their solution comprises several optimizations used to transform XQueries in a way that allows the execution of the transformed queries with a single pass over the input data. Further, they provide a methodology for deciding whether such a single pass evaluation is possible for a given, possibly transformed query. Their approach also entails support for user-defined aggregates, including recursive functions. Lim et al. (2006) exploit the duality of data and queries to devise a radically different approach to continuous query processing. They propose a solution that is based on the transformation of the continuous query processing problem to a multi-dimensional spatial join problem. The join identifies pairs of overlapping regions from the set of data elements and the set of queries, respectively. A one-dimensional data index, obtained by linearizing the multi-dimensional data space using a space filling curve, together with a multi-dimensional query index enable an efficient join computation. A performance evaluation asserts the effectiveness of the proposed query processing algorithm. Finally, Krämer and Seeger (2005) provide a formal temporal semantics for continuous queries over data streams ensuring deterministic query results.

Botan et al. (2007) propose extensions to XQuery and to the XQuery data model (XDM) for supporting window-based continuous queries and infinite sequences. Fischer et al. (2006) provide an accompanying collection of use cases. The proposed window syntax and semantics supports all types of data windows found in the literature and the authors plan to submit their proposal to the W3C for possible standardization in the upcoming XQuery 1.1 standard. The window extensions are implemented in the Java-based streaming XQuery engine MXQuery[1]. The basic idea of introducing `for` loops that iterate over a sequence of data windows and bind the corresponding sequences of window contents to a variable is identical to the concept of our window extensions in WXQuery.

We defer a discussion of related work in the area of aggregate result sharing to Section 5.7.

4.7 Summary

In this chapter, we have presented a subscription language, a properties approach, a cost model, and algorithms for registering continuous queries over data streams in a distributed DSMS using data stream sharing. Our approach takes three steps. First, we construct the properties of a newly registered subscription. Second, we identify shareable data streams generated for answering previously registered subscriptions in the network by matching properties. We choose an appropriate stream for answering the new subscription according to a cost model that focuses on the reduction of network traffic and peer load as well as on load balancing aspects. Finally, we generate and install a distributed query evaluation plan to execute the new subscription.

In the next chapter, we introduce an enhanced properties structure for representing continuous queries in StreamGlobe. The enhanced structure supports nested queries and enables us to widen data streams. This allows the system to consider data streams for sharing that initially do not contain all the necessary data for a new query but can be altered to do so by changing some operators in the network. We also devise support for join queries over multiple input data streams in the enhanced approach. Apart from this, an interesting opportunity for future work in the context of data stream sharing is the dynamic optimization of the set of registered subscriptions to retain an optimized data flow in the network even if network conditions or data stream statistics change over time.

---

[1] http://www.mxquery.org

CHAPTER 5

Advanced Data Stream Sharing: Matching and Merging Queries and Data

---

Multi-query optimization aims at sharing common work among multiple queries and thus requires the identification of shareable query parts. As stated in Chapter 1, this is especially important for distributed DSMSs with multiple continuous queries running concurrently over long periods of time. In this chapter, we introduce an abstract property tree (APT) and its extension, an abstract property forest (APF), for representing, matching, and merging queries and data in a distributed DSMS. The presented techniques enable data stream sharing as introduced in Chapter 4. In addition, data stream widening increases the possibilities for sharing streams. The combination of data stream sharing and data stream widening thus allows for efficient resource usage and further increases the number of queries that can be processed concurrently.

5.1 Introduction

Deciding whether a certain query result or a data set contains all the relevant information for answering another query is strongly related to the query containment problem [Dong et al. (2004)]. Further, it is a common problem for many applications such as view selection [Levy et al. (1995)] and semantic caching [Dar et al. (1996)]. Data stream sharing in a distributed DSMS is a new area where this problem arises.

We have shown in Chapter 4 how data stream sharing can improve performance in a distributed DSMS such as StreamGlobe. However, the optimization quality of the presented solution depends on the properties of the registered queries and on the query registration sequence. Only if the result data stream of a previously registered query contains at least all the data required as input for a new query, sharing the previous result for satisfying the new query is possible. In this chapter, we introduce *data stream widening* as an additional technique for making the optimization quality more independent of the specific query properties and the query registration sequence. Data stream widening is able to widen an existing data stream to additionally contain all the necessary data for a new query. We also devise the inverse *data stream narrow-*

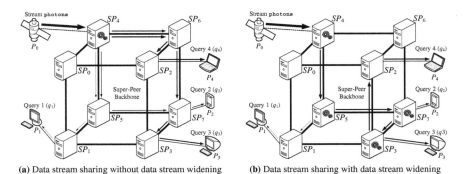

(a) Data stream sharing without data stream widening   **(b)** Data stream sharing with data stream widening

Figure 5.1: Example DSMS scenario

ing approach for downsizing a data stream in case a dependent query has been deleted from the system. Furthermore, the techniques we introduce in this chapter support a larger class of queries. While the previous approach supports flat selection, projection, and aggregate queries, the new approach additionally supports nested queries and joins.

As a motivating example for the application of our advanced data stream sharing technique with data stream widening in StreamGlobe, we continue to use the astrophysical e-science application introduced in Chapter 2. Consider Figure 5.1 which illustrates the exemplary network of Figure 2.1 on page 9 employing data stream sharing once without and once with data stream widening. The example scenario used in this chapter is identical to that used in Chapter 4 except for the sequence in which queries are registered. For the example scenario used in this chapter, we reversed the query registration sequence. In Chapter 4, each query was able to share the result stream of a previously registered query. In this chapter, no sharing is possible since each new query to be registered requires more input data from stream photons than the result data streams of all previously registered queries provide. We will show how data stream widening enables us to share preprocessed data streams in such a scenario anyway. Figure 5.2 shows Queries 1 (q_1) to 4 (q_4) of the example scenario used in this chapter.

Queries q_1, q_2, and q_4 select the area in the sky that contains the *Vela supernova remnant*. Queries q_1 and q_2 are window-based aggregate queries returning the average energy of detected photons in the input stream. While q_1 computes the average for all photons with det_time values within the last 60 time units and produces an aggregate value every 40 time units, q_2 computes the average for all photons with det_time values within the last 20 time units and produces an aggregate value every 10 time units. Query q_3 is a simple selection and projection query delivering the celestial coordinates, the energy, and the detection time of all the photons detected in the area of the *RX J0852.0-4622 supernova remnant*.

Assuming that we register queries q_1 to q_4 one after another in ascending order, data stream sharing without data stream widening is not able to reuse any query results of previously registered queries for satisfying later registered queries. This is due to the fact that the later registered queries in this example always require more information than the result data streams of all previously installed queries provide. Therefore, multi-subscription optimization has no effect and the optimizer creates a new data stream for each query that needs to be routed through the network individually. Figure 5.1(a) illustrates this situation.

```
<photons>
  { for $w in stream("photons")/photons/photon
      [coord/cel/ra >= 120.0 and
       coord/cel/ra <= 138.0 and
       coord/cel/dec >= -49.0 and
       coord/cel/dec <= -40.0]
      |det_time diff 60 step 40|
    let $a := avg($w/en)
    where $a >= 1.3
    return <avg_en> { $a } </avg_en> }
</photons>
```

(a) Query 1 (q_1)

```
<photons>
  { for $w in stream("photons")/photons/photon
      [coord/cel/ra >= 120.0 and
       coord/cel/ra <= 138.0 and
       coord/cel/dec >= -49.0 and
       coord/cel/dec <= -40.0]
      |det_time diff 20 step 10|
    let $a := avg($w/en)
    return <avg_en> { $a } </avg_en> }
</photons>
```

(b) Query 2 (q_2)

```
<photons>
  { for $p in stream("photons")/photons/photon
    where $p/en >= 1.3
      and $p/coord/cel/ra >= 130.5
      and $p/coord/cel/ra <= 135.5
      and $p/coord/cel/dec >= -48.0
      and $p/coord/cel/dec <= -45.0
    return
      <rxj>
        { $p/coord/cel/ra } { $p/coord/cel/dec }
        { $p/en } { $p/det_time }
      </rxj> }
</photons>
```

(c) Query 3 (q_3)

```
<photons>
  { for $p in stream("photons")/photons/photon
    where $p/coord/cel/ra >= 120.0
      and $p/coord/cel/ra <= 138.0
      and $p/coord/cel/dec >= -49.0
      and $p/coord/cel/dec <= -40.0
    return
      <vela>
        { $p/coord/cel/ra } { $p/coord/cel/dec }
        { $p/phc } { $p/en } { $p/det_time }
      </vela> }
</photons>
```

(d) Query 4 (q_4)

Figure 5.2: Example queries

By using data stream sharing with data stream widening, we are able to alter data streams generated for satisfying previously registered queries to additionally contain all the necessary data for a new query. This yields a larger data stream that constitutes the union of the input data of all dependent queries. We can then replicate the stream at appropriate super-peers in the network and further process each of its copies to form the query result for each dependent query. Figure 5.1(b) shows the corresponding result for our example scenario. Note that now, with the exception of q_1 which is registered first, each newly registered query shares the widened result data stream of a previously registered query. The effect can be seen when comparing the number of arrows indicating the data flow in the backbone network in Figures 5.1(a) and 5.1(b). Without data stream widening, there are nine arrows in the backbone network. With data stream widening, there are only five.

In detail, we make the following contributions in this chapter:

- We introduce the *Abstract Property Tree (APT)*, a structure used for representing, matching, and merging queries and data which naturally supports data stream widening and data stream narrowing (Section 5.2). We focus on queries over XML data streams formulated in our XQuery-based subscription language *WXQuery* introduced in Section 4.3. We initially consider selection, projection, and aggregate queries and subsequently introduce an extension called *Abstract Property Forest (APF)* to additionally support join queries (Section 5.4).

- We show how to translate an arbitrary WXQuery into a corresponding APT and how to translate an APT back into a corresponding WXQuery. We define inference rules for the translation of a WXQuery into an APT and query templates for the inverse translation. We discuss the soundness and completeness of the translation in both directions (Section 5.2).

- We present an algorithm for matching and merging two APTs, yielding a new APT that represents the union of the input APTs (Section 5.3) and generalize the algorithm for the use with APFs (Section 5.4). We further discuss the soundness and completeness of the matching and merging algorithm.

- Some performance experiments conducted using our StreamGlobe prototype implementation assess the effectiveness of data stream sharing with data stream widening as introduced in this chapter (Section 5.6).

5.2   The Abstract Property Tree (APT)

The abstract property tree (APT) is a data structure for representing, matching, and merging queries and data as needed for data stream sharing and data stream widening. This section introduces APTs and shows how to translate a WXQuery into a corresponding APT and vice versa. Further, we discuss the completeness and correctness of these translations.

5.2.1   Definition

An *abstract property tree (APT)* consists of two main parts. The first part is a path tree representing all paths referenced in the corresponding query and the second part is a set of annotations. The path tree reflects the *structural* aspects of the query while the annotations reflect its *content-based* aspects, e. g., selection predicates, join predicates, data window definitions, and aggregates. Note that an APT is an *abstract* representation of a query, i. e., it represents only the relevant parts of the query as needed for data stream sharing or, more generally, query result sharing. With the exception of aggregate and join queries, APTs abstract from any complex restructuring of the query result relative to the query inputs as described in Section 4.3. This abstraction makes the difficult task of matching and merging queries and data feasible in practice. The loss of information about the original query due to abstraction is the reason why the translation of an APT back into a corresponding WXQuery generally yields a query that is different from the original.

Definition 5.1 (Query abstraction) The abstraction $\hat{q}$ of a query q reflects all the properties of q that are relevant for in-network query processing. Compared to the original query q, the corresponding abstraction $\hat{q}$ does not contain any query details that are postponed to the postprocessing step, such as any restructuring of the query result involving element construction, reordering, or renaming. Let q be a query, $\mathsf{APT}(x)$ a function that returns the corresponding APT of a query x, and $\mathsf{Query}(y)$ a function that returns the corresponding query of an APT y. Then, the abstraction $\hat{q}$ of q is obtained as follows:

$$\hat{q} := \mathsf{Query}(\mathsf{APT}(q)) \qquad\qquad \Box$$

Figure 5.3 shows the APTs of the four example queries of Figure 5.2. The path tree in each case reflects all the paths referenced in the corresponding query. The APT of q_4 in Figure 5.3(d) for example contains the path /photons/photon/phc because the phc element is returned and therefore referenced in the query. However, the phc element does not occur in the APTs of queries q_1 to q_3 because these queries do not reference this element. Note that all paths referenced in a query are always expanded to absolute paths starting at the data stream root element in the corresponding APT.

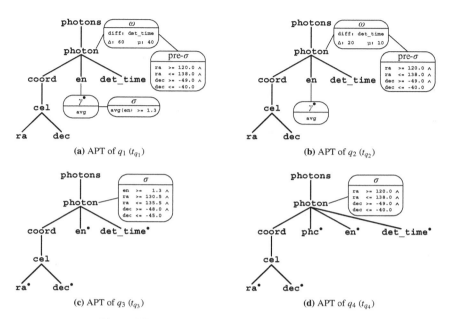

Figure 5.3: APTs of example queries from Section 5.1

The boxes in Figure 5.3 represent annotations that augment the structural information of the path tree with additional content-based information. There are three types of annotations reflecting the characteristics of the three content-based operators for selection (σ), window construction (ω), and aggregation (γ).

Selection annotations are associated either with output elements in the path tree, i. e., with elements that are actually contained in the query result, or with aggregate annotations denoting returned aggregate values. A selection annotation indicates under which condition the corresponding element or aggregate value is returned by the query. Output elements are marked with bullets in an APT. In Figure 5.3(c), for example, the output elements are ra, dec, en, and det_time. Queries returning aggregate values are special since, in their APTs, bullets also mark the aggregate annotations of the aggregate values returned by the query as shown in Figures 5.3(a) and 5.3(b). Also, Figures 5.3(c) and 5.3(d) indicate that common selection annotations of multiple elements can be pulled up to a common ancestor node. Pulled-up annotations are implicitly considered valid for all output elements further below in the path tree as long as these do not have any other selection annotations associated with them.

Window annotations are always associated with the window root element, i. e., the element whose instances are actually contained in the window. In q_1 and q_2, photon is the window root element. Two different kinds of selection predicates can be associated with window annotations. Predicates in the location steps of a window-defining XPath expression filter the items selected by the XPath expression *before* the items enter the data window. We call selection annotations representing such predicates *window preselection annotations* since the selection takes place before window construction. The symbol pre-σ indicates these annotations which appear in the APTs of q_1 and q_2 in Figure 5.3. Furthermore, predicates in a where clause filter the entire data window *after* it has been constructed in accordance with XQuery existential semantics, treating the window contents as a sequence. We call selection annotations representing these predicates *window postselection annotations*, since the selection takes place after window construction. The symbol post-σ indicates such annotations.

Finally, aggregate annotations are always associated with the aggregated element, which is en in q_1 and q_2. Like window annotations, aggregate annotations can be associated with two different kinds of selection annotations. An *aggregate preselection annotation* reflects a selection predicate occurring within the XPath expression that references the aggregated element in the argument of the aggregate function call. Such a predicate filters elements *before* the actual aggregate computation, i. e., elements not fulfilling the predicate of the aggregate preselection annotation do not contribute to the aggregate. Furthermore, an ordinary selection annotation associated with an aggregate annotation indicates that the aggregate result value is only returned if the respective condition is satisfied. Figure 5.3(a) shows such an annotation indicating that the average energy of photons in the specified data window is only to be returned if it is greater than or equal to 1.3 keV. We denote aggregate preselection annotations by the same symbol pre-σ as window preselection annotations. The meaning of the overloaded symbol is unambiguous in an actual APT since the corresponding annotation is either associated with a window or an aggregate annotation.

For simplicity, we allow window postselection conditions to appear only in where clauses of the FLWR expression that defines the corresponding window. Note that element references in annotations are actually absolute paths starting from the data stream root element. In our figures, however, we only show the element name for better readability. Projection operators are structural operators which remove elements from the query inputs. Their effects are therefore already reflected by the path tree. If a query removes elements using a projection, these elements do not appear in the path tree of that query. Thus, there is no explicit projection annotation. We introduce an additional join annotation for representing join operators in Section 5.4.

Definition 5.2 (Abstract Property Tree (APT)) The *abstract property tree (APT)* of a query q is denoted $t_q := (P, A, O, id, d)$ and consists of the set of referenced paths P, the set of annotations A, and the set of returned paths and aggregate values O of q, as well as the identifier id and the DTD d of q's input stream or input document.

Structural part The set P contains all the paths referenced in the corresponding query. The APT internally represents these paths as a tree with merged common prefixes as shown in Figure 5.3, i. e., each path element occurs as a tree node exactly once. The tree thus constitutes a prefix tree where each node represents an element occurring in the paths in P. A node v_1 is the parent of a node v_2 in the tree if the element represented by v_1 is the parent of the element represented by v_2 in a path in P. The root of the tree is the root of the query input data stream or document. We expand relative paths referenced in the query to absolute paths before adding them to P. The construction of the path tree uses the DTD d to preserve the stream or document order of the elements in the tree. The set O of returned paths and aggregate values identifies the elements in the path tree that we need to mark as output elements. Aggregate values in O, indicated by a path with an aggregate function applied to it, cause the corresponding aggregate annotation to be marked with an output marker. As with P, we expand all relative paths to absolute paths before adding them to O.

Content-based part An annotation $a := (\tau, C, R)$ has a type $\tau \in \{\sigma, \omega, \gamma, \text{pre-}\sigma, \text{post-}\sigma\}$ indicating a selection annotation, a window annotation, an aggregate annotation, a window preselection annotation or an aggregate preselection annotation, and a window postselection annotation, respectively. The annotation further consists of its contents C. In case of a selection annotation, a window preselection annotation, an aggregate preselection annotation, or a window postselection annotation, C is a set of selection predicates. The predicates in the set are meant to be conjunctively combined. We take a closer look at the form and handling of predicates in the context of data stream sharing and data stream widening in Chapter 6. A window annotation representing a count-based window contains the window type, the window size, and the step size of the window. In case of a time-based window, the annotation additionally contains the absolute path to the reference element of the window. An aggregate annotation contains the corresponding aggregate function. Finally, R denotes the parents of the annotation, i. e., the objects the annotation is associated with. For selection annotations, R is a set that can contain elements in the path tree as well as aggregate annotations. For window annotations and for aggregate annotations, the parent always is a single element in the path tree. For window preselection and window postselection annotations, the parent always is a window annotation. For aggregate preselection annotations, the parent always is an aggregate annotation. □

Note that, for simplicity, the visualization of APTs in Figure 5.3 does not explicitly show stream identifiers and DTDs. Also, for ease of exposition concerning the inference rules of Section 5.2.2 further below, we formally define the path tree as a set of paths instead of as an actual tree structure. For implementation purposes, it is however advisable to represent the tree in the latter form, which we did in our StreamGlobe prototype implementation.

We define *structure-preserving* and *structure-mutating* APTs similar to structure-preserving and structure-mutating queries.

Definition 5.3 (Structure-preserving APT) A *structure-preserving APT* is an APT that results in a structure-preserving query when applying the translation described in Section 5.2.3. □

Example 5.1 (Structure-preserving APTs) The APTs of queries q_3 and q_4 in Figures 5.3(c) and 5.3(d) are structure-preserving APTs. □

Definition 5.4 (Structure-mutating APT) A *structure-mutating APT* is an APT that results in a structure-mutating query when applying the translation described in Section 5.2.3. □

Example 5.2 (Structure-mutating APTs) The APTs of queries q_1 and q_2 in Figures 5.3(a) and 5.3(b) are structure-mutating APTs. □

5.2.2 Translating WXQueries into APTs

The StreamGlobe optimizer translates each newly registered query into a corresponding APT as follows.

Assembling the Path Tree

We assemble the path tree of a query by extracting all paths occurring in the respective query. Paths in a query can occur in `for` and `let` expressions, in XPath predicates, in `where` clauses, in window definitions for time-based data windows, in conditional expressions, as parameters of aggregate function calls, and as standalone path expressions or path expressions in return clauses. Each path in a query is either absolute or relative. The query parser extracts all paths occurring in a query and expands each relative path to the corresponding absolute path. In case of paths in XPath predicates and time-based data windows, the expansion concatenates the absolute path of the corresponding context element and the relative path in the predicate or window definition. In all other cases, relative paths start with a variable that can be recursively expanded using a symbol table that contains the bindings for all the variables in the query.

We merge all extracted absolute paths into one path tree by adding the paths to the tree one by one. The process identifies common prefixes which occur in the resulting tree only once. Path tree construction also preserves the document or stream order of the respective query inputs. The order of elements on each level of the path tree, from left to right, reflects their order in the query input. Note that up to now, we assume that each query has exactly one input stream. If a query has more than one input stream, we need to build an individual path tree for each input stream. We extend our ideas to this class of queries in Section 5.4.

Example 5.3 As an example for path tree assembly consider q_1 in Figure 5.2(a) and its APT t_{q_1} in Figure 5.3(a). The query contains the absolute path /photons/photon and the relative paths coord/cel/ra and coord/cel/dec in the XPath predicate, det_time in the reference element specification of the time-based data window, and $w/en as parameter of the aggregate function call. The context element for the XPath predicate and the data window definition is photon. Therefore, we expand the corresponding relative paths to absolute paths by prepending /photons/photon/, yielding the absolute paths /photons/photon/coord/cel/ra, /photons/photon/coord/cel/dec, and /photons/photon/det_time. The variable $w is bound to a sequence of photon elements, i. e. the photons contained in the current data window. We therefore expand the relative path in the aggregate function call by replacing $w with the path /photons/photon yielding /photons/photon/en as the final path. When merging the resulting absolute paths into one path tree, we get /photons/photon/ as common prefix of all paths and further /photons/photon/coord/cel/ as common prefix of the two paths in the XPath predicate. The APT of Figure 5.3(a) contains the resulting path tree.   □

Determining the Annotations

The next step in APT construction is to determine the annotations. We consider this issue for each of the three main types of annotations, i. e., selection annotations, window annotations, and aggregate annotations. We further treat the three subtypes of selection annotations, i. e., window preselection annotations, aggregate preselection annotations, and window postselection annotations.

Selection annotations We must associate each output element of the path tree and each aggregate annotation representing a returned aggregate value with the condition under which the corresponding element or aggregate value is returned by the query. This condition depends on the context of the respective output element or aggregate value. The relevant conditions can appear as XPath predicates in the location steps of certain XPath expressions, in where clauses of FLWR expressions (expression 3 in Definition 4.5 on page 44), and in conditional expressions (expression 4 in Definition 4.5). Since FLWR expressions and conditional expressions can be nested, the query parser needs to keep track of the current context for each output element. We do this by storing the predicates defined in each FLWR expression or conditional expression in a list and pushing this list on a stack. Whenever an output element is encountered, all predicates in all lists on the stack are conjunctively combined, thus forming the predicate for this element's selection annotation.

For conditional expressions, the predicate defined in the conditional expression is used for the then part and the negation of this predicate is used for the else part. When the scope of a FLWR expression or conditional expression ends, the corresponding predicate list is popped from the stack and will therefore not be part of the selection annotations of subsequent output elements. If the query returns several output elements under the same condition, we try to avoid associating the selection annotation with each output element individually. This is possible by pulling up the selection annotation to a common ancestor node as long as no other output elements with different selection annotations occur between this ancestor node and the output elements.

Aggregate annotations Whenever the query parser discovers a call of an aggregate function, it creates an aggregate annotation indicating the type of the aggregation (min, max, sum, count, or avg) and associates it with the aggregated element referenced in the aggregate function argument. We associate a corresponding aggregate preselection annotation with the aggregate annotation if the query filters the sequence of elements to be aggregated prior to aggregation.

Window annotations Whenever the query parser discovers a window definition, it creates an according window annotation and associates it with the context element of the window, i. e., the element the window is defined on. Each window annotation contains the window type (count-based or time-based), the reference element (only in case of a time-based window), the window size, and the step size. Optionally, we associate a window preselection annotation, a window postselection annotation, or both with the window annotation if indicated by the query.

We introduce an additional join annotation in Section 5.4.

Example 5.4 The APTs of queries q_3 and q_4 in Figures 5.3(c) and 5.3(d) show examples for selection annotation pull-up. In both queries, all output elements are returned under the same condition. Therefore, the corresponding selection annotation is not associated with each output element individually. Instead, a single copy of the annotation is pulled up to the first common ancestor node, which is the node representing the photon element in both cases.

In the APT of q_2 in Figure 5.3(b), the window annotation is associated with the window context element photon. Furthermore, a window preselection annotation representing the XPath predicate of the query is associated with the window annotation. Finally, an aggregate annotation marks the en element as the aggregated element using an avg aggregate operator. The aggregate annotation also contains an output marker since the corresponding aggregate value is returned by the query. The situation is similar for the APT of q_1 in Figure 5.3(a). The only difference, besides different values in the window annotation, is the additional selection annotation associated with the aggregate annotation. It indicates that the query returns the corresponding aggregate value only under the annotated condition. □

Determining the Output Elements

All elements occurring in the path tree of a query are *input elements* of that query, i. e., they must be present in the query input—possibly only under certain conditions expressed by selection annotations. Otherwise, the query probably will not be answered correctly. The *output elements* of a query are the elements returned by the query, i. e., the elements contained in the query result. Except for aggregate values, each output element also is an input element. However, there can be input elements which are no output elements, e. g., elements that only occur in selection predicates but are never returned by the query. We mark output elements with bullets in APTs as in Figure 5.3. A special case occurs for queries returning aggregate values. Here, we mark the corresponding aggregate annotations with bullets.

Determining the output elements of a query is a little more difficult than assembling the path tree. The reason is that for building the path tree, we can treat all paths occurring in the query equally. But for determining output elements, we need to distinguish whether an element referenced in a query q is actually returned by the abstraction $\hat{q}$ of that query. Starting with q as the initial expression α, we determine the set of output elements O_q of q recursively as follows:

- If α is a path expression as in expressions 5 or 6 of Definition 4.5 on page 44, then add the element referenced by α to O_q.

- If α is a sequence of expressions as in expressions 2 or 7 of Definition 4.5, recursively process each expression in the sequence.

- If α is a conditional expression as in expression 4 of Definition 4.5, recursively process the expressions in both branches of α.

- If α is a FLWR expression as in expression 3 of Definition 4.5, recursively process the expression returned by α.

The current StreamGlobe prototype implementation performs the restructuring of the result data stream of structure-preserving queries in the postprocessing step by applying the original query to the data stream created during in-network query processing. Consequently, we need to assure that each input element required by the original query is present in this stream. We achieve this by additionally marking all input elements of a structure-preserving original query as output elements in the corresponding APT. It is possible to optimize this approach such that elements referenced but not returned by the query are not marked as output elements and remain in the APT only as input elements. This requires rewriting the original query to obtain the correct query for restructuring. The rewriting needs to remove any elements that are referenced but not returned by the original query and that are no longer needed during restructuring. This can be the case, e. g., because the elements only occur in a selection predicate that has already been evaluated during in-network query processing. The predicate is therefore assured to be satisfied for all remaining data items. Optimizing the APT and the postprocessing query in this way further reduces network traffic for queries for which the set of referenced elements is a proper superset of the set of returned elements. Note that this is not an issue for our example queries since q_1 and q_2 are not structure-preserving and q_3 and q_4 return all referenced elements anyway. Generating complex restructuring queries is an issue of future work.

Example 5.5 In the APTs of q_1 and q_2 in Figures 5.3(a) and 5.3(b), we mark the aggregate annotation with an output marker since these queries return the corresponding aggregate value. The set of output elements of q_3 marked with bullets in Figure 5.3(c) is $\{\texttt{ra},\texttt{dec},\texttt{en},\texttt{det\_time}\}$ and that of q_4 marked with bullets in Figure 5.3(d) is $\{\texttt{ra},\texttt{dec},\texttt{phc},\texttt{en},\texttt{det\_time}\}$. Note that, in our current implementation, the set of output elements of q_3 would not change if the query would not return the elements $\texttt{ra}$, $\texttt{dec}$, or $\texttt{en}$. Also, the set of output elements of q_4 would not change if the query would not return the elements $\texttt{ra}$ or $\texttt{dec}$. This is due to the fact that these elements are referenced in selection predicates in the respective queries. With the optimization described above, however, these elements would be removed from the set of output elements if they were not returned by the query.   □

Inference Rules

In this section, we introduce formal rules for the translation of a WXQuery into a corresponding APT. There is one rule for each WXQuery expression of Definition 4.5. We use the inference rule notation of the XQuery formal semantics specification [W3C (2007e)]. Marian and Siméon (2003a,b) use a similar notation to describe rules for projecting XML documents to reduce the memory requirements of XML query processors. The judgment

$$Env \vdash \alpha \Rightarrow (P, A, O, id, d)$$

holds if and only if, under the environment *Env*, the expression α references the paths in *P*, defines the annotations in *A*, returns the paths and aggregate values in *O*, and references an input source, i.e., a data stream or a document, with identifier *id* and DTD *d*. The environment *Env* holds the symbol table needed for converting relative paths in a WXQuery to absolute paths. Note that all paths are expanded to absolute paths using the variable bindings from *Env*. The set of returned paths *O* contains absolute paths to returned elements, e.g., /photons/photon/en, as well as absolute paths to aggregated elements of returned aggregate values together with the corresponding aggregate function calls, e.g., avg(/photons/photon/en). Inference rules are of the form

$$\frac{premise_1 \ \dots \ premise_n}{conclusion}$$

where all premises and the conclusion are judgments of the above form. Additionally, premises may constitute expressions of the form $Env' = Env + (\$var \Rightarrow Path)$ that extend the environment *Env* by adding the binding of the variable $\$var$ to the path represented by *Path*, thus yielding the extended environment *Env'*. An inference rule expresses that, if all premises hold, then the conclusion holds as well.

We now give the inference rules for each of the WXQuery expressions of Definition 4.5. Since each APT has exactly one identifier *id* and exactly one DTD *d*, rules 5.2, 5.7, and 5.10 assume that all subexpressions have the same values for *id* and *d*. As *id* and *d* might also be undefined ($\perp$) in certain subexpressions, we implicitly ignore undefined values unless *id* and *d* are undefined in all subexpressions of an expression.

Empty direct element constructor   The empty direct element constructor does not reference or return any paths. It further does not induce any annotations.

$$\frac{}{Env \vdash \langle t/\rangle \Rightarrow (\emptyset, \emptyset, \emptyset, \perp, \perp)} \tag{5.1}$$

This inference rule has no premises and therefore, nothing is written above the rule.

Direct element constructor   The direct element constructor contains zero or more WXQuery expressions. The additions to the APT induced by the direct element constructor are the unions of the additions induced by the enclosed WXQuery expressions. Since an APT always references exactly one input data stream or document, the input identifier *id* and the DTD *d* are the same in all expressions, ignoring undefined values as described above.

$$\frac{Env \vdash \alpha_1 \Rightarrow (P_1, A_1, O_1, id, d) \ \dots \ Env \vdash \alpha_n \Rightarrow (P_n, A_n, O_n, id, d)}{Env \vdash \langle t \rangle \alpha_1 \dots \alpha_n \langle /t \rangle \Rightarrow (\bigcup_{i=1}^n P_i, \bigcup_{i=1}^n A_i, \bigcup_{i=1}^n O_i, id, d)} \tag{5.2}$$

Note that we have rephrased the WXQuery expression for direct element constructors in the inference rule compared to the WXQuery definition to better support the inference rule notation. Although not explicitly shown in the inference rule for simplicity, an expression α_i still needs to be enclosed in curly braces if representing one of the expressions 3 to 7 of Definition 4.5.

FLWR expression We split the inference rule for FLWR expressions into four separate rules. Three rules cover `for` loops without data windows and with count-based and time-based data windows, respectively. The fourth rule covers `let` expressions. For better readability, we use shortcuts for certain patterns in the following inference rules. The shortcut $Path_1$ denotes the path $\$y[\![/\pi]\!]^?$ bound to a variable in a `for` loop, $Path_2$ represents the window reference element $[\![/]\!]^?\bar{\pi}$ of a time-based data window, and $Path_3$ stands for the path $\$y[\![/\pi]\!]^?$ in the argument of an aggregate function call.

The path function used in the inference rules can be applied to any path or aggregate function call. If the argument path is a relative path, the function converts it to the corresponding absolute path. Further, the function removes any conditions from the argument path before returning it. Any aggregate function that is applied to the argument path is preserved by the path function. The $\overline{\text{path}}$ function can be applied to paths and conditions. It leaves an absolute argument path unchanged and expands a relative argument path to the corresponding absolute path. If the argument path contains any conditions, the paths referenced in these conditions are also extracted, expanded, and returned. The return value of $\overline{\text{path}}$ therefore is a set of paths. When applied to a condition, the $\overline{\text{path}}$ function extracts all the paths referenced in the condition and expands any relative paths to the corresponding absolute paths. When encountering an aggregate function call, the function expands a relative path in the aggregate function argument to an absolute path before returning it. The aggregate function call is removed. The cond function can be applied to paths and conditions. When applied to a path, it extracts all XPath conditions contained in the argument path. Also, the function expands any relative paths in these conditions to the corresponding absolute paths. The return value of the cond function therefore is a set of conditions. When applied to a condition, the function expands any relative paths in the condition to absolute paths. Finally, the id and dtd functions take a path as argument. If the path starts with a reference to a stream or document node (i. e., with a call to the `stream` or `doc` function), the id function returns the corresponding stream identifier or document name. The dtd function uses the stream identifier or document name to retrieve the corresponding DTD of the referenced stream or document from a metadata repository. The stream identifier or document name is read from the argument of the `stream` or `doc` function, respectively. If the argument path does not reference a stream or document node, the id and dtd functions return $\perp$. This is safe since we require each query and therefore also each APT to reference exactly one input data stream or document. We deal with queries having multiple inputs in Section 5.4.

A `for` loop without a window operator references the path bound to the new variable and the paths in the optional XPath conditions and `where` clauses. These XPath conditions and `where` clauses also define the selection annotation which is associated with the set of returned paths and aggregate values. If no XPath conditions and `where` clauses are present in the query, the corresponding paths and annotations are not generated. The set of returned paths contains the paths returned by the WXQuery expression α in the `return` clause. The first premise in the rule reflects the variable binding in the `for` loop.

$$
\begin{array}{c}
Env' = Env + (\$x \Rightarrow \mathsf{path}(Path_1)) \\
\underline{Env' \vdash \alpha \Rightarrow (P,A,O,id,d)} \\
Env \vdash \mathtt{for}\ \$x\ \mathtt{in}\ Path_1\ \mathtt{where}\ \chi\ \mathtt{return}\ \alpha \\
\Rightarrow (P \cup \overline{\mathsf{path}}(Path_1) \cup \overline{\mathsf{path}}(\chi), \\
A \cup \{(\sigma, \mathsf{cond}(Path_1) \cup \mathsf{cond}(\chi), O)\}, O, \mathsf{id}(Path_1), \mathsf{dtd}(Path_1))
\end{array}
\tag{5.3}
$$

The above rule reflects the optimized translation of a WXQuery into an APT in the sense described in the previous section on determining the output elements. If the original query should be used for restructuring the resulting intermediate result data stream, then $\overline{\text{path}}(Path_1)$ and $\overline{\text{path}}(\chi)$ need to be added to the set O of returned paths and to the set of parents of the selection annotation that is added to A.

The next rule describes the translation of a `for` loop with a count-based data window. The only change compared to the previous rule affects the set of annotations. This set now contains a window annotation for the count-based data window. The window annotation is associated with the element referenced by $Path_1$. Furthermore, we need to break up the selection annotation into a window preselection annotation for the conditions contained in $Path_1$ and a window postselection annotation for the conditions contained in the `where` clause. Both selection annotations are associated with the window annotation ω. The selection annotations are optional, just as the corresponding conditions in the query.

$$
\frac{
\begin{array}{c}
Env' = Env + (\$x \Rightarrow \text{path}(Path_1)) \\
Env' \vdash \alpha \Rightarrow (P, A, O, id, d)
\end{array}
}{
\begin{array}{c}
Env \vdash \text{for } \$x \text{ in } Path_1 \text{ | count } \Delta \text{ step } \mu \text{ | where } \chi \text{ return } \alpha \\
\Rightarrow (P \cup \overline{\text{path}}(Path_1) \cup \overline{\text{path}}(\chi), \\
A \cup \{(\omega, (\text{count}, \Delta, \mu), \text{path}(Path_1)), (\text{pre-}\sigma, \text{cond}(Path_1), \omega), (\text{post-}\sigma, \text{cond}(\chi), \omega)\}, \\
O, \text{id}(Path_1), \text{dtd}(Path_1))
\end{array}
} \tag{5.4}
$$

In the same way as in the previous rule, the rule without optimization additionally adds the paths in $\overline{\text{path}}(Path_1)$ and $\overline{\text{path}}(\chi)$ to the set O of returned paths.

The inference rule describing the translation of `for` loops with time-based data windows is similar to the previous rule for count-based windows. The only difference is the additional handling of a path $Path_2$ which identifies the window reference element.

$$
\frac{
\begin{array}{c}
Env' = Env + (\$x \Rightarrow \text{path}(Path_1)) \\
Env' \vdash \alpha \Rightarrow (P, A, O, id, d)
\end{array}
}{
\begin{array}{c}
Env \vdash \text{for } \$x \text{ in } Path_1 \text{ | } Path_2 \text{ diff } \Delta \text{ step } \mu \text{ | where } \chi \text{ return } \alpha \\
\Rightarrow (P \cup \overline{\text{path}}(Path_1) \cup \overline{\text{path}}(Path_2) \cup \overline{\text{path}}(\chi), \\
A \cup \{(\omega, (\text{diff}, \text{path}(Path_2), \Delta, \mu), \text{path}(Path_1)), (\text{pre-}\sigma, \text{cond}(Path_1), \omega), \\
(\text{post-}\sigma, \text{cond}(\chi), \omega)\}, O, \text{id}(Path_1), \text{dtd}(Path_1))
\end{array}
} \tag{5.5}
$$

The window reference element path occurs in the set of referenced paths and in the window annotation. The rule without optimization additionally adds the paths in $\overline{\text{path}}(Path_1)$, $\overline{\text{path}}(Path_2)$, and $\overline{\text{path}}(\chi)$ to the set O of returned paths.

Finally, the following inference rule defines the translation of `let` expressions which are used to bind the result of an aggregate function call to a variable in WXQuery. The first premise of the rule reflects the binding of the new variable. The rule adds the path $Path_3$ of the aggregated element and, if present, the paths referenced in the condition to the set of referenced paths. It further adds an aggregate annotation to the set of annotations. The aggregate annotation is associated with the aggregated element. Optionally, an aggregate preselection annotation is associated with the aggregate annotation and an ordinary selection annotation is associated with the set of returned elements and aggregate values in O.

$$\frac{\begin{array}{c} Env' = Env + (\$a \Rightarrow \Phi(\mathsf{path}(Path_3))) \\ Env' \vdash \alpha \Rightarrow (P,A,O,id,d) \end{array}}{\begin{array}{c} Env \vdash \mathtt{let}\ \$a := \Phi(Path_3)\ \mathtt{where}\ \chi\ \mathtt{return}\ \alpha \\ \Rightarrow (P \cup \overline{\mathsf{path}}(Path_3) \cup \overline{\mathsf{path}}(\chi), \\ A \cup \{(\gamma,\Phi,\mathsf{path}(Path_3)),(\mathsf{pre}\text{-}\sigma,\mathsf{cond}(Path_3),\gamma),(\sigma,\mathsf{cond}(\chi),O)\}, \\ O,\mathsf{id}(Path_3),\mathsf{dtd}(Path_3)) \end{array}} \quad (5.6)$$

In the non-optimized case, the rule additionally adds the paths in $\overline{\mathsf{path}}(Path_3)$ and $\overline{\mathsf{path}}(\chi)$ to the set O of returned paths and consequently also to the set of parents of the selection annotation added to A.

Conditional expression A conditional expression returns the returned paths and aggregate values of α_1 under the condition χ and those of α_2 under the condition $\neg\chi$. The inference rule adds the corresponding selection annotations to the set of annotations A. It further adds the paths referenced in the condition to the set of referenced paths P. Apart from that, the rule propagates the referenced paths, the annotations, and the returned paths and aggregate values of α_1 and α_2.

$$\frac{\begin{array}{c} Env \vdash \alpha_1 \Rightarrow (P_{\alpha_1},A_{\alpha_1},O_{\alpha_1},id,d) \\ Env \vdash \alpha_2 \Rightarrow (P_{\alpha_2},A_{\alpha_2},O_{\alpha_2},id,d) \end{array}}{\begin{array}{c} Env \vdash \mathtt{if}\ \chi\ \mathtt{then}\ \alpha_1\ \mathtt{else}\ \alpha_2 \\ \Rightarrow (P_{\alpha_1} \cup P_{\alpha_2} \cup \overline{\mathsf{path}}(\chi), \\ A_{\alpha_1} \cup A_{\alpha_2} \cup \{(\sigma,\mathsf{cond}(\chi),O_{\alpha_1}),(\sigma,\mathsf{cond}(\neg\chi),O_{\alpha_2})\},O_{\alpha_1} \cup O_{\alpha_2},id,d) \end{array}} \quad (5.7)$$

The non-optimized version of the above rule additionally adds the paths in $\overline{\mathsf{path}}(\chi)$ to the set of returned paths $O_{\alpha_1} \cup O_{\alpha_2}$ and to each of the sets of parents of the two selection annotations added to $A_{\alpha_1} \cup A_{\alpha_2}$.

Output of subtrees reachable from node $\$y$ through path π A path expression of this form adds the corresponding path to the sets of referenced and returned paths and generates an additional selection annotation if the path contains predicates. In the inference rule, $Path_4$ represents the pattern $\$y/\pi$.

$$\frac{}{\begin{array}{c} Env \vdash Path_4 \\ \Rightarrow (\overline{\mathsf{path}}(Path_4),\{(\sigma,\mathsf{cond}(Path_4),\{\mathsf{path}(Path_4)\})\},\{\mathsf{path}(Path_4)\},\bot,\bot) \end{array}} \quad (5.8)$$

This rule has no premises.

Output of a subtree rooted at node $\$z$ The inference rule for this expression adds the path referenced by $\$z$ to the set of returned paths. The path may also contain an aggregate function call. Note that we do not need to add the path to the set of referenced paths since this will be done when processing the expression that defines the variable binding.

$$\frac{}{Env \vdash \$z \Rightarrow (\emptyset,\emptyset,\{\mathsf{path}(\$z)\},\bot,\bot)} \quad (5.9)$$

This rule has no premises.

Sequence   The inference rule for a sequence propagates the union of the sets of referenced paths, annotations, and returned paths and aggregate values of all expressions contained in the sequence.

$$\frac{Env \vdash \alpha_1 \Rightarrow (P_1, A_1, O_1, id, d) \ \ldots \ Env \vdash \alpha_n \Rightarrow (P_n, A_n, O_n, id, d)}{Env \vdash (\alpha_1, \ldots, \alpha_n) \Rightarrow (\bigcup_{i=1}^{n} P_i, \bigcup_{i=1}^{n} A_i, \bigcup_{i=1}^{n} O_i, id, d)} \tag{5.10}$$

Note that, similar to the rule for direct element constructors, we have rephrased the WXQuery expression for sequences in the inference rule compared to the WXQuery definition to better support the inference rule notation.

Example 5.6   We use query q_1 of Figure 5.2(a) to illustrate the translation of a WXQuery into a corresponding APT following the inference rules introduced above. We start by applying rules 5.5 and 5.6. Note that the four decomposed rules for FLWR expressions always need to be applied in combination since they are actually responsible for handling a single language construct, namely the FLWR expression of expression 3 in Definition 4.5. We decomposed the rule for FLWR expressions only to make the individual rules more concise.

First, the inference rules 5.5 and 5.6 update the environment *Env* yielding the extended environment *Env′* by adding the bindings $\$w \Rightarrow$ stream("photons")/photons/photon and $\$a \Rightarrow$ avg(stream("photons")/photons/photon/en). Using the updated environment whose contents are needed by the path, $\overline{path}$, and cond functions during the expansion of relative paths to absolute paths, the returned expression <avg_en> { $\$a$ } <avg_en> is evaluated next. This is the task of rule 5.2 which in turn triggers rule 5.9 on the returned variable $\$a$. Rule 5.9 adds the aggregate function call avg(stream("photons")/photons/photon/en) to the set of returned paths and aggregate values O. The set of referenced paths P and the set of annotations A remain empty. Further, the input stream identifier *id* and the input stream DTD *d* remain undefined. Afterwards, rule 5.2 simply returns the current state to rules 5.5 and 5.6 for handling the FLWR expression.

Applying rule 5.5, $Path_1$ becomes stream("photons")/photons/photon and $Path_2$ becomes det_time. Further, the value of Δ is 60 and the value of μ is 40. The rule adds the following paths to P:

- stream("photons")/photons/photon
  which corresponds to $Path_1$,

- stream("photons")/photons/photon/coord/cel/ra
  and
  stream("photons")/photons/photon/coord/cel/dec
  corresponding to the condition within $Path_1$,

- stream("photons")/photons/photon/det_time
  which is the absolute path of $Path_2$, and

- stream("photons")/photons/photon/en
  reflecting the path referenced via $\$a$ in the where clause.

The rule further adds to the set of annotations A the window annotation

$$(\omega, (\text{diff}, \text{stream}(\text{"photons"})/\text{photons}/\text{photon}/\text{det\_time}, 60, 40),$$
$$\text{stream}(\text{"photons"})/\text{photons}/\text{photon})$$

and subsequently the window preselection annotation

$$(\text{pre-}\sigma, \{\texttt{stream("photons")/photons/photon/coord/cel/ra} >= \texttt{120.0} \wedge$$
$$\texttt{stream("photons")/photons/photon/coord/cel/ra} <= \texttt{138.0} \wedge$$
$$\texttt{stream("photons")/photons/photon/coord/cel/dec} >= \texttt{-49.0} \wedge$$
$$\texttt{stream("photons")/photons/photon/coord/cel/dec} <= \texttt{-40.0}\}, \omega).$$

The set O of output elements remains unchanged to that returned by rule 5.2 before. Eventually, id is set to photons and d is set to the DTD of stream photons shown in Figure 2.2 on page 9.

Applying rule 5.6, $Path_3$ becomes $w/en. Subsequently, the rule adds to P the path

$$\texttt{stream("photons")/photons/photon/en}$$

which results from both applications of the $\overline{\text{path}}$ function to $Path_3$ and to the condition χ in the where clause. Further, the rule adds to A the aggregate annotation

$$(\gamma, \texttt{avg}, \texttt{stream("photons")/photons/photon/en})$$

as well as the selection annotation

$$(\sigma, \{\texttt{avg(stream("photons")/photons/photon/en)} >= \texttt{1.3}\},$$
$$\{\texttt{avg(stream("photons")/photons/photon/en)}\})$$

induced by the condition χ in the where clause of the query. Again, O remains unchanged. Since $Path_3$ does not contain a stream or doc function call, $\text{id}(Path_3)$ and $\text{dtd}(Path_3)$ both return $\perp$.

Figure 5.3(a) shows a graphical representation of the final APT t_{q_1} of q_1. □

Completeness and Correctness of the Translation

The translation of WXQueries into APTs according to the inference rules of the previous section needs to be complete and correct.

Statement 5.1 (Completeness) *Any WXQuery q referencing a single input stream and obeying Definition 4.5 can be translated into a corresponding APT t_q.* □

DISCUSSION: The statement follows from the fact that each WXQuery expression in Definition 4.5 is associated with an according inference rule. Therefore, any expression that can be contained in a valid WXQuery with a single input stream can be translated accordingly into a corresponding APT. ∎

Statement 5.2 (Correctness) *The translation of any WXQuery q with a single input stream into a corresponding APT t_q always yields an APT which represents the abstraction $\hat{q}$ of q.* □

DISCUSSION: The correctness of the translation follows by induction over the inference rules for each WXQuery expression:

Empty direct element constructor The empty direct element constructor does not contribute anything to the APT. It does not reference or return any paths and it does not induce any annotations. Neither does it yield any input identifier or DTD.

Direct element constructor A direct element constructor may contain zero or more subexpressions. Assuming that we have correctly determined the sets of referenced and returned paths of the subexpressions as well as the sets of annotations induced by them, the direct element constructor expression needs to be associated with the unions of these sets, respectively. The input identifier and the DTD of the subexpressions are simply forwarded.

FLWR expression Assuming that we have correctly determined the APT of the expression returned by a FLWR expression, we need to add the paths referenced in the FLWR expression to P. These include the path bound to the new variable and any paths in optional conditions, either in XPath predicates or in a where clause. We further need to add the according selection annotations to A. The set O of returned paths is the same as that of the returned expression. When data windows are involved, we need to distinguish window preselection and window postselection annotations. Further, we need to add the window annotation. In case of a time-based data window, the path of the reference element becomes part of the set of referenced paths. Eventually, a let expression induces an according aggregate annotation. We need to add the path in the aggregate function argument to the set of referenced paths. Furthermore, we need to take into account any aggregate preselection specified by conditions in the XPath expression identifying the aggregated element. Finally, the FLWR expression also determines the identifier and the DTD of the input stream or document.

Conditional expression If we have correctly determined the APTs of both subexpressions of a conditional expression, we can construct the APT of the conditional expression by taking the unions of the sets of referenced paths, annotations, and returned paths of the subexpressions. Additionally, we need to add the paths in the condition to the set of referenced paths. Further, we add two new selection annotations. One for the if-then part, using the original condition and associating the annotation with the returned paths of the if-then part. The other one for the else part, using the negation of the original condition and associating the annotation with the returned paths of the else part. The input identifier and the DTD of the subexpressions are just forwarded.

Output of subtrees reachable from node y through path π Here, the sets of referenced and returned paths each contain the referenced path. If the path contains an XPath predicate, the paths referenced in the predicate are added to the set of referenced paths and a corresponding selection annotation is added to the set of annotations. Otherwise, the set of annotations is empty. The expression does not yield any input identifier or DTD.

Output of a subtree rooted at node z A variable yields no referenced paths or annotations. These will be determined when the FLWR expression binding the variable is encountered. The variable, however, yields a returned path. It does not provide an input identifier or a DTD.

Sequence Similar to direct element constructors, sequences can contain zero or more subexpressions. We can therefore determine the set of referenced paths, the set of annotations, and the set of returned paths and aggregate values of a sequence by computing the unions of these sets over all subexpressions. Furthermore, a sequence simply forwards the input identifier and the DTD of its subexpressions.

Summary   Each inference rule correctly propagates the set of referenced paths P, the set of annotations A, and the set of returned paths and aggregate values O, as well as the input identifier id and the DTD d of its subexpressions. Thus, the inference rule of the top-level expression yields the corresponding correct sets and values for the entire query.   ∎

5.2.3   Translating APTs into WXQueries

The purpose of representing queries using APTs is to abstract from the restructuring details of the query and to enable a feasible way of identifying reusable data streams for data stream sharing. Furthermore, we show in Section 5.3 how APTs can be merged in order to represent multiple queries, i. e., the union of the corresponding result data streams, to increase possibilities for data stream sharing. The merged APT then reflects a subscription that can serve as a prefilter for the corresponding original queries. Therefore, each APT represents either the abstraction of a single query or the abstraction of the union of a set of queries. For creating the data streams represented by APTs in a distributed DSMS, we need to install and execute according queries in the system. We distinguish between structure-preserving and structure-mutating APTs.

Structure-Preserving APT

A structure-preserving APT represents a query with selection and projection operators but without more complex operators such as window construction and aggregation. We use the query template of Figure 5.4 for translating such an APT into a corresponding query. We concentrate on queries referencing data streams as input in the following. Queries on documents can be handled analogously. The template contains template variables which are replaced by actual values when generating a query for a given APT. In the template, the template variable *ROOT* stands for the root element of the input data stream (photons in our running example), *VAR* represents an arbitrary variable name, *STREAM* denotes the input data stream (again photons in our running example), and *ITEM* references the name of the elements actually contained in the stream (photon in the running example). Further, *PRED1* to *PREDn* represent selection predicates, and *PATH1* to *PATHn* represent paths to output elements starting from $VAR. These paths can be empty in an actual instance of the template variable, in which case the corresponding preceding slash also disappears from the template.

   The replacement of the template variables is straightforward for a given APT except for the predicate template variables *PRED1* to *PREDn*. These represent the predicates of the selection annotations of the APT. The query template returns each output element in the APT under the condition indicated by the corresponding selection annotation. If there is no selection annotation for a certain output element, the query simply returns the element without a surrounding if expression. In this case, we also need to remove the if expression guarding the output of the *ITEM* tags from the template. The query preserves the stream order, i. e., it returns all elements in the correct order of the data stream schema. We reference an output element in the return clause of the generated query by starting an XPath expression with $VAR and concatenating the remaining path steps leading to the output element. The APT yields the paths *PATH1* to *PATHn* by taking the absolute path of the respective output element and removing the prefix bound to $VAR. An according prefix replacement also takes place for any paths in the predicates *PRED1* to *PREDn*. The generated query needs to enclose each returned element in the correct sequence of direct element constructors to correctly retain the schema of the original data stream. We can easily derive the necessary information from the paths to the returned elements in the original

```
<ROOT>
  { for $VAR in stream("STREAM")/ROOT/ITEM
    return
      if (PRED1 or ... or PREDn) then
        <ITEM>...
          { if (PRED1) then $VAR/PATH1 else () }
          ...
          { if (PREDn) then $VAR/PATHn else () }
        ...</ITEM>
      else () }
</ROOT>
```

Figure 5.4: Structure-preserving query template

stream schema. These details vary for each actual query which is suggested by the dots in the template of Figure 5.4.

Example 5.7 The APTs of the structure-preserving queries q_3 and q_4 as shown in Figures 5.3(c) and 5.3(d) are translated into the queries of Figures 5.6(c) and 5.6(d), respectively. Since the original queries each return all output elements under the same condition as indicated by the selection annotation pull-up in the APT, only one `if` expression is used in the generated query to return all the output elements. This illustrates how selection annotation pull-up can be used to optimize query generation and reduce query size. In general, if all output elements of a query are returned under the same condition, the `if` expression guarding the output of the *ITEM* element constructor and the `if` expressions guarding the output of the single output elements are all equivalent. We can therefore leave them all out of the generated query except for the outermost expression which then guards the entire output of the query. □

Structure-Mutating APT

A structure-mutating APT represents a window query or an aggregate query. We concentrate on window-based aggregate queries since these are most common in practice and present a query template for aggregate queries with time-based windows. Query templates for aggregate queries with count-based windows, for queries defining data windows without aggregation, and for aggregate queries without data windows look similar. Figure 5.5 shows the query template for structure-mutating APTs with aggregation and a time-based data window. In addition to the *ROOT*, *VAR*, *STREAM*, and *ITEM* template variables already known from the template for structure-preserving queries, we introduce the following additional variables. The *PATH* template variable stands for a relative XPath expression with predicates allowed in each location step. We use *REFPATH* to denote a predicateless relative or absolute path. The variable *SIZE* denotes the window size and the variable *STEP* denotes the step size of the data window. The *PRED* variable represents a selection predicate. Further, *AGGVAR1* to *AGGVARn* stand for arbitrary aggregate variable names, *AGGFUNC1* to *AGGFUNCn* each denote one of the aggregate functions `min`, `max`, `sum`, `count`, or `avg`, and *AGGPATH1* to *AGGPATHn* represent paths to the corresponding aggregated element relative to *VAR*. Moreover, *AGGPRED1* to *AGGPREDn* are optional selection predicates for filtering aggregate values and *AGGELEM1* to *AGGELEMn* are generic aggregate element names. Accordingly, *WINPATH1* to *WINPATHm* denote paths to window elements relative to *VAR*, and *WINPRED1* to *WINPREDm* are optional selection predicates for filtering window elements. Further, the *WINELEM* template variable represents a generic window root element. The `where`

```
<ROOT>
  { for $VAR in stream("STREAM")/PATH|REFPATH diff SIZE step STEP|
    where PRED
    return
    let $AGGVAR1 := AGGFUNC1($VAR/AGGPATH1)
    ...
    let $AGGVARn := AGGFUNCn($VAR/AGGPATHn)
    return
    if (AGGPRED1 or ... or AGGPREDn or WINPRED1 or ... or WINPREDm) then
      <ITEM>
        { if (AGGPRED1) then <AGGELEM1> { $AGGVAR1 } </AGGELEM1> else () }
        ...
        { if (AGGPREDn) then <AGGELEMn> { $AGGVARn } </AGGELEMn> else () }
        { if (WINPRED1 or ... or WINPREDm) then
            <WINELEM>
              { if (WINPRED1) then $VAR/WINPATH1  else () }
              ...
              { if (WINPREDm) then $VAR/WINPATHm  else () }
            </WINELEM>
          else () }
      </ITEM>
    else () }
</ROOT>
```

Figure 5.5: Structure-mutating query template with time-based data window

clause, the if expressions, and the PATH, AGGPATHi, and WINPATHi variables are optional depending on the characteristics of the corresponding APT. If PATH or any AGGPATHi or WINPATHi is empty in an actual instance of the template variable, the corresponding preceding slash also disappears from the template. If there is no selection annotation for a certain returned aggregate value or window element, the query simply returns the value or element without a surrounding if expression. In such a case, we also need to remove any if expressions guarding the output of the surrounding ITEM and WINELEM tags from the template.

The query templates for queries defining data windows without aggregation are the same as those for window-based aggregate queries except that the let expressions for computing the aggregate values and the corresponding if expressions in the return clause are missing. Note that sharing window operators without aggregation during in-network query processing yields no optimization benefit in our setting since we assume potentially overlapping sliding windows that cover the entire input stream. Window operators therefore do not reduce the data volume of the stream. Rather, in case of overlapping windows, the transmitted data volume is increased by repeating the overlapping parts of subsequent windows. The query templates for aggregate queries without data windows are also the same as those for window-based aggregate queries except that the for loop, its optional where clause, and the window-specific parts in the return clause are missing. The query then needs to reference the input data stream via the stream function from within the aggregate function argument. Original queries that contain a for loop without a window definition and compute individual aggregate values for each item in the iteration are not meaningful in practice but, for the sake of completeness, are treated internally as if they would define a count-based window with a window size and a step size of one item each. Their APT representation therefore also contains a corresponding window

```
<photons>
  { for $w in stream("photons")/photons/photon
    [coord/cel/ra >= 120.0 and
     coord/cel/ra <= 138.0 and
     coord/cel/dec >= -49.0 and
     coord/cel/dec <= -40.0]
     |det_time diff 60 step 40|
    let $a := avg($w/en)
    return
    if ($a >= 1.3) then
      <photon>
        <avg_en> { $a } </avg_en>
      </photon>
    else () }
</photons>
```

(a) Abstract Query 1 $(\hat{q}_1)$

```
<photons>
  { for $w in stream("photons")/photons/photon
    [coord/cel/ra >= 120.0 and
     coord/cel/ra <= 138.0 and
     coord/cel/dec >= -49.0 and
     coord/cel/dec <= -40.0]
     |det_time diff 20 step 10|
    let $a := avg($w/en)
    return
    <photon>
      <avg_en> { $a } </avg_en>
    </photon> }
</photons>
```

(b) Abstract Query 2 $(\hat{q}_2)$

```
<photons>
  { for $p in stream("photons")/photons/photon
    return
    if ($p/en >= 1.3 and
        $p/coord/cel/ra >= 130.5 and
        $p/coord/cel/ra <= 135.5 and
        $p/coord/cel/dec >= -48.0 and
        $p/coord/cel/dec <= -45.0)
    then <photon>
           <coord>
             <cel>
               { $p/coord/cel/ra }
               { $p/coord/cel/dec }
             </cel>
           </coord>
           { $p/en } { $p/det_time }
         </photon>
    else () }
</photons>
```

(c) Abstract Query 3 $(\hat{q}_3)$

```
<photons>
  { for $p in stream("photons")/photons/photon
    return
    if ($p/coord/cel/ra >= 120.0 and
        $p/coord/cel/ra <= 138.0 and
        $p/coord/cel/dec >= -49.0 and
        $p/coord/cel/dec <= -40.0)
    then <photon>
           <coord>
             <cel>
               { $p/coord/cel/ra }
               { $p/coord/cel/dec }
             </cel>
           </coord>
           { $p/phc } { $p/en }
           { $p/det_time }
         </photon>
    else () }
</photons>
```

(d) Abstract Query 4 $(\hat{q}_4)$

Figure 5.6: Abstractions of example queries from Section 5.1

annotation. This is necessary to distinguish such queries from semantically different queries that do not contain any `for` loop and compute a single aggregate value over the entire input. Of course, such queries are only viable on finite inputs.

Again, the determination of the template variable values for a given APT is straightforward. One important issue, however, is that selection predicates in window preselection annotations become XPath predicates in `PATH` whereas selection predicates in window postselection annotations become predicates in `PRED` in a `where` clause. Selection predicates in aggregate preselection annotations become XPath predicates in `AGGPATHi` of the corresponding aggregate function call. We create the generic aggregate element name `AGGELEM` by concatenating the actual aggregate function name and the actual name of the aggregated element with an underscore in between, e. g., avg_en in our example queries. This is the element name for the aggregate value in the intermediate result data stream generated during in-network query processing. Similarly, we create the generic window root element name `WINELEM` by concatenating a fixed prefix with the name of the actual window root element, e. g., win_photon.

We reference both, aggregated elements in the arguments of aggregate function calls as well as output elements in the return clause of the generated query by starting an XPath expression with `$VAR` and concatenating the remaining path steps leading to the respective aggregated or returned element. Note that `$VAR` represents a variable bound to a data window, i. e., to a sequence of elements, in the template of Figure 5.5. The APT yields the paths `AGGPATH1` to `AGGPATHn` and `WINPATH1` to `WINPATHm` by taking the absolute path of the respective aggregated or returned element and removing the prefix bound to `$VAR`, ignoring the window definition. Again, an according prefix replacement also takes place for any paths in the predicates `AGGPRED1` to `AGGPREDn` and `WINPRED1` to `WINPREDm`.

Note that sharing a previously computed stream of aggregate values as input for a new aggregate query requires the installation of an appropriate reusing query based on Algorithm 4.4 as described in Section 4.4.6. This reusing query can be complemented by an additional selection query for performing any aggregate postselection.

Example 5.8 Figures 5.6(a) and 5.6(b) show the abstractions of queries q_1 and q_2 of Figures 5.2(a) and 5.2(b), respectively. Note the missing `if` expression guarding the output of the `photon` element constructor in $\hat{q}_2$ compared to $\hat{q}_1$. This is due to the fact that $\hat{q}_2$ does not filter the returned aggregate value and therefore unconditionally produces an output for each data window. We have also optimized $\hat{q}_1$ by removing the `if` expression guarding the output of the `avg_en` element constructor. As in queries $\hat{q}_3$ and $\hat{q}_4$, this is again possible since the query returns elements only under a single condition which is already tested by the surrounding `if` expression guarding the output of the `photon` element constructor.   □

DTD Generation

To be able to further use and process an intermediate data stream generated during in-network query processing, we need to determine the schema of each such stream. For simplicity, StreamGlobe uses DTDs since these provide a practical and concise means for describing data stream schemas and are easy to handle. Nevertheless, it is possible to extend the system to use the more expressive XML Schema. Creating the DTD for the result data stream of a structure-preserving query requires removing all elements from the DTD of the input data stream that are removed by a projection operator specified by the query. Furthermore, if the query returns multiple output elements under different conditions, we need to mark those output elements that are not necessarily part of every returned query result item as optional in the DTD. For structure-mutating queries, we construct a completely new DTD which contains the data stream root element (`photons` in our running example) as its root and the data stream item (`photon` in the example) as the only child of the root, with multiple occurrence. The data stream item has as its children either a sequence of generic aggregate elements, a generic window element, or both. The generic window element contains, as direct subelements, the complete DTD subtrees of the elements contained in the windows returned by the query.

Example 5.9 Figure 5.7 shows the DTDs of the result data streams of the abstract example queries shown in Figure 5.6.   □

Completeness and Correctness of the Translation

Similar to the translation of WXQueries into APTs, the inverse translation also needs to be complete and correct.

Statement 5.3 (Completeness) *Any APT t_q obtained by translating a WXQuery q using the inference rules of Section 5.2.2 can be translated back into a corresponding WXQuery $\hat{q}$.*   □

DISCUSSION: The statement follows from the fact that for both kinds of APTs, structure-preserving as well as structure-mutating, corresponding query templates for translating an APT into a corresponding WXQuery exist.   ■

```
<!ELEMENT photons (photon*)>
<!ELEMENT photon  (avg_en)>
<!ELEMENT avg_en  (#PCDATA)>
```

(a) Abstract Query 1 ($\hat{q}_1$)

```
<!ELEMENT photons (photon*)>
<!ELEMENT photon  (avg_en)>
<!ELEMENT avg_en  (#PCDATA)>
```

(b) Abstract Query 2 ($\hat{q}_2$)

```
<!ELEMENT photons  (photon*)>
<!ELEMENT photon   (coord, en, det_time)>
<!ELEMENT coord    (cel)>
<!ELEMENT cel      (ra, dec)>
<!ELEMENT ra       (#PCDATA)>
<!ELEMENT dec      (#PCDATA)>
<!ELEMENT en       (#PCDATA)>
<!ELEMENT det_time (#PCDATA)>
```

(c) Abstract Query 3 ($\hat{q}_3$)

```
<!ELEMENT photons  (photon*)>
<!ELEMENT photon   (coord, phc, en, det_time)>
<!ELEMENT coord    (cel)>
<!ELEMENT cel      (ra, dec)>
<!ELEMENT ra       (#PCDATA)>
<!ELEMENT dec      (#PCDATA)>
<!ELEMENT phc      (#PCDATA)>
<!ELEMENT en       (#PCDATA)>
<!ELEMENT det_time (#PCDATA)>
```

(d) Abstract Query 4 ($\hat{q}_4$)

Figure 5.7: Result DTDs of abstract example queries

Statement 5.4 (Correctness) *The translation of any APT t_q into a corresponding WXQuery always yields a WXQuery which represents the abstraction $\hat{q}$ of the original query q on which t_q is based.*   □

DISCUSSION: The correctness of the translation follows directly from the definitions of APTs and query abstractions as well as from the fact that the template variables in the query templates are replaced by the corresponding values of the APT.   ■

5.3   Matching and Merging APTs

We next introduce a tree algebra comprising two operators for matching and merging a pair of APTs. Matching APTs is equivalent to a containment check of the represented queries. We use this check for identifying shareable data streams in the network. Merging APTs enables us to compute the union of two queries. This is necessary for data stream widening.

Merging also enables data stream narrowing which can be applied when a query is deleted from the system. Several queries might reference the same intermediate data stream generated during in-network query processing as their inputs. If one of these queries is deleted from the system, we can potentially narrow this intermediate data stream. Narrowing requires replacing the stream with a reduced version that contains less data. Merging the APTs of the remaining queries yields an APT that represents the properties of the narrowed stream. If the deleted query required some data that is not needed by any of the other queries, narrowing will remove this data and the intermediate data stream will therefore become smaller. The narrowing can be propagated backwards from peer to peer towards the original stream source until no more data can be removed from the intermediate stream in the network. However, narrowing is expensive when dealing with large numbers of queries. Also, preserving the original intermediate stream in the system might ease sharing for future queries. Therefore, narrowing should only be performed on demand if network bandwidth or computational resources need to be freed. An interesting aspect for future work is to assess the benefits of preserving result streams of deleted queries with respect to anticipated requirements of future subscriptions. This is in a way similar to forward-looking caching strategies for one-time queries over persistent data in distributed environments as introduced by Kossmann et al. (2000).

It is possible to extend the tree algebra introduced in this section by additional operators. One interesting extension is support for subtraction. Subtracting APTs from each other could for example be used for generating remainder queries in semantic caching [Dar et al. (1996)].

In our application scenario, we always perform matching and merging of APTs in combination. For efficiency reasons, we therefore combine the matching and merging steps in one operation. The operation takes two APTs as input. These correspond to the stream APT and the query APT. The stream APT represents the result data stream of a query already installed in the system while the query APT represents a newly arriving query. In the matching step, the matching and merging operation examines whether the data stream represented by the stream APT can be shared for satisfying the query represented by the query APT. If this is not the case, the merging step appropriately merges both APTs, yielding a new APT that represents the union of both input APTs. The resulting APT can be translated into a WXQuery according to Section 5.2.3. Appropriately installing this query in the system generates a data stream that is shareable by both, the new query and the query represented by the original stream APT. The matching and merging of APTs needs to match and merge the path trees, the annotations, and the returned elements of the query APT and the stream APT under consideration.

5.3.1 Matching and Merging the Tree Structures

We match and merge the tree structures of two APTs by checking whether the path tree of the stream APT contains each path in the path tree of the query APT. If any path is missing, the APTs do not match and we need to merge them by adding to the stream APT all the paths of the query APT that are not already contained in the stream APT. Adding a path works in the same way as described for path tree construction in Section 5.2.2.

There is a special case where we do not need to add all missing elements to the path tree of the stream APT. This case occurs if, in the path tree of the stream APT, an ancestor of the subelement to be added is already present and is marked as an output element under the same or a less restrictive condition than the new subelement. In this case, the new subelement is already implicit and therefore does not need to be added explicitly.

5.3.2 Matching and Merging the Annotations

We match and merge annotations by traversing the APTs and comparing any corresponding annotations, i. e., annotations that are associated with the same elements in both trees, along the way. We need to handle each kind of annotation separately.

Selection annotations For each selection annotation in the stream APT, there must be a corresponding selection annotation in the query APT and the selection predicate in the query APT must imply the corresponding predicate of the stream APT. If these conditions are not met, we widen the stream APT by appropriately relaxing the selection predicate. We will examine predicate implication checking and relaxation in detail in Chapter 6. If the query APT contains no selection annotation for a path tree element for which the stream APT contains a selection annotation, then the widening consists of removing the selection annotation in the resulting merged APT.

Aggregate annotations An aggregate annotation, apart from being associated with the same element, must reference the same aggregate operator in both APTs. Further, we require the predicates of any aggregate preselection annotations to be semantically equivalent.

Otherwise, we must remove the aggregate annotation in the merged APT. We must also remove the aggregate annotation if the aggregate is window-based and the corresponding window annotation needs to be removed during merging (see below).

Window annotations The window annotations of the stream APT and the query APT can only match if they are defined over the same element in the same data stream, e. g., element photon in stream photons in our example queries q_1 and q_2 of Figure 5.2 on page 81. Further, we require the predicates of any window preselection annotations to be semantically equivalent. The predicates of any window postselection annotation in the query APT must imply the predicate of a corresponding window postselection annotation in the stream APT. Finally, the window definitions need to fulfill the following conditions for the window sizes Δ and Δ' and the step sizes μ and μ' of the window definition in the stream APT and the window definition in the query APT, respectively:

- $\Delta' \bmod \Delta = 0$
- $\Delta \bmod \mu = 0$
- $\mu' \bmod \mu = 0$

Furthermore, the window type (count-based or element-based) must be the same and time-based data windows must have identical reference elements. We have already presented the details on sharing window-based aggregate values without widening in Section 4.4.6. These continue to be applicable without any changes. If any of the above requirements is not fulfilled, we remove the window annotation and all dependent aggregate annotations from the merged APT and mark all elements required by the removed annotations as output elements. We make an exception from this rule for differing window sizes and step sizes of the two data windows. In this case, we perform data stream widening by computing the window size and the step size of a new window. This new window is the basis for a new window annotation that replaces the window annotations of the stream APT and the query APT in the merged APT. The query represented by the resulting APT yields a result data stream that can be used to generate the original data stream as well as to satisfy the new query. The next section details the algorithm for computing the window size and the step size of the new window annotation.

5.3.3 Relaxing Data Windows

The relaxation of data windows computes a window size and a step size for a new data window that all dependent windows can share. This requires that, for each dependent window, we can combine multiple instances of the new data window to form an instance of the dependent window. Therefore, we do not need to compute the dependent windows or any aggregates on these windows from scratch. Rather, we can determine them by appropriately combining the results of the relaxed window.

The window size $\bar{\Delta}$ and the step size $\bar{\mu}$ of the new window and the window and step sizes Δ, μ, Δ', and μ' of the stream window and the query window, respectively, must satisfy the following conditions:

- $\bar{\Delta} \bmod \bar{\mu} = 0$
- $\Delta \bmod \bar{\Delta} = 0$

Algorithm 5.1 RELAXWINDOW

Input: Window sizes Δ and Δ', step sizes μ and μ' of stream and query window, respectively.
Output: Window size $\bar{\Delta}$ and step size $\bar{\mu}$ of relaxed window.

1. *Initialize.* Compute the list $L_{\Delta,\Delta'}$ of all common divisors of Δ and Δ'. Similarly, compute the list $L_{\mu,\mu'}$ of all common divisors of μ and μ'. These are the sets of potential values for $\bar{\Delta}$ and $\bar{\mu}$, respectively.

2. *Check for compatible pairs.* Iterate $L_{\Delta,\Delta'}$ and $L_{\mu,\mu'}$ in decreasing order, i.e., examine larger values first. For each $\bar{\mu} \in L_{\mu,\mu'}$ compare $\bar{\mu}$ to each $\bar{\Delta} \in L_{\Delta,\Delta'}$ until the condition $\bar{\Delta} \bmod \bar{\mu} = 0$ is satisfied.

3. *Return result.* Return $\bar{\Delta}$ and $\bar{\mu}$.

- $\mu \bmod \bar{\mu} = 0$

- $\Delta' \bmod \bar{\Delta} = 0$

- $\mu' \bmod \bar{\mu} = 0$

The task of the window relaxation algorithm therefore is to find suitable values for $\bar{\Delta}$ and $\bar{\mu}$ under the above conditions. Furthermore, to support the optimization goal of reducing network traffic, the resulting data stream should consume as few bandwidth as possible. The major parameter in this respect is the step size. Note that, for example, a window-based aggregate with a count-based data window, a window size of 10, and a step size of 1 causes twice as much network traffic as a window with window size 5 and step size 2. The reason is that the first window produces an aggregate value after *every* data stream item while the second window produces an aggregate value only after *every second* data stream item.

Algorithm 5.1 shows how to compute $\bar{\Delta}$ and $\bar{\mu}$ from Δ, μ, Δ', and μ'. The algorithm takes all potential combinations of $\bar{\Delta}$ and $\bar{\mu}$ into account and chooses the one with the largest value for $\bar{\mu}$ and the largest value of $\bar{\Delta}$ for the chosen value of $\bar{\mu}$ such that the first of the above conditions, which is $\bar{\Delta} \bmod \bar{\mu} = 0$, is satisfied. We choose the largest possible value for $\bar{\mu}$ to minimize network traffic as described above and the largest possible value for $\bar{\Delta}$ for the chosen value of $\bar{\mu}$ to minimize computational effort. Algorithm 5.1 always finds optimal values for $\bar{\Delta}$ and $\bar{\mu}$. Note that it always finds valid values since, in the worst case, $\bar{\Delta}$ and $\bar{\mu}$ will be set to 1 each.

Example 5.10 Let $\Delta = 45$, $\mu = 30$, $\Delta' = 30$, and $\mu' = 20$. Then, all three conditions for window shareability as introduced in Section 5.3.2 are violated:

- $\Delta' \bmod \Delta = 30 \bmod 45 = 30 \neq 0$

- $\Delta \bmod \mu = 45 \bmod 30 = 15 \neq 0$

- $\mu' \bmod \mu = 20 \bmod 30 = 20 \neq 0$

Consider the lists of all divisors $L_\Delta = [45, 15, 9, 5, 3, 1]$, $L_{\Delta'} = L_\mu = [30, 15, 10, 6, 5, 3, 2, 1]$, and $L_{\mu'} = [20, 10, 5, 4, 2, 1]$ of Δ, Δ', μ, and μ', respectively. In the first step, Algorithm 5.1 determines the lists of common divisors of Δ and Δ' as $L_{\Delta,\Delta'} = [15, 5, 3, 1]$ and of μ and μ' as $L_{\mu,\mu'} = [10, 5, 2, 1]$. In the second step, the algorithm tests the largest possible value for $\bar{\mu}$, which is 10, against all possible values for $\bar{\Delta}$. This yields the invalid combinations $15 \bmod 10 = 5 \neq 0$,

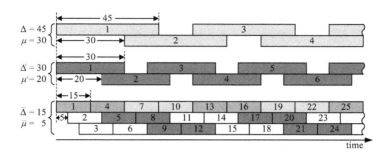

Figure 5.8: Window relaxation example

5 mod $10 = 5 \neq 0$, 3 mod $10 = 3 \neq 0$, and 1 mod $10 = 1 \neq 0$. In practice, the algorithm immediately continues with the next value for $\bar{\mu}$ as soon as the current value of $\bar{\Delta}$ becomes smaller than the current value of $\bar{\mu}$. The algorithm then takes into account the second largest possible value for $\bar{\mu}$, which is 5, and starts again by comparing this value to the largest possible value for $\bar{\Delta}$, which is 15, immediately arriving at the first valid combination 15 mod $5 = 0$. In the third step, the algorithm returns the final result $\bar{\Delta} = 15$ and $\bar{\mu} = 5$.

Figure 5.8 illustrates the correlations between the window sequences of, from top to bottom, the stream window, the query window, and the relaxed window for the above example. The individual shading of the relaxed windows indicates whether a particular relaxed window is shared for building a stream window (light gray), a query window (dark gray), or both (medium gray). Unshaded windows are not shared for any of the two. ☐

5.3.4 Example Matchings

Consider the APTs of the four example queries in Figure 5.3 on page 83. Assuming that the APT of q_1 is the query APT and the APT of q_2 is the stream APT, applying the rules described above yields a match without widening. If we interchange the roles of the query APT and the stream APT, i. e., match the APT of q_2 with the APT of q_1, the APTs do not match and need to be merged. The resulting APT is semantically equivalent to the APT of q_2 in this example, i. e., both APTs represent the same data stream.

The situation is analogous for the APTs of q_3 and q_4. Again, matching the APT of q_3 with the APT of q_4 yields a match without widening since the path tree of q_4 contains all the paths in the path tree of q_3 and the selection predicate of q_3 implies the selection predicate of q_4. When interchanging the roles of q_3 and q_4, we have no match since the path tree of q_3 does not contain the phc element and the inverse implication between the selection predicates is not valid. Therefore, we need to merge the APTs, adding the phc element and relaxing the selection predicate in the process. Again, the resulting APT is semantically equivalent to the APT of q_4 in this particular example.

Matching the APT of q_3 with the APT of q_1 leads to the removal of the window annotation and the aggregate annotation together with its associated selection annotation in the merged APT. The window preselection annotation becomes a selection annotation associated with the photon element and all elements at the leaves of the path tree are marked as output elements. The resulting APT therefore is similar to the APT of q_3. The only difference consists in the selection predicate of the selection annotation. Interchanging the roles of the queries here and matching the APT of q_1 with the APT of q_3 leads to the same result. In this case, the selection predicate of q_3 needs to be relaxed and becomes semantically equivalent to the window preselection predicate in q_1.

5.3.5 Completeness and Correctness of Matching and Merging APTs

The matching and merging of two APTs needs to be complete and correct.

Statement 5.5 (Completeness) *The algorithm for matching and merging two APTs is able to match and merge any two arbitrary APTs complying to Definition 5.2.* □

DISCUSSION: The statement follows directly from the discussion of the matching and merging process for APTs. ∎

Statement 5.6 (Correctness) *Matching and merging two APTs t_1 and t_2 always results in an APT t representing the union of the two input APTs. This result APT can be translated into a query $\hat{q}$ that represents the union of the corresponding queries $\hat{q}_1$ and $\hat{q}_2$ of the input APTs, i. e., the results of both queries $\hat{q}_1$ and $\hat{q}_2$ are contained in the result of query $\hat{q}$.* □

DISCUSSION: The tree structure of the merged APT t results from merging the tree structures of both input APTs t_1 and t_2. Therefore, t contains all the paths, and only those paths, that are referenced by either t_1 or t_2, or both. The same rationale applies to the set of output elements of the result APT. Incompatible annotations are either removed or relaxed whenever they prevent the implication of the stream result by the query result. ∎

5.4 Handling Join Queries

In the following, we extend our findings on APTs from the previous sections to additionally support join queries. Join queries are queries that either reference multiple inputs or that reference the same input multiple times in case of a self-join. Therefore, for each individual input, the abstract property representation of the query contains an individual APT describing the referenced and returned parts of the corresponding input source. Consequently, we call the resulting abstract property representation of such a query an *abstract property forest (APF)*. If inputs are combined, i. e., joined, their respective APTs are interconnected using a new kind of annotation, called a *join annotation*. We begin by introducing our notion of join and query semantics. Then, we describe how APFs are defined on the basis of APTs. Finally, we extend the previously introduced algorithm for matching and merging APTs to support the matching and merging of APFs. Hence, the extensions presented in this section enable the sharing, widening, and narrowing of join query results.

5.4.1 Preliminaries

Before describing the extensions for handling join queries, we first introduce our notion of join and query semantics.

Join Semantics

Considering a window-based binary join on two input streams, we define the join semantics as follows. Whenever one of the windows is updated, i.e., the window slides along by the extent defined by its step size, all items entering the window during the update are joined with the contents of the current data window of the other input stream. Consequently, newly arriving data items need to be buffered until the next update is triggered. In case of a count-based data window, the update is triggered after as many items as indicated by the window's step size have arrived on the stream. In case of a time-based data window, the update is triggered when the first item is encountered in the input stream whose reference element value is larger than the projected new upper bound of the window. Due to the sort order of the stream, we can be sure that no more items fitting into the updated window will arrive afterwards.

Whenever a window update occurs, the new items entering the updated window are joined with the current contents of the window of the other input stream. Afterwards, the updated window slides along, removing invalidated items from the window and adding the newly arrived ones. This process easily generalizes to multi-way joins by appropriately joining the new items of the updated window with the current contents of the windows of all other join inputs [Golab and Özsu (2003c)]. For simplicity, we only consider binary joins here.

The step-based join semantics introduced above leads to non-deterministic join results. This is due to the fact that the join result depends on the arrival sequence of data items on the joined input streams. Figure 5.9(a) illustrates this issue. We assume that the data windows are generated in the sequence indicated by the numbers next to the window intervals in the figure, i.e., the initial window of stream B arrives before the three windows of stream A. Finally, the second window of stream B arrives. Note that the time axes in the figure indicate the timestamp values contained in the arriving data items. These represent application time and are independent of the actual arrival time of the data items in the data window. We further assume that the contents of the initial windows of streams A and B in Figure 5.9(a) have already been joined appropriately. We now consider joins triggered by subsequent window updates. This leads to the three joins indicated in the figure. First, when updating the window over stream A, the new parts of the windows numbered 3 and 4, respectively, are joined with the contents of the window numbered 1. This corresponds to the first two joins of the data items a_4 and a_5 with the data items b_1, b_2, and b_3 in the figure. Subsequently, the new part of the window numbered 5 consisting of b_4 and b_5 is joined with the complete contents of the window numbered 4 comprising a_4 and a_5. We can see that a change in the arrival sequence of the windows of both streams—which depends on the arrival sequence of the data items on both streams—can lead to a different join result. For example, if the two windows of stream B arrive between the first and the second window of stream A, then a_4 and a_5 entering the data window of stream A during its first and second update would never be joined with b_1 and b_2 contained in the first window of stream B in our example. This is different from the window sequence shown in Figure 5.9(a).

Despite its non-determinism, we make the case for this join semantics. In a multitude of application domains, joining most recent data instead of computing purely timestamp-based joins is of great importance. Prominent examples comprise sensor monitoring, surveillance, traffic supervision, logistics, and process automation control. All of these application scenarios have in common that they need to quickly recognize and react to the newest developments and to exceptional events such as unusual sensor readings, alarms, traffic jams, or malfunctions. Thus, in many cases it is not of primary importance to join data items that have been generated at about the same time and to produce deterministic join results. Instead, it is more important to join the latest, most current values that have arrived on the input streams in order to get the most

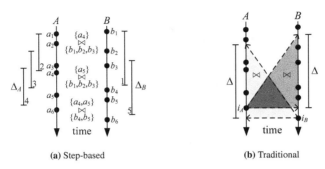

(a) Step-based   (b) Traditional

Figure 5.9: Window join semantics

up-to-date combinations. Our step-based join semantics supports this requirement as long as windows have reasonably small step sizes, e. g., one data item for count-based windows in the extreme case. In the business world, SAP Executive Board member Claus Heinrich has coined the term Real World Awareness [Heinrich (2005)], emphasizing the importance of monitoring and reacting to most recent data for corporate success. One of the main enabling technologies in this direction is Radio Frequency IDentification (RFID). In logistics, for example, reading RFID tags generates streams of events that need to be processed. As a more concrete example, consider stock exchange tickers. When joining the tickers of two companies to compare their relative performance, it is imperative to always combine the latest available values. Since only the most current results are of interest, the fact that the overall join result depends on the arrival sequence of data items is irrelevant. A similar example is to compare the relative performance of the same company at different stock exchanges. In this case, each stock exchange provides one of the input data streams to be joined and the join predicate checks for equality of the company id, assuming that each ticker provides data about multiple companies. The example join queries of Figure 5.10 stick to our astrophysics application scenario. In this scenario, combining measurements of multiple photon detectors of various telescopes and satellites provides for another possible application of our join semantics. For example, it might be interesting to join photons detected in the same celestial area, i. e., having similar celestial coordinates, and to retrieve their energy and detection time for comparison. For brevity and clarity of exposition, the actual example queries of Figure 5.10 use simpler join conditions that are not necessarily meaningful in practice. However, our approach also works for more complex join queries. Another advantage of our join semantics is that no synchronization between join input streams is necessary since we correlate the streams based on their local window definitions which solely depend on the respective input stream. We assume that newly arriving data items from both input streams are processed sequentially to guarantee the synchronization of window updates and associated join computations. Furthermore, the problem of large and growing operator states that requires the introduction of heartbeats or punctuations to limit memory usage when joining slow or bursty input streams is not an issue in our join semantics.

Note that WXQuery can also support different variants of traditional window join semantics over data streams as found in the literature[1]. One of these variants, for example, specifies

---

[1]See, for example, [Chandrasekaran and Franklin (2002); Golab and Özsu (2003c); Hammad et al. (2003b); Kang et al. (2003); Krämer and Seeger (2005); Madden et al. (2002b)].

```
<photons>
  { for $x in stream("photons1")/photons/photon
      |det_time diff 10 step 5|
    for $y in stream("photons2")/photons/photon
      |det_time diff 20 step 10|
    where $x/en >= $y/en + 0.5
    return
      <result>
        { $x/en } { $x/phc }
        { $y/en } { $y/phc }
      </result> }
</photons>
```

(a) Query 5 (q_5)

```
<photons>
  { for $x in stream("photons1")/photons/photon
      |det_time diff 10 step 5|
    for $y in stream("photons2")/photons/photon
      |det_time diff 20 step 10|
    where $x/en >= $y/en
    return
      <result>
        { $x/en } { $x/det_time }
        { $y/en } { $y/det_time }
      </result> }
</photons>
```

(b) Query 6 (q_6)

```
<photons>
  { for $x in stream("photons1")/photons/photon
      |det_time diff 30 step 5|
    for $y in stream("photons2")/photons/photon
      |det_time diff 15 step 10|
    where $x/en >= $y/en
    return
      <result>
        { $x/en } { $x/det_time }
        { $y/en } { $y/det_time }
      </result> }
</photons>
```

(c) Query 7 (q_7)

```
<photons>
  { for $x in stream("photons1")/photons/photon
      |det_time diff 15 step 10|
    for $y in stream("photons2")/photons/photon
      |det_time diff 30 step 15|
    where $x/phc >= $y/phc
    return
      <result>
        { $x/en } { $x/det_time }
        { $y/en } { $y/det_time }
      </result> }
</photons>
```

(d) Query 8 (q_8)

Figure 5.10: Example join queries

that each newly arriving data item from one stream is joined with all the data items arriving on the other stream whose timestamps are contained in a certain interval around the timestamp of the new data item. Figure 5.11 shows an according example WXQuery with $\Delta = 10$. Streams photons1 and photons2 are supposed to be photon data streams of the same schema as introduced in Figure 2.2 on page 9 in all our example join queries. The above semantics has the advantage of producing deterministic join results when using time-based data windows. Count-based data windows always lead to non-deterministic join results. Hammad et al. (2003b) have already extensively studied efficient join result sharing for join queries using another variant of time-based window join semantics. In this variant, data items receive their timestamp on arrival at the join operator. Each data item arriving on an input stream is joined with all data items of the other input stream that arrived previously within a certain time interval. Consider Fig-

```
<photons>
  { for $x in stream("photons1")/photons/photon
    for $y in stream("photons2")/photons/photon
    where $x/det_time - $y/det_time <= 10
      or $y/det_time - $x/det_time < 10
    return
      <result>
        { $x/en } { $x/phc }
        { $y/en } { $y/phc }
      </result> }
</photons>
```

Figure 5.11: WXQuery with traditional join semantics

ure 5.9(b) that shows an illustrative example. The newly arriving data item i_A with timestamp value t_{i_A} in stream A is joined with all data items of stream B which have arrived previously and whose timestamp values are greater than or equal to $t_{i_A} - \Delta$, with Δ being the common window size of streams A and B. Since each newly arriving data item i_B with timestamp value t_{i_B} in stream B is accordingly joined with all data items of stream A which have arrived previously and whose timestamp values are greater than or equal to $t_{i_B} - \Delta$, i_A will eventually be joined with all data items i_B from stream B for which $(t_{i_A} - t_{i_B} \leq \Delta) \vee (t_{i_B} - t_{i_A} \leq \Delta)$ holds.

The results of Hammad et al. (2003b) are applicable without any changes in our setting when the corresponding join semantics is applied. Note that the optimizations introduced by Hammad et al. (2003b) impose restrictions on the queries that may be taken into account for join result sharing. These restrictions include identical signatures of the join queries, i. e., identical join predicates, and an equal window size Δ for all input streams of a query as indicated in Figure 5.9(b). In contrast, our step-based semantics and the accompanying join sharing approach introduced further below allow for different join predicates in the queries taken into account for sharing. We also support varying window and step sizes in the windows of various input streams of a query.

Query Semantics

In SQL, joins can simply be formulated by referencing the relations to be joined in the `from` clause and by including the join predicates as conditions in the `where` clause. The query does not imply a certain evaluation strategy for computing the join. Therefore, SQL-based continuous query languages such as CQL [Arasu et al. (2006)] extend the query language by introducing window syntax constructs without having to change the basic underlying SQL query semantics.

In XQuery and consequently also in WXQuery, joins are expressed by nested `for` loops with accompanying conditions reflecting the join predicates. The usual semantics of nested loops is, however, not applicable when formulating window-based joins over possibly infinite data streams since this leads to infinite loops that do not produce the desired results. To illustrate this issue, consider Query 5 (q_5) of Figure 5.10(a). Both `for` loops in the query reference unbounded data streams with data windows defined on them. Under conventional XQuery semantics, the inner loop would iterate indefinitely over an infinite number of windows on stream `photons2` while the outer loop would never leave its first iteration. Therefore, we redefine the query semantics for join queries in WXQuery as follows. Whenever a WXQuery contains more than one `for` loop over a windowed input, we compute the corresponding window join as described in the previous section on join semantics. During join computation in combination with a window update, we consider the variables bound by the `for` loops to iterate over the new items of the updated data window and the current items of the other data window in a nested loops fashion. Due to this change in semantics, we currently do not deal with queries mixing aggregates and joins. Introducing a dedicated WXQuery syntax extension for expressing window-based joins over unbounded data streams is an issue of future work.

5.4.2   The Abstract Property Forest (APF)

In the following, we define APFs and show how to translate a join query into a corresponding APF and vice versa.

Definition

The definition of an APF builds on Definition 5.2 of an APT.

Definition 5.5 (Abstract Property Forest (APF)) An *abstract property forest (APF)* $f_q := T$ of a query q with m input data streams consists of a list $T := [t_q^i \mid 1 \leq i \leq m]$ of property trees, one for each input source referenced in q.

Structural part The structural part of f_q consists of the union of the structural parts of the contained APTs, i.e., it is a forest consisting of the path trees of the input sources. If a query references the same input source multiple times, e.g., for self-join purposes, then each reference has its own path tree in f_q.

Content-based part In addition to the annotations of the APTs as introduced in Section 5.2, f_q can also contain *join annotations*. A join annotation $a := (\tau, C, R)$ is a selection annotation that is associated with elements from multiple APTs. It consists of its type $\tau = \bowtie$, its contents C which represent a set of join predicates, and a set R of parents. Similar to selection annotations, the predicates in the contents C of a join annotation are meant to be conjunctively combined. A join annotation can be associated with elements from each participating APT. As a special kind of a selection annotation, a join annotation is associated with the returned elements of a query and determines under which condition these elements are returned as part of the join result. □

Translating WXQueries into APFs

We extend the translation rules introduced in Section 5.2.2 to support join queries referencing multiple input streams.

Determining Join Annotations Generating the APTs of the multiple input sources, i.e., assembling the path trees, determining the annotations, and identifying the output elements, works exactly as described in Section 5.2.2 for each input source. The only additional aspect is the identification of join annotations. This is similar to determining selection annotations. If the corresponding predicate is a join predicate, i.e., the predicate correlates elements from different input sources, a join annotation is generated and associated with the returned elements of the involved sources' APTs. Determining the input source an element belongs to is straightforward since the path to each element is expanded to the corresponding absolute path if necessary. The absolute path contains the respective stream or document identifier as an argument to the `stream` or `doc` function.

Example 5.11 Figure 5.12 shows the APFs of the example join queries q_5 to q_8. Note the join annotations connecting the returned elements of both input streams in each APF. □

Inference Rules This section extends the formal rules for translating a WXQuery into a corresponding APT introduced in Section 5.2.2 to additionally support join queries and their translation into APFs.

The construction of the APTs of each individual input stream works as described in Section 5.2.2. For queries with multiple input data streams, instead of generating a single APT, we generate a list of APTs containing one APT per input data stream. The length of the list

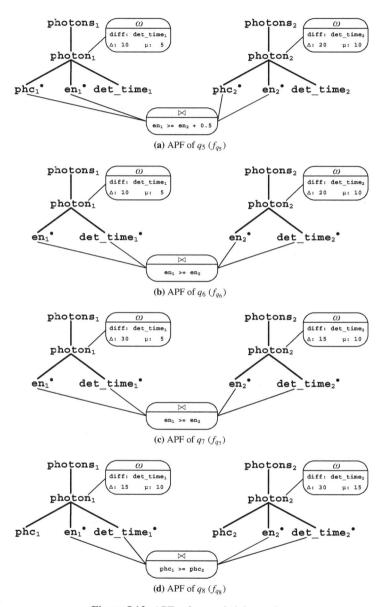

(a) APF of q_5 (f_{q_5})

(b) APF of q_6 (f_{q_6})

(c) APF of q_7 (f_{q_7})

(d) APF of q_8 (f_{q_8})

Figure 5.12: APFs of example join queries

can be derived from the query in advance. For each input source i, we also determine the input stream identifier or document name id^i and the corresponding DTD d^i in advance during a preprocessing phase by scanning the query for any stream or doc function calls which contain an input source identifier as parameter. We use the input source identifier to retrieve the corresponding DTD from a metadata repository. Therefore, id^i and d^i are already present for each input source i and the following rules simply forward them. This is important since we need the corresponding input source identifier during APF generation to add paths, annotations, and output elements to the correct APTs. In this context, we also slightly redefine the semantics of the path, $\overline{\text{path}}$, and cond functions. These now only return those paths or conditions referring to the corresponding input source as indicated by a superscript. For example, if $Path_1$ represents a path belonging to APT t^i, then $\overline{\text{path}}^i(Path_1)$ returns this path and $P^i \cup \{\overline{\text{path}}^i(Path_1)\}$ adds it to P^i. At the same time, $\overline{\text{path}}^j(Path_1)$ does not return any path and therefore $P^j \cup \{\overline{\text{path}}^j(Path_1)\}$ does not add any path to P^j for all $1 \leq j \leq m, j \neq i$. Finally, we define the $cond^i$ function to only return conditions that exclusively reference elements from input source i, i.e., simple selection conditions. Further, we additionally introduce a variant $\overline{cond}^i$ that only returns conditions that reference additional input sources besides i, i.e., join conditions involving input source i.

We again use the inference rule notation of the XQuery formal semantics specification [W3C (2007e)]. The judgment

$$Env \vdash \alpha \Rightarrow [(P^1, A^1, O^1, id^1, d^1), \ldots, (P^m, A^m, O^m, id^m, d^m)]$$

holds if and only if, under the environment Env, the expression α induces the construction of the APTs $(P^1, A^1, O^1, id^1, d^1)$ to $(P^m, A^m, O^m, id^m, d^m)$ as described in Section 5.2.2. Inference rules are again of the form

$$\frac{premise_1 \ \ldots \ premise_n}{conclusion}$$

where all premises and the conclusion are judgments of the above form. Additionally, premises may again constitute expressions of the form $Env' = Env + (\$var \Rightarrow Path)$ that extend the environment Env yielding the environment Env' by adding the binding of the variable $\$var$ to the path represented by $Path$. The inference rule expresses that, if all premises hold, then the conclusion holds as well.

We now give the extended inference rules for each WXQuery expression of Definition 4.5.

Empty direct element constructor   An empty direct element constructor induces a list of empty APTs.

$$\overline{Env \vdash <t/> \Rightarrow [(\emptyset^1, \emptyset^1, \emptyset^1, id^1, d^1), \ldots, (\emptyset^m, \emptyset^m, \emptyset^m, id^m, d^m)]} \tag{5.11}$$

Direct element constructor   For each input source, the rule generates the corresponding APT just as for the single APT in the original rule of Section 5.2.2.

$$Env \vdash \alpha_1 \Rightarrow [(P_1^1, A_1^1, O_1^1, id^1, d^1), \ldots, (P_1^m, A_1^m, O_1^m, id^m, d^m)]$$

$$\cdots$$

$$\frac{Env \vdash \alpha_n \Rightarrow [(P_n^1, A_n^1, O_n^1, id^1, d^1), \ldots, (P_n^m, A_n^m, O_n^m, id^m, d^m)]}{Env \vdash <t>\alpha_1 \ldots \alpha_n</t>} \tag{5.12}$$

$$\Rightarrow [(\bigcup_{i=1}^n P_i^1, \bigcup_{i=1}^n A_i^1, \bigcup_{i=1}^n O_i^1, id^1, d^1), \ldots, (\bigcup_{i=1}^n P_i^m, \bigcup_{i=1}^n A_i^m, \bigcup_{i=1}^n O_i^m, id^m, d^m)]$$

Note that, as described in Section 5.2.2, we have again rephrased the WXQuery expression for direct element constructors in the inference rule compared to the WXQuery definition to better support the inference rule notation.

FLWR expression   We again split the inference rule for FLWR expressions into four separate rules as in Section 5.2.2. We use the same shortcuts and functions as in the introduction of the original rules. Additionally, as introduced above, the functions path^i and $\overline{\text{path}}^i$ with $1 \leq i \leq m$ return only those paths that reference the input source with identifier id^i. Furthermore, the cond function only considers non-join conditions, i.e., conditions that reference elements from only one APT. We introduce the $\overline{\text{cond}}$ function to exclusively handle join conditions referencing elements from more than one APT. Both functions are applied as described in Section 5.2.2 on the respective conditions.

First, we consider a `for` loop without any data window. The first premise in the rule again reflects the variable binding in the `for` loop.

$$
\frac{
\begin{array}{c}
Env' = Env + (\$x \Rightarrow \text{path}(Path_1)) \\
Env' \vdash \alpha \Rightarrow [(P^1, A^1, O^1, id^1, d^1), \dots, (P^m, A^m, O^m, id^m, d^m)]
\end{array}
}{
\begin{array}{c}
Env \vdash \texttt{for } \$x \texttt{ in } Path_1 \texttt{ where } \chi \texttt{ return } \alpha \\
\Rightarrow [(P^1 \cup \overline{\text{path}}^1(Path_1) \cup \overline{\text{path}}^1(\chi), \\
A^1 \cup \{(\sigma, \text{cond}^1(Path_1) \cup \text{cond}^1(\chi), O^1), (\bowtie, \overline{\text{cond}}^1(Path_1) \cup \overline{\text{cond}}^1(\chi), O^1)\}, \\
O^1, id^1, d^1), \\
\dots, \\
(P^m \cup \overline{\text{path}}^m(Path_1) \cup \overline{\text{path}}^m(\chi), \\
A^m \cup \{(\sigma, \text{cond}^m(Path_1) \cup \text{cond}^m(\chi), O^m), (\bowtie, \overline{\text{cond}}^m(Path_1) \cup \overline{\text{cond}}^m(\chi), O^m)\}, \\
O^m, id^m, d^m)]
\end{array}
}
\tag{5.13}
$$

Note that an annotation is only added to the set A^i of annotations of a certain APT t^i if O^i is not empty, i.e., the annotation is associated with at least one returned element in O^i. As stated in Section 4.3, $O := O^1 \cup \dots \cup O^m$ must not be empty, i.e., each query must return at least one element of the input sources or an aggregate value based on the input sources. Therefore, each annotation is associated with at least one element in at least one of the APTs of the APF.

The next rule describes the translation of a `for` loop with a count-based data window. The selection annotations are again optional, just as the corresponding conditions in the query.

$$
\frac{
\begin{array}{c}
Env' = Env + (\$x \Rightarrow \text{path}(Path_1)) \\
Env' \vdash \alpha \Rightarrow [(P^1, A^1, O^1, id^1, d^1), \dots, (P^m, A^m, O^m, id^m, d^m)]
\end{array}
}{
\begin{array}{c}
Env \vdash \texttt{for } \$x \texttt{ in } Path_1 \texttt{ |count } \Delta \texttt{ step } \mu \texttt{ | where } \chi \texttt{ return } \alpha \\
\Rightarrow [(P^1 \cup \overline{\text{path}}^1(Path_1) \cup \overline{\text{path}}^1(\chi), \\
A^1 \cup \{(\omega, (\text{count}, \Delta, \mu), \text{path}^1(Path_1)), (\text{pre-}\sigma, \text{cond}^1(Path_1), \omega), \\
(\text{post-}\sigma, \text{cond}^1(\chi), \omega), (\bowtie, \overline{\text{cond}}^1(Path_1) \cup \overline{\text{cond}}^1(\chi), O^1)\}, O^1, id^1, d^1), \\
\dots, \\
(P^m \cup \overline{\text{path}}^m(Path_1) \cup \overline{\text{path}}^m(\chi), \\
A^m \cup \{(\omega, (\text{count}, \Delta, \mu), \text{path}^m(Path_1)), (\text{pre-}\sigma, \text{cond}^m(Path_1), \omega), \\
(\text{post-}\sigma, \text{cond}^m(\chi), \omega), (\bowtie, \overline{\text{cond}}^m(Path_1) \cup \overline{\text{cond}}^m(\chi), O^m)\}, O^m, id^m, d^m)]
\end{array}
}
\tag{5.14}
$$

Note that $\mathsf{path}^i(Path_1)$ only returns a path for the input source with identifier id^i. Therefore, the rule generates the window annotation only once and associates it with the correct input source. The rule does not generate the same window annotation for the other input sources since for the other sources, the parent of the annotation specified by $\mathsf{path}^j(Path_1)$ with $j \neq i$ is empty.

The inference rule describing the translation of `for` loops with time-based data windows again handles an additional path $Path_2$ which identifies the window reference element.

$$
\frac{\begin{array}{c} Env' = Env + (\$x \Rightarrow \mathsf{path}(Path_1)) \\ Env' \vdash \alpha \Rightarrow [(P^1, A^1, O^1, id^1, d^1), \ldots, (P^m, A^m, O^m, id^m, d^m)] \end{array}}{\begin{array}{c} Env \vdash \texttt{for } \$x \texttt{ in } Path_1 \mid Path_2 \texttt{ diff } \Delta \texttt{ step } \mu \mid \texttt{ where } \chi \texttt{ return } \alpha \\ \Rightarrow [(P^1 \cup \overline{\mathsf{path}}^1(Path_1) \cup \overline{\mathsf{path}}^1(Path_2) \cup \overline{\mathsf{path}}^1(\chi), \\ A^1 \cup \{(\omega, (\mathsf{diff}, \mathsf{path}^1(Path_2), \Delta, \mu), \mathsf{path}^1(Path_1)), (\mathsf{pre}\text{-}\sigma, \mathsf{cond}^1(Path_1), \omega), \\ (\mathsf{post}\text{-}\sigma, \mathsf{cond}^1(\chi), \omega), (\bowtie, \overline{\mathsf{cond}}^1(Path_1) \cup \overline{\mathsf{cond}}^1(\chi), O^1)\}, O^1, id^1, d^1), \\ \ldots, \\ (P^m \cup \overline{\mathsf{path}}^m(Path_1) \cup \overline{\mathsf{path}}^m(Path_2) \cup \overline{\mathsf{path}}^m(\chi), \\ A^m \cup \{(\omega, (\mathsf{diff}, \mathsf{path}^m(Path_2), \Delta, \mu), \mathsf{path}^m(Path_1)), (\mathsf{pre}\text{-}\sigma, \mathsf{cond}^m(Path_1), \omega), \\ (\mathsf{post}\text{-}\sigma, \mathsf{cond}^m(\chi), \omega), (\bowtie, \overline{\mathsf{cond}}^m(Path_1) \cup \overline{\mathsf{cond}}^m(\chi), O^m)\}, O^m, id^m, d^m)] \end{array}} \quad (5.15)
$$

Although we do not deal with queries mixing aggregates and joins due to the semantic differences described in Section 5.4.1, we introduce the inference rule for translating `let` expressions which are used to bind the result of an aggregate function call to a variable in WXQuery. This sets the stage for supporting mixed queries in future work.

$$
\frac{\begin{array}{c} Env' = Env + (\$a \Rightarrow \Phi(\mathsf{path}(Path_3))) \\ Env' \vdash \alpha \Rightarrow [(P^1, A^1, O^1, id^1, d^1), \ldots, (P^m, A^m, O^m, id^m, d^m)] \end{array}}{\begin{array}{c} Env \vdash \texttt{let } \$a := \Phi(Path_3) \texttt{ where } \chi \texttt{ return } \alpha \\ \Rightarrow [(P^1 \cup \overline{\mathsf{path}}^1(Path_3) \cup \overline{\mathsf{path}}^1(\chi), \\ A^1 \cup \{(\gamma, \Phi, \mathsf{path}^1(Path_3)), (\mathsf{pre}\text{-}\sigma, \mathsf{cond}^1(Path_3), \gamma), (\sigma, \mathsf{cond}^1(\chi), O^1), \\ (\bowtie, \overline{\mathsf{cond}}^1(Path_3) \cup \overline{\mathsf{cond}}^1(\chi), O^1)\}, O^1, id^1, d^1), \\ \ldots, \\ (P^m \cup \overline{\mathsf{path}}^m(Path_3) \cup \overline{\mathsf{path}}^m(\chi), \\ A^m \cup \{(\gamma, \Phi, \mathsf{path}^m(Path_3)), (\mathsf{pre}\text{-}\sigma, \mathsf{cond}^m(Path_3), \gamma), (\sigma, \mathsf{cond}^m(\chi), O^m), \\ (\bowtie, \overline{\mathsf{cond}}^m(Path_3) \cup \overline{\mathsf{cond}}^m(\chi), O^m)\}, O^m, id^m, d^m)] \end{array}} \quad (5.16)
$$

Similar to the window annotations, the rule generates the aggregate annotation only once and associates it with the APT t^i for which $\mathsf{path}^i(Path_3)$ actually returns a path. For the remaining input sources, the parent of the aggregate annotation remains empty and the annotation is therefore not generated.

Conditional expression   Apart from handling multiple input streams, the rule for conditional expressions further differs from the corresponding rule in Section 5.2.2 in that it creates join annotations in addition to normal selection annotations if dictated by the query to be translated.

$$Env \vdash \alpha_1 \Rightarrow [(P^1_{\alpha_1}, A^1_{\alpha_1}, O^1_{\alpha_1}, id^1, d^1), \ldots, (P^m_{\alpha_1}, A^m_{\alpha_1}, O^m_{\alpha_1}, id^m, d^m)]$$

$$\frac{Env \vdash \alpha_2 \Rightarrow [(P^1_{\alpha_2}, A^1_{\alpha_2}, O^1_{\alpha_2}, id^1, d^1), \ldots, (P^m_{\alpha_2}, A^m_{\alpha_2}, O^m_{\alpha_2}, id^m, d^m)]}{Env \vdash \text{if } \chi \text{ then } \alpha_1 \text{ else } \alpha_2} \quad (5.17)$$

$$\Rightarrow [(P^1_{\alpha_1} \cup P^1_{\alpha_2} \cup \overline{\text{path}}^1(\chi), A^1_{\alpha_1} \cup A^1_{\alpha_2} \cup \{(\sigma, \text{cond}^1(\chi), O^1_{\alpha_1}), (\sigma, \text{cond}^1(\neg\chi), O^1_{\alpha_2}),$$
$$(\bowtie, \overline{\text{cond}}^1(\chi), O^1_{\alpha_1}), (\bowtie, \overline{\text{cond}}^1(\neg\chi), O^1_{\alpha_2})\}, O^1_{\alpha_1} \cup O^1_{\alpha_2}, id^1, d^1),$$
$$\ldots,$$
$$(P^m_{\alpha_1} \cup P^m_{\alpha_2} \cup \overline{\text{path}}^m(\chi), A^m_{\alpha_1} \cup A^m_{\alpha_2} \cup \{(\sigma, \text{cond}^m(\chi), O^m_{\alpha_1}), (\sigma, \text{cond}^m(\neg\chi), O^m_{\alpha_2}),$$
$$(\bowtie, \overline{\text{cond}}^m(\chi), O^m_{\alpha_1}), (\bowtie, \overline{\text{cond}}^m(\neg\chi), O^m_{\alpha_2})\}, O^m_{\alpha_1} \cup O^m_{\alpha_2}, id^m, d^m)]$$

Output of subtrees reachable from node $\$y$ through path π In addition to the corresponding rule of Section 5.2.2, this inference rule handles multiple input streams and join annotations. In the rule, $Path_4$ again represents the pattern $\$y/\pi$.

$$\frac{}{Env \vdash Path_4} \quad (5.18)$$
$$\Rightarrow [(\overline{\text{path}}^1(Path_4),$$
$$\{(\sigma, \text{cond}^1(Path_4), \{\text{path}^1(Path_4)\}), (\bowtie, \overline{\text{cond}}^1(Path_4), \{\text{path}^1(Path_4)\})\},$$
$$\{\text{path}^1(Path_4)\}, id^1, d^1),$$
$$\ldots,$$
$$(\overline{\text{path}}^m(Path_4),$$
$$\{(\sigma, \text{cond}^m(Path_4), \{\text{path}^m(Path_4)\}), (\bowtie, \overline{\text{cond}}^m(Path_4), \{\text{path}^m(Path_4)\})\},$$
$$\{\text{path}^m(Path_4)\}, id^m, d^m)]$$

Output of a subtree rooted at node $\$z$ This rule is similar to the corresponding rule of Section 5.2.2 except that it handles multiple input streams and propagates the identifier id^i and the DTD d^i of each input stream i determined in the preprocessing phase described further above.

$$\frac{}{Env \vdash \$z \Rightarrow [(\emptyset, \emptyset, \{\text{path}^1(\$z)\}, id^1, d^1), \ldots, (\emptyset, \emptyset, \{\text{path}^m(\$z)\}, id^m, d^m)]} \quad (5.19)$$

Sequence For each individual input stream, the sequence rule behaves just like the original rule of Section 5.2.2.

$$Env \vdash \alpha_1 \Rightarrow [(P^1_1, A^1_1, O^1_1, id^1, d^1), \ldots, (P^m_1, A^m_1, O^m_1, id^m, d^m)]$$
$$\ldots$$
$$\frac{Env \vdash \alpha_n \Rightarrow [(P^1_n, A^1_n, O^1_n, id^1, d^1), \ldots, (P^m_n, A^m_n, O^m_n, id^m, d^m)]}{Env \vdash (\alpha_1, \ldots, \alpha_n)} \quad (5.20)$$
$$\Rightarrow [(\bigcup_{i=1}^n P^1_i, \bigcup_{i=1}^n A^1_i, \bigcup_{i=1}^n O^1_i, id^1, d^1), \ldots, (\bigcup_{i=1}^n P^m_i, \bigcup_{i=1}^n A^m_i, \bigcup_{i=1}^n O^m_i, id^m, d^m)]$$

Similar to the rule for direct element constructors, we have again rephrased the WXQuery expression for sequences in the inference rule compared to the corresponding expression in the WXQuery definition to better support the inference rule notation.

Example 5.12 As an example for the translation of a join query into a corresponding APF, consider query q_5 of Figure 5.10(a). For both input streams of q_5, the translation builds a corresponding APT just as described in Section 5.2.2. Additionally, the inference rules introduce a new join annotation each time they encounter a selection annotation that references elements from more than one APT. The join annotation

$$(\bowtie, \{\texttt{stream("photons1")/photons/photon/en}$$

$$\texttt{>= stream("photons2")/photons/photon/en + 0.5}\},$$

$$\{\texttt{stream("photons1")/photons/photon/en, stream("photons1")/photons/photon/phc,}$$

$$\texttt{stream("photons2")/photons/photon/en, stream("photons2")/photons/photon/phc}\})$$

of q_5 is associated with the returned elements of all affected APTs. Figure 5.12(a) shows the resulting APF f_{q_5} of q_5. □

Completeness and Correctness of the Translation   Similar to the translation of a WXQuery with a single input stream into a corresponding APT, the translation of a WXQuery with multiple input streams into a corresponding APF needs to be complete and correct.

Statement 5.7 (Completeness) *Any WXQuery q obeying Definition 4.5 can be translated into a corresponding APF f_q.* □

DISCUSSION: The discussion is analogous to the discussion of Statement 5.1 on page 94. ∎

Statement 5.8 (Correctness) *The translation of any WXQuery q into a corresponding APF f_q always yields an APF which represents the abstraction $\hat{q}$ of q.* □

DISCUSSION: The discussion is analogous to the discussion of Statement 5.2 on page 94. ∎

Translating APFs into WXQueries

Similar to APTs, we can translate an arbitrary APF back into a corresponding WXQuery. In contrast to APTs, APFs are always structure-mutating since they represent join queries and joins are structure-mutating operators.

Figure 5.13 shows the query template for translating an arbitrary APF representing a join query with time-based data windows into a corresponding WXQuery. The template variables *VARi*, *STREAMi*, *PATHi*, *REFPATHi*, *SIZEi*, and *STEPi* have the same meaning as in Section 5.2.3. The index *i* indicates the input stream the respective template variable belongs to. The *JOINROOT* variable represents the root element name of the join result. For intermediate results created during in-network processing, we generate a generic name by concatenating the root element names of the joined input streams with underscores in between. This yields `photons_photons` in our example queries since `photons` is the root element name of both input streams. The variable *JOINPREDS* represents the join predicates. We use *PREDij* to denote the *j*-th selection predicate concerning stream *i*. The *JOINITEM* variable refers to the element name of one join result item. We generically create this name by concatenating the names of the data stream items of the joined streams. This yields `photon_photon` in our example queries since the data stream items are named `photon` in both streams. Finally, *PATHij* is the path referencing the *j*-th returned element of stream *i*, relative to *VARi*. The values of the template variables other than *JOINROOT* and *JOINITEM* are determined from an APF in a similar way as described for the translation of APTs in Section 5.2.3.

```
<JOINROOT>
   { for $VAR1 in stream("STREAM1")/PATH1|REFPATH1 diff SIZE1 step STEP1|
      ...
     for $VARm in stream("STREAMm")/PATHm|REFPATHm diff SIZEm step STEPm|
     where JOINPREDS
     return
       if (PRED11 or ... or PRED1n or ... or PREDm1 or PREDmk) then
         <JOINITEM>
           { if (PRED11 or ... or PRED1n) then
               <STREAM1>...
                 { if (PRED11) then $VAR1/PATH11 else () }
                   ...
                 { if (PRED1n) then $VAR1/PATH1n else () }
                 ...</STREAM1>
             else () }
             ...
           { if (PREDm1 or ... or PREDmk) then
               <STREAMm>...
                 { if (PREDm1) then $VARm/PATHm1 else () }
                   ...
                 { if (PREDmk) then $VARm/PATHmk else () }
                 ...</STREAMm>
             else () }
         </JOINITEM>
       else () }
</JOINROOT>
```

Figure 5.13: Join query template

The where clause, the if expressions, and the *PATHi* and *PATHij* variables are optional depending on the characteristics of the corresponding APF. If any *PATHi* or *PATHij* is empty in an actual instance of the template variable, the respective preceding slash also disappears from the template. If there is no selection annotation for a certain returned element, the query simply returns the element without a surrounding if expression. In such a case, we also need to remove any if expressions guarding the output of the surrounding *JOINITEM* and *STREAMi* tags from the template. Each returned element is enclosed in the correct sequence of surrounding elements as in the original input stream schema, starting with the first element below the stream item, which is the photon element in our example stream. This is necessary to uniquely identify the elements during postprocessing and is indicated by dots in the query template of Figure 5.13.

Example 5.13 Figure 5.14 shows the abstractions of queries q_5 to q_8 of Figure 5.10.   □

DTD Generation For structure-mutating join queries, we construct a completely new DTD which contains the join root element (photons_photons in our example queries) as the root and the join result item (photon_photon in the example queries) as the only child of the root, with multiple occurrence. The join result item has as its children a sequence of generic stream elements representing the joined input streams. Each generic stream element contains the elements of the respective stream that are returned by the query. The returned elements are embedded in the correct sequence of surrounding elements as in the original stream schema, starting with the first element below the data stream item.

```
<photons_photons>
  { for $x in stream("photons1")/photons/photon
    |det_time diff 10 step 5|
    for $y in stream("photons2")/photons/photon
    |det_time diff 20 step 10|
    where $x/en >= $y/en + 0.5
    return
      <photon_photon>
        <photons1>
          { $x/phc } { $x/en }
        </photons1>
        <photons2>
          { $y/phc } { $y/en }
        </photons2>
      </photon_photon> }
</photons_photons>
```

(a) Abstract Query 5 ($\hat{q}_5$)

```
<photons_photons>
  { for $x in stream("photons1")/photons/photon
    |det_time diff 10 step 5|
    for $y in stream("photons2")/photons/photon
    |det_time diff 20 step 10|
    where $x/en >= $y/en
    return
      <photon_photon>
        <photons1>
          { $x/en } { $x/det_time }
        </photons1>
        <photons2>
          { $y/en } { $y/det_time }
        </photons2>
      </photon_photon> }
</photons_photons>
```

(b) Abstract Query 6 ($\hat{q}_6$)

```
<photons_photons>
  { for $x in stream("photons1")/photons/photon
    |det_time diff 30 step 5|
    for $y in stream("photons2")/photons/photon
    |det_time diff 15 step 10|
    where $x/en >= $y/en
    return
      <photon_photon>
        <photons1>
          { $x/en } { $x/det_time }
        </photons1>
        <photons2>
          { $y/en } { $y/det_time }
        </photons2>
      </photon_photon> }
</photons_photons>
```

(c) Abstract Query 7 ($\hat{q}_7$)

```
<photons_photons>
  { for $x in stream("photons1")/photons/photon
    |det_time diff 15 step 10|
    for $y in stream("photons2")/photons/photon
    |det_time diff 30 step 15|
    where $x/phc >= $y/phc
    return
      <photon_photon>
        <photons1>
          { $x/en } { $x/det_time }
        </photons1>
        <photons2>
          { $y/en } { $y/det_time }
        </photons2>
      </photon_photon> }
</photons_photons>
```

(d) Abstract Query 8 ($\hat{q}_8$)

Figure 5.14: Abstractions of example join queries

Example 5.14 Figure 5.15 shows the DTDs of the result data streams of the abstract example join queries in Figure 5.14. □

Completeness and Correctness of the Translation As with APTs, the translation of APFs into corresponding WXQueries needs to be complete and correct.

Statement 5.9 (Completeness) *Any APF f_q obtained by translating a WXQuery q using the inference rules introduced earlier in Section 5.4.2 can be translated back into a corresponding WXQuery $\hat{q}$.* □

DISCUSSION: The discussion is analogous to the discussion of Statement 5.3 on page 100. ■

```
<!ELEMENT photons_photons (photon_photon*)>
<!ELEMENT photon_photon   (photons1, photons2)>
<!ELEMENT photons1        (phc, en)>
<!ELEMENT photons2        (phc, en)>
<!ELEMENT phc             (#PCDATA)>
<!ELEMENT en              (#PCDATA)>
```

(a) Abstract Query 5 ($\hat{q}_5$)

```
<!ELEMENT photons_photons (photon_photon*)>
<!ELEMENT photon_photon   (photons1, photons2)>
<!ELEMENT photons1        (en, det_time)>
<!ELEMENT photons2        (en, det_time)>
<!ELEMENT en              (#PCDATA)>
<!ELEMENT det_time        (#PCDATA)>
```

(b) Abstract Queries 6, 7, and 8 ($\hat{q}_6, \hat{q}_7, \hat{q}_8$)

Figure 5.15: Result DTDs of abstract join queries

Statement 5.10 (Correctness) *The translation of any APF f_q into a corresponding WXQuery always yields a WXQuery which represents the abstraction $\hat{q}$ of the original query q on which f_q is based.* □

DISCUSSION: The discussion is analogous to the discussion of Statement 5.4 on page 101. ∎

5.4.3 Matching and Merging APFs

This section describes how to match and merge APFs for data stream sharing and data stream widening. It further discusses possibilities for join result sharing.

Basics

As with APTs, we perform the matching and merging of APFs in one operation which takes two APFs as input, the stream APF and the query APF. The stream APF represents the result data stream of a join query already installed in the system while the query APF represents a newly registered join query. In the matching step, the matching and merging operation examines whether the data stream represented by the stream APF can be shared for satisfying the query represented by the query APF. If this is not the case, the merging step appropriately merges both APFs, yielding either a new APF or—if the join needs to be removed during the merge—a set of APTs representing the necessary inputs for both original APFs. The resulting APF or APTs can be translated into one or more WXQueries according to Sections 5.4.2 and 5.2.3, respectively. Appropriately installing these queries in the system generates one or more data streams that are shareable by both, the new query and the query represented by the original stream APF. The matching and merging of APFs needs to match and merge the path trees as well as the annotations of both input APFs.

Note that it is also possible to match and merge the APF of a multiple input join query with the APT of a single input non-join query. If the single input query should share the result of the join query, widening will involve removing the join from the merging result. This leads to a set of independent APTs that represent single input queries to be installed in the system. The result data streams of these queries can then be combined later to form the original join result while a copy of one of the streams can further be used to satisfy the new single input query. If the APF of a newly arriving join query is matched with the APT of an already installed single input query, it might be possible to use the result stream of the single input query as one of the inputs to the join query. To determine this, the APT of the corresponding input stream contained in the APF of the join query needs to be matched and merged with the APT of the query whose result shall be shared. This process can be repeated for each input stream of the join query to find suitable streams for all inputs. An open question to be dealt with in future work is where to place the join operator in the network to combine the inputs and to compute the actual join result. Network-aware operator placement has already been the subject of some research work, e. g., by Ahmad and Çetintemel (2004), Pietzuch et al. (2006), and Srivastava et al. (2005). A simple solution is to route all input streams to the final super-peer which is connected to the peer that registered the new query and to compute the join there. This approach is beneficial if the join result stream is larger than the sum of the sizes of all input streams. Another possibility is to compute the join at any super-peer at which one of the shareable inputs has been found and to route the remaining inputs there. The join result can subsequently be routed to the querying peer. This approach may be beneficial if the join result size is smaller compared to the sum of the sizes of the join inputs. More sophisticated solutions would make dynamic decisions, e. g., based on statistics and join result size estimations.

Sharing Join Results

In the following, we concentrate on the matching and merging of the APFs of two binary join queries. Using the join and the query semantics introduced in Section 5.4.1, we distinguish three cases that allow for different levels of sharing. The cases differ in the relation between the window sizes Δ and Δ' as well as the step sizes μ and μ' of each of the data windows in the properties of an already installed query whose result data stream is considered for sharing and a newly arriving query, respectively.

Full join result sharing   Full join result sharing is the simplest and most effective case. It occurs if $\Delta = \Delta'$ and $\mu = \mu'$ for each pair of corresponding data windows in the properties of the installed query and the properties of the new query. In this case, the join only needs to be computed once and the join result can be shared for both queries. However, different selection predicates and projections might be applied to the shared join result to obtain the exact result for each query. We demonstrate this case using q_5 of Figure 5.10(a) as the query already installed and q_6 as the newly arriving query. Figure 5.16(a) illustrates the evaluation of both queries. The figure uses subscripts to distinguish equally named elements from different input streams. The upper part of the figure depicts the resulting APF *after* matching and merging the APFs of the two queries. The window definitions stay the same since both queries use the same windows. The join annotation reflects the relaxed join condition which is equal to the join condition of q_6 in this case. This is due to the fact that the join condition of q_5 implies the join condition of q_6. The lower part of the figure shows the application of further selection and projection operators to generate the final results for queries q_5 and q_6. Since both queries use the same window definitions for their corresponding input streams, the basic join is computed only once as result of the widening. The join result is then further processed using according selection and projection operators in the postprocessing phase to obtain the final results for both queries.

Selective join result sharing   Selective join result sharing also allows to compute the join result once and to share it for both queries. This case occurs if $\Delta \neq \Delta'$ for at least one pair and $\mu = \mu'$ for each pair of corresponding data windows in the properties of the installed query and the properties of the new query. Apart from the selection and projection operators as in full join result sharing, an additional selection of join results is necessary in the selection phase. The reason is that during widening, the window size of each data window that has non-equal size in the properties of the installed query and the properties of the new query is set to the maximum of the corresponding window sizes in both properties. Figure 5.16(b) illustrates this aspect using queries q_5 and q_7 as an example. Query q_5 defines a window size of 10 for the input stream photons1 and a window size of 20 for the input stream photons2. Accordingly, query q_7 defines a window size of 30 for the input stream photons1 and a window size of 15 for the input stream photons2. Consequently, the shareable window size for stream photons1 is $\max(10, 30) = 30$ and the shareable window size for stream photons2 is $\max(20, 15) = 20$. In the selection phase, the operator SELECTJOINRESULT(10,20) selects only those join result items where the joined item from the left input is within the first 10 units of the widenend data window of the left input stream, i. e., it selects only the first third of the entire widened window which has a total size of 30 units. Furthermore, the joined item from the right input of each selected join result item

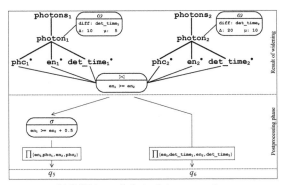

(a) Full join result sharing between q_5 and q_6

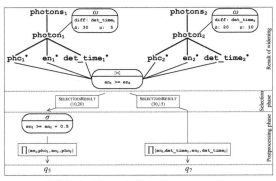

(b) Selective join result sharing between q_5 and q_7

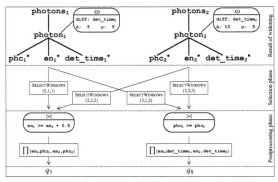

(c) Selective window sharing between q_5 and q_8

Figure 5.16: Join result sharing

is situated within the first 20 units of the widened data window of the right input stream, i. e., the operator selects the entire widened window which has a total size of 20 units to obtain the correct results for q_5. Units may either be time units or the number of elements, depending on whether time-based or count-based windows are used. The situation is similar for the operator SELECTJOINRESULT(30,15) which selects the entire widenend window of the left input stream and only the first three quarters of the widened window of the right input stream to obtain the correct results for q_7. Again, the final results for both queries are obtained by applying adequate selection and projection operators in the postprocessing phase.

The SELECTJOINRESULT operator requires additional information for each join result item during the selection phase. For time-based data windows, the timestamps of the individual input items forming a join result item need to be preserved if the join query removes the timestamp elements from the join result. For count-based data windows, we associate each individual input item with a monotonically increasing integer value when the item enters the corresponding data window. Furthermore, each input item is associated with the lower bound of the corresponding data window instance the input item belonged to when the respective join result item was generated. Join computations are triggered by window updates in our join semantics. Therefore, the corresponding window instance of the join input stream that triggered the join computation corresponds to the window instance of the updated window. Window bounds are time values in case of time-based data windows and counter values in case of count-based data windows. Knowing the window lower bounds and the timestamp or counter values of the joined data items enables us to decide which join result items qualify for the result of a certain join query. Note that the counter value for count-based windows does not need to grow indefinitely. It can be reset during any window update process by subtracting the minimum of the counter values of all the data items contained in the window from the current window bounds and from the counter values of all the items remaining in the window after the update. Newly added items subsequently need to be consistently associated with further incremental counter values.

Selective window sharing The third and final case is called selective window sharing and occurs if $\mu \neq \mu'$ for at least one pair of corresponding data windows in the properties of the installed query and the properties of the new query. In this case, the join result cannot be shared due to the incompatible window definitions. Instead, we can compute relaxed window definitions according to Algorithm 5.1 that are shareable by both queries, just as we do for aggregate queries. Figure 5.16(c) shows an example using queries q_5 and q_8. Widening computes the new window definitions using Algorithm 5.1 for both input streams and removes the join annotation. In the selection phase, a window selection operator selects the appropriate windows in the appropriate order to generate windows of the window size and the step size required by the respective query. Window selection works just as aggregate value selection as described in Algorithm 4.4 on page 67 except that complete window contents instead of window-based aggregate values are selected. For example, in Figure 5.16(c), SELECTWINDOWS(2,1,1) selects two consecutive windows of window size 5 and step size 5 and combines them to generate a window of window size 10 and step size 5 corresponding to the window over the left input of q_5. SELECTWINDOWS(2,2,2) analogously combines two windows of window size 10 and step size 5 to generate the window over the right input of q_5 with window size 20 and step size 10. But it only takes into account every second window in the input when generating a particular window. This provides for the combination of contiguous non-overlapping windows. Also, only after every second window arriving on the input stream, the window of q_5 is updated. This leads to the required step size of 10 whereas the shared windows have a step size of 5. Similarly, for q_8, SELECTWINDOWS(3,1,2) selects three consecutive windows of window size 5 and step size 5 to form one window of window size 15 over the left input of q_8. Only after every second window arriving on the input stream, the window of q_8 is updated. This leads to the required step size of 10, which is two times the step size of the shared window. Finally, SELECTWIN-DOWS(3,2,3) combines three windows of window size 10 to form one window of window size 30 over the right input of q_8. Only every second input window is used to get a sequence of contiguous non-overlapping windows for a particular window instance. To obtain the correct window update interval of 15 for the window over the right input of q_8, three windows of step size 5 must have arrived on the shared input before updating the window of q_8. Depending on the actual window and step sizes, certain data windows might have to be temporarily buffered for later reference as detailed in Algorithm 4.4. The postprocessing phase then generates the final join result for both queries by applying appropriate join and projection operators.

The joins in the postprocessing phase obey the join semantics introduced in Section 5.4.1. The join operators can derive the updated parts of the data windows delivered by the SE-LECTWINDOWS operators by means of the window definition, i.e., by examining the window bounds and the step size. If the SELECTWINDOWS operators and the join operators are kept separate as indicated in Figure 5.16(c), overlapping parts of subsequent data windows are delivered to the join operators multiple times. This can be avoided by integrating the SELECTWIN-DOWS operators of the selection phase with the join operators of the postprocessing phase and by applying appropriate optimizations.

Finally, it is worth noting that it might be more efficient in practice to execute each window join operator individually on the ungrouped inputs instead of computing and sharing common windows among queries via selective window sharing. Deciding which solution is the better choice depends on cost function and network characteristics.

Completeness and Correctness of Matching and Merging APFs

Similar to APTs, the matching and merging of two APFs needs to be complete and correct.

Statement 5.11 (Completeness) *The algorithm for matching and merging two APFs is able to match and merge any two arbitrary APFs complying to Definition 5.5.* □

DISCUSSION: The statement follows directly from the discussion of the matching and merging process for APFs. ∎

Statement 5.12 (Correctness) *Matching and merging two APFs f_1 and f_2 always results either in an APF f or a set of APTs T representing the necessary inputs of the two original APFs. A resulting APF can be translated into a query $\hat{q}$ that represents the union of the corresponding queries $\hat{q}_1$ and $\hat{q}_2$ of the original APFs, i.e., the results of both queries $\hat{q}_1$ and $\hat{q}_2$ are contained in the result of query $\hat{q}$. A resulting set of APTs can be translated into a set of queries Q whose results may again be joined to form the results of f_1 and f_2.* □

DISCUSSION: The tree structures of the APTs contained in the merged APF f or the resulting set of APTs T result from merging the tree structures of the corresponding APTs in the input APFs f_1 and f_2. Therefore, f or T contains all the paths, and only those paths, that are referenced by either f_1 or f_2, or both. The same rationale applies to the set of output elements of the merged APF f or the sets of output elements of the resulting APTs in T. Incompatible annotations are either removed or relaxed whenever they prevent the implication of the stream result by the query result. Therefore, the merged APF f or the resulting set of APTs T represents all the data required for obtaining the correct results for the queries represented by f_1 and f_2. ∎

5.5 Adapting the StreamGlobe Optimization Framework

Integrating the previously introduced approaches for supporting data stream widening, data stream narrowing, and join queries into StreamGlobe requires the following adaptations to the StreamGlobe optimization framework.

5.5.1 Cost Model

The widening of data streams involves the replacement and therefore the deletion of parts of distributed query evaluation plans in the StreamGlobe system. Thus, the cost model must be able to handle the removal of operators. This can easily be achieved by taking into account negative costs for removed operators. Thus, the cost function accumulates positive costs for added operators and negative costs for removed operators. This yields an estimation of the additional costs caused by replacing an existing plan with a new plan involving stream widening.

5.5.2 Deleting Queries

Data stream widening and data stream narrowing require the deletion of previously installed query operators. This functionality is also desirable to support the explicit deletion of previously installed continuous queries in StreamGlobe. Operator deletion requires an augmentation of the query plan specification by introducing a means for specifying the removal of operators.

5.5.3 Data Stream Widening and Data Stream Narrowing

Besides the extensions described above, support for data stream widening and data stream narrowing in StreamGlobe also requires changes to the discovery algorithm for finding shareable streams in the network. Instead of pruning a stream during the search as soon as the algorithm recognizes that the stream does not contain all the necessary data for satisfying a new query, a query plan using this stream and employing appropriate data stream widening must be generated. The widening must be propagated backwards towards the source of the original data stream in the network until all necessary data for the widened stream is available. In the worst case, the widening can propagate all the way back to the stream source which always contains all the data. During widening, the properties of any other streams depending on the stream to be widened must be preserved. This may require reversing the effects of the widening for certain dependencies by installing appropriate compensating operators that correspond to the properties of the data stream required by the dependency.

For data stream narrowing, no stream discovery is necessary. But after the deletion of an operator, the narrowing needs to propagate backwards towards the data stream source in a similar fashion as during data stream widening. After the removal of an operator from a certain peer, the necessary data at the respective peer can be determined by merging the properties of the remaining parts of each of the streams affected by the removal. This yields the unified properties of the remaining parts of the according original data streams required at that peer. Each of these properties needs to be propagated backwards to the previous peer en route to the corresponding data stream source. There, the unified properties replace the respective previous properties and are merged with the properties of all other instances of the same stream required at that peer. This process continues until it cannot remove any more data from the stream or it reaches the super-peer where the original stream is registered.

As stated earlier, data stream narrowing can be an expensive task due to the necessity of merging a possibly large number of properties of remaining data streams at numerous peers in the network. Therefore, narrowing should rather be used as a means for freeing system resources on demand by identifying and removing unnecessary parts of streams flowing through the network instead of employing it as a required step during query deletion. In addition, preserving parts of data streams that become unnecessary after the deletion of a query increases the possibilities for finding shareable input streams when registering future queries. Unnecessary parts of streams can still be removed later when system resources become scarce.

5.5.4 Handling Join Queries

Data stream sharing for join queries involves further changes to the stream discovery algorithm. The algorithm must search for shareable versions of each input stream of a join query. After it has found shareable streams for each input, the system needs to decide where to place the join operator to combine the streams. As mentioned previously, join operator placement in distributed environments has already been examined in the literature, e. g., by Pietzuch et al. (2006). Dealing with this issue in the context of StreamGlobe is part of future work. Alternatively, the discovery algorithm might also find a shareable join result in which case the system does not need to recompute the join.

5.6 Evaluation

To assess the benefits of data stream widening, we have conducted some performance experiments using our StreamGlobe prototype implementation. We have implemented data stream sharing and data stream widening for non-join queries in StreamGlobe, together with the naive data shipping strategy known from Section 4.5. The results for data shipping merely serve as a baseline. For each query, data shipping transmits a copy of each original input stream referenced by the query from the original stream source to the peer that registered the query. The transmission uses a shortest path in the network and does not share or fork the stream in any way. We implemented data stream widening using Java 6 and again ran our tests on a blade server. Depending on the scenario, we used 8 or 16 blades, one for each peer in the backbone network. Each blade had a 2.8 GHz Intel Xeon processor and at least 1 GB of main memory.

We conducted performance tests using various scenarios differing in the number of peers in the backbone network (8 or 16) and in the number of queries registered (from 4 to 100). We used three- and four-dimensional hypercubes as network topologies. The data streams were of the form described in Section 2.2. Since the results were similar for all scenarios, we selected one scenario for presentation. The chosen scenario uses a three-dimensional hypercube network topology consisting of 8 super-peers as shown in Figure 2.1 on page 9. We used a single photons data stream and registered 32 randomly generated queries. The query generator generates queries that return a randomly chosen subset of the elements contained in their single input stream. It further generates random selection predicates. Selections were performed either on the detector pixel coordinates (dx, dy) or on the energy (en) of a photon, or on both. Selections consist of conjunctive and disjunctive combinations of atomic predicates. An atomic predicate in turn consists of an element, a comparison operator, and a constant, e. g., en >= 1.3. The constants are chosen randomly from a predefined set of reasonable values from our photons data set using a normal distribution. The resulting overlap between queries reflects the assumption of regional query hotspots which are common in astrophysics when several researchers investigate

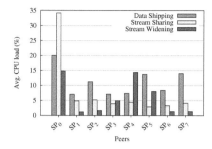 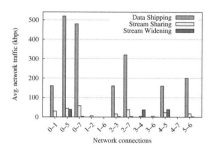

Figure 5.17: Average CPU load and network traffic

interesting events in a certain, relatively small area of the sky. Further, the overlap increases the probability that there will be some queries that can readily share the result streams of previously registered queries using plain data stream sharing without data stream widening.

Figure 5.17 shows the results in terms of average CPU load in percent on the peers in the example network and in terms of average network traffic in kilobits per second on the network connections between peers. Additionally, Table 5.1 presents the accumulated and average CPU load and network traffic in the overall backbone network. The accumulated overall values are computed by adding up the average CPU load and network traffic values shown in Figure 5.17 for all peers and network connections. The average overall values are computed by dividing the accumulated values by the number of peers or network connections, respectively. The percentage in the table illustrates the relation between the three strategies compared to the values of data shipping which serve as a baseline at 100%.

As expected, data shipping causes the highest amount of CPU load and network traffic throughout the network since it requires to forward the entire data stream multiple times, once for each query. In contrast, stream sharing potentially shares one result data stream for satisfying multiple subscriptions. Thus, it reduces computational load and network traffic due to result sharing. Also, by installing subscriptions in the network close to the data sources, early filtering and early aggregation at the stream source further reduce resource usage within the backbone network. Only at SP_0, which is the peer where the original photons data stream is registered, the CPU load increases using stream sharing. The reason is that stream sharing installs a query directly at the stream source and routes the resulting stream to the querying peer on a shortest path in the network if the query is unable to share any preprocessed streams. In our scenario, 14 of the 32 queries registered were able to share preprocessed streams without widening. Using data stream widening, this value increased to 31, i. e., every query except for the very first one was able to reuse a possibly widened result data stream of a previously registered query. This leads to a further reduction of CPU load and network traffic compared to data stream sharing without data stream widening. In the presented scenario, the average CPU load in the overall network, i. e., averaged over all 8 peers, dropped from 7.85% to 5.95%. This corresponds to a reduction of about 25%. The average network traffic in the overall network, i. e., averaged over all 12 network connections, dropped from 20.3 kbps to 10.6 kbps, corresponding to a reduction of about 48%.

Summarizing, the results show that data stream widening serves the important purpose of making optimization quality more independent of the actual query characteristics and the query

	CPU Load (%)		
	Accumulated	Average	Percentage
Data Shipping	89.0	11.13	100.0%
Stream Sharing	62.8	7.85	70.6%
Stream Widening	47.6	5.95	53.5%
	Network Traffic (kbps)		
	Accumulated	Average	Percentage
Data Shipping	1999.7	166.6	100.0%
Stream Sharing	243.6	20.3	12.2%
Stream Widening	127.8	10.6	6.4%

Table 5.1: Accumulated and average overall CPU load and network traffic

registration sequence. Thus, the approach achieves good optimization results and efficient resource usage for arbitrary query loads.

Due to the increased optimization overhead, registering a query usually takes longer when using stream widening compared to plain stream sharing without widening. Query registration times tend to become longer for both strategies with an increasing number of previously registered queries in the system. This is due to the fact that the optimizer has more alternatives to take into account. In our experiments, data stream widening caused an increase in query registration times of up to double the amount of time used by data stream sharing without data stream widening. Nevertheless, registering a query never took longer than 45 seconds in the largest scenario with 100 queries registered. Since we deal with continuous queries which are supposed to run for long periods of time, optimization delays of several seconds up to some minutes for a single query are acceptable. Further, we may stop the optimization process after a certain amount of time and use the best solution found so far if query registration times should not exceed a certain threshold.

5.7 Related Work

In addition to the work related to data stream sharing presented in Section 4.6, this section discusses existing approaches for computing and sharing aggregate and join results over streams.

Starting with aggregation, Zhang et al. (2003a) deal with temporal and spatio-temporal aggregates occurring in applications that maintain time-evolving data. Their approach uses different time granularities for data of different age and employs specialized indexing schemes to dynamically and progressively maintain temporal and spatio-temporal aggregates over data streams. Li et al. (2005b) focus on general semantics and evaluation techniques for window aggregates over data streams. The importance of sharing work and resources to achieve efficient and scalable query processing has been observed multiple times in the literature, especially in the context of data streams. Precise sharing of common work while avoiding unnecessary work is the focus of TULIP [Krishnamurthy et al. (2004)], which keeps track of predicate evaluation results using the concept of tuple lineage known, e. g., from Eddies [Avnur and Hellerstein (2000)]. However, TULIP focuses on selection predicates and does not deal with aggregation. Zhang et al. (2005) enable the shared computation of multiple related aggregates over data streams that differ only in the choice of grouping attributes. Resource sharing for continuous sliding window aggregates is an aspect that has sparked special interest. Arasu and Widom

(2004c), for example, propose several algorithms for solving various instances of this problem. A possible approach for enabling sharing for overlapping sliding windows is to divide the windows into disjoint *panes* [Li et al. (2005a)]. These can be used to compute window aggregates containing the respective panes. Therefore, work on the overlapping parts of the windows is done only once. However, the approach described by Li et al. (2005a) only deals with sharing within a single query. An improvement over panes allows sharing among various queries involving different window definitions *and* selection predicates at the same time using so-called *shards* [Krishnamurthy et al. (2006)]. Golab et al. (2006a,b) show how to enable multi-query optimization for sliding window aggregates by means of schedule synchronization. Further, Babcock et al. (2004) deal with load shedding for aggregate queries over data streams. Their approach handles system overload during aggregate computation by dropping unprocessed input tuples. The challenge is to minimize the degree of inaccuracy introduced in query results due to load shedding. All of the above approaches are centralized and tuple-based, whereas our approach in StreamGlobe is distributed and based on XML data. Huebsch et al. (2007) examine shared aggregate computation for aggregates with different selection predicates in distributed tuple-based environments but do not deal with continuous queries over data streams. Finally, aggregation also is a major topic in sensor networks. Work in this direction comprises TAG [Madden et al. (2002a)], a service for aggregation in distributed, wireless sensor networks. In TAG, users can state simple declarative queries which are then distributed and executed in the sensor network using in-network query processing. Manjhi et al. (2005) aim at reducing power consumption and at improving the result quality of aggregation in sensor networks by combining a tree-based approach for reduced power consumption with a multi-path-based approach for increased robustness. In contrast to StreamGlobe, which is based on a stationary backbone network, the solutions for sensor networks are tuple-based and focus on energy efficient query evaluation in networks of battery-powered sensors.

Joins over data streams are another interesting topic that is widely covered in the literature. Several join algorithms for streamed join processing have been proposed. The Symmetric Hash Join by Wilschut and Apers (1991) is an early approach that aims at achieving a high degree of parallelism in parallel database systems by lowering the synchronization requirements of join operators. Based on the Symmetric Hash Join, the XJoin [Urhan and Franklin (2000)] is a nonblocking pipelined join operator able to produce initial results quickly. The XJoin pays special attention to reactively scheduling background processing in order to hide intermittent delays in data arrival, making it an appropriate choice for join query processing in slow and bursty wide-area networks. Rate-based query optimization [Viglas and Naughton (2002)] turns away from traditional cardinality-based query optimization used in database management systems and aims at optimizing query plans for maximum output rate instead. In this context, RPJ [Tao et al. (2005)] is another join algorithm for progressively joining streams. Its goal is to produce first results early on and to generate result tuples at a fast rate. The MJoin [Viglas et al. (2003)] addresses the problem of varying stream arrival rates in complex query evaluation plans in an innovative way. Instead of dynamically reorganizing the query plan in response to variations in stream input rates, it augments existing symmetric binary join operators to support multiple inputs, therefore also eliminating intermediate results in the execution tree. Ripple joins [Haas and Hellerstein (1999)] are a class of join algorithms designed to support multi-table online aggregation in relational database management systems. In contrast to traditional offline join algorithms which always produce exact answers, ripple joins aim at yielding reasonably precise online estimates in less time. As in our work, most approaches use windows to limit the memory requirements of streaming joins. Many of these solutions, e. g., PSoup [Chandrasekaran and

Franklin (2002)] and CACQ [Madden et al. (2002b)], use join semantics similar to the traditional window join semantics introduced in Section 5.4.1. Some approaches, including CACQ, also use a basic approach for sharing join results among multiple queries that have equal inputs and join predicates but differ in their window definitions. This involves computing the join of the contents of the largest windows and then filtering the result multiple times with different filter conditions to obtain the exact results for all queries. However, this might impose considerable delays on queries using relatively small windows since these queries have to wait for their results until the join of the larger windows completes. Alternative algorithms for shared window join scheduling introduced by Hammad et al. (2003b) alleviate this problem. Hong et al. (2007) describe several techniques for enabling efficient multi-query optimization for join queries over streaming as well as persistent XML inputs in a publish&subscribe setting. The literature furthermore provides efficient algorithms for processing sliding window multi-joins in continuous queries over data streams [Golab and Özsu (2003c)] and a binary sliding window join variant of the symmetric hash join [Kang et al. (2003)]. A new paradigm of multi-query optimization for window queries over data streams suggests the slicing of window states and introduces a new pipelining method to reduce the number of total joins [Wang et al. (2006)]. Babu et al. (2005) examine adaptive caching for continuous queries to improve performance and adaptivity for queries involving continuous multi-way joins. Hammad et al. (2003a) consider sliding window joins over streaming data in the context of sensor networks, e. g., for tracking moving objects in the sensor space. Finally, Ganguly et al. (2004) introduce skimmed sketches for estimating the result size of stream-based binary joins.

5.8   Summary

In this chapter, we have introduced an abstract property tree (APT) for representing, matching, and merging queries and data in a distributed DSMS. The presented approach enables data stream sharing as well as data stream widening and data stream narrowing. We have established formal rules for the translation of a query formulated in our XQuery-based subscription language WXQuery into a corresponding APT. Query templates provide for the inverse translation. Further, we have extended our approach to support queries with multiple inputs, e. g., join queries, by introducing abstract property forests (APFs). The results of performance experiments conducted using the prototype implementation of our distributed DSMS StreamGlobe demonstrate the effectiveness of data stream sharing in combination with data stream widening at a reasonable optimization cost.

An interesting problem for future work is the cost-efficient placement of join operators in the StreamGlobe network. Techniques from distributed databases may be useful in this direction. Furthermore, the problem of dynamic plan migration, i. e., of replacing a query evaluation plan with its widened or narrowed pendant in the network without losing data, is of great importance. Examining previously proposed solutions to this problem by Zhu et al. (2004), Krämer et al. (2006), and Yang et al. (2007) with regard to their applicability in our setting can give directions on how to solve this issue. Additional difficulties for dynamic plan migration in the context of data stream widening in StreamGlobe arise from the fact that other queries may depend on an existing plan. These dependencies must be preserved during plan migration. A further interesting aspect is the extension of the WXQuery subscription language, e. g., by introducing a general let expression similar to that of standard XQuery. Finally, the tree algebra introduced in this chapter can be extended, e. g., to support tree subtraction. Among other things, tree subtraction would be a useful approach for computing remainder queries in semantic caching.

CHAPTER 6

Matching and Evaluation Strategies
for Disjunctive Predicates

Traditional query optimization largely neglects the handling of disjunctive predicates. However, new and evolving applications and optimization techniques such as data stream sharing and data stream widening make the treatment of disjunctive predicates a necessity. In this chapter, we develop, compare, and discuss methods for matching and evaluating disjunctive predicates in StreamGlobe in the context of data stream sharing and data stream widening. Nevertheless, the presented techniques are generic and can be applied to other domains as well.

6.1 Introduction

Except for a few publications[1] which have dealt with the issue in the database field, disjunctive predicates have largely been neglected in the context of query optimization for traditional database management systems (DBMSs). This is also true for other domains such as active databases [Widom and Ceri (1996)] and publish&subscribe systems [Hanson et al. (1990); Hanson and Johnson (1996); Wu et al. (2004a,b)]. Disjunctive predicates are known to be complex to handle. Hence, query optimization often limits itself to considering conjunctive query predicates since well-known ways for efficiently managing such predicates exist. The main argument for justifying the neglect of disjunctive predicates has been that such predicates do not occur often in practice. While this argument might be true for traditional database systems and applications, it is not correct for new and evolving applications and optimization techniques, e. g., in semantic caching [Dar et al. (1996)] and in data stream management. Considering DSMSs for example, new network-aware optimization strategies that take into account the current network state for deciding how to distribute query processing operators among network nodes and how to route data streams through the network can introduce disjunctions in predicates. That

---

[1]See, for example, [Bry (1989); Chang and Lee (1997); Claussen et al. (2000); Hellerstein and Stonebraker (1993); Kemper et al. (1994); Muralikrishna and DeWitt (1988)].

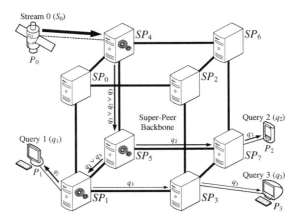

Figure 6.1: Example DSMS scenario

includes the data stream widening optimization technique introduced in Chapter 5. In the following, we focus on disjunctive predicates consisting of disjunctively combined conjunctive predicates. Each conjunctive predicate forms a multi-dimensional hyperrectangle in the data space with edges parallel to the coordinate axes. Such predicates are typical, e. g., for region-based queries in astrophysics. Our approaches can also be used as an approximation for more complex shaped predicates. However, we do not explicitly deal with this issue in this thesis. Although we use a DSMS example scenario, it is worth noting that the techniques presented in this chapter are generic and can be applied to any other domain as well.

As an example for a DSMS that needs to handle disjunctive predicates during query optimization and query processing, consider data stream sharing in combination with data stream widening in a StreamGlobe network with the network topology shown in Figure 6.1. We assume that three queries q_1, q_2, and q_3 are registered one after another in the given order. Since sharing a data stream is only possible if the stream contains all the necessary information for answering a new subscription, optimization quality depends on the characteristics and the registration sequence of queries. If queries selecting smaller parts of the data streams are registered first, their result data streams as produced by in-network query processing are not reusable for satisfying later registered queries that require larger parts of the streams. For example, assuming that the result data stream of q_2 does not contain all the necessary data for satisfying q_1, registering query q_2 before q_1 in the example network would prevent any sharing of result data streams among q_1 and q_2. To alleviate this problem, data stream widening as introduced in Chapter 5 can be employed, e. g., by relaxing some selection predicate in the network. Thus, an existing result data stream is widened to deliver not only the result data for the query it was originally computed for, but also the data for a newly registered query. Since, in its simplest form, relaxing a predicate in this way consists of disjunctively combining the predicates of the two queries, data stream widening can introduce additional disjunctions in the predicates of selection operators in the network. To illustrate this, suppose that q_3 in Figure 6.1 is registered after q_1 but needs some more data of stream S_0 than q_1. The query processing operators at SP_4 and SP_5 can then be relaxed to produce a result stream containing at least the necessary information for both queries. This causes the selection predicate for producing the combined stream to become the disjunction of the selection predicates of the two individual queries ($q_1 \vee q_3$). Note that the additional disjunction can make future predicate matchings and evaluations more expensive. Further processing at SP_1 can then produce the final result data streams of queries q_1 and q_3. The resulting stream for query q_1 can subsequently be delivered directly to P_1. The stream generated for query q_3 can be routed to P_3 via SP_3.

Deciding whether a certain data stream can be used for satisfying a newly registered query involves the matching of the selection predicates of the new query with those of the query that produced the data stream considered for reuse. The matching process consists of an implication check and an optional predicate relaxation. If the selection predicate of the new query does not imply the selection predicate of the stream-producing query, predicate relaxation computes the relaxed predicate covering all the necessary information for both queries. To speed up the predicate matching and evaluation processes, predicates can be indexed using a multi-dimensional index structure. This corresponds to a change in perspective similar to predicate indexing in active databases and publish&subscribe systems. In traditional DBMSs, data is relatively static and queries are dynamic, i. e., different queries are posed and answered using the already present data. Therefore, the data is indexed to support efficient answering of certain query types. In a DSMS, the set of registered continuous queries is relatively static and the data arriving in the form of continuous, possibly infinite data streams is highly dynamic. Thus, the queries—or, in our case, the query predicates—are indexed for efficient predicate matching and evaluation.

In detail, we provide the following contributions in this chapter:

- We develop, compare, and discuss various methods for matching and evaluating interval-based disjunctive predicates (Sections 6.3 and 6.4). We propose heuristics as well as an exact solution for the predicate matching problem (Section 6.3) and investigate the use of multi-dimensional indexing for speeding up the matching (Section 6.3.6) and evaluation (Section 6.4.2) processes for disjunctive predicates.

- We analyze the space and the time complexities of the presented algorithms (Section 6.5).

- We have implemented all presented algorithms and show the results of an extensive experimental study comparing and evaluating the various approaches (Section 6.6). The study reveals that performance gains of several orders of magnitude are achievable for predicate matching and evaluation by using multi-dimensional predicate indexes.

6.2 Preliminaries

Before describing the algorithms for predicate matching and predicate evaluation, we first introduce our notion of predicates in the context of this chapter and define the problems of predicate matching and predicate evaluation. We further introduce some notation used for describing the algorithms in the following sections.

6.2.1 Predicates

We define predicates in this chapter as follows.

Definition 6.1 (Predicates) Predicates in our context are of the following three forms:

Atomic predicate An atomic predicate is a comparison of the form $v \, \theta \, c$, where v is a variable, c is a constant, and $\theta \in \{=, \neq, <, \leq, >, \geq\}$.
Example: $a \leq 5$

Conjunctive predicate A conjunctive predicate is a conjunction of atomic predicates.
Example: $(a \leq 5) \wedge (b \geq 7)$

Disjunctive predicate A disjunctive predicate is a disjunction of conjunctive predicates.
Example: $((a \leq 5) \wedge (b \geq 7)) \vee ((a \geq 0) \wedge (b < 9))$ □

We call the distinct variables referenced in a predicate the *dimensions* of the predicate. For example, the disjunctive predicate shown above has two dimensions named a and b. Atomic predicates define intervals in the various dimensions of a predicate by setting lower and upper bounds that can be included in or excluded from the interval itself. For example, $a \geq 0$ defines an included lower bound of 0 for the interval in dimension a. In contrast, $b < 9$ defines an excluded upper bound of 9 for the interval in dimension b. Intervals can also be unbounded on one or both ends, i. e., the lower bound of an interval can be negative infinity and the upper bound can be positive infinity. Atomic predicates of the form $v = c$, where v is a variable and c is a constant, can be replaced by $(v \leq c) \wedge (v \geq c)$. Similarly, atomic predicates of the form $v \neq c$ can be replaced by $(v < c) \vee (v > c)$. The disjunctively combined conjunctive predicates making up a disjunctive predicate are called the (conjunctive) *subpredicates* of the respective disjunctive predicate.

Note that the above definition defines a predicate hierarchy, i. e., any atomic predicate can be regarded as a special case of a conjunctive predicate and any conjunctive predicate can in turn be regarded as a special case of a disjunctive predicate but not vice versa. Also note that any conjunctive and disjunctive combination of atomic predicates can always be transformed into the form of a disjunctive predicate as defined above. This requires transforming the predicate into disjunctive normal form (DNF) with the atomic predicates being treated as literals.

6.2.2   Predicate Matching

Predicate matching in our context is the problem of deciding whether a predicate implies another predicate and, if this is not the case, how the other predicate can be altered in order for the implication to become valid. More formally, given two predicates p and p', matching p' with p returns $(true, p)$ if $p' \Rightarrow p$ and $(false, \bar{p})$, where $\bar{p}$ is a relaxed version of p such that $p' \Rightarrow \bar{p}$ (and also $p \Rightarrow \bar{p}$), otherwise.

While the implication problem for conjunctive predicates can be solved efficiently according to Rosenkrantz and Hunt (1980) and Sun et al. (1989), the general implication problem for disjunctive predicates is proven to be NP-hard [Sun et al. (1989)]. Since disjunctive predicates can be created during data stream widening in a DSMS, matching such predicates is a necessity when optimizing stream processing in such a system.

In the following, we always consider the matching of the *query predicate* of a newly registered query with the *stream predicate* of a stream-producing query that is already being executed in a DSMS. Nevertheless, the presented techniques are generic and can be applied to any predicates of the form described in Section 6.2.1 and in any domain.

6.2.3   Predicate Evaluation

Predicate evaluation in our context is the problem of deciding whether a data item satisfies a predicate or not. More formally, given a predicate p and a data item i, evaluating p against i returns true if, for all dimensions referenced in p, the value of i in the corresponding dimension is contained within the interval defined for that dimension in p.

VARIABLE	DESCRIPTION
p	disjunctive stream predicate
p'	disjunctive query predicate
c	conjunctive subpredicate of stream predicate p
c'	conjunctive subpredicate of query predicate p'
n	number of conjunctive subpredicates c in p
m	number of conjunctive subpredicates c' in p'
d	dimension of a conjunctive subpredicate c in p
d'	dimension of a conjunctive subpredicate c' in p'
I_d	interval defined by c in dimension d
$I_{d'}$	interval defined by c' in dimension d'
D	data space
k	number of dimensions in the data space
k_c	number of dimensions referenced by c

Table 6.1: Variables used in algorithm descriptions and during complexity analysis

6.2.4 Notation

Table 6.1 shows important variables used in the algorithm descriptions and during the complexity analysis of Section 6.5. In the pseudocode representations of the predicate matching and evaluation algorithms in Appendix F on page 207, assignments of the value of a variable y to a variable x are written $x \leftarrow y$. Assignments are supposed to assign a copy of the value of y to x. Furthermore, function calls are supposed to use call-by-value. Unless explicitly stated, queues used in the algorithm descriptions can be either FIFO or LIFO queues.

6.3 Predicate Matching

This section presents three algorithms for matching disjunctive predicates. The first two algorithms are heuristics that are very efficient, yet do not deliver exact results. The third algorithm is an exact method whose worst case running time is exponential in the number of subpredicates contained in the predicates to be matched.

6.3.1 Example Predicates

We use the following predicates as a running example for illustrating the matching algorithms introduced in this section.

Example 6.1 (Predicates) Consider predicates p_1 and p_2 defined below as examples and suppose we want to match p_2 with p_1, i.e., determine whether p_2 implies p_1 or how p_1 could be modified in order for the implication to be valid.

p_1: $((a \geq 3) \wedge (a \leq 12) \wedge (b \geq 0) \wedge (b \leq 5)) \vee$
$\quad ((a \geq 9) \wedge (a \leq 14) \wedge (b \geq 2) \wedge (b \leq 8)) \vee$
$\quad ((a \geq 0) \wedge (a \leq 5) \wedge (b \geq 1) \wedge (b \leq 6))$

p_2: $((a \geq 1) \wedge (a \leq 8) \wedge (b \geq 2) \wedge (b \leq 4))$

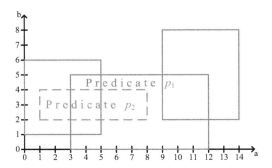

Figure 6.2: Graphical representation of predicates p_1 (solid boxes) and p_2 (dashed box)

Note that predicate p_1 constitutes a disjunction of conjunctive predicates and that, for simplicity and a shorter presentation, predicate p_2 consists of only one conjunctive subpredicate and does not contain any disjunctions. However, our algorithms are also capable of handling the general case of more than one subpredicate in p_2. Figure 6.2 shows a graphical representation of the example predicates p_1 and p_2.   □

6.3.2 Quick Check (QC)

We start by first introducing a simple *quick check* (QC) algorithm that can be combined with each of the matching algorithms. It is described in Algorithm 6.1 and tests for a conjunctive subpredicate c', whether c' implies at least one of the conjunctive subpredicates c of a given stream predicate p. The implication check for conjunctive predicates can easily be done by checking the bounds of c' for containment in the intervals defined by the atomic predicates in c for all dimensions [Rosenkrantz and Hunt (1980); Sun et al. (1989)]. If the quick check returns true, nothing more remains to be done for the tested subpredicate since it is clear that this subpredicate already matches the stream predicate as is.

Concerning our running example, comparing the only conjunctive subpredicate of p_2 to each conjunctive subpredicate of p_1 obviously yields no match, i. e., the quick check returns false. This is due to the fact that none of the tested implications is valid which can easily be seen from Figure 6.2. The dashed box of p_2 is not completely contained in any one of the three solid boxes of p_1.

Algorithm 6.1 Quick Check (QC)

Input: Stream predicate p and a conjunctive subpredicate c' of query predicate p'.
Output: true, if $c' \Rightarrow c$ for at least one conjunctive subpredicate c in p; false, otherwise.

1. *Compare subpredicates.* Compare c' to each conjunctive subpredicate c in p, i. e., check if $c' \Rightarrow c$.

2. *Return result.* As soon as $c' \Rightarrow c$ for the current values of c' and c, return true. If no conjunctive subpredicate c in p with $c' \Rightarrow c$ exists, return false.

Since the QC algorithm has to iterate over the conjunctive subpredicates of p and, for each subpredicate, over all dimensions referenced in that subpredicate, the worst case complexity of this algorithm is in $O(n \cdot k)$, where n is the number of conjunctive subpredicates c in p and k is the number of dimensions in the data space. Algorithm F.1 on page 207 shows a pseudocode representation of the quick check.

6.3.3 Heuristics with Simple Relaxation (HSR)

The easiest way to perform predicate matching is to completely skip the predicate implication checking and to go directly to the relaxation part. This is the idea of the *heuristics with simple relaxation* (HSR) shown in Algorithm 6.2. When matching a predicate p' with a predicate p, all conjunctive subpredicates of p' are disjunctively added to p. Since this solution does not perform any implication checking at all, it misses matches that are already present in the original predicates and it therefore performs unnecessary predicate relaxations in general.

The situation can be improved by combining the approach with the quick check algorithm of Section 6.3.2. The matching problem for disjunctive predicates is thereby basically reduced to the implication problem for conjunctive predicates. In this solution, two nested loops compare each conjunctive subpredicate of the query predicate to each conjunctive subpredicate of the stream predicate, checking for implication. If, for each subpredicate of the query predicate, a matching subpredicate in the stream predicate is found, the matching succeeds, else it fails. Obviously, this approach might fail even though the query and the stream predicates do match. In the running example, the only subpredicate $((a \geq 1) \wedge (a \leq 8) \wedge (b \geq 2) \wedge (b \leq 4))$ of predicate p_2 does not match any of the three subpredicates $((a \geq 3) \wedge (a \leq 12) \wedge (b \geq 0) \wedge (b \leq 5))$, $((a \geq 9) \wedge (a \leq 14) \wedge (b \geq 2) \wedge (b \leq 8))$, or $((a \geq 0) \wedge (a \leq 5) \wedge (b \geq 1) \wedge (b \leq 6))$ of predicate p_1 directly. However, p_2 matches with the entire predicate p_1 as can be seen from Figure 6.2, which this algorithm does not realize. Therefore, the algorithm reports a mismatch although the predicates actually do match.

Predicate relaxation in the case of a mismatch is simply done by adding the concerned query subpredicate to the stream predicate using a disjunction. This yields $((a \geq 3) \wedge (a \leq 12) \wedge (b \geq 0) \wedge (b \leq 5)) \vee ((a \geq 9) \wedge (a \leq 14) \wedge (b \geq 2) \wedge (b \leq 8)) \vee ((a \geq 0) \wedge (a \leq 5) \wedge (b \geq 1) \wedge (b \leq 6)) \vee ((a \geq 1) \wedge (a \leq 8) \wedge (b \geq 2) \wedge (b \leq 4))$ for $\bar{p}_1$ in our example and clearly causes the number of disjunctions in the stream predicate to increase by one. In general, even more than one disjunction might be added—one for each conjunctive subpredicate of the query predicate in the worst case. Note that, if one or more subpredicates of the query predicate already matched the stream predicate before the relaxation and the algorithm just was not able to detect these matches, this strategy still adds unnecessary disjunctions to the stream predicate. This should be avoided since additional disjunctions can cause future predicate matchings and predicate evaluations to become more expensive because the number of subpredicates has direct impact on algorithm complexities.

The worst case complexity of Algorithm 6.2 is in $O(m)$ without the quick check and in $O((m \cdot n + m^2) \cdot k)$ with the quick check, where m is the number of conjunctive subpredicates c' in p', n is the number of conjunctive subpredicates c in p, and k is the number of dimensions in the data space.

The advantages of the HSR algorithm without as well as with the quick check are that it is fast and easy to implement. The disadvantages of the approach obviously are that it misses matches in general—actually all matches if it is used without the quick check—and that it can therefore cause unnecessary predicate relaxations which affects the performance of future

---

Algorithm 6.2 Heuristics with Simple Relaxation (HSR)

Input: Stream predicate p and query predicate p'.

Output: (true, p), if the quick check of Algorithm 6.1 is activated and, for all conjunctive subpredicates c' in p', $c' \Rightarrow c$ for at least one conjunctive subpredicate c in p; $(\text{false}, \bar{p})$, where $\bar{p}$ is a relaxed version of p such that the above condition is satisfied, otherwise.

1. *Relax predicate.* Disjunctively add each conjunctive subpredicate c' in p' to p. Optionally, perform the quick check of Algorithm 6.1 for p and each c' in p' and only append those conjunctive subpredicates c' in p' to p for which the quick check returns false.

2. *Return result.* Return (true, p), if no changes have been made to p, i. e., no conjunctive subpredicates c' of p' have been disjunctively added to p. Otherwise, return $(\text{false}, \bar{p})$, where $\bar{p}$ is the modified version of p after the addition of one or more conjunctive subpredicates c' of p'.

---

predicate matching and predicate evaluation processes. Algorithm F.2 on page 208 shows a pseudocode representation of the HSR approach.

6.3.4 Heuristics with Complex Relaxation (HCR)

The *heuristics with complex relaxation* (HCR) avoids the increase in the number of subpredicates in the stream predicate induced by HSR at the expense of potentially producing only approximate results. Algorithm 6.3 shows the approach. For each conjunctive subpredicate in the query predicate, HCR relaxes one of the conjunctive subpredicates in the stream predicate in order for it to match the query subpredicate if no direct match between subpredicates has been found. Relaxing a subpredicate means employing a less restrictive filter on the corresponding data stream, therefore increasing network traffic. Thus, the subpredicate of the stream predicate that needs the least amount of relaxation in order to match the query subpredicate should be relaxed. In our running example, this is $((a \geq 3) \wedge (a \leq 12) \wedge (b \geq 0) \wedge (b \leq 5))$ which becomes $((a \geq 1) \wedge (a \leq 12) \wedge (b \geq 0) \wedge (b \leq 5))$. Figure 6.3 illustrates the situation. In general, this kind of relaxation causes the data stream to contain unnecessary data, e. g., the data with $((a \geq 1) \wedge (a < 3) \wedge (b \geq 0) \wedge (b < 2)) \vee ((a \geq 1) \wedge (a < 3) \wedge (b > 4) \wedge (b \leq 5))$ in our example. However, in the example, parts of these areas are already covered by another conjunctive subpredicate of p_1 as can be seen from Figure 6.3. Therefore, additional unnecessary network traffic is only caused by the inclusion of the hatched area $((a \geq 1) \wedge (a < 3) \wedge (b \geq 0) \wedge (b < 1))$ in Figure 6.3 in this specific case.

Deciding which subpredicate should be chosen for relaxation is a complex issue. As the example indicates, minimizing the extensions that have to be made to the intervals covered by the subpredicate in the various dimensions of the data space is generally not enough in order to maximize the quality of the solution. The reason is that the parts of the data space that are unnecessarily covered by the relaxed subpredicate might or might not already be covered by other subpredicates. Therefore, the coverage of these parts of the data space might or might not cause additional unnecessary network traffic. Recognizing whether or not the unnecessary parts of the intervals added to the relaxed subpredicate are covered by other subpredicates leads to the same kind of matching problem that we initially intended to solve—without the relaxation aspect. We use heuristics to solve this problem and choose the subpredicate with the lowest number of infinite interval bounds for relaxation. If the number of infinite interval bounds is

---

Algorithm 6.3 Heuristics with Complex Relaxation (HCR)

Input: Stream predicate p and query predicate p'.

Output: (true, p), if, for all conjunctive subpredicates c' in p', $c' \Rightarrow c$ for at least one conjunctive subpredicate c in p; (false, $\bar{p}$), where $\bar{p}$ is a relaxed version of p such that the above condition is satisfied, otherwise.

1. *Compare subpredicates.* Compare each conjunctive subpredicate c' in p' to each conjunctive subpredicate c in p in step 2. Optionally, perform the quick check of Algorithm 6.1 for p and c' and only consider c' in the following if the quick check returns false.

2. *Compare dimensions.* Compare each dimension d of c to the corresponding dimension d' of c', i. e., in the following, $d = d'$ holds. For each pair of corresponding dimensions d and d', if the interval $I_{c'}^{d'}$ of c' in d' is not completely contained in the interval I_c^d of c in d, compute the amount a by which I_c^d has to be extended, i. e., the sum of the amounts by which its lower bound has to be decreased and its upper bound has to be increased in order for the containment to be valid. Multiply a with the product of the non-zero extents of all finite intervals in all other dimensions of c and add up the results for all dimensions, yielding an accumulated value e. Replace I_c^d in c with its extended version. If, after the comparison of all dimensions, the relaxed version of c has less unbounded interval ends than the current best solution (the initial best solution has an infinite number of unbounded interval ends) or the same number of unbounded interval ends and a smaller value for e (again, the initial value for e is infinite), the relaxed version of c is saved as the new current best solution. If, after the comparison of c' with all c in p, no match for c' without relaxation has been found, replace the original version of the current best solution in p with the relaxed version computed above.

3. *Return result.* Return (true, p), if no changes have been made to p, i. e., no conjunctive subpredicates c of p have been replaced with relaxed versions. Otherwise, return (false, $\bar{p}$), where $\bar{p}$ is the modified version of p after the relaxation of one or more conjunctive subpredicates c in p.

---

equal for two subpredicates, we choose the subpredicate that yields the lowest increase in the volume of the data space it covers when ignoring dimensions with infinite interval length.

Figure 6.4 illustrates a case where relaxation is actually necessary. In this example, the third subpredicate of predicate p_1 has been altered from $((a \geq 0) \wedge (a \leq 5) \wedge (b \geq 1) \wedge (b \leq 6))$ to $((a \geq 0) \wedge (a \leq 5) \wedge (b \geq 3) \wedge (b \leq 6))$ to form predicate p'_1. This leads to the necessary inclusion of the hatched area described by $((a \geq 1) \wedge (a < 3) \wedge (b \geq 2) \wedge (b < 3))$ in Figure 6.4, whereas the other hatched area described by $((a \geq 1) \wedge (a < 3) \wedge (b \geq 0) \wedge (b < 2))$ is unnecessarily included in addition.

Like the HSR approach, HCR can be combined with the quick check algorithm of Section 6.3.2 to detect obvious matches before starting the more complex relaxation algorithm. The worst case complexity of the algorithm is in $O(m \cdot n \cdot k^2)$ with as well as without the quick check, with m, n, and k as defined before.

Some advantages of HCR are similar to those of HSR, i. e., the approach is relatively fast and easy to implement. Furthermore, other than the HSR approach, HCR does not introduce any additional disjunctions in the stream predicate. Some disadvantages are also similar since the approach still misses matches and therefore performs unnecessary predicate relaxations in general. Additionally, in contrast to HSR, the HCR approach can lead to the inclusion of unneeded

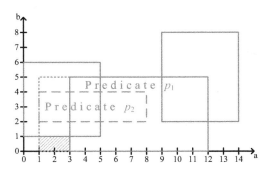

Figure 6.3: Relaxation of predicate p_1 (solid boxes) to match predicate p_2 (dashed box)

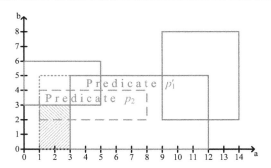

Figure 6.4: Partial match of predicates p_1' (solid boxes) and p_2 (dashed box)

parts of the data space in the relaxed predicate and therefore cause unnecessary network traffic due to false drops. This leads to a deterioration of the optimization effect in our distributed DSMS scenario and necessitates additional filtering to obtain the exact result if approximate results are not acceptable. Algorithm F.3 on page 209 shows a detailed pseudocode representation of the HCR algorithm.

6.3.5 Exact Matching (EM)

The *exact matching* (EM) algorithm is a split algorithm that always correctly detects a match of a query predicate p' with a stream predicate p. It does not miss matches like the heuristics above nor does it report false matches. The query predicate is split along its dimensions according to the boundaries of the overlapping intervals of the stream predicate. Only if all parts of the query predicate have been successfully matched at the end of the matching process, a match is reported. Otherwise, the stream predicate is relaxed. Algorithm 6.4 describes the approach.

Concerning the two dimensions a and b of our running example, we first match the intervals $[3, 12]$ for a and $[0,5]$ for b of the first subpredicate $((a \geq 3) \wedge (a \leq 12) \wedge (b \geq 0) \wedge (b \leq 5))$ of p_1 with the intervals $[1,8]$ for a and $[2,4]$ for b corresponding to $((a \geq 1) \wedge (a \leq 8) \wedge (b \geq 2) \wedge (b \leq 4))$ of p_2. Since the interval for b of p_2 is completely contained in the interval for b of p_1, we do

---

Algorithm 6.4 Exact Matching (EM)

Input: Stream predicate p and query predicate p'.
Output: (true, p), if $p' \Rightarrow p$; (false, $\bar{p}$), where $\bar{p}$ is a relaxed version of p such that $p' \Rightarrow \bar{p}$, otherwise.

1. *Compare subpredicates.* Compare each conjunctive subpredicate c' in p' to each conjunctive subpredicate c in p in step 2. Optionally, perform the quick check of Algorithm 6.1 for p and c' and only consider c' in the following if the quick check returns false.

2. *Compare dimensions.* Compare each dimension d of c to the corresponding dimension d' of c', i.e., in the following, $d = d'$ holds. Let I_c^d and $I_{c'}^{d'}$ be the intervals defined by c and c' in dimensions d and d', respectively. We distinguish four cases:

   (a) If I_c^d and $I_{c'}^{d'}$ are disjoint, continue with the next conjunctive subpredicate c in p to be matched with c'.

   (b) If $I_{c'}^{d'}$ is completely contained in I_c^d, continue with the next pair of dimensions from c and c'.

   (c) If I_c^d is completely contained in $I_{c'}^{d'}$, split c' along dimension d' into the part c_i' that is overlapping with c in dimension d' and the remaining parts c_{o1}' and c_{o2}'. Enqueue c_{o1}' and c_{o2}' in a queue Q_c'.

   (d) If I_c^d and $I_{c'}^{d'}$ overlap, split c' along dimension d' into the part c_i' that is overlapping with c in dimension d' and the remaining part c_o'. Enqueue c_o' in a queue Q_c'.

   Match the remaining parts of c' contained in Q_c' with the remaining conjunctive subpredicates c in p as above. As soon as Q_c' does not contain any more unmatched parts of c', continue with the next c' in p' from the beginning. If not all parts of c' could be matched, disjunctively add c' to p.

3. *Return result.* Return (true, p), if no changes have been made to p, i.e., no conjunctive subpredicates c' of p' have been disjunctively added to p. Otherwise, return (false, $\bar{p}$), where $\bar{p}$ is the modified version of p after the addition of one or more conjunctive subpredicates c' of p'.

---

not have to split the interval for b of p_2. We simply keep this interval and only split the interval for a of p_2 into the two intervals $[1,3[$ and $[3,8]$. The second of these two intervals is covered by the first subpredicate of p_1 and therefore does not have to be considered any further. Thus, in the following, we only need to match the intervals $[1,3[$ for a and $[2,4]$ for b of p_2. This corresponds to a *rest predicate* of $((a \geq 1) \wedge (a < 3) \wedge (b \geq 2) \wedge (b \leq 4))$. Matching this rest predicate with intervals $[9,14]$ and $[2,8]$ of the second subpredicate $((a \geq 9) \wedge (a \leq 14) \wedge (b \geq 2) \wedge (b \leq 8))$ of p_1 does not yield any additional matches. So we continue with the third and final subpredicate $((a \geq 0) \wedge (a \leq 5) \wedge (b \geq 1) \wedge (b \leq 6))$ of p_1, which yields intervals $[0,5]$ for a and $[1,6]$ for b. These intervals completely contain the intervals for a and b of the rest predicate of p_2. Thus, the resulting rest predicate of p_2 is empty and the entire predicate has been matched. Therefore, the algorithm correctly recognizes that p_1 is implied by p_2.

The above example illustrates the case of a complete match between predicates. In case of a mismatch, the resulting rest predicate will not be empty. In order to appropriately relax the

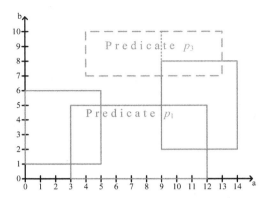

Figure 6.5: Partial match of predicates p_1 (solid boxes) and p_3 (dashed box)

query predicate, either the rest predicate or the original query predicate has to be disjunctively added to the stream predicate. While the former solution does not cause any additional overlap in the stream predicate, the latter always introduces only one additional stream subpredicate per mismatched query subpredicate. Overlap is not that critical for predicate matching and predicate evaluation. This is indicated by our performance evaluation presented in Section 6.6 and is also due to our short-circuit optimization introduced in Section 6.4.2. In contrast, the number of subpredicates has direct impact on the efficiency of matching and evaluation algorithms and should therefore be kept small. Consequently, we choose to add the original query predicate in case of a mismatch. Note that, in each case, no unnecessary parts of the data space are added to the predicate during relaxation as opposed to the HCR algorithm.

To demonstrate the case of a partial match, we introduce predicate p_3.

p_3: $((a \geq 4) \land (a \leq 13) \land (b \geq 7) \land (b \leq 10))$

We now want to match p_3 with p_1. Figure 6.5 illustrates the situation. Considering the intervals $[4, 13]$ for a and $[7, 10]$ for b of p_3, we want to match these with intervals $[3, 12]$ for a and $[0, 5]$ for b of the first subpredicate $((a \geq 3) \land (a \leq 12) \land (b \geq 0) \land (b \leq 5))$ of p_1. Since the intervals for b of both predicates are disjoint, no match is found. We therefore continue by matching the intervals of p_3 with intervals $[9, 14]$ for a and $[2, 8]$ for b of the second subpredicate of p_1. Since the intervals for a of both predicates overlap, we have to split the interval for a of p_3 into the two intervals $[4, 9[$ and $[9, 13]$. As the first interval does not overlap with the currently examined subpredicate of p_1, this part of p_3 is saved for future comparisons with other subpredicates of p_1. The second interval completely overlaps with the current subpredicate of p_1 and is therefore compared with this subpredicate in the remaining dimensions. Since there is also an overlap of the intervals for b, another split is made. The resulting intervals for b are $[7, 8]$ and $]8, 10]$. After the decomposition, p_3 looks as follows:

$$((a \geq 4) \land (a < 9) \land (b \geq 7) \land (b \leq 10)) \lor$$
$$((a \geq 9) \land (a \leq 13) \land (b > 8) \land (b \leq 10)) \lor$$
$$((a \geq 9) \land (a \leq 13) \land (b \geq 7) \land (b \leq 8))$$

The three disjoint parts of this predicate are indicated by the dotted lines within the rectangle of p_3 in Figure 6.5. The third of the three disjoint subpredicates of the decomposed predicate

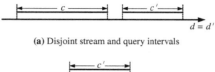

(a) Disjoint stream and query intervals

(b) Query interval contained in stream interval

(c) Stream interval contained in query interval

(d) Overlapping stream and query intervals

Figure 6.6: Cases distinguished during dimension comparison

p_3 above has now been completely matched with the second subpredicate of p_1. The other two subpredicates of the decomposed predicate p_3 have to be matched with the remaining subpredicates of p_1. This yields no further matches. Therefore, p_3 does not match p_1. In order to force the match, p_1 has to be relaxed by disjunctively adding the entire subpredicate of p_3, which in our example happens to be p_3 itself. The relaxed predicate looks as follows:

$$((a \geq 3) \wedge (a \leq 12) \wedge (b \geq 0) \wedge (b \leq 5)) \vee$$
$$((a \geq 9) \wedge (a \leq 14) \wedge (b \geq 2) \wedge (b \leq 8)) \vee$$
$$((a \geq 0) \wedge (a \leq 5) \wedge (b \geq 1) \wedge (b \leq 6)) \vee$$
$$((a \geq 4) \wedge (a \leq 13) \wedge (b \geq 7) \wedge (b \leq 10))$$

Figure 6.4 shows another example for a partial match. In this case, the EM algorithm would split predicate p_2 into the three disjoint parts $(a \geq 3) \wedge (a \leq 8) \wedge (b \geq 2) \wedge (b \leq 4)$, $(a \geq 1) \wedge (a < 3) \wedge (b \geq 3) \wedge (b \leq 4)$, and $(a \geq 1) \wedge (a < 3) \wedge (b \geq 2) \wedge (b < 3)$. The third of these three parts remains unmatched.

The EM algorithm needs to compare the intervals defined by stream subpredicates in the various dimensions of the data space to the intervals defined by query subpredicates in the corresponding dimensions. This dimension comparison distinguishes four cases which are illustrated in Figure 6.6. The intervals defined by the stream and the query subpredicate may either be disjoint (Figure 6.6(a)), overlapping (Figure 6.6(d)), or contained in each another (Figures 6.6(b) and 6.6(c)). Algorithm F.4 on page 210 shows the details of the dimension comparison.

Again, the quick check presented in Section 6.3.2 can be executed in combination with the EM approach to check for matching subpredicates in advance before starting the more complex relaxation algorithm. The worst case time complexity of the EM algorithm without the quick check is in $O(\sum_{i=0}^{m-1}\sum_{j=0}^{n+i-1}(2k)^j \cdot k)$ and thus in $O(k \cdot (2k)^{m+n})$, with m, n, and k defined as before. Section 6.5 presents the details of the complexity analysis.

The advantages of the exact solution are that it determines matches between predicates in an exact way, i. e., all existing matches are found—as opposed to the heuristics—and no false matches are reported. Therefore, the approach does not cause any unnecessary predicate relaxations. Also, the non-matching parts of the query predicate are exactly identified. The major disadvantage of the exact solution is its high algorithmic complexity which is exponential in the number of subpredicates in the predicates to be matched. This might slow down the optimization process considerably for predicates with many disjunctions and makes the algorithm inapplicable for larger problem sizes. In such cases, the heuristics have to be used instead.

We have developed three different split strategies for use with the EM algorithm. The strategies differ in the order in which they process unmatched parts of previously split subpredicates. These differences have impact on the average execution time—though not on the theoretical worst case time complexity—and on the space complexity of the EM algorithm. We call the (unmatched) parts resulting from the splitting of a conjunctive subpredicate the (unmatched) *subparts* of the subpredicate and the original subpredicate itself the corresponding *superpart* of these subparts. Note that each subpart and each superpart by itself constitutes a conjunctive predicate. Figure 6.7 shows a schematic illustration of the split strategies for a small example with a query subpredicate c', $n = 3$ stream subpredicates, and $k = 2$ dimensions in the data space. The figure assumes the worst case of the query subpredicate and each of its resulting subparts in turn being split into $2k$ unmatched parts during the matching. Note that this is a conservative approximation since it is impossible in reality that each of the subparts originating from the same superpart is split into $2k$ unmatched parts. This is due to the fact that all the subparts of the same superpart are pairwise disjoint and $2k$ unmatched parts only result from the splitting if the stream subpredicate is completely contained in the query subpredicate that is to be split. However, a stream subpredicate cannot be completely contained in more than one subpart of a set of disjoint subparts. Nevertheless, we use this approximation for the EM algorithm, yielding exponential worst case time complexity. Since the general implication problem involving disjunctive predicates is proven to be NP-hard [Sun et al. (1989)], the actual worst case time complexity—although lower than our approximation—still is exponential.

Breadth-First Split Strategy (BFS)

The breadth-first split strategy (BFS) starts by splitting a query subpredicate c' by comparing it to the first stream subpredicate c of a stream predicate p. The remaining unmatched parts of c' are then split in turn by comparing them to the next stream subpredicate in p until no more unmatched parts remain, in which case the matching succeeds, or until no more stream subpredicates remain, in which case the matching fails and the stream predicate needs to be relaxed. Figure 6.7(a) shows the resulting tree of unmatched parts for the worst case. The tree has a maximum of $n + 1$ levels, one for each stream subpredicate and one for the root, which is the original query subpredicate c'. On each level, every subpart on that level is split into $2k$ new subparts that belong to the next level of the tree. Thus, the leaf level contains a total of $(2k)^n$ subparts. Algorithm F.5 on page 211 shows the details of the EM algorithm with BFS strategy.

Using the BFS strategy leads to building up the aforementioned tree in a breadth-first manner, i. e., each level of the tree is completely filled with all subparts belonging to that level before the next level is built. This leads to a maximum in computational cost and memory usage, since the algorithm performs every possible split and creates the maximum possible number of subparts that need to be stored.

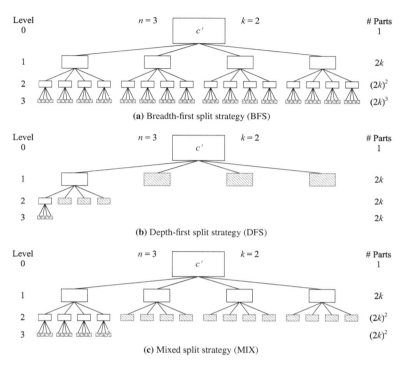

Figure 6.7: Exact matching algorithm split strategies

Depth-First Split Strategy (DFS)

The situation can be vastly improved by using the depth-first split strategy (DFS), which is illustrated in Figure 6.7(b). Using this strategy, only one of the subparts on each level of the tree is split further by comparing it to the next stream subpredicate. If all parts on one tree level have been successfully matched, the matching continues with the next subpart on the corresponding parent level. In the worst case, each level of the tree contains $2k$ parts. Thus, the tree has a total of $(n-1) \cdot (2k-1) + 2k$ leaf nodes. Algorithm F.6 on page 212 shows the details of the EM algorithm with DFS strategy.

Using the DFS strategy leads to building up the aforementioned tree in a depth-first manner. Since matched parts are removed from the tree, each level contains at most $2k$ parts at each time, except for the root level which always contains at most one part—the original query subpredicate c'. This reduces the space complexity of the algorithm to quadratic in k and to linear in all other parameters. Further, the DFS strategy reduces the average execution time of the algorithm since mismatches can be detected early and therefore many comparisons between subparts and stream subpredicates can be saved compared to the BFS strategy. On the other hand, the DFS strategy is a little more difficult to implement and has a slightly higher data structure maintenance overhead than the BFS strategy. However, the differences between the two strategies are small in this respect.

Mixed Split Strategy (MIX)

The mixed split strategy (MIX) is a compromise between the BFS and the DFS strategies. The memory consumption of the MIX strategy is higher than that of the DFS strategy. Also, the MIX strategy might perform some unnecessary splits before detecting a mismatch. But it still needs much less memory than the BFS strategy and it can be implemented with less data structure maintenance overhead than the DFS strategy. The idea is to always compare all the subparts that belong to the same superpart against the next stream subpredicate at once, splitting them as needed. Figure 6.7(c) illustrates the approach. Using this strategy, the tree of subparts has one node in level 0, $2k$ nodes in level 1, and $(2k)^2$ nodes in all remaining levels in the worst case. Therefore, the number of leaf nodes is $(n-2) \cdot (2k-1) \cdot 2k + (2k)^2$ in the worst case. Algorithm F.7 on page 213 shows the details of the EM algorithm with MIX strategy.

The MIX strategy potentially detects mismatches later than the DFS strategy but still earlier than the BFS strategy. It furthermore has cubic space complexity in k, whereas the DFS and BFS strategies have quadratic and exponential space complexities in k, respectively. Section 6.5 contains the details of the complexity analysis. The MIX strategy is supposed to be slower than the DFS strategy for large numbers of stream subpredicates n and for large numbers of dimensions k if many mismatches occur. In these cases, the DFS strategy benefits from detecting mismatches earlier. However, if only few mismatches occur, the reduction in maintenance overhead achieved in the MIX strategy might cause it to outperform the DFS strategy. Similar to the DFS strategy, the MIX strategy is a little more difficult to implement than the BFS strategy. However, all three variants are comparatively easy to implement.

6.3.6   Multi-Dimensional Indexing

The previously described algorithms can be supported by multi-dimensional indexing as follows. The quick check of Algorithm 6.1 can use such an index to retrieve all conjunctive subpredicates of the stream predicate p that overlap with the current conjunctive subpredicate c' of the query predicate p'. Only the overlapping subpredicates instead of all subpredicates of the stream predicate need to be iterated and compared to c' in subsequent steps.

Algorithm 6.2 without the quick check offers no possibility for indexing. Algorithm 6.3 cannot be supported directly by an index either. It must always take all subpredicates of the stream predicate into consideration for relaxation since it is not clear—and cannot be decided using a multi-dimensional index—which of these subpredicates should be relaxed to minimize the cost. However, as with all matching algorithms presented in this chapter, the quick check that can be combined with these algorithms can use an index.

The exact solution of Algorithm 6.4 can benefit the most from a multi-dimensional index. In addition to the indexed quick check, the index can also be used during the splitting step to quickly identify the subpredicates of the stream predicate that overlap with the current subpredicate of the query predicate. Only these overlapping subpredicates have to be considered during splitting instead of iterating over all subpredicates of the stream predicate.

Various multi-dimensional index structures with different characteristics have been developed over the years [Gaede and Günther (1998)]. In this chapter, we use main memory versions of different variants of the R-tree [Beckmann et al. (1990); Guttman (1984)]. Since R-trees index boxes in multi-dimensional space, they can naturally index the multi-dimensional intervals described by our predicates without any additional postprocessing. We do not deal with arbitrary intervals that form complex structures rather than rectangular boxes in the data space in this thesis. But we could approximate such arbitrary intervals by minimum bounding boxes in

---

Algorithm 6.5 Standard Evaluation (SE)

Input: Predicate p and data item i.
Output: true, if i satisfies p; false, otherwise.

1. *Iterate subpredicates.* Compare i to each conjunctive subpredicate c in p. For each such subpredicate, compare each dimension d_c in c to the corresponding dimension d_i in i in step 2.

2. *Compare dimensions.* For each pair of corresponding dimensions d_c and d_i, i. e., $d_c = d_i$, check if the value for d_i in i lies within the interval defined for d_c in c. If so, continue with the next dimension in c. Otherwise, continue with the next conjunctive subpredicate c in p.

3. *Return result.* As soon as, for a certain conjunctive subpredicate c in p, the intervals of all dimensions d_c in c contain the values of all the corresponding dimensions d_i in i, return true. If there is no conjunctive subpredicate c in p such that the above condition is satisfied, return false.

---

an R-tree. This may necessitate a non-trivial postprocessing step in addition to an index access. Note that the index does not need to comprise all dimensions of the data space. It only needs to contain the dimensions that are actually referenced by the indexed predicate. These are usually few, compared to the potentially many dimensions of the data space. If the dimensions referenced by predicates can change dynamically, e. g., due to predicate relaxation as in our DSMS scenario, a subset of the dimensions of the data space containing the most selective dimensions can be indexed. This yields a quick and efficient reduction of the data volume. If a predicate references non-indexed dimensions, these can subsequently be evaluated conventionally. Alternatively, the index can be rebuilt each time the set of referenced dimensions changes.

6.4 Predicate Evaluation

Apart from predicate matching, efficient predicate evaluation is also important in a DSMS. The goal is to evaluate a given predicate against as many data items per time unit as possible, i. e., to achieve a high throughput. In the following, we present two approaches for predicate evaluation.

6.4.1 Standard Evaluation (SE)

We use the term *standard evaluation* (SE) to denote a simple sequential scan that is shown in Algorithm 6.5. The algorithm evaluates a given predicate p against a given data item i by iterating over the conjunctive subpredicates c of p and by testing for each dimension whether the value of i in that dimension is contained in the interval defined for the same dimension in c. As soon as a subpredicate containing the values of i in each dimension is found, the algorithm terminates and returns true. Only if no subpredicate containing i could be found after inspecting all conjunctive subpredicates c of p, the algorithm returns false.

The worst case complexity of the standard evaluation algorithm is in $O(n \cdot k)$, where n denotes the number of conjunctive subpredicates in the predicate p to be evaluated and k is the number of dimensions in the data space. Algorithm F.8 on page 214 shows a pseudocode representation of the standard evaluation algorithm.

6.4.2 Index-based Evaluation (IE)

Considering the facts that the exact matching algorithm is only applicable for small problem sizes and the approximate results of the HCR algorithm are often not desirable, a switch to the HSR algorithm for larger problem sizes, i. e., larger numbers of dimensions and subpredicates, seems necessary in many cases. Since the HSR algorithm—with as well as without the quick check—can introduce a considerable number of additional disjunctions in predicates, the simple standard evaluation algorithm above will quickly become inefficient. Therefore, an optimized predicate evaluation strategy that better handles large numbers of subpredicates is needed.

Predicate evaluation can benefit even more from multi-dimensional indexing than the predicate matching algorithms of Section 6.3. We call the evaluation algorithm with index support *index-based evaluation* (IE). It differs from standard evaluation in that it does not iterate over the conjunctive subpredicates of the predicate to be evaluated. Instead, it indexes the predicate using a multi-dimensional index structure. To evaluate the predicate against a data item, the algorithm simply executes the containment method of the index with the data item as a parameter. The evaluation is then completely performed by the index, returning true if the predicate covers the data item and false otherwise. If a predicate references a very large number of dimensions, it is possible to index only a subset, i. e., the most selective of these dimensions, to obtain a quick index-based prefiltering with only a small number of false drops in the result. The remaining dimensions can then be evaluated conventionally using standard evaluation. Furthermore, predicate evaluation can be dynamically adapted to available computing resources by limiting the index level to which the evaluation descends before deciding whether a data item satisfies the indexed predicate. This will in general lead to approximate results, i. e., the resulting data stream will contain data items that do not satisfy the original predicate. In a DSMS scenario, this can be corrected by an additional filtering step at another peer in the network further downstream. Note that this approach does not remove any qualifying data items from the stream. In the remainder of this chapter, we always assume that an index contains all dimensions referenced in a predicate and that the index-based evaluation is exact, i. e., that it does not use the dynamic adaptation described above.

It has been noted several times in the literature[1] that multi-dimensional index structures are not suitable for predicate indexing in active databases and publish&subscribe systems. The reason is that overlap between regions tends to be high in these settings and multi-dimensional index structures are prone to deteriorate under such circumstances. Searching the regions containing a certain multi-dimensional point in an R-tree with highly overlapping regions could, for example, lead to a full tree traversal in the worst case. However, this is only true if *all* containing regions for a data item have to be returned as in traditional use cases. In our application scenario, we index disjunctive predicates and the first hit determines the result, i. e., it suffices to determine whether there is *at least one* region containing the data item. If such a region is found, the search can be stopped and true can be returned as the evaluation result. If no containing region is present in the index, the mismatch can potentially be detected early at higher index levels. Using this *short-circuit* optimization on an R-tree proves to be a beneficial evaluation strategy as the performance evaluation in Section 6.6 shows. Even better results could be achieved by using adaptive index structures such as the TV-tree [Lin et al. (1994)]. In contrast to R-trees, such index structures are able to dynamically adapt the set of indexed dimensions. They can thus help to avoid indexing unbounded dimensions in a predicate. This is desirable since unbounded dimensions in the index can cause excessive overlap between index regions

---

[1]See, for example, [Hanson and Johnson (1996)].

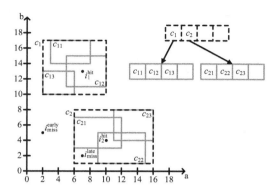

Figure 6.8: Index-based predicate evaluation

and therefore degrade index performance. Examining the use of such advanced indexing techniques as well as integrating application-specific improvements and tuning into the index itself are possibilities for future research.

Figure 6.8 illustrates an example where a disjunctive predicate consisting of 6 conjunctive subpredicates is represented by an R-tree and evaluated against 4 different data items. The figure shows the graphical representation of the predicate in the data space and the corresponding R-tree. For data item $i_{\text{miss}}^{\text{early}}$, the fact that the data item does not satisfy the predicate can already be determined by comparing the data item to the root of the index tree. In contrast, for $i_{\text{miss}}^{\text{late}}$, the mismatch is not detected before the leaf level of the index tree. While i_1^{hit} can be identified as a match by traversing one single path in the index tree, i_2^{hit} would normally require to visit two different leaf nodes. However, by using our short-circuit optimization, we can stop the evaluation and return true after the first matching leaf node has been found.

6.5 Complexity Analysis

This section analyzes the best case, average case, and worst case time and space complexities of the matching and evaluation algorithms introduced in Sections 6.3 and 6.4.

6.5.1 Prerequisites

Table 6.2 repeats from Table 6.1 on page 135 the variables used during complexity analysis together with their meaning. We assume $m, n, k \in \mathbb{N}^+$ in the following. We consider a dimension in the data space as the most fine-grained unit for time and space complexity analysis. For time complexity, comparing two dimensions is the most fine-grained unit. Note that comparing two dimensions always consists of comparing the upper and the lower bounds of the two dimensions, i.e., the comparison always leads to two value comparisons. Since this is the same for each comparison between two dimensions, we abstract from the actual value comparisons and choose the comparison between two dimensions as the most fine-grained unit for time complexity analysis. Equally, for space complexity analysis, the most fine-grained unit is the memory required to store the information associated with a single dimension in the data space. Again,

VARIABLE	DESCRIPTION
p	disjunctive stream predicate
p'	disjunctive query predicate
c	conjunctive subpredicate of stream predicate p
c'	conjunctive subpredicate of query predicate p'
n	number of conjunctive subpredicates c in p
m	number of conjunctive subpredicates c' in p'
k	number of dimensions in the data space

Table 6.2: Variables used during complexity analysis

for each dimension, its corresponding upper and lower bound need to be stored. We again abstract from these values and choose the memory needed for storing all the information for a single dimension as the most fine-grained unit for space complexity analysis.

6.5.2 Quick Check (QC)

Time Complexity

- Best Case:
  The best case for the QC algorithm occurs when the query subpredicate c' already implies the first stream subpredicate c in p and c only references one of the k dimensions of the data space. Then, only a single comparison between two dimensions of the data space is necessary. In this case, the time complexity of the QC algorithm is constant and is in

$$\Omega(1)$$

- Worst Case:
  The worst case for the QC algorithm occurs when the query subpredicate c' does not imply any of the n stream subpredicates c in p and each stream subpredicate references all of the k dimensions of the data space. Then, for each of the n conjunctive subpredicates c in p, all of the k dimensions of the data space need to be considered. In this case, the time complexity of the QC algorithm is linear in n and k, and is in

$$O(n \cdot k)$$

- Average Case:
  The average case for the QC algorithm occurs when the query subpredicate c' is found to imply a stream subpredicate c in p after checking half of the n subpredicates c in p and each subpredicate c in p on average references half of the k dimensions of the data space. In this case, the time complexity of the QC algorithm is linear in n and k, and is in

$$\Theta\left(\frac{n}{2} \cdot \frac{k}{2}\right) = \Theta(n \cdot k)$$

Space Complexity

- Best Case:
  The best case for the QC algorithm occurs when each stream subpredicate c in p as well as the query subpredicate c' only reference one of the k dimensions of the data space. Then, for each of the n stream subpredicates c in p as well as for the query subpredicate c', the information for only one dimension needs to be stored. In this case, the space complexity of the QC algorithm is linear in n and is in

$$\Omega(n+1)$$

- Worst Case:
  The worst case for the QC algorithm occurs when each stream subpredicate c in p as well as the query subpredicate c' reference all of the k dimensions of the data space. Then, for each of the n stream subpredicates c in p as well as for the query subpredicate c', the information for all k dimensions of the data space needs to be stored. In this case, the space complexity of the QC algorithm is linear in n and k, and is in

$$O((n+1) \cdot k)$$

- Average Case:
  The average case for the QC algorithm occurs when each stream subpredicate c in p as well as the query subpredicate c' reference half of the k dimensions of the data space. Then, for each of the n stream subpredicates c in p as well as for the query subpredicate c', the information for half of the k dimensions of the data space needs to be stored. In this case, the space complexity of the QC algorithm is linear in n and k, and is in

$$\Theta\left((n+1) \cdot \frac{k}{2}\right)$$

Summary

The QC algorithm is an efficient algorithm for quickly determining obvious matches of a query subpredicate with a stream predicate. Its time and space complexities are at most linear in the number n of subpredicates in the stream predicate and the number k of dimensions in the data space. Note that the worst and average case time complexities are the same. The complexity of the index-based QC algorithm depends on the complexity of the employed index structure.

6.5.3 Heuristics with Simple Relaxation (HSR)

Time Complexity

For the HSR algorithm without the quick check, the best case, worst case, and average case time complexities are linear in m and are in $\Omega(m)$, $O(m)$, and $\Theta(m)$, respectively. This is due to the fact that, without the quick check, the HSR algorithm simply iterates over all m conjunctive subpredicates in the query predicate and disjunctively adds each of these subpredicates to the stream predicate one after another. The situation is different when combining the HSR algorithm with the quick check as described in the following.

- Best Case:
  The best case for the HSR algorithm with the quick check occurs if, for each of the m query subpredicates c' in p', the quick check finds a matching subpredicate in the first stream subpredicate c in p and c only references one of the k dimensions of the data space. Then, the algorithm only has to iterate over all m subpredicates of the query predicate and to perform a single dimension comparison for each query subpredicate. In this case, the time complexity of the HSR algorithm with the quick check is linear in m and is in

  $$\Omega(m)$$

- Worst Case:
  The worst case for the HSR algorithm with the quick check occurs if, for each of the m query subpredicates c' in p', the quick check iterates over all of the n stream subpredicates c in p without finding a match and each subpredicate in the stream predicate references all of the k dimensions of the data space. Since each of the unmatched query subpredicates is disjunctively added to the stream predicate, the number of conjunctive subpredicates in the stream predicate increases by one each time the algorithm starts to consider the next conjunctive subpredicate of the query predicate. Therefore, the number of comparisons between dimensions can be estimated as

  $$\sum_{i=0}^{m-1}(n+i)\cdot k \;\; = \;\; \left(m\cdot n+\sum_{i=0}^{m-1}i\right)\cdot k$$
  $$\overset{\text{arith.}}{\underset{\text{series}}{=}} \;\; \left(m\cdot n+\frac{(m-1)\cdot m}{2}\right)\cdot k$$
  $$\leq \;\; \left(m\cdot n+m^2\right)\cdot k$$

  Consequently, the worst case time complexity of the HSR algorithm with the quick check is quadratic in m, linear in n and k, and is in

  $$O\left(\left(m\cdot n+m^2\right)\cdot k\right)$$

- Average Case:
  The average case for the HSR algorithm with the quick check occurs if, for each of the m query subpredicates c' in p', the quick check iterates over half of the n stream subpredicates c in p before finding a match and each subpredicate in the stream predicate references half of the k dimensions of the data space. Furthermore, we assume that half of the m query subpredicates remain unmatched and are therefore disjunctively added to the stream predicate, thus increasing the number of conjunctive subpredicates in the stream predicate by one for half of the query subpredicates. Therefore, the number of comparisons between dimensions can be estimated as

  $$\sum_{i=0}^{m-1}\left(\frac{n+\frac{i}{2}}{2}\right)\cdot\frac{k}{2} \;\; = \;\; \left(m\cdot n+\frac{1}{2}\cdot\sum_{i=0}^{m-1}i\right)\cdot\frac{k}{4}$$
  $$\overset{\text{arith.}}{\underset{\text{series}}{=}} \;\; \left(m\cdot n+\frac{1}{2}\cdot\frac{(m-1)\cdot m}{2}\right)\cdot\frac{k}{4}$$
  $$\leq \;\; \left(m\cdot n+m^2\right)\cdot k$$

  Consequently, the average case time complexity of the HSR algorithm with the quick check is quadratic in m, linear in n and k, and is in

  $$\Theta\left(\left(m\cdot n+m^2\right)\cdot k\right)$$

Space Complexity

The space complexity of the HSR algorithm is independent of whether the algorithm is executed with or without the quick check.

- Best Case:
  The best case for the HSR algorithm occurs when each subpredicate only references one of the k dimensions of the data space. Then, for each of the m query subpredicates c' in p' as well as for each of the n stream subpredicates c in p, the information for only one dimension needs to be stored. In this case, the space complexity of the HSR algorithm is linear in m and n, and is in

$$\Omega(m+n)$$

- Worst Case:
  The worst case for the HSR algorithm occurs when each subpredicate references all of the k dimensions of the data space. Then, for each of the m query subpredicates c' in p' as well as for each of the n stream subpredicates c in p, the information for all k dimensions of the data space needs to be stored. In this case, the space complexity of the HSR algorithm is linear in m, n, and k, and is in

$$O((m+n)\cdot k)$$

- Average Case:
  The average case for the HSR algorithm occurs when each subpredicate references half of the k dimensions of the data space. Then, for each of the m query subpredicates c' in p' as well as for each of the n stream subpredicates c in p, the information for half of the k dimensions of the data space needs to be stored. In this case, the space complexity of the HSR algorithm is linear in m, n, and k, and is in

$$\Theta\left((m+n)\cdot\frac{k}{2}\right)$$

Summary

The HSR algorithm without the quick check is a simple relaxation algorithm with linear time complexity in m and with linear space complexity. Combining the HSR algorithm with the QC algorithm does not affect the space complexity but leads to quadratic time complexity in m in the worst and average case. Note that, as for the QC algorithm, the worst and average case time complexities of the HSR algorithm are the same. Still, the HSR approach is a simple and relatively fast algorithm. The HSR algorithm can only indirectly be supported by an index when using an index-supported quick check. In this case, the complexity of the algorithm depends on the complexity of the employed index structure.

6.5.4 Heuristics with Complex Relaxation (HCR)

Time Complexity

- Best Case:
  The best case for the HCR algorithm without the quick check occurs if, for each of the m query subpredicates c' in p', the algorithm finds a matching subpredicate in the first stream subpredicate c in p and c only references one of the k dimensions of the data space. Then,

the algorithm only has to iterate over all m subpredicates of the query predicate and to perform a single dimension comparison for each query subpredicate. In this case, the time complexity of the HCR algorithm without the quick check is linear in m and is in

$$\Omega(m)$$

The best case complexity of the HCR algorithm remains the same when combining it with the quick check. The best case then occurs when the quick check finds a match for each query subpredicate c' in p' when comparing it to the first stream subpredicate c in p and furthermore, c references only one of the k dimensions of the data space.

- Worst Case:
  The worst case for the HCR algorithm without the quick check occurs if, for each of the m query subpredicates c' in p', the algorithm iterates over all of the n stream subpredicates c in p without finding a match and each subpredicate in the stream predicate references all of the k dimensions of the data space. Since, for each pair of subpredicates c' in p' and c in p as well as for each dimension in the data space, the list of all k dimensions has to be iterated to compute v in line 20 of Algorithm F.3 on page 209, the worst case time complexity of the HCR algorithm without the quick check is linear in m and n, quadratic in k, and is in

$$O\left(m \cdot n \cdot k^2\right)$$

The worst case complexity of the HCR algorithm with the quick check has to additionally take into account the worst case complexity of the QC algorithm. The quick check is executed before the actual HCR algorithm and in case the quick check does not yield a match, the normal HCR algorithm is executed. Thus, the numbers of dimension comparisons of the QC algorithm and the HCR algorithm have to be added. This yields

$$m \cdot n \cdot k + m \cdot n \cdot k^2 = m \cdot n \cdot \left(k + k^2\right)$$
$$\leq 2 \cdot m \cdot n \cdot k^2$$

Therefore, the worst case complexity of the HCR algorithm with the quick check is still linear in m and n, quadratic in k, and is in

$$O\left(m \cdot n \cdot k^2\right)$$

- Average Case:
  The average case for the HCR algorithm without the quick check occurs if, for each of the m query subpredicates c' in p', the algorithm iterates over half of the n stream subpredicates c in p before finding a match and each subpredicate in the stream predicate references half of the k dimensions of the data space. Furthermore, we assume that half of the m query subpredicates remain unmatched and thus lead to a relaxation of the stream predicate during the execution of the algorithm. Therefore, the average case time complexity of the HCR algorithm without the quick check is linear in m and n, quadratic in k, and is in

$$\Theta\left(m \cdot \frac{n}{2} \cdot \left(\frac{k}{2}\right)^2\right) = \Theta\left(m \cdot n \cdot k^2\right)$$

The average case complexity of the HCR algorithm with the quick check is determined analogously to the worst case. For the number of dimension comparisons, this yields

$$m \cdot \frac{n}{2} \cdot \frac{k}{2} + \frac{m}{2} \cdot n \cdot \left(\frac{k}{2}\right)^2 \leq m \cdot n \cdot \left(k + k^2\right)$$
$$\leq 2 \cdot m \cdot n \cdot k^2$$

Therefore, the average case complexity of the HCR algorithm with the quick check is still linear in m and n, quadratic in k, and is in

$$\Theta\left(m \cdot n \cdot k^2\right)$$

Space Complexity

The space complexity of the HCR algorithm is identical to the space complexity of the HSR algorithm since both algorithms only need to store the query and the stream predicate. In contrast to the EM algorithm which is analyzed below, the HSR and HCR algorithms do not split subpredicates and therefore do not create additional subpredicates either.

Summary

The time and space complexities of the HCR algorithm are independent of whether the quick check is activated or deactivated. Also note that the worst and average case time complexities are again the same. Although they are quadratic in k, the algorithm still is relatively fast compared to the exact solution analyzed below. Like the HSR algorithm, the HCR algorithm only offers the possibility of indirect index support via an index-supported quick check. In this case, the complexity of the algorithm depends on the complexity of the employed index structure.

6.5.5   Exact Matching (EM)

Time Complexity

The time complexity of the EM algorithm is the same for each of the three split strategies introduced in Section 6.3.5. This is due to the fact that all strategies need to examine the same number of subparts in the best, worst, and average case. They only do so in different order. We therefore only consider the time complexity of the EM algorithm with and without the quick check in general, without distinguishing the different split strategies.

- Best Case:
  The best case for the EM algorithm without the quick check occurs if, for each of the m query subpredicates c' in p', the algorithm finds a matching subpredicate in the first stream subpredicate c in p and c only references one of the k dimensions of the data space. Then, the algorithm only has to iterate over all m subpredicates of the query predicate and to perform a single dimension comparison for each query subpredicate. In this case, the time complexity of the EM algorithm without the quick check is linear in m and is in

$$\Omega(m)$$

  Similar to the HCR algorithm, the best case complexity of the EM algorithm remains the same when combining it with the quick check. The best case then occurs when the quick check finds a match for each query subpredicate c' in p' when comparing it to the first stream subpredicate c in p and furthermore, c references only one of the k dimensions of the data space.

- Worst Case:
  The worst case for the EM algorithm without the quick check occurs if, for each of the m query subpredicates c' in p', the algorithm iterates over all of the n stream subpredicates c in p without finding a match, each subpredicate in the stream predicate references all of the k dimensions of the data space, and the intervals defined by the stream subpredicate in each dimension are completely contained in the respective intervals defined by the query subpredicate in the corresponding dimensions. Then, the algorithm needs to split the query subpredicate into three parts during each comparison (lines 7–9 in Algorithm F.4 on page 210). Two of these three parts need to be taken into account in future comparisons. Since each of the unmatched query subpredicates is disjunctively added to the stream predicate, the number of conjunctive subpredicates in the stream predicate increases by one each time the algorithm starts to consider the next conjunctive subpredicate of the query predicate. Thus, we can estimate the number of dimension comparisons as

$$
\sum_{i=0}^{m-1}\sum_{j=0}^{n+i-1}(2k)^j\cdot k \overset{\text{geom.}}{\underset{\text{series}}{=}} \sum_{i=0}^{m-1}\frac{(2k)^{n+i}-1}{2k-1}\cdot k
$$

$$
= \frac{k}{2k-1}\cdot\sum_{i=0}^{m-1}\left((2k)^{n+i}-1\right)
$$

$$
= \frac{k}{2k-1}\cdot\left(\left((2k)^n\cdot\sum_{i=0}^{m-1}(2k)^i\right)-m\right)
$$

$$
\overset{\text{geom.}}{\underset{\text{series}}{=}} \frac{k}{2k-1}\cdot\left((2k)^n\cdot\frac{(2k)^m-1}{2k-1}-m\right)
$$

$$
\leq k\cdot(2k)^{m+n}
$$

Therefore, the worst case time complexity of the EM algorithm without the quick check is polynomial in k, exponential in m and n, and is in

$$
O\left(k\cdot(2k)^{m+n}\right)
$$

Similar to the HCR algorithm, the worst case time complexity of the EM algorithm with the quick check has to additionally take into account the worst case time complexity of the quick check algorithm. Again, the quick check is executed before the actual EM algorithm. In case the quick check does not yield a match, the normal EM algorithm is executed. Thus, the number of dimension comparisons of the quick check algorithm and the EM algorithm have to be added. This yields

$$
\sum_{i=0}^{m-1}\left((n+i)\cdot k+\sum_{j=0}^{n+i-1}(2k)^j\cdot k\right) = \sum_{i=0}^{m-1}(n+i)\cdot k+\sum_{i=0}^{m-1}\sum_{j=0}^{n+i-1}(2k)^j\cdot k
$$

$$
\leq (m\cdot n+m^2)\cdot k+k\cdot(2k)^{m+n}
$$

$$
= (m\cdot n+m^2+(2k)^{m+n})\cdot k
$$

Therefore, the worst case time complexity of the EM algorithm with the quick check is polynomial in k, exponential in m and n, and is in

$$
O\left((m\cdot n+m^2+(2k)^{m+n})\cdot k\right)
$$

- Average Case:
  The average case for the EM algorithm without the quick check occurs if, for each of the m query subpredicates c' in p', the algorithm iterates over half of the n stream subpredicates c in p before finding a match, each subpredicate in the stream predicate references half of the k dimensions of the data space, and the intervals defined by the stream subpredicate in each dimension overlap with the respective intervals defined by the query subpredicate in the corresponding dimensions. Then, the algorithm needs to split the query subpredicate into two parts during each comparison (lines 10–13 in Algorithm F.4 on page 210), one of which needs to be taken into account in future comparisons. Furthermore, we assume that half of the m query subpredicates remain unmatched and are therefore disjunctively added to the stream predicate, increasing the number of conjunctive subpredicates in the stream predicate by one for half of the query subpredicates. Therefore, assuming $k > 3$, the number of comparisons between dimensions can be estimated as

$$
\sum_{i=0}^{m-1} \sum_{j=0}^{\left\lceil \frac{n+\frac{i}{2}}{2} \right\rceil - 1} \left(\frac{k}{2}\right)^j \cdot \frac{k}{2} \overset{\text{geom.}}{\underset{\text{series}}{=}} \sum_{i=0}^{m-1} \frac{\left(\frac{k}{2}\right)^{\left\lceil \frac{n+\frac{i}{2}}{2} \right\rceil} - 1}{\frac{k}{2} - 1} \cdot \frac{k}{2}
$$

$$
= \frac{k}{k-2} \cdot \left(\left(\sum_{i=0}^{m-1} \left(\frac{k}{2}\right)^{\left\lceil \frac{n+\frac{i}{2}}{2} \right\rceil} \right) - m \right)
$$

$$
\leq \frac{k}{k-2} \cdot \left(\left(\sum_{i=0}^{m-1} \left(\frac{k}{2}\right)^{\left\lceil \frac{n}{2} \right\rceil} \cdot \left(\frac{k}{2}\right)^{\left\lceil \frac{i}{4} \right\rceil} \right) - m \right)
$$

$$
\leq \frac{k \cdot \left(\frac{k}{2}\right)^n}{k-2} \cdot \sum_{i=0}^{m-1} \left(\frac{k}{2}\right)^i
$$

$$
\overset{\text{geom.}}{\underset{\text{series}}{=}} \frac{k \cdot \left(\frac{k}{2}\right)^n}{k-2} \cdot \frac{\left(\frac{k}{2}\right)^m - 1}{\frac{k}{2} - 1}
$$

$$
\leq k \cdot \left(\frac{k}{2}\right)^{m+n}
$$

Therefore, the average case time complexity of the EM algorithm without the quick check is polynomial in k, exponential in m and n, and is in

$$
\Theta\left(k \cdot \left(\frac{k}{2}\right)^{m+n} \right)
$$

The average case complexity of the EM algorithm with the quick check is determined analogously to the worst case. For the number of dimension comparisons, this yields

$$\sum_{i=0}^{m-1}\left(\left(\frac{n+\frac{i}{2}}{2}\right)\cdot\frac{k}{2}+\sum_{j=0}^{\left\lceil\frac{n+\frac{i}{2}}{2}\right\rceil-1}\left(\frac{k}{2}\right)^j\cdot\frac{k}{2}\right)=\sum_{i=0}^{m-1}\left(\frac{n+\frac{i}{2}}{2}\right)\cdot\frac{k}{2}+\sum_{i=0}^{m-1}\sum_{j=0}^{\left\lceil\frac{n+\frac{i}{2}}{2}\right\rceil-1}\left(\frac{k}{2}\right)^j\cdot\frac{k}{2}$$

$$\leq (m\cdot n+m^2)\cdot k+k\cdot\left(\frac{k}{2}\right)^{m+n}$$

$$=\left(m\cdot n+m^2+\left(\frac{k}{2}\right)^{m+n}\right)\cdot k$$

Therefore, the average case time complexity of the EM algorithm with the quick check is polynomial in k, exponential in m and n, and is in

$$\Theta\left(\left(m\cdot n+m^2+\left(\frac{k}{2}\right)^{m+n}\right)\cdot k\right)$$

Space Complexity

The space complexity of the EM algorithm is independent of whether the algorithm is executed with or without the quick check.

- Best Case:
  The best case for all variants of the EM algorithm occurs when each subpredicate only references one of the k dimensions of the data space and no splitting of subpredicates occurs during the execution of the algorithm. Then, for each of the m query subpredicates c' in p' as well as for each of the n stream subpredicates c in p, the information for only one dimension needs to be stored. In this case, the space complexity of the EM algorithm is linear in m and n, and is in

$$\Omega(m+n)$$

- Worst Case:
  The worst case for the EM algorithm occurs when each subpredicate references all of the k dimensions of the data space and each query subpredicate c' in p' needs to be split in three parts in each dimension (lines 7–9 in Algorithm F.4 on page 210). Two of these three parts need to be stored in a queue for later matching. Thus, in the worst case, two additional conjunctive subpredicates are created during each split. Using the BFS strategy, this leads to $2k$ additional subpredicates after comparing all dimensions and to $(2k)^n$ additional subpredicates after comparing a query subpredicate c' to all n stream subpredicates c in p in the worst case. This is indicated by the hatched subparts in Figure 6.7(a). All subparts at the leaf level of the tree need to be stored in memory. Then, for each of the m query subpredicates c' in p' as well as for each of the n stream subpredicates c in p, the information for all of the k dimensions of the data space needs to be stored. This analogously applies to each of the conjunctive subpredicates that were newly created by the algorithm due to the splitting of existing query subpredicates. Thus, in this case, the space complexity of the EM algorithm is linear in m, polynomial in k, exponential in n, and is in

$$O\left((m+n+(2k)^n)\cdot k\right)$$

The DFS strategy only produces up to $(n-1) \cdot (2k-1) + 2k$ subparts during matching as indicated by the hatched subparts in Figure 6.7(b). Therefore, its worst case space complexity is linear in m and n, quadratic in k, and is in

$$O((m+n+(n-1) \cdot (2k-1) + 2k) \cdot k)$$

The MIX strategy produces up to $(n-2) \cdot (2k-1) \cdot 2k + (2k)^2$ subparts during matching as indicated by the hatched subparts in Figure 6.7(c). Therefore, its worst case space complexity is linear in m and n, cubic in k, and is in

$$O\left((m+n+(n-2) \cdot (2k-1) \cdot 2k + (2k)^2) \cdot k\right)$$

- Average Case:
  The average case for the EM algorithm occurs when each subpredicate references half of the k dimensions of the data space and half of the query subpredicates c' in p' need to be split in two parts in half of the dimensions (lines 10–13 in Algorithm F.4 on page 210). One of these two parts needs to be stored in a queue for later matching. Thus, in the average case, one additional conjunctive subpredicate is created during each split. Using the BFS strategy, this leads to $k/2$ additional subpredicates after comparing half of the dimensions and to $(k/2)^{n/2} = \sqrt{(k/2)^n}$ additional subpredicates after comparing a query subpredicate to half of the n stream subpredicates on average. Then, for each of the m query subpredicates c' in p' as well as for each of the n stream subpredicates c in p, the information for half of the k dimensions of the data space needs to be stored. This analogously applies to each of the conjunctive subpredicates that were newly created by the algorithm due to the splitting of existing query subpredicates. Thus, in this case, the space complexity of the EM algorithm is linear in m, polynomial in k, exponential in n, and is in

$$\Theta\left(\left(m+n+\sqrt{(k/2)^n}\right) \cdot \frac{k}{2}\right)$$

The DFS strategy only produces $((n-1)/2) \cdot (k/2-1) + k/2$ subparts on average during matching. Therefore, its average case space complexity is linear in m and n, quadratic in k, and is in

$$\Theta\left(\left(m+n+\frac{n-1}{2} \cdot \left(\frac{k}{2}-1\right) + \frac{k}{2}\right) \cdot \frac{k}{2}\right)$$

The MIX strategy produces $((n-2)/2) \cdot (k/2-1) \cdot (k/2) + (k/2)^2$ subparts on average during matching. Therefore, its average case space complexity is linear in m and n, cubic in k, and is in

$$\Theta\left(\left(m+n+\frac{n-2}{2} \cdot \left(\frac{k}{2}-1\right) \cdot \frac{k}{2} + \left(\frac{k}{2}\right)^2\right) \cdot \frac{k}{2}\right)$$

Summary

The EM algorithm with BFS strategy shows exponential time and space complexity in the worst and average case. Since Sun et al. (1989) have proven the general implication problem for disjunctive predicates to be NP-hard, the exponential time complexity cannot be improved substantially. However, it is possible to improve the space complexity to cubic in the number of dimensions in the data space and to linear in all other parameters using the MIX strategy instead of the BFS strategy. Using the DFS strategy even reduces the space complexity to quadratic in the number of dimensions in the data space and to linear in all other parameters. The complexity of the index-based EM algorithm depends on the complexity of the employed index structure.

6.5.6   Standard Evaluation (SE)

Time Complexity

- Best Case:
  The best case for the SE algorithm occurs when the first conjunctive subpredicate c in the predicate p to be evaluated references only one of the k dimensions of the data space and the interval defined for that dimension in c contains the value of the corresponding dimension in i. Then, only a single value to interval comparison is necessary to evaluate the predicate to true. In this case, the time complexity of the SE algorithm is constant and is in

$$\Omega(1)$$

- Worst Case:
  The worst case for the SE algorithm occurs when every conjunctive subpredicate c in the predicate p to be evaluated references all of the k dimensions of the data space but none of the subpredicates matches the data item i and the mismatch in each case is only detected after all dimensions have been considered. Then, all of the n subpredicates of predicate p and, for each subpredicate, all of the k dimensions of the data space need to be iterated and compared to the values in i. In this case, the time complexity of the SE algorithm is linear in n and k, and is in

$$O(n \cdot k)$$

- Average Case:
  The average case for the SE algorithm occurs when every conjunctive subpredicate c in the predicate p to be evaluated references half of the k dimensions of the data space, a match is found after considering half of the n subpredicates of predicate p, and mismatches are detected on average after considering half of the dimensions referenced in the corresponding subpredicate. Then, half of the n subpredicates of predicate p and, for each subpredicate, one quarter of the k dimensions of the data space need to be iterated and compared to the values in i. In this case, the time complexity of the SE algorithm is linear in n and k, and is in

$$\Theta\left(\frac{n}{2} \cdot \frac{k}{4}\right) = \Theta(n \cdot k)$$

Space Complexity

- Best Case:
  The best case for the SE algorithm occurs when each conjunctive subpredicate c in the predicate p to be evaluated references only one of the k dimensions of the data space. Additionally, the k values of the data item i need to be stored. In this case, the space complexity of the SE algorithm is linear in n and k, and is in

$$\Omega(n+k)$$

- Worst Case:

  The worst case for the SE algoritm occurs when each conjunctive subpredicate c in the predicate p to be evaluated references all of the k dimensions of the data space. Additionally, the k values of the data item i need to be stored. In this case, the space complexity of the SE algorithm is again linear in n and k, and is in

$$O(n \cdot k + k) = O((n+1) \cdot k)$$

- Average Case:

  The average case for the SE algorithm occurs when each conjunctive subpredicate c in the predicate p to be evaluated references half of the k dimensions of the data space. Additionally, the k values of the data item i need to be stored. In this case, the space complexity of the SE algorithm is also linear in n and k, and is in

$$\Theta\left(n \cdot \frac{k}{2} + k\right) = \Theta\left(\left(\frac{n}{2}+1\right) \cdot k\right)$$

Summary

The SE algorithm shows linear time and space complexity in the worst and average case. This causes the evaluation to slow down for large numbers of subpredicates n and for large numbers of dimensions k. We introduced the index-based evaluation strategy to alleviate this problem.

6.5.7   Index-based Evaluation (IE)

The best case, worst case, and average case time and space complexities of the index-based evaluation depend on the respective complexities of the employed index structure.

6.5.8   Summary

Tables 6.3 and 6.4 summarize the time complexities and the space complexities of the predicate matching algorithms, respectively. Since the time complexity of the EM algorithm is the same for all three split strategies, Table 6.3 shows the time complexity only once for the generic EM algorithm. Also, in Table 6.4, the space complexities of the algorithms with the quick check are omitted since they are the same as for the corresponding algorithms without the quick check.

Tables 6.5 and 6.6 summarize the time complexities and the space complexities of the predicate evaluation algorithms, respectively. In Table 6.5, $I_\Omega^{\text{point}}(n,k)$, $I_\Theta^{\text{point}}(n,k)$, and $I_O^{\text{point}}(n,k)$ denote the best case, average case, and worst case time complexity of a point containment query on the corresponding index structure. Analogously, in Table 6.6, $I_\Omega^{\text{space}}(n,k)$, $I_\Theta^{\text{space}}(n,k)$, and $I_O^{\text{space}}(n,k)$ denote the best case, average case, and worst case space complexity of the corresponding index structure. In addition to the index, the values of the data item i in the k dimensions need to be stored.

6.6   Performance Evaluation

This section presents our experimental evaluation results. First, we describe the implementation of the algorithms presented in this chapter and the evaluation setting. Second, we show some comparative evaluation results for predicate matching and predicate evaluation.

		TIME COMPLEXITY	
	Best Case	Worst Case	Average Case
QC	$\Omega(1)$	$O(n \cdot k)$	$\Theta(n \cdot k)$
HSR	$\Omega(m)$	$O(m)$	$\Theta(m)$
HSR+QC	$\Omega(m)$	$O\left((m \cdot n + m^2) \cdot k\right)$	$\Theta\left((m \cdot n + m^2) \cdot k\right)$
HCR	$\Omega(m)$	$O\left(m \cdot n \cdot k^2\right)$	$\Theta\left(m \cdot n \cdot k^2\right)$
HCR+QC	$\Omega(m)$	$O\left(m \cdot n \cdot k^2\right)$	$\Theta\left(m \cdot n \cdot k^2\right)$
EM	$\Omega(m)$	$O\left(k \cdot (2k)^{m+n}\right)$	$\Theta\left(k \cdot (k/2)^{m+n}\right)$
EM+QC	$\Omega(m)$	$O\left((m \cdot n + m^2 + (2k)^{m+n}) \cdot k\right)$	$\Theta\left((m \cdot n + m^2 + (k/2)^{m+n}) \cdot k\right)$

Table 6.3: Time complexities of predicate matching algorithms

		SPACE COMPLEXITY	
	Best Case	Worst Case	
QC	$\Omega(n+1)$	$O((n+1) \cdot k)$	
HSR	$\Omega(m+n)$	$O((m+n) \cdot k)$	
HCR	$\Omega(m+n)$	$O((m+n) \cdot k)$	
EM-BFS	$\Omega(m+n)$	$O((m+n+(2k)^n) \cdot k)$	
EM-DFS	$\Omega(m+n)$	$O((m+n+(n-1) \cdot (2k-1) + 2k) \cdot k)$	
EM-MIX	$\Omega(m+n)$	$O\left((m+n+(n-2) \cdot (2k-1) \cdot 2k + (2k)^2) \cdot k\right)$	

	SPACE COMPLEXITY
	Average Case
QC	$\Theta((n+1) \cdot k/2)$
HSR	$\Theta((m+n) \cdot k/2)$
HCR	$\Theta((m+n) \cdot k/2)$
EM-BFS	$\Theta\left(\left(m+n+\sqrt{(k/2)^n}\right) \cdot (k/2)\right)$
EM-DFS	$\Theta((m+n+((n-1)/2) \cdot ((k/2)-1) + (k/2)) \cdot (k/2))$
EM-MIX	$\Theta\left((m+n+((n-2)/2) \cdot ((k/2)-1) \cdot (k/2) + (k/2)^2) \cdot (k/2)\right)$

Table 6.4: Space complexities of predicate matching algorithms

6.6.1 Implementation and Setting

We have implemented all algorithms presented in this chapter using Java 5. We use double values to represent constants in atomic predicates in our implementation. The internal representation of a disjunctive predicate contains a collection of conjunctive subpredicates. The entries in this collection are automatically kept sorted in decreasing order in terms of the volume of the hyperrectangle representing the predicate in multi-dimensional space. In our terminology, if predicates have unbounded interval ends, a predicate is "smaller" than another one if it has less unbounded interval ends or an equal number of unbounded interval ends and less volume when restricting the volume computation to the finite dimensions. The purpose of the sorting is to compare larger subpredicates first when iterating the subpredicate list of a disjunctive predicate. This helps to find matches earlier or to match large parts of a subpredicate early on in order to potentially reduce the number of necessary matching steps. Also, the intervals for each dimension within a conjunctive predicate are kept sorted in increasing order according to interval length. Considering shorter intervals first increases the probability of comparing two disjoint intervals early on. With the exception of the HCR algorithm, we can stop the comparison with

	TIME COMPLEXITY		
	Best Case	Worst Case	Average Case
SE	$\Omega(1)$	$O(n \cdot k)$	$\Theta(n \cdot k)$
IE	$\Omega(I_{\Omega}^{\text{point}}(n,k))$	$O(I_{O}^{\text{point}}(n,k))$	$\Theta(I_{\Theta}^{\text{point}}(n,k))$

Table 6.5: Time complexities of predicate evaluation algorithms

	SPACE COMPLEXITY		
	Best Case	Worst Case	Average Case
SE	$\Omega(n+k)$	$O((n+1) \cdot k)$	$\Theta((n/2+1) \cdot k)$
IE	$\Omega(I_{\Omega}^{\text{space}}(n,k)+k)$	$O(I_{O}^{\text{space}}(n,k)+k)$	$\Theta(I_{\Theta}^{\text{space}}(n,k)+k)$

Table 6.6: Space complexities of predicate evaluation algorithms

the current subpredicate when encountering disjoint intervals and continue with the next sub-predicate without having to consider the remaining dimensions. These optimizations are used for all the matching and evaluation algorithms throughout.

A generic interface allows the integration and usage of various index structures in our implementation. For each index, the interface is implemented by an adapter class that delegates the interface method calls to the appropriate method calls of the underlying index structure and performs any necessary conversions. We have compared various implementations of R-tree variants for our evaluation. For the evaluation of the matching algorithms, we have decided to use an efficient lightweight main memory implementation of a standard R-tree with quadratic split strategy [Guttman (1984)]. This specific implementation turned out to be the fastest of all the index structures that we have tested for predicate matching and predicate evaluation. For the predicate evaluation tests, however, we have switched to a more generic and flexible main memory implementation of an R*-tree [van den Bercken et al. (2001)]. Although this specific implementation of the R*-tree was slightly slower in our tests than the lightweight R-tree implementation, it already supports our short-circuit evaluation optimization without having to edit the index source code. We have also repeated the evaluation of the matching algorithms using this R*-tree implementation. In our tests, all index structures use a minimum node capacity of 5 and a maximum node capacity of 10.

All tests ran on a single server blade with two 2.8 GHz Intel Xeon processors (only one of which was used), 4 GB of main memory, and SuSE Linux Enterprise Server 9.

6.6.2 Predicate Matching

For the evaluation of the predicate matching algorithms, we randomly generated a set of query predicates and a set of stream predicates by appropriately setting the number of dimensions and subpredicates, and by randomly choosing the constant values for the interval bounds of each dimension in each subpredicate. The values were chosen from a list of 21 distinct values between 0 and 100 using a normal distribution for query predicates and a uniform distribution for stream predicates. Each subpredicate defines a finite interval in each dimension of the data space. For the tests shown in this section, we used a set of 60 query predicates that were matched against a set of 20 stream predicates. We matched each query predicate against each stream predicate, i. e., 1200 predicate pairs were matched in total. Figures 6.9 to 6.11 show the average matching time per predicate pair in milliseconds for the heuristics with simple relaxation (HSR+QC), the heuristics with complex relaxation (HCR+QC), and the exact matching algorithm with breadth-first split strategy without index support (EM+QC) as well as with index support (EM+QC+I). All algorithms use the quick check (QC). Note that the matching time is scaled logarithmically on each of the three diagrams. If nothing else is stated, the default settings used for the tests were 6 dimensions, 2 subpredicates per query predicate, and 20 subpredicates per stream predicate. We use relatively low values for the numbers of dimensions and subpredicates in the matching tests to be able to include the EM approach in the comparison. Due to its exponential complexity, the EM approach is not feasible for large problem sizes. Note that matching time is a part of query compilation time in our DSMS scenario. It is therefore less important if dealing with long-running continuous queries.

In Figure 6.9, we varied the number of distinct dimensions in the data space that are referenced in each predicate. We can clearly see that the matching time of the EM algorithm without index support grows exponentially with an increasing number of dimensions. Using the index approach significantly reduces matching time and can therefore keep the approach feasible for larger problem sizes. The index-supported EM approach does not even differ that much from the HCR approach which has polynomial complexity and whose running time increases linearly. The matching time of the HSR approach also increases linearly but is generally lower than for the other algorithms since less complex computations need to be performed.

Figures 6.10 and 6.11 show the effects of a varying number of subpredicates in the query and the stream predicate, respectively. Again, the index-based version of the EM algorithm clearly outperforms the version without index and can compete roughly with the HCR approach. In each case, the performance gain achieved through multi-dimensional indexing is about two orders of magnitude.

We repeated the above tests with predicates containing infinite intervals. The predicates were generated by randomly choosing the finite dimensions of the data space for each subpredicate using a uniform distribution. The remaining dimensions were not referenced by the subpredicate and were therefore unbounded. In this setting, the performance gain of the index was about an order of magnitude less. However, the index-based EM algorithm was still superior to the version without an index, especially for larger numbers of dimensions and subpredicates.

We furthermore repeated the matching tests using the R*-tree index that we also used for the predicate evaluation tests further below instead of the lightweight R-tree index implementation. Also, we included the exact matching algorithms with depth-first (EM-DFS) and mixed split strategy (EM-MIX) in addition to the exact matching algorithm with breadth-first split strategy (EM-BFS). The results shown in Figures 6.12 to 6.14 indicate that the R*-tree is a little bit slower in our tests than the R-tree index of the previous tests. Also, with growing number of dimensions and subpredicates in the query and the stream predicates, the EM-DFS and EM-MIX algorithm variants increasingly outperform the EM-BFS variant without as well as with index support. The difference in matching time between the EM-DFS and EM-MIX variants is marginal in our tests. We did not investigate index support for the EM-DFS and EM-MIX variants in detail. But we expect that an index could also improve the performance of these algorithm variants. However, the achievable performance improvements through indexing are supposed to be smaller than for the EM-BFS variant since the EM-DFS and EM-MIX algorithms already avoid lots of unnecessary work compared to the EM-BFS algorithm. In fact, in extreme cases, index overhead might even exceed index benefits.

An interesting observation from Figure 6.12 is that the EM-BFS algorithm with index support and the EM-DFS and EM-MIX algorithm variants become faster when increasing the number of dimensions referenced in each predicate from 5 to 6. Further, Figures 6.12 to 6.14 show

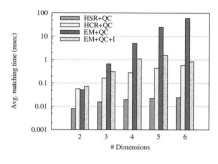

Figure 6.9: Varying number of dimensions   **Figure 6.10:** Varying query predicate size

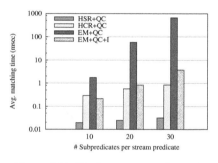

Figure 6.11: Varying stream predicate size   **Figure 6.12:** Varying number of dimensions

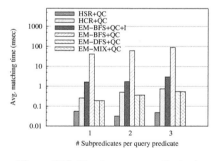

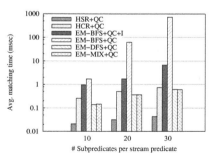

Figure 6.13: Varying query predicate size   **Figure 6.14:** Varying stream predicate size

that the EM-DFS and EM-MIX algorithm variants are actually faster than the HCR algorithm if the number of dimensions referenced in the predicates is greater than 4. Note that the tests shown in Figures 6.13 and 6.14 use the default value of 6 dimensions per predicate. These results are most likely due to the fact that an increasing number of dimensions also increases the probability of encountering disjoint intervals when comparing the extents of two conjunctive

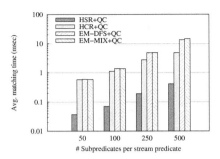

Figure 6.15: Matching large predicates

subpredicates in the various dimensions. This reduces the total number of matching predicates and enables the EM algorithm variants to stop the comparison early, thus preventing the corresponding query subpredicate from being split. In contrast, the HCR algorithm does not benefit from encountering disjoint intervals since it always needs to consider each dimension in each stream subpredicate to obtain the desired result if the predicates under consideration do not match without relaxation.

In another test, we investigated how the matching algorithms perform for larger predicates, i. e., stream predicates with a larger number of subpredicates. Figure 6.15 shows the results. The EM-BFS algorithm variant is missing in the figure since it was not able to process stream predicates with more than 30 subpredicates without running out of main memory. As the figure shows, the performance of the EM-DFS and EM-MIX algorithm variants is comparable to that of the HCR algorithm for up to 50 subpredicates in the stream predicate. For 500 subpredicates, HCR is about a factor of 3 faster than the exact matching variants.

To illustrate the differences in predicate relaxation between the matching algorithms, we randomly generated a predicate with 6 dimensions and 20 subpredicates representing a stream predicate. We also generated 4 predicates with 6 dimensions and 2 subpredicates each, which represent query predicates. We generated the predicates as described above except that the values for the interval bounds were chosen among 6 distinct values between 0 and 100 for the query predicates and among 4 distinct values for the stream predicate. We then matched the stream predicate with the first query predicate to obtain predicate p_A. Predicate p_A was then matched with the second query predicate to obtain predicate p_B. Predicate p_B was again matched with the third query predicate to obtain predicate p_C which was in turn matched with the fourth query predicate to obtain predicate p_D. Matching was performed with the HSR, the HSR+QC, the HCR, and the EM algorithms. Note that the use of the quick check for HCR and EM and the use of index-based matching for all algorithms has no influence on the structure of the resulting predicates. Predicates p_A to p_D were then evaluated using one million uniformly distributed data items. Table 6.7 shows the results for the observed selectivities of all four predicates depending on the matching algorithm that produced them. As expected, HSR, HSR+QC, and EM yield predicates with identical selectivities because these algorithms produce exact predicates that do not cause any false drops. Also, we can see that predicates p_A and p_C need to be relaxed to obtain predicates p_B and p_D, respectively. The HCR algorithm relaxes the predicate during each matching step and yields higher selectivity values which shows that this algorithm causes false drops. However, the increase in selectivity induced by the false drops

	p_A	p_B	p_C	p_D
HSR	66.31	66.37	66.37	66.44
HSR+QC	66.31	66.37	66.37	66.44
HCR	66.31	67.93	69.26	69.82
EM	66.31	66.37	66.37	66.44

Table 6.7: Selectivities for combined test (%)

never exceeds 3.5%. This indicates that the approximation made by the HCR algorithm stays close to the exact solution in this test.

The difference between the various matching algorithms in the ability to detect matching predicates that do not need to be relaxed is illustrated by the following test. Using a randomly generated set of 60 query and 20 stream predicates with 3 possibly unbounded dimensions, 3 subpredicates per query predicate, and 30 subpredicates per stream predicate, the EM algorithm successfully matched 933 out of the 1200 predicate pairs without relaxation. The remaining algorithms, with the exception of the HSR algorithm without QC, detected only 660 matching pairs. This means that the heuristics missed 273 matches in this example. The HSR algorithm without QC never detects any matches at all.

Summarizing, we can state that the EM algorithm is applicable in practice as long as the problem size, i.e., the number of dimensions in the data space and the number of subpredicates in the stream predicate, is reasonably low. However, performance quickly degrades with increasing problem size. This effect can be alleviated by combining the EM algorithm with a multi-dimensional index on the subpredicates of the stream predicate. Since the DFS and MIX split strategies outperform the BFS split strategy by far in all tests and are applicable for larger problem sizes due to the profoundly reduced memory consumption, they are the preferred choice. For very large problem sizes, the exponential time complexity of the EM algorithm becomes prohibitive. In this case, we need to use the heuristics instead. Both heuristics, HSR as well as HCR, perform and scale well with increasing problem size. Also, the increase in predicate selectivity induced by the approximation made when using HCR proves to be relatively low in our tests.

6.6.3 Predicate Evaluation

In contrast to predicate matching time, predicate evaluation time is performance critical in our DSMS scenario. We carried out the predicate evaluation tests by evaluating a given predicate against one million randomly generated data items with values distributed uniformly between 0 and 100 for each dimension. We also again randomly generated predicates using a certain number of subpredicates for disjunctively covering an area of the data space. We placed the remaining subpredicates in the middle of that area using a normal distribution for placing the center point of each subpredicate. Since data items are distributed uniformly in the data space, the percentage of the data space covered by the predicate yields the predicate's selectivity. Unless otherwise stated, all parameters take default values which are 3 dimensions, 100 subpredicates in the predicate to be evaluated, and a predicate selectivity of 1%. We choose a larger number of subpredicates for the evaluation benchmark than for the matching benchmark since we expect many subpredicates to be introduced by predicate relaxation in the EM and especially the HSR matching approaches. In our tests, predicates have an overlap of 50%. We achieve this by using half of the subpredicates for disjunctively covering the area of the data space needed to obtain

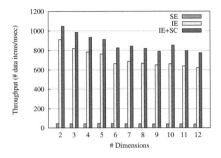

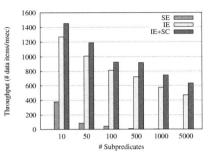

Figure 6.16: Varying number of dimensions   **Figure 6.17:** Varying predicate size

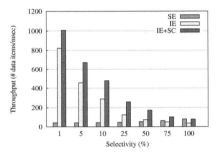

Figure 6.18: Varying predicate selectivity

the desired selectivity and by placing the remaining subpredicates within this area as described above. Figures 6.16 to 6.18 show the throughput of predicate evaluation in data items per millisecond for the standard evaluation (SE), the index-based evaluation (IE), and the index-based evaluation with short-circuit optimization (IE+SC).

Figure 6.16 shows the throughput for a varying number of dimensions in the data space. Clearly, index-based evaluation is superior for the given settings. Short-circuiting the evaluation yields an additional performance gain of about 20%. For all three algorithms, throughput decreases only moderately for an increasing number of dimensions.

In Figure 6.17, we vary the number of subpredicates in the predicate to be evaluated. Again, index-based evaluation is clearly superior to standard evaluation and the performance of the index-based approach degrades slower with an increasing number of subpredicates than the performance of the standard approach. For 5000 subpredicates, the index-based approach is still better than the standard evaluation for 10 subpredicates.

In another test, we varied the selectivity of the predicate to be evaluated between 1%, meaning that only one in a hundred data items satisfies the predicate, and 100%, which means that all data items satisfy the predicate. Figure 6.18 shows the results. Obviously, the lower the selectivity, the better the index-based solutions perform. In contrast, the standard evaluation performs better for higher selectivities. This is due to the fact that the index can identify a non-qualifying data item early on, e. g., when comparing it to the root of the index tree if the data

SELECTIVITY	$\sigma = 10\%$					$\sigma = 75\%$				
OVERLAP	0%	15%	25%	30%	50%	0%	15%	25%	30%	50%
SE	100	100	100	100	100	100	100	100	100	100
IE	644	690	670	633	655	74	85	89	84	79
IE+SC	1215	1120	1114	1015	1088	160	156	185	181	160

Table 6.8: Relative throughput for varying predicate overlap (%)

item is situated outside the root area of the index. In contrast, the evaluation needs to descend to the leaves of the tree if the data item qualifies. For the standard evaluation, the situation is vice versa. A qualifying data item can be identified early on because as soon as the data item is contained within the current subpredicate, no further comparisons with the remaining subpredicates are necessary. But if a data item does not qualify, all subpredicates need to be considered in order to be sure that no matching subpredicate exists.

We can roughly expect from Figure 6.18 that for our default settings and for 50% subpredicate overlap, standard evaluation is better than index-based evaluation for selectivity values above about 70% and better than index-based evaluation with short-circuit optimization for selectivity values above about 90%. With less overlap between subpredicates, the situation changes in favor of the index-based solutions. For overlap ratios of up to 40%, the index-based evaluation with short-circuit optimization was superior for all selectivities in our tests when using default values for the other parameters. Higher overlap reduces the benefit of the index-based solutions as more overlap means that more paths need to be traversed in the tree. This effect is worse for the index-based evaluation without short-circuit optimization. However, selectivities are expected to be low in practice since users are mostly interested in very specific parts of the available information. Also, the number of dimensions in our DSMS scenario is supposed to be moderate since, e. g., sensor data streams rarely contain more than about 10 to 20 dimensions per data item. Further, queries often only reference a small subset of the available dimensions. In contrast, the number of subpredicates can become large (in the order of many thousand) if many queries are registered. This is due to the effects of data stream widening, especially if the HSR approach is used.

Table 6.8 shows the relative throughput of the three predicate evaluation algorithms for varying subpredicate overlap ratios of the evaluated predicate with low ($\sigma = 10\%$) and high ($\sigma = 75\%$) selectivities. The baseline is the throughput of the standard evaluation (SE) which is set to 100% in each case. For low selectivity values, the index-based evaluation (IE) and the index-based evaluation with short-circuit optimization yield a performance gain of about a factor of 6 and a factor of 11, respectively. For high selectivity values, the index-based evaluation is already inferior to the standard evaluation. The index-based evaluation with short-circuit optimization is however still superior by about 55% to 85%. This shows that the short-circuit optimization yields a major improvement over the non-optimized index approach and makes index use beneficial even for high predicate overlap ratios and selectivity values.

The throughput of the individual algorithms does not show a stable trend for increasing overlap ratios in Table 6.8. This is due to the fact that we have randomly generated a new predicate for each overlap ratio. Therefore, the characteristics of the various predicates cannot be fully controlled. However, variations are similar in relation for all three algorithms.

Summarizing, the index-based evaluation is beneficial especially for predicates with many subpredicates and realistically low selectivity values. It yields performance gains of up to three orders of magnitude for predicates with 50% overlap and even more if overlap is less. The tests also show that the short-circuit optimization alleviates the disadvantages of multi-dimensional index structures such as the R-tree when indexing highly overlapping regions.

6.7   Related Work

Efficient handling of predicates has been a research topic for many years. Rosenkrantz and Hunt (1980) have already examined the handling of conjunctive predicates in the early 1980s. They deal with problems such as predicate representation and predicate minimization as well as with equivalence and satisfiability checking. Sun et al. (1989) address implication checking for conjunctive predicates. Guo et al. (1996) conducted detailed studies for solving satisfiability, implication, and equivalence problems for conjunctive predicates concerning different domains and operator sets. Denny and Franklin (2005) introduce predicate result range caching for speeding up the evaluation of continuous queries. Instead of merely memorizing the predicate evaluation results of single input values, which may be ineffective if values are diverse and drawn from a large domain, predicate result range caching computes and caches predicate evaluation results for ranges of input values. This allows for more effective cache usage and saves potentially expensive predicate evaluations. Predicate result range caching is also in a sense related to stream sharing. However, instead of sharing result streams, range caching shares predicate evaluation results for ranges of input values. Furthermore, since predicate result range caching also performs range expansion to increase the value ranges for which the predicate evaluation result is known, range caching is also somehow related to data stream widening. However, all of the above works are restricted to conjunctive predicates.

Predicate indexing has been and still is an active research area, especially in the domains of active databases [Widom and Ceri (1996)] and publish&subscribe systems such as Le Subscribe [Fabret et al. (2001)] and MDV [Keidl et al. (2002)]. Two index structures that have been proposed for predicate indexing in active databases are the IBS-tree [Hanson et al. (1990)] and interval skip lists [Hanson and Johnson (1996)]. These are one-dimensional index structures for indexing a set of independent intervals on one attribute. Another approach for indexing a set of independent one-dimensional intervals are virtual construct intervals (VCIs) [Wu et al. (2004b)]. There also exists a two-dimensional variant, the virtual construct rectangles (VCRs) [Wu et al. (2004a)], for indexing a set of independent two-dimensional intervals. In contrast, we propose using a multi-dimensional index structure for indexing a set of multi-dimensional conjunctive predicates that are all part of the disjunctive normal form of the same disjunctive predicate. Wang et al. (2004) study multi-dimensional predicate indexing for event filtering in publish&subscribe systems using the UB-tree as an index structure. Their approach accordingly transforms the dimensions using a space filling curve to map the multi-dimensional universe to a one-dimensional space. Further, Enderle et al. (2005) have examined index support for the evaluation of queries over data sets containing interval-valued attributes.

There are only few works on predicate handling for disjunctive predicates in the database field. These approaches deal with the efficient evaluation of disjunctive predicates by merging disjuncts [Muralikrishna and DeWitt (1988)] or by using a special form of relational algebra translation [Bry (1989)]. Other work focuses on bypassing the evaluation of expensive predicate terms if possible [Claussen et al. (2000); Kemper et al. (1994)] and on union pushdown techniques for optimizing the processing of disjunctive predicates [Chang and Lee (1997)]. Hellerstein and Stonebraker (1993) also consider disjunctive predicates in their work on optimizing query evaluation by appropriately moving expensive predicates in the query plan.

Multi-dimensional indexing has originally been motivated by the needs of spatial databases.

One of the most well-known spatial index structures is the R-tree introduced by Guttman (1984). It uses minimum bounding boxes to index spatial objects and stores multi-dimensional rectangles such as our conjunctive subpredicates without any further transformation or clipping. The R*-tree by Beckmann et al. (1990) is an advanced version of the R-tree aiming at improved performance by reducing the area, margin, and overlap of the rectangles stored in the index. These goals are achieved by employing a modified insertion strategy that uses a forced reinsert policy. Overlap between index regions is known to be responsible for performance degradation in an R-tree during a search due to the necessity of traversing all paths covering or intersecting the searched data point or region. To completely eliminate any overlap between index regions, Sellis et al. (1987) developed the R^+-tree which uses clipping to distribute non-overlapping parts of rectangles over different index regions. While the problem of overlapping regions is thus avoided, the clipping approach may lead to a high fragmentation of indexed regions. The TV-tree of Lin et al. (1994) indexes high-dimensional data by dynamically choosing an appropriate subset of dimensions for indexing on each index level. A similar indexing approach could be beneficial in our setting. It could be used to dynamically adapt the index to a changing set of dimensions referenced in the indexed predicate during predicate relaxation. Investigating such advanced predicate indexing approaches is an interesting aspect for future work. Finally, Gaede and Günther (1998) have published an extensive survey on multi-dimensional access methods including a classification and comparative studies.

6.8 Summary

In this chapter, we have presented various methods for matching and evaluating interval-based disjunctive predicates. Matching involves deciding whether a predicate implies another and, if this is not the case, how the other predicate can be altered in order for the implication to become valid. We have concentrated on predicates in disjunctive normal form consisting of conjunctive subpredicates that form multi-dimensional hyperrectangles with edges parallel to the coordinate axes in the data space. The approach can also be used as an approximation for more complex shaped predicates. This affords a non-trivial postprocessing step that we do not elaborate on in this thesis. We have introduced two heuristics that can be executed efficiently but either cause the number of subpredicates of a disjunctive predicate to increase or deliver only approximate results. We have further shown an exact solution that is applicable for small input sizes, i. e., small numbers of dimensions and subpredicates. Achieving high throughput during predicate evaluation is a major goal in most application scenarios. We therefore have further dealt with the evaluation of disjunctive predicates and examined the use of multi-dimensional indexing for speeding up predicate matching and predicate evaluation. We have implemented and evaluated all our algorithms in a comparative experimental study asserting the effectiveness of the index-based approach which yields a performance gain of up to several orders of magnitude compared to the corresponding solution without indexing.

There are numerous opportunities for future work. First, the applicability and efficiency of other multi-dimensional index structures in the context of predicate matching and predicate evaluation could be examined. Second, implementing a specialized index structure that is based on existing index techniques but specifically fits the needs of indexing disjunctive predicates is an interesting approach. In this course, the functionality of predicate matching could be fully or partially integrated into the index itself.

CHAPTER 7

Conclusion and Outlook

Data streams constitute a relatively new paradigm for data management and data processing. Despite its novelty, this paradigm forms a natural way of modelling actual data in many application scenarios, e. g., in sensor networks or in scientific experiments and observations. In many of these application domains and especially in e-science, cooperative nodes for delivering, processing, and requesting streaming data are often—also geographically—distributed over various administrative domains. We target such application scenarios with our StreamGlobe system which constitutes a model as well as a prototype implementation of a distributed data stream management system (DSMS) based on techniques known from P2P systems and Grid computing. An astrophysical flavor of StreamGlobe, called StarGlobe, augments StreamGlobe with user-defined operators from the astrophysics domain and proves that stream-based processing including parallelization and early filtering is a valuable computing approach for actual astrophysical e-science workflows.

In DSMSs in general and in distributed DSMSs in particular, multi-query optimization offers huge optimization potentials. This is due to the fact that long-running continuous queries enable larger amortized optimization benefits in terms of computational load and network traffic than short-lived one-time queries known from traditional database management systems (DBMSs). Data stream sharing is an optimization technique that aims at reducing computational load on peers and network traffic on network connections between peers in a distributed DSMS such as StreamGlobe. The optimization employs in-network query processing and multi-subscription optimization to achieve these goals. Using a cost model to generate query plans that share result data streams of previously registered queries, multi-subscription optimization avoids redundant processing and transfer of data streams in the network. Additionally, in-network query processing increases the flexibility of the system by allowing any device to register arbitrarily complex queries and by delegating query processing to the super-peers in the backbone network. Further, in-network query processing enables load balancing and the reduction of network traffic by means of early filtering and early aggregation. Data stream sharing shows significantly improved performance in our experiments compared to traditional distributed query processing techniques such as data shipping and query shipping.

We have further improved data stream sharing by introducing data stream widening. Relaxing selection predicates, projection operators, and data window definitions for aggregates or joins can greatly improve the possibilities for sharing the result data streams of previously registered queries in the network. Furthermore, data stream widening makes optimization quality more independent from actual query characteristics and the query registration sequence. We have introduced an abstract property tree (APT) and an abstract property forest (APF) representation of queries and data streams. APTs enable the matching and merging of queries and data in the context of data stream sharing and data stream widening for queries with a single input stream. APFs provide the same possibilities for queries with multiple input streams. Formal inference rules and query templates describe the process of translating a query into the internal APT or APF representation and vice versa. Experiments using our StreamGlobe prototype implementation indicate that data stream widening further improves the effectiveness and applicability of data stream sharing.

Finally, we have investigated in detail possible approaches for matching, relaxing, and evaluating disjunctive predicates that may occur in user queries or result from data stream widening. For solving the matching problem, we have described and compared two heuristics and an exact solution that is, however, only applicable for reasonably small problem sizes due to its exponential complexity. Furthermore, we have investigated possible improvements to predicate matching and predicate evaluation through multi-dimensional indexing. We analyzed the complexities of the proposed matching and evaluation algorithms. An extensive comparative performance evaluation shows how the algorithms relate to each other and reveals the benefits of speeding up predicate matching and predicate evaluation using multi-dimensional indexing.

The techniques presented in this thesis form the basis of a network-aware optimizer for continuous queries over streaming data in a distributed DSMS. There are several worthwile directions for extending this work. Among the most important ones are the following:

- In an architectural sense, it would be interesting to investigate the hierarchical network organization proposed in Section 2.3.6 in more detail, e. g., with respect to the determination of optimal subnet sizes. Another aspect is the dynamic selection of speaker-peers and the dynamic growth or shrinkage of subnets in environments where super-peers may dynamically join or leave the network and in case of node failures.

- The WXQuery language introduced in Section 4.3 offers possibilities for further language extensions. One issue would be the introduction of a general `let` expression similar to the `let` expression in standard XQuery. Such extensions need to be investigated under the light of their potential implications for the internal query and stream representation and the matching process in the context of data stream sharing and data stream widening.

- An important aspect concerning queries with multiple input streams is the question of optimal network-aware operator placement. While previous work in this direction exists in the field of distributed databases [Kossmann (2000)] as well as in the area of data stream processing [Pietzuch et al. (2006); Srivastava et al. (2005)], the applicability of such solutions in the context of network-aware optimization in distributed DSMSs still needs to be evaluated.

- Data stream widening as introduced in Chapter 5 already introduces increased dynamics into the data stream sharing optimization process. Instead of only considering streams for reuse that are available at the time of optimization as in Chapter 4, widening allows to dynamically change the current network state. This also affects the query evaluation plans of previously registered queries and increases the possibilities for sharing preprocessed streams. Yet, the incremental optimization and integration of newly arriving queries might lead to a suboptimal global state of the distributed DSMS over time. Periodic or event-based reoptimization can help to alleviate this problem. Since global reoptimization in large-scale systems is prohibitively expensive, reoptimization should be combined with a hierarchical network organization. This allows for the feasible independent reoptimization of smaller individual subnets.

- Eventually, dynamic plan migration for distributed query evaluation plans is a topic of major importance in the context of data stream widening. Previous solutions to the dynamic plan migration problem [Krämer et al. (2006); Yang et al. (2007); Zhu et al. (2004)] focus on migrating a logical algebra operator plan to a semantically equivalent plan if the original plan has become suboptimal during query processing due to changing conditions such as stream rates or operator selectivities. In contrast, data stream widening requires migrating existing plans to widened plans that result from widening-enabled optimization. This makes the migration problem potentially more difficult. Additional difficulties arise from the fact that query plans are distributed in StreamGlobe and that existing dependencies that share the results of the migrated plan must be preserved. Research in this direction needs to investigate whether existing methods can be applied to the new problem—possibly with some changes or extensions—or whether new solutions need to be developed.

Altogether, these topics constitute many interesting future research directions in both, data stream management in general as well as network-aware continuous query optimization in distributed DSMSs in particular.

APPENDIX A

StreamGlobe Client Interface

A.1 Example Scenario

A StreamGlobe scenario is an XML document describing the network topology and the streams and queries to be registered in the system. The StreamGlobe prototype provides a client for reading and executing such a scenario description. The following example scenario reflects the example network of Figure 4.1 on page 38.

```xml
<?xml version="1.0" encoding="UTF-8"?>
<scenario name="example"
          xmlns:xsi="http://www.w3.org/2001/XMLSchema-instance"
          xmlns="http://www-db.in.tum.de/research/projects/
              StreamGlobe/scenario">

  <statistix dbPath="${user.home}/statistiX" reportType="file"/>

  <graph>
    <vertex vid="0" label="000"/>
    <vertex vid="1" label="001"/>
    <vertex vid="2" label="010"/>
    <vertex vid="3" label="011"/>
    <vertex vid="4" label="100"/>
    <vertex vid="5" label="101"/>
    <vertex vid="6" label="110"/>
    <vertex vid="7" label="111"/>
    <edge source="0" target="1"/>
    <edge source="0" target="2"/>
    <edge source="0" target="4"/>
    <edge source="1" target="3"/>
    <edge source="1" target="5"/>
    <edge source="2" target="3"/>
```

```
    <edge source="2" target="6"/>
    <edge source="3" target="7"/>
    <edge source="4" target="5"/>
    <edge source="4" target="6"/>
    <edge source="5" target="7"/>
    <edge source="6" target="7"/>
  </graph>

  <streams>
    <kindDefinition>
      <kind name="file" class="streamglobe.client.p2p.
        FileContentServer"/>
    </kindDefinition>
    <stream sid="photons" type="file">
      <dtd filename="/home/strglobe/schema/vela.dtd"/>
      <param name="stream.filename">
        /home/strglobe/data/vela.xml
      </param>
      <param name="stream.server.port">
        9009
      </param>
      <param name="stream.sleep.time">
        100
      </param>
    </stream>
  </streams>

  <queries>
    <query qid="1">
      <![CDATA[
        <photons>
        {
          for $p in stream("photons")/photons/photon
          where $p/coord/cel/ra >= 120.0
            and $p/coord/cel/ra <= 138.0
            and $p/coord/cel/dec >= -49.0
            and $p/coord/cel/dec <= -40.0
          return
            <vela>
              {$p/coord/cel/ra} {$p/coord/cel/dec}
              {$p/phc} {$p/en} {$p/det_time}
            </vela>
        }
        </photons>
      ]]>
    </query>
    <query qid="2">
      <![CDATA[
        <photons>
        {
```

```
          for $p in stream("photons")/photons/photon
          where $p/en >= 1.3
            and $p/coord/cel/ra >= 130.5
            and $p/coord/cel/ra <= 135.5
            and $p/coord/cel/dec >= -48.0
            and $p/coord/cel/dec <= -45.0
          return
            <rxj>
              {$p/coord/cel/ra} {$p/coord/cel/dec}
              {$p/en} {$p/det_time}
            </rxj>
      }
      </photons>
    ]]>
  </query>
  <query qid="3">
    <![CDATA[
      <photons>
      {
        for $w in stream("photons")/photons/photon
          [coord/cel/ra >= 120.0 and
           coord/cel/ra <= 138.0 and
           coord/cel/dec >= -49.0 and
           coord/cel/dec <= -40.0]
          |det_time diff 20 step 10|
        let $a := avg($w/en)
        return
          <avg_en>
            {$a}
          </avg_en>
      }
      </photons>
    ]]>
  </query>
  <query qid="4">
    <![CDATA[
      <photons>
      {
        for $w in stream("photons")/photons/photon
          [coord/cel/ra >= 120.0 and
           coord/cel/ra <= 138.0 and
           coord/cel/dec >= -49.0 and
           coord/cel/dec <= -40.0]
          |det_time diff 60 step 40|
        let $a := avg($w/en)
        where $a >= 1.3
        return
          <avg_en>
            {$a}
          </avg_en>
```

```
      }
      </photons>
    ]]>
  </query>
 </queries>

 <injectorMapping>
   <mapping peer="4" stream="photons"/>
 </injectorMapping>

 <queryMapping>
   <mapping peer="1" query="1"/>
   <mapping peer="7" query="2"/>
   <mapping peer="3" query="3"/>
   <mapping peer="2" query="4"/>
 </queryMapping>

</scenario>
```

Listing A.1: Example scenario

A.2 Scenario Schema

StreamGlobe scenarios adhere to the following XML Schema:

```
<?xml version="1.0" encoding="UTF-8"?>
<xs:schema attributeFormDefault="unqualified"
           elementFormDefault="qualified"
           xmlns:xs="http://www.w3.org/2001/XMLSchema"
           targetNamespace="http://www-db.in.tum.de/research/
              projects/StreamGlobe/scenario"
           xmlns:sg="http://www-db.in.tum.de/research/projects/
              StreamGlobe/scenario">

  <xs:element name="scenario">
    <xs:complexType>
      <xs:sequence>
        <xs:element ref="sg:statistix" minOccurs="0"/>
        <xs:element ref="sg:graph"/>
        <xs:element ref="sg:streams"/>
        <xs:element ref="sg:queries" minOccurs="0"/>
        <xs:element ref="sg:injectorMapping"/>
        <xs:element ref="sg:queryMapping" minOccurs="0"/>
      </xs:sequence>
      <xs:attribute name="name" type="xs:string" use="required"/>
    </xs:complexType>

    <xs:key name="vertexKey">
      <xs:selector xpath="sg:graph/sg:vertex"/>
      <xs:field xpath="@vid"/>
    </xs:key>
    <xs:keyref name="vertexRefForSource" refer="sg:vertexKey">
      <xs:selector xpath="sg:graph/sg:edge"/>
      <xs:field xpath="@source"/>
    </xs:keyref>
    <xs:keyref name="vertexRefForTarget" refer="sg:vertexKey">
      <xs:selector xpath="sg:graph/sg:edge"/>
      <xs:field xpath="@target"/>
    </xs:keyref>
    <xs:keyref name="vertexRefForStreamInjector" refer="sg:
       vertexKey">
      <xs:selector xpath="sg:injectorMapping/sg:mapping"/>
      <xs:field xpath="@peer"/>
    </xs:keyref>
    <xs:keyref name="vertexRefForQueryMapping" refer="sg:vertexKey
       ">
      <xs:selector xpath="sg:queryMapping/sg:mapping"/>
      <xs:field xpath="@peer"/>
    </xs:keyref>

    <xs:key name="streamKey">
      <xs:selector xpath="sg:streams/sg:stream"/>
```

```
      <xs:field xpath="@sid"/>
    </xs:key>
    <xs:keyref name="streamRef" refer="sg:streamKey">
      <xs:selector xpath="sg:injectorMapping/sg:mapping"/>
      <xs:field xpath="@stream"/>
    </xs:keyref>

    <xs:key name="queryKey">
      <xs:selector xpath="sg:queries/sg:query"/>
      <xs:field xpath="@qid"/>
    </xs:key>
    <xs:keyref name="queryRef" refer="sg:queryKey">
      <xs:selector xpath="sg:queryMapping/sg:mapping"/>
      <xs:field xpath="@query"/>
    </xs:keyref>

    <xs:key name="kindKey">
      <xs:selector xpath="sg:streams/sg:kindDefinition/sg:kind"/>
      <xs:field xpath="@name"/>
    </xs:key>

</xs:element>

<xs:element name="statistix">
  <xs:complexType>
    <xs:attribute name="dbPath" type="xs:string" use="required"/>
    <xs:attribute name="reportType" default="file" use="optional
      ">
      <xs:simpleType>
        <xs:restriction base="xs:NMTOKEN">
          <xs:enumeration value="file"/>
          <xs:enumeration value="rrdb"/>
          <xs:enumeration value="combined"/>
        </xs:restriction>
      </xs:simpleType>
    </xs:attribute>
  </xs:complexType>
</xs:element>

<xs:element name="graph">
  <xs:complexType>
    <xs:sequence>
      <xs:element name="vertex" maxOccurs="unbounded">
        <xs:complexType>
          <xs:attribute name="vid" type="xs:unsignedByte" use="
            required"/>
          <xs:attribute name="label" type="xs:string" use="
            optional"/>
          <xs:attribute name="pid" type="xs:string" use="optional
            "/>
```

```
            </xs:complexType>
          </xs:element>
          <xs:element name="edge" minOccurs="0" maxOccurs="unbounded
            ">
            <xs:complexType>
              <xs:attribute name="source" type="xs:unsignedByte" use
                ="required"/>
              <xs:attribute name="target" type="xs:unsignedByte" use
                ="required"/>
            </xs:complexType>
          </xs:element>
        </xs:sequence>
      </xs:complexType>
    </xs:element>

    <xs:element name="streams">
      <xs:complexType>
        <xs:sequence>
          <xs:element name="kindDefinition">
            <xs:complexType>
              <xs:sequence>
                <xs:element name="kind" maxOccurs="unbounded">
                  <xs:complexType>
                    <xs:attribute name="name" type="xs:string" use="
                      required"/>
                    <xs:attribute name="class" type="xs:string" use="
                      required"/>
                  </xs:complexType>
                </xs:element>
              </xs:sequence>
            </xs:complexType>
          </xs:element>
          <xs:element name="stream" maxOccurs="unbounded">
            <xs:complexType>
              <xs:sequence>
                <xs:element name="dtd">
                  <xs:complexType>
                    <xs:attribute name="filename" type="xs:string"
                      use="required"/>
                  </xs:complexType>
                </xs:element>
                <xs:element name="param" maxOccurs="unbounded">
                  <xs:complexType>
                    <xs:simpleContent>
                      <xs:extension base="xs:string">
                        <xs:attribute name="name" type="xs:string"
                          use="required"/>
                      </xs:extension>
                    </xs:simpleContent>
                  </xs:complexType>
```

```xml
              </xs:element>
            </xs:sequence>
            <xs:attribute name="sid" type="xs:string" use="required
              "/>
            <xs:attribute name="type" type="xs:string" use="
              required"/>
          </xs:complexType>
        </xs:element>
      </xs:sequence>
    </xs:complexType>
  </xs:element>

  <xs:element name="queries">
    <xs:complexType>
      <xs:sequence>
        <xs:element name="query" maxOccurs="unbounded">
          <xs:complexType mixed="true">
            <xs:sequence minOccurs="0">
              <xs:element name="resource">
                <xs:complexType>
                  <xs:attribute name="filename" type="xs:string"
                    use="required"/>
                </xs:complexType>
              </xs:element>
            </xs:sequence>
            <xs:attribute name="qid" type="xs:unsignedByte" use="
              required"/>
          </xs:complexType>
        </xs:element>
      </xs:sequence>
    </xs:complexType>
  </xs:element>

  <xs:element name="injectorMapping">
    <xs:complexType>
      <xs:sequence>
        <xs:element name="mapping" maxOccurs="unbounded">
          <xs:complexType>
            <xs:attribute name="peer" type="xs:unsignedByte" use="
              required"/>
            <xs:attribute name="stream" type="xs:string" use="
              required"/>
          </xs:complexType>
        </xs:element>
      </xs:sequence>
    </xs:complexType>
  </xs:element>

  <xs:element name="queryMapping">
    <xs:complexType>
```

```
      <xs:sequence>
        <xs:element name="mapping" maxOccurs="unbounded">
          <xs:complexType>
            <xs:attribute name="peer" type="xs:unsignedByte" use="
              required"/>
            <xs:attribute name="query" type="xs:unsignedByte" use="
              required"/>
            <xs:attribute name="install_interval" type="xs:int" use
              ="optional"/>
          </xs:complexType>
        </xs:element>
      </xs:sequence>
    </xs:complexType>
  </xs:element>

</xs:schema>
```

Listing A.2: Scenario schema

A.3   Distributed Query Evaluation Plan

Similar to scenarios, distributed query evaluation plans are also represented as XML documents in StreamGlobe. Each plan consists of a sequence of nested `plan` elements. Each `plan` element belongs to a certain peer in the network and contains information about all the stream operators to be installed, removed, or replaced locally at the respective peer. Furthermore, the `plan` element contains nested subplans for all neighbor peers that are affected by the plan. The nested subplans are again `plan` elements themselves. In an actual distributed query evaluation plan, the outermost `plan` element contains the local plan for the super-peer at which the query is registered. The innermost `plan` elements correspondingly contain the local plans for the peers at which the input streams of the query are available.

The following example plan was generated by the StreamGlobe optimizer for installing the example query q_1 of Chapter 4 in the example network of Figure 4.1 on page 38.

```
<?xml version="1.0" encoding="UTF-8"?>
<plan atPeer="http://192.168.0.1:8080/wsrf/services/streamglobe/
   PeerFactory?1"
      id="query-1:plan-1"
      xmlns="urn:streamglobe.in.tum.de/pdc"
      xmlns:pdc="urn:streamglobe.in.tum.de/pdc"
      xmlns:xsi="http://www.w3.org/2001/XMLSchema-instance">
  <add>
    <streamoperator id="query-1:plan-1:query-1:q1#"
                    xmlns:xsi="http://www.w3.org/2001/XMLSchema-
                       instance"
                    xsi:type="queryStreamoperatorType">
      <dependencies>
        <streamreference id="query-1:plan-1"/>
      </dependencies>
      <source>
        <![CDATA[
          <photons>
          {
            for $p in /photons/photon
            return
              <vela>
                {$p/coord/cel/ra} {$p/coord/cel/dec}
                {$p/phc} {$p/en} {$p/det_time}
              </vela>
          }
          </photons>
        ]]>
      </source>
      <input-dtd>
        <![CDATA[
          <!ELEMENT photons (photon)*>
          <!ELEMENT photon (coord, phc, en, det_time)>
          <!ELEMENT coord (cel)>
          <!ELEMENT cel (ra, dec)>
          <!ELEMENT ra (#PCDATA)>
```

```
            <!ELEMENT dec (#PCDATA)>
            <!ELEMENT phc (#PCDATA)>
            <!ELEMENT en (#PCDATA)>
            <!ELEMENT det_time (#PCDATA)>
          ]]>
        </input-dtd>
        <output-dtd>
          <![CDATA[
            <!ELEMENT photons (photon)*>
            <!ELEMENT photon (coord, phc, en, det_time)>
            <!ELEMENT coord (cel)>
            <!ELEMENT cel (ra, dec)>
            <!ELEMENT ra (#PCDATA)>
            <!ELEMENT dec (#PCDATA)>
            <!ELEMENT phc (#PCDATA)>
            <!ELEMENT en (#PCDATA)>
            <!ELEMENT det_time (#PCDATA)>
          ]]>
        </output-dtd>
      </streamoperator>
      <streamoperator id="query-1:plan-1"
                      xmlns:xsi="http://www.w3.org/2001/XMLSchema-
                         instance"
                      xsi:type="counterStreamoperatorType">
        <dependencies>
          <streamreference id="query-1:plan-0"/>
        </dependencies>
        <stream-item>photon</stream-item>
        <neighbor>
          http://192.168.0.1:8080/wsrf/services/streamglobe/
            PeerFactory?5
        </neighbor>
      </streamoperator>
    </add>
    <plan atPeer="http://192.168.0.1:8080/wsrf/services/streamglobe/
      PeerFactory?5"
        id="query-1:plan-0"
        xmlns="urn:streamglobe.in.tum.de/pdc"
        xmlns:pdc="urn:streamglobe.in.tum.de/pdc"
        xmlns:xsi="http://www.w3.org/2001/XMLSchema-instance">
      <add>
        <streamoperator id="query-1:plan-0"
                        xmlns:xsi="http://www.w3.org/2001/XMLSchema-
                           instance"
                        xsi:type="counterStreamoperatorType">
          <dependencies>
            <streamreference id="query-1"/>
          </dependencies>
          <stream-item>photon</stream-item>
          <neighbor>
```

```
            http://192.168.0.1:8080/wsrf/services/streamglobe/
               PeerFactory?4
         </neighbor>
      </streamoperator>
   </add>
<plan atPeer="http://192.168.0.1:8080/wsrf/services/streamglobe
   /PeerFactory?4"
         id="query-1"
         xmlns="urn:streamglobe.in.tum.de/pdc"
         xmlns:pdc="urn:streamglobe.in.tum.de/pdc"
         xmlns:xsi="http://www.w3.org/2001/XMLSchema-instance">
   <add>
      <streamoperator id="query-1:q0"
                      xmlns:xsi="http://www.w3.org/2001/XMLSchema
                         -instance"
                      xsi:type="queryStreamoperatorType">
         <dependencies>
           <stream id="photons"/>
         </dependencies>
         <source>
           <![CDATA[
             <photons>
             {
               for $p in /photons/photon
               where $p/coord/cel/ra >= 120.0
                 and $p/coord/cel/ra <= 138.0
                 and $p/coord/cel/dec >= -49.0
                 and $p/coord/cel/dec <= -40.0
               return
                 <photon>
                   <coord>
                     <cel>
                       {$p/coord/cel/ra}
                       {$p/coord/cel/dec}
                     </cel>
                   </coord>
                   {$p/phc}
                   {$p/en}
                   {$p/det-time}
                 </photon>
             }
             </photons>
           ]]>
         </source>
         <input-dtd>
           <![CDATA[
             <!ELEMENT photons (photon)* >
             <!ELEMENT photon (coord, phc, en, det_time)>
             <!ELEMENT coord (cel, det)>
             <!ELEMENT cel (ra, dec)>
```

```
                    <!ELEMENT ra (#PCDATA)>
                    <!ELEMENT dec (#PCDATA)>
                    <!ELEMENT det (dx, dy)>
                    <!ELEMENT dx (#PCDATA)>
                    <!ELEMENT dy (#PCDATA)>
                    <!ELEMENT phc (#PCDATA)>
                    <!ELEMENT en (#PCDATA)>
                    <!ELEMENT det_time (#PCDATA)>
                 ]]>
            </input-dtd>
            <output-dtd>
               <![CDATA[
                  <!ELEMENT photons (photon)*>
                  <!ELEMENT photon (coord, phc, en, det_time)>
                  <!ELEMENT coord (cel)>
                  <!ELEMENT cel (ra, dec)>
                  <!ELEMENT ra (#PCDATA)>
                  <!ELEMENT dec (#PCDATA)>
                  <!ELEMENT phc (#PCDATA)>
                  <!ELEMENT en (#PCDATA)>
                  <!ELEMENT det_time (#PCDATA)>
               ]]>
            </output-dtd>
         </streamoperator>
      </add>
   </plan>
  </plan>
</plan>
```

Listing A.3: Distributed query evaluation plan

A.4   Plan Schema

Distributed query evaluation plans in StreamGlobe adhere to the following XML Schema:

```
<?xml version="1.0" encoding="UTF-8"?>
<xs:schema attributeFormDefault="unqualified"
           elementFormDefault="qualified">
           xmlns:xs="http://www.w3.org/2001/XMLSchema"
           targetNamespace="urn:streamglobe.in.tum.de/pdc"
           xmlns:pdc="urn:streamglobe.in.tum.de/pdc">

  <xs:element name="plan">
    <xs:complexType>
      <xs:sequence>
        <xs:element name="delete" type="pdc:
          deleteOperatorsAtPeerType" minOccurs="0"/>
        <xs:element name="replace" type="pdc:
          replaceOperatorsAtPeerType" minOccurs="0" maxOccurs="
          unbounded"/>
        <xs:element name="add" type="pdc:addOperatorsAtPeerType"
          minOccurs="0"/>
        <xs:element ref="pdc:plan" minOccurs="0" maxOccurs="
          unbounded"/>
      </xs:sequence>
      <xs:attribute name="atPeer" type="xs:string" use="required"/>
      <xs:attribute name="id" type="xs:string" use="required"/>
    </xs:complexType>

    <xs:key name="planIdOrOperatorId">
      <xs:selector xpath="./pdc:add/pdc:streamoperator|./pdc:plan
        "/>
      <xs:field xpath="@id"/>
    </xs:key>
    <xs:keyref name="validReferences" refer="pdc:planIdOrOperatorId
      ">
      <xs:selector xpath="./pdc:add/pdc:streamoperator/pdc:
        dependencies/pdc:streamreference"/>
      <xs:field xpath="@id"/>
    </xs:keyref>
    <xs:unique name="doNotDeleteNewOperators">
      <xs:selector xpath=".//pdc:streamoperator"/>
      <xs:field xpath="@id"/>
    </xs:unique>
  </xs:element>

  <xs:complexType name="deleteOperatorsAtPeerType">
    <xs:sequence>
      <xs:element name="streamoperator" type="pdc:
        abstractStreamoperatorType" maxOccurs="unbounded"/>
    </xs:sequence>
  </xs:complexType>
```

```
<xs:complexType name="replaceOperatorsAtPeerType">
  <xs:sequence>
    <xs:element name="delete" type="pdc:deleteOperatorsAtPeerType
      " minOccurs="0"/>
    <xs:element name="add" type="pdc:addOperatorsAtPeerType"
      minOccurs="0"/>
  </xs:sequence>
</xs:complexType>
<xs:complexType name="addOperatorsAtPeerType">
  <xs:sequence>
    <xs:element name="streamoperator" type="pdc:
      abstractStreamoperatorType" maxOccurs="unbounded"/>
  </xs:sequence>
</xs:complexType>

<xs:complexType name="parameterType">
  <xs:sequence>
    <xs:element name="key" type="xs:string"/>
    <xs:element name="value" type="xs:string"/>
  </xs:sequence>
</xs:complexType>

<xs:complexType name="abstractStreamoperatorType" abstract="true
  ">
  <xs:sequence>
    <xs:element name="dependencies">
      <xs:complexType>
        <xs:choice maxOccurs="unbounded">
          <xs:element name="streamreference" type="pdc:
            streamreferenceType"/>
          <xs:element name="stream" type="pdc:streamType"/>
        </xs:choice>
      </xs:complexType>
    </xs:element>
  </xs:sequence>
  <xs:attribute name="id" type="xs:string" use="required"/>
</xs:complexType>
<xs:complexType name="streamreferenceType">
  <xs:attribute name="id" type="xs:string" use="required"/>
</xs:complexType>
<xs:complexType name="streamType">
  <xs:attribute name="id" type="xs:string" use="required"/>
</xs:complexType>
<xs:complexType name="queryStreamoperatorType">
  <xs:complexContent>
    <xs:extension base="pdc:abstractStreamoperatorType">
      <xs:sequence>
        <xs:element name="source" type="xs:string"/>
        <xs:element name="input-dtd" type="xs:string"/>
        <xs:element name="output-dtd" type="xs:string"/>
```

```
          <xs:element name="udf" minOccurs="0" maxOccurs="unbounded
            ">
            <xs:complexType>
              <xs:attribute name="name" type="xs:string" use="
                required"/>
              <xs:attribute name="codebase" type="pdc:codebaseType"
                use="required"/>
            </xs:complexType>
          </xs:element>
        </xs:sequence>
        <xs:attribute name="name" default="query" use="optional"/>
      </xs:extension>
    </xs:complexContent>
  </xs:complexType>
  <xs:complexType name="builtInStreamoperatorType">
    <xs:complexContent>
      <xs:extension base="pdc:abstractStreamoperatorType">
        <xs:attribute name="name" use="required">
          <xs:simpleType>
            <xs:restriction base="xs:NMTOKEN">
              <xs:enumeration value="forward"/>
              <xs:enumeration value="display"/>
              <xs:enumeration value="statistics"/>
              <xs:enumeration value="counter"/>
              <xs:enumeration value="null"/>
            </xs:restriction>
          </xs:simpleType>
        </xs:attribute>
      </xs:extension>
    </xs:complexContent>
  </xs:complexType>
  <xs:complexType name="hopStreamoperatorType">
    <xs:complexContent>
      <xs:extension base="pdc:abstractStreamoperatorType">
        <xs:sequence>
          <xs:element name="roottag" type="xs:string"/>
          <xs:element name="blocktag" type="xs:string"/>
          <xs:element name="stream_win" type="xs:int"/>
          <xs:element name="stream_step" type="xs:int"/>
          <xs:element name="query_win" type="xs:int"/>
          <xs:element name="query_step" type="xs:int"/>
        </xs:sequence>
        <xs:attribute name="name" default="hop" use="optional"/>
      </xs:extension>
    </xs:complexContent>
  </xs:complexType>
  <xs:complexType name="counterStreamoperatorType">
    <xs:complexContent>
      <xs:extension base="pdc:abstractStreamoperatorType">
        <xs:sequence>
```

```
            <xs:element name="stream-item" type="xs:string"/>
            <xs:element name="neighbor" type="xs:anyURI"/>
          </xs:sequence>
        </xs:extension>
      </xs:complexContent>
    </xs:complexType>
    <xs:complexType name="externalStreamoperatorType">
      <xs:complexContent>
        <xs:extension base="pdc:abstractStreamoperatorType">
          <xs:sequence>
            <xs:element name="authorizedby" type="xs:string"/>
            <xs:element name="inputstreamdata" type="pdc:
                inputStreamDataType" maxOccurs="unbounded"/>
            <xs:element name="outputstreamdata" type="pdc:
                outputStreamDataType"/>
            <xs:element name="parameter" type="pdc:parameterType"
                minOccurs="0" maxOccurs="unbounded"/>
          </xs:sequence>
          <xs:attribute name="name" type="xs:string" use="required"/>
          <xs:attribute name="codebase" type="pdc:codebaseType" use="
              required"/>
          <xs:attribute name="dependencyToEnrich" type="xs:string"
              use="optional"/>
        </xs:extension>
      </xs:complexContent>
    </xs:complexType>

    <xs:complexType name="streamDataType">
      <xs:sequence>
        <xs:element name="dtd" type="xs:string" minOccurs="0"/>
      </xs:sequence>
    </xs:complexType>
    <xs:complexType name="inputStreamDataType">
      <xs:complexContent>
        <xs:extension base="pdc:streamDataType">
          <xs:sequence>
            <xs:element name="variable" type="pdc:
                typedVariableMapping" minOccurs="0" maxOccurs="
                unbounded"/>
          </xs:sequence>
          <xs:attribute name="id" type="xs:string" use="required"/>
        </xs:extension>
      </xs:complexContent>
    </xs:complexType>
    <xs:complexType name="outputStreamDataType">
      <xs:complexContent>
        <xs:extension base="pdc:streamDataType">
          <xs:sequence>
            <xs:element name="variable" type="pdc:
                untypedVariableMapping" minOccurs="0" maxOccurs="
```

```
            unbounded"/>
        </xs:sequence>
      </xs:extension>
    </xs:complexContent>
  </xs:complexType>

  <xs:complexType name="untypedVariableMapping">
    <xs:attribute name="name" use="required"/>
    <xs:attribute name="select" type="pdc:mappingPathType" use="
      required"/>
    <xs:attribute name="position" use="optional">
      <xs:simpleType>
        <xs:restriction base="xs:NMTOKEN">
          <xs:enumeration value="FIRST"/>
          <xs:enumeration value="LAST"/>
        </xs:restriction>
      </xs:simpleType>
    </xs:attribute>
  </xs:complexType>
  <xs:complexType name="typedVariableMapping">
    <xs:complexContent>
      <xs:extension base="pdc:untypedVariableMapping">
        <xs:attribute name="type" use="required"/>
      </xs:extension>
    </xs:complexContent>
  </xs:complexType>
  <xs:simpleType name="mappingPathType">
    <xs:restriction base="xs:string">
      <xs:pattern value="\./.*"/>
    </xs:restriction>
  </xs:simpleType>

  <xs:simpleType name="codebaseType">
    <xs:restriction base="xs:anyURI">
      <xs:pattern value="http://.*"/>
      <xs:pattern value="file:///.*"/>
      <xs:pattern value="urn:streamglobe:internalCodeBase"/>
    </xs:restriction>
  </xs:simpleType>

</xs:schema>
```

Listing A.4: Plan schema

APPENDIX B

Proof of Theorem 3.1

Theorem B.1 (repeated from Theorem 3.1) *Let* $A := \{[a_1, \ldots, a_l]\}$, $B := \{[b_1, \ldots, b_m]\}$, *and* $C := \{[c_1, \ldots, c_n]\}$ *be relations and let* $A.id \in \{a_1, \ldots, a_l\}$, $B.id \in \{b_1, \ldots, b_m\}$, *and* $C.id \in \{c_1, \ldots, c_n\}$ *be their corresponding join attributes, respectively. Then the following applies:*

$$(A \bowtie_{A.id=B.id} B) \bowtie_{A.id=C.id} C \equiv A \bowtie_{A.id=B.id \vee A.id=C.id} (B \bowtie_{B.id=C.id} C) \qquad \square$$

PROOF: We show the above equivalence using the relational tuple calculus. Since all joins are equi-joins over the same attribute, we omit the join condition in the following for the sake of readability.

In terms of the relational tuple calculus, the relational left-outer join $\bowtie$ is defined as

$$
\begin{aligned}
A \bowtie B \Leftrightarrow \{ & [t_a.a_1, \ldots, t_a.a_l, t_b.b_1, \ldots, t_b.b_m] \mid \\
& t_a \in A \wedge t_b \in \{B \cup \bot\} \wedge \\
& (t_a.id = t_b.id \vee \\
& (t_b = \bot \wedge \forall t_b' \in B : (t_b'.id \neq t_a.id))) \}
\end{aligned}
\tag{B.1}
$$

and the relational full-outer join $\bowtie$ is defined as

$$
\begin{aligned}
B \bowtie C \Leftrightarrow \{ & [t_b.b_1, \ldots, t_b.b_m, t_c.c_1, \ldots, t_c.c_n] \mid \\
& t_b \in \{B \cup \bot\} \wedge t_c \in \{C \cup \bot\} \wedge \\
& (t_b.id = t_c.id \vee \\
& (t_b = \bot \wedge \forall t_b' \in B : (t_b'.id \neq t_c.id)) \vee \\
& (t_c = \bot \wedge \forall t_c' \in C : (t_c'.id \neq t_b.id))) \}.
\end{aligned}
\tag{B.2}
$$

Hence

$$
\begin{aligned}
(A \bowtie B) \bowtie C \Leftrightarrow \{ & [t_a.a_1,\ldots,t_a.a_l,t_b.b_1,\ldots,t_b.b_m,t_c.c_1,\ldots,t_c.c_n] \mid \\
& t_a \in A \land t_b \in \{B \cup \bot\} \land t_c \in \{C \cup \bot\} \land \\
& ((t_a.id = t_b.id \land t_b.id = t_c.id) \lor \\
& (t_a.id = t_b.id \land t_c = \bot \land \forall t_c' \in C : (t_c'.id \neq t_a.id)) \lor \\
& (t_a.id = t_c.id \land t_b = \bot \land \forall t_b' \in B : (t_b'.id \neq t_a.id)) \lor \\
& (t_b = \bot \land \forall t_b' \in B : (t_b'.id \neq t_a.id) \land \\
& t_c = \bot \land \forall t_c' \in C : (t_c'.id \neq t_a.id)))\}
\end{aligned}
\tag{B.3}
$$

and

$$
\begin{aligned}
A \bowtie (B \bowtie C) \Leftrightarrow \{ & [t_a.a_1,\ldots,t_a.a_l,t_b.b_1,\ldots,t_b.b_m,t_c.c_1,\ldots,t_c.c_n] \mid \\
& t_a \in A \land t_b \in \{B \cup \bot\} \land t_c \in \{C \cup \bot\} \land \\
& ((t_a.id = t_b.id \land t_b.id = t_c.id) \lor \\
& (t_a.id = t_b.id \land t_c = \bot \land \forall t_c' \in C : (t_c'.id \neq t_a.id)) \lor \\
& (t_a.id = t_c.id \land t_b = \bot \land \forall t_b' \in B : (t_b'.id \neq t_a.id)) \lor \\
& (t_b = \bot \land \forall t_b' \in B : (t_b'.id \neq t_a.id) \land \\
& t_c = \bot \land \forall t_c' \in C : (t_c'.id \neq t_a.id))) \land \\
& (t_b.id = t_c.id \lor \\
& (t_b = \bot \land \forall t_b' \in B : (t_b'.id \neq t_c.id)) \lor \\
& (t_c = \bot \land \forall t_c' \in C : (t_c'.id \neq t_b.id)))\}.
\end{aligned}
\tag{B.4}
$$

Now it remains to be proven that the sets of tuples defined in (B.3) and (B.4) are equivalent. We do this by comparing the conditions. Obviously, the complete condition of (B.3) is already contained in the condition of (B.4). Additionally, (B.4) conjunctively adds to the overall condition an additional disjunctive term represented by the last three lines in (B.4). We next show that the additional term in (B.4) is redundant since it is already expressed by other terms in (B.4). We do this via a pairwise comparison of the respective disjunctively combined terms.

The following implication

$$
\begin{aligned}
& ((t_a.id = t_b.id \land t_b.id = t_c.id) \lor \\
& (t_a.id = t_b.id \land t_c = \bot \land \forall t_c' \in C : (t_c'.id \neq t_a.id)) \lor \\
& (t_a.id = t_c.id \land t_b = \bot \land \forall t_b' \in B : (t_b'.id \neq t_a.id)) \lor \\
& (t_b = \bot \land \forall t_b' \in B : (t_b'.id \neq t_a.id) \land t_c = \bot \land \forall t_c' \in C : (t_c'.id \neq t_a.id))) \\
\Rightarrow & (t_b.id = t_c.id \lor \\
& (t_b = \bot \land \forall t_b' \in B : (t_b'.id \neq t_c.id)) \lor (t_c = \bot \land \forall t_c' \in C : (t_c'.id \neq t_b.id)))
\end{aligned}
\tag{B.5}
$$

applies because of

$$
(t_a.id = t_b.id \land t_b.id = t_c.id) \Rightarrow (t_b.id = t_c.id)
$$

and

$$
(t_a.id = t_b.id \land t_c = \bot \land \forall t_c' \in C : (t_c'.id \neq t_a.id)) \Rightarrow (t_c = \bot \land \forall t_c' \in C : (t_c'.id \neq t_b.id)) \tag{B.6}
$$

and

$$
(t_a.id = t_c.id \land t_b = \bot \land \forall t_b' \in B : (t_b'.id \neq t_a.id)) \Rightarrow (t_b = \bot \land \forall t_b' \in B : (t_b'.id \neq t_c.id)).
$$

Thus, we can omit the third term in (B.4) and the equivalence of (B.3) and (B.4) is proven to be valid. Hence, Theorem 3.1 applies. ∎

APPENDIX C

Alternative XQuery Window Implementations

This section presents alternative XQuery implementations of count-based and time-based data windows with the gather and the run semantics introduced in Section 4.3.

C.1 Count-based Data Windows

Figures C.1 and C.2 show alternative XQuery implementations of count-based data windows. The implementation of Figure C.1 gathers the remaining elements in a final window at the end of the stream according to the gather semantics. In the implementation of Figure C.2, the window slides along until it contains no more elements as specified by the run semantics.

```
declare function local:cwin($count as xs:integer,
                            $step as xs:integer,
                            $data as node()*) as node()*
{
  let $cwin := fn:subsequence($data, 1, $count)
  let $tail := fn:subsequence($data, $step + 1)
  return
    if (fn:count($data) <= $count) then
      (<cw> { $cwin } </cw>)
    else
      (<cw> { $cwin } </cw>, local:cwin($count, $step, $tail))
};

for $x in doc("data.xml")/a
return
  <result>
    { for $w in local:cwin(4, 2, $x/b)
      return
        <win> { $w/* } </win> }
  </result>
```

Figure C.1: Gathering remaining elements in final window

```
declare function local:cwin($count as xs:integer,
                            $step as xs:integer,
                            $data as node()*) as node()*
{
  let $cwin := fn:subsequence($data, 1, $count)
  let $tail := fn:subsequence($data, $step + 1)
  return
    if (fn:empty($tail)) then
      (<cw> { $cwin } </cw>)
    else
      (<cw> { $cwin } </cw>, local:cwin($count, $step, $tail))
};

for $x in doc("data.xml")/a
return
  <result>
    { for $w in local:cwin(4, 2, $x/b)
      return
        <win> { $w/* } </win> }
  </result>
```

Figure C.2: Sliding windows until no elements remain

C.2   Time-based Data Windows

Figures C.3 and C.4 show alternative XQuery implementations of time-based data windows. The implementation of Figure C.3 gathers the remaining elements in a final window at the end of the stream according to the gather semantics. In the implementation of Figure C.4, the window slides along until it contains no more elements as specified by the run semantics.

```
declare function local:dwin($start as xs:integer,
                            $diff as xs:integer,
                            $step as xs:integer,
                            $data as node()*,
                            $refs as node()*) as node()*
{
  let $dwin := for $i in $data
               let $ds := for $d in $i/descendant-or-self::node()
                          where some $r in $refs satisfies $r is $d
                          return $d
               where $ds[1] >= $start and $ds[1] < $start + $diff
               return $i
  let $tail := for $i in $data
               let $ds := for $d in $i/descendant-or-self::node()
                          where some $r in $refs satisfies $r is $d
                          return $d
               where $ds[1] >= $start + $step
               return $i
  return
    if (fn:count($dwin) = fn:count($data)) then
      (<dw> { $dwin } </dw>)
    else
      (<dw> { $dwin } </dw>, local:dwin($start + $step, $diff, $step,
                                        $tail, $refs))
};

for $x in doc("data.xml")/a
return
  <result>
    { for $w in local:dwin(0, 4, 2, $x/b, $x/b/c)
      return
        <win> { $w/* } </win> }
  </result>
```

Figure C.3: Gathering remaining elements in final window

```
declare function local:dwin($start as xs:integer,
                            $diff as xs:integer,
                            $step as xs:integer,
                            $data as node()*,
                            $refs as node()*) as node()*
{
  let $dwin := for $i in $data
                 let $ds := for $d in $i/descendant-or-self::node()
                            where some $r in $refs satisfies $r is $d
                            return $d
                 where $ds[1] >= $start and $ds[1] < $start + $diff
                 return $i
  let $tail := for $i in $data
                 let $ds := for $d in $i/descendant-or-self::node()
                            where some $r in $refs satisfies $r is $d
                            return $d
                 where $ds[1] >= $start + $step
                 return $i
  return
    if (fn:empty($tail)) then
      (<dw> { $dwin } </dw>)
    else
      (<dw> { $dwin } </dw>, local:dwin($start + $step, $diff, $step,
                                        $tail, $refs))
};

for $x in doc("data.xml")/a
return
  <result>
    { for $w in local:dwin(0, 4, 2, $x/b, $x/b/c)
      return
        <win> { $w/* } </win> }
  </result>
```

Figure C.4: Sliding windows until no elements remain

APPENDIX D

WXQuery EBNF Grammar

The notation of the following WXQuery EBNF grammar is based on the notation of the XQuery EBNF grammar in [W3C (2007d)]. In particular, the grammar uses a special notation to reference externally defined parts via URLs.

[1]	QueryBody	::=	Expr
[2]	Expr	::=	ExprSingle ("," ExprSingle)*
[3]	ExprSingle	::=	FLWRExpr | PathExpr | ElementConstructor | ParenthesizedExpr | IfExpr
[4]	FLWRExpr	::=	(ForClause | LetClause)+ WhereClause? "return" ExprSingle
[5]	ForClause	::=	"for" VarRef "in" WindowedPathExpr
[6]	VarRef	::=	"$" VarName
[7]	VarName	::=	QName
[8]	QName	::=	[http://www.w3.org/TR/REC-xml-names/#NT-QName]^Names
[9]	WindowedPathExpr	::=	PathExpr ("|" WindowSpec "|")?
[10]	PathExpr	::=	PrimaryExpr | ((PrimaryExpr "/")? RelativePathExpr) | ("/" RelativePathExpr?)

[11]	PrimaryExpr	::=	VarRef | XMLFunctionCall

[12] XMLFunctionCall   ::= (("stream" | "doc")
                                     "(" StringLiteral ")")
                                     | ("collection"
                                     "(" StringLiteral? ")")

[13] StringLiteral   ::= ('"' (PredefinedEntityRef
                                     | CharRef
                                     | EscapeQuot
                                     | [^"&])* '"')
                                     | ("'" (PredefinedEntityRef
                                     | CharRef
                                     | EscapeApos
                                     | [^'&])* "'")

[14] PredefinedEntityRef   ::= "&" ("lt" | "gt" | "amp"
                                     | "quot" | "apos") ";"

[15] CharRef   ::= [http://www.w3.org/TR/REC-xml#NT-CharRef]^XML

[16] EscapeQuot   ::= '""'

[17] EscapeApos   ::= "''"

[18] RelativePathExpr   ::= StepExpr ("/" StepExpr)*

[19] StepExpr   ::= StepExprNoPredicates Predicate?

[20] StepExprNoPredicates   ::= ContextItemExpr | QName

[21] ContextItemExpr   ::= "."

[22] Predicate   ::= "[" WherePredicate "]"

[23] WherePredicate   ::= PredicateOrExpr

[24] PredicateOrExpr   ::= PredicateAndExpr
                                     ("or" PredicateAndExpr)*

[25] PredicateAndExpr   ::= (PredicateComparisonExpr
                                     | ParenPredOrExpr)
                                     ("and" (PredicateComparisonExpr
                                     | ParenPredOrExpr))*

[26] PredicateComparisonExpr ::= AdditiveExpr
                                     (ComparisonOperator AdditiveExpr)?

[27] AdditiveExpr   ::= PredicateValue
                                     (("+" | "-") PredicateValue)*

[28] PredicateValue   ::= (("-" | "+")? Literal)
                                     | RelPathExprNoPred
                                     | PredicateVariablePath

[29] Literal   ::= NumericLiteral | StringLiteral

[30] NumericLiteral   ::= IntegerLiteral
                                     | DecimalLiteral
                                     | DoubleLiteral

[31] IntegerLiteral   ::= Digits

[32] Digits   ::= [0-9]+

[33] DecimalLiteral   ::= ("." Digits) | (Digits "." [0-9]*)

[34] DoubleLiteral   ::= (("." Digits)
                                     | (Digits ("." [0-9]*)?))
                                     [eE] [+-]? Digits

[35] RelPathExprNoPred   ::= StepExprNoPredicates
                                     ("/" StepExprNoPredicates)*

[36] PredicateVariablePath   ::= VarRef ("/" RelPathExprNoPred)?

[37] ComparisonOperator   ::= "=" | "!=" | "<" | "<=" | ">" | ">="

[38] ParenPredOrExpr   ::= "(" PredicateOrExpr ")"

[39] WindowSpec   ::= (("count" IntegerLiteral)
                                     | (PathExprNoPredicates
                                     "diff" IntegerLiteral))
                                     ("step" IntegerLiteral)?

[40] PathExprNoPredicates   ::= ("/")? RelPathExprNoPred

[41] LetClause   ::= "let" VarRef ":=" AggFunctionCall

[42] AggFunctionCall   ::= AggFunctionName "(" PathExpr ")"

[43] AggFunctionName   ::= "min" | "max" | "sum" | "count" | "avg"

[44] WhereClause   ::= "where" WherePredicate

[45] ElementConstructor   ::= "<" QName
                                     ("/>"
                                     | (">" ElementContent*
                                     "</" QName ">"))

[46] ElementContent   ::= ElementConstructor | EnclosedExpr

[47] EnclosedExpr   ::= "{" Expr "}"

[48] ParenthesizedExpr   ::= "(" Expr? ")"

[49] IfExpr   ::= "if" "(" PredicateOrExpr ")"
                                           "then" ExprSingle "else" ExprSingle

APPENDIX E

Alternative Aggregate Value Selection Algorithm

Algorithm E.1 is an alternative to the aggregate value selection algorithm introduced in Algorithm 4.4 on page 67. The alternative algorithm avoids buffering data items that are never used and thus potentially saves memory. Despite the overhead caused by additional sequence numbers, the alternative algorithm reduces the overall memory consumption compared to Algorithm 4.4 if enough unused data items exist in the input stream to compensate for the overhead. The sequence numbers are used to decide which data items to buffer and which items to send to the query engine in each step of the alternative algorithm. In Algorithm 4.4, the buffer for the data items is generally larger but the algorithm does not need to introduce any additional sequence numbers.

Example E.1 (Reusing aggregate values) Applying Example 4.6 on page 67 with $\Delta = 40$, $\mu = 10$, $\Delta' = 80$, and $\mu' = 20$ to Algorithm E.1 causes the first $((\Delta' - \Delta)\ \mathrm{div}\ \mu) + 1 = ((80 - 40)\ \mathrm{div}\ 10) + 1 = 5$ values to be initially read from the input stream with sequence numbers from 0 to $((\Delta' - \Delta)\ \mathrm{div}\ \mu) = ((80 - 40)\ \mathrm{div}\ 10) = 4$. Due to $(\Delta'\ \mathrm{div}\ \Delta) = (80\ \mathrm{div}\ 40) = 2$ and $(\mu'\ \mathrm{div}\ \mu) = (20\ \mathrm{div}\ 10) = 2$, the values with sequence numbers $1 \cdot 2 = 2$ and $2 \cdot 2 = 4$ are inserted into the buffer. These are the values numbered 3 and 5 in Figure 4.20 on page 67. Only these two values of the five values read from the stream actually need to be buffered at this stage. Accordingly, due to $(\Delta\ \mathrm{div}\ \mu) = (40\ \mathrm{div}\ 10) = 4$, the values with sequence numbers $0 \cdot 4 = 0$ and $1 \cdot 4 = 4$ are sent to the query engine. These are the values numbered 1 and 5 in Figure 4.20, which are needed to compute the aggregate value corresponding to the first data window of the reusing query. The remaining values with sequence numbers 1 and 3 corresponding to the values numbered 2 and 4 in Figure 4.20 are ignored since they are not needed for computing the aggregate values of the reusing query. Subsequently, the algorithm removes all values with sequence numbers from 0 to $(\mu'\ \mathrm{div}\ \mu) - 1 = (20\ \mathrm{div}\ 10) - 1 = 1$ from the buffer. This affects no values in the initial iteration since the values currently contained in the buffer have sequence numbers 2 and 4. The algorithm next decreases the sequence numbers of the values contained in the buffer by $(\Delta'\ \mathrm{div}\ \Delta) = (80\ \mathrm{div}\ 40) = 2$, i.e., from 2 to 0 and from 4 to 2 in the example. The next iteration of the for loop reads the next $(\Delta'\ \mathrm{div}\ \Delta) = (80\ \mathrm{div}\ 40) = 2$ values from the input stream and assigns increasing sequence num-

---

Algorithm E.1 SELECTAGGREGATEVALUES

Input: Window sizes Δ and Δ' as well as step sizes μ and μ' of the data window to be reused and the new data window, respectively.
Output: The correct sequence of aggregate values for reuse.

1: during the initial iteration of the `for` loop in line 3, read first $((\Delta' - \Delta) \text{ div } \mu) + 1$ values v_0 to $v_{(\Delta' - \Delta) \text{ div } \mu}$ from the input stream and assign sequence numbers from 0 to $((\Delta' - \Delta) \text{ div } \mu)$ to them;
2: **repeat**
3:    **for** value v_n with sequence number n contained in buffer or read from input stream **do**
4:       **if** $n \in \{i \cdot (\mu' \text{ div } \mu) \mid i > 0 \land i \le (\Delta' \text{ div } \Delta)\}$ **then**
5:          **if** v_n is not yet contained in the buffer **then**
6:             insert v_n into buffer;
7:          **end if**
8:       **end if**
9:       **if** $n \in \{i \cdot (\Delta \text{ div } \mu) \mid i \ge 0 \land i < (\Delta' \text{ div } \Delta)\}$ **then**
10:          send v_n to the query engine;
11:       **end if**
12:    **end for**
13:    remove values v_0 to $v_{(\mu' \text{ div } \mu)-1}$ from buffer if present;
14:    decrease sequence number of each value contained in buffer by $(\Delta' \text{ div } \Delta)$;
15:    during the next iteration of the `for` loop in line 3, read next $(\Delta' \text{ div } \Delta)$ values from the stream and assign increasing sequence numbers starting from $((\Delta' - \Delta) \text{ div } \mu) - (\Delta' \text{ div } \Delta) + 1$ to them;
16: **until** the buffer contains no more values;

---

bers starting from $((\Delta' - \Delta) \text{ div } \mu) - (\Delta' \text{ div } \Delta) + 1 = ((80 - 40) \text{ div } 10) - (80 \text{ div } 40) + 1 = 3$ to them, i. e., the two new values receive the sequence numbers 3 and 4. The algorithm inserts the new value with sequence number 4 that now corresponds to the value numbered 7 in Figure 4.20 into the buffer. The value with sequence number 2 that now corresponds to the value numbered 5 in Figure 4.20 is already contained in the buffer and is therefore not inserted again. The values with sequence numbers 0 and 4 corresponding to the values numbered 3 and 7 in Figure 4.20 are sent to the query engine where they are used to compute the aggregate value corresponding to the second data window of the reusing query. The remaining value with sequence number 3 corresponding to the value numbered 6 in Figure 4.20 is not needed and is therefore ignored. This process continues until the buffer contains no more values.   □

APPENDIX F

Predicate Matching and Evaluation Algorithms

All algorithms in this chapter assume that each stream predicate p and each query predicate p' contains at least one conjunctive subpredicate c and c', respectively. Extensions for the handling of special cases such as empty predicates and predicates that constitute tautologies or contradictions are straightforward but would clutter the algorithm presentations. It is also possible to deal with these special cases beforehand. In our StreamGlobe prototype implementation, for example, we handle these cases within the data stream sharing optimizer.

F.1 Quick Check (QC)

Algorithm F.1 Quick Check (QC)

Input: Stream predicate p and a conjunctive subpredicate c' of query predicate p'.

Output: 1, if $c' \Rightarrow c$ for at least one conjunctive subpredicate c in p; 0, if c' overlaps with at least one conjunctive subpredicate c in p and $c' \not\Rightarrow c$ for every c in p; -1, if c' does not overlap with any conjunctive subpredicate c in p.

1: $overlap \leftarrow -1$;
2: **for all** conjunctive subpredicates c in p **do**
3:    **if** $c' \Rightarrow c$ **then**
4:       **return** 1;
5:    **end if**
6:    **if** c' overlaps with c **then**
7:       $overlap \leftarrow 0$;
8:    **end if**
9: **end for**
10: **return** $overlap$;

The pseudocode version of the QC algorithm in Algorithm F.1 is an extension of the QC algorithm presented in Algorithm 6.1 on page 136. Algorithm 6.1 returns true if $c' \Rightarrow c$ for at least one c in p, and false otherwise. Algorithm F.1 returns 1 if $c' \Rightarrow c$ for at least one c in p, 0 if c' overlaps with at least one c in p and $c' \not\Rightarrow c$ for every c in p, and -1 if c' does not overlap with any c in p. The pseudocode versions of the exact matching algorithms use this additional information to optimize their execution in Algorithms F.5, F.6, and F.7. If a c' does not overlap with any c in p, we do not need to start the complex split algorithm since we already know that there are no overlapping parts. Instead, we disjunctively add c' to $\bar{p}$ right away. If it is not required to exactly determine the non-matching parts of a subpredicate c', we can even further optimize the algorithms. In this case, we may return 0 in the QC algorithm under the stricter condition that c' does not imply any c in p and at the same time, c' overlaps with at least *two* c in p. If c' overlaps with at most *one* c in p, we may return -1. This is possible since it is clear that overlap with only one c in p without containment cannot make the implication valid.

F.2 Heuristics with Simple Relaxation (HSR)

Algorithm F.2 Heuristics with Simple Relaxation (HSR)

Input: Stream predicate p and query predicate p'.

Output: (true, p), if the quick check of Section F.1 is activated and, for all conjunctive subpredicates c' in p', $c' \Rightarrow c$ for at least one conjunctive subpredicate c in p; $(\text{false}, \bar{p})$, where $\bar{p}$ is a relaxed version of p such that the above condition is satisfied, otherwise.

1: $\bar{p} \leftarrow p$; *match* $\leftarrow$ true;
2: **for all** conjunctive subpredicates c' in p' **do**
3:     **if** quick check is activated $\land \, \text{QC}(\bar{p}, c') = 1$ **then**
4:         **continue**;
5:     **else**
6:         *match* $\leftarrow$ false;
7:         $\bar{p} \leftarrow \bar{p} \lor c'$;
8:     **end if**
9: **end for**
10: **return** $(match, \bar{p})$;

F.3 Heuristics with Complex Relaxation (HCR)

In Algorithm F.3 on the facing page, k denotes the number of dimensions in the data space and k_c denotes the number of dimensions that are referenced in subpredicate c. Further, I_d indicates an interval in dimension d and $\bar{I}_d$ indicates the extent of interval I_d.

Algorithm F.3 Heuristics with Complex Relaxation (HCR)

Input: Stream predicate p and query predicate p'.

Output: (true, p), if, for all conjunctive subpredicates c' in p', $c' \Rightarrow c$ for at least one conjunctive subpredicate c in p; $(\text{false}, \bar{p})$, where $\bar{p}$ is a relaxed version of p such that the above condition is satisfied, otherwise.

```
 1: p̄ ← p; match ← true;
 2: for all conjunctive subpredicates c' in p' do
 3:    if quick check is activated ∧ QC(p̄, c') = 1 then
 4:       continue;
 5:    else
 6:       i_b ← +∞; e_b ← +∞; c_b ← null; c_orig ← null; m ← true;
 7:       for all conjunctive subpredicates c in p̄ do
 8:          i ← 2(k − k_c); e ← 0; c_c ← c; m ← true;
 9:          for all pairs of corresponding dimensions d, d' in c_c, c' with d = d' do
10:             if (lowerBound(I_d) = −∞) ∨ (lowerBound(I_d' = −∞)) then
11:                i ← i + 1;
12:             end if
13:             if (upperBound(I_d) = +∞) ∨ (upperBound(I_d' = +∞)) then
14:                i ← i + 1;
15:             end if
16:             if I_d ∩ I_d' ≠ I_d' then
17:                m ← false;
18:                a ← max(0, lowerBound(I_d) − lowerBound(I_d')) +
19:                       max(0, upperBound(I_d') − upperBound(I_d));
20:                v ← ∏_{d*∈D:((d*≠d)∧(0<Ī_{d*}<+∞))} Ī_{d*};
21:                e ← e + (a · v);
22:                replace I_d in c_c with I_{d_c} := [min(lowerBound(I_d), lowerBound(I_d')),
23:                                           max(upperBound(I_d), upperBound(I_d'))];
24:             end if
25:          end for
26:          if m = true then
27:             break;
28:          else if (i < i_b) ∨ ((i = i_b) ∧ (e < e_b)) then
29:             i_b ← i; e_b ← e; c_b ← c_c; c_orig ← c;
30:          end if
31:       end for
32:       if m = false then
33:          match ← false;
34:          replace c_orig in p̄ with c_b;
35:       end if
36:    end if
37: end for
38: return (match, p̄);
```

F.4 Exact Matching (EM)

Algorithm F.4 Compare Dimensions (CD)

Input: Conjunctive stream subpredicate c and conjunctive query subpredicate c'_c.
Output: Queue Q'_c of unmatched parts of query subpredicate c'_c.

1: $Q'_c \leftarrow \emptyset$; $c'_{\text{orig}} \leftarrow c'_c$;
2: **for all** pairs of corresponding dimensions d, d' in c, c'_c with $d = d'$ **do**
3:     **if** $I_d \cap I_{d'} = \emptyset$ **then**
4:         $Q'_c \leftarrow \emptyset$; enqueue($Q'_c, c'_{\text{orig}}$); **break**;
5:     **else if** $I_d \cap I_{d'} = I_{d'}$ **then**
6:         **continue**;
7:     **else if** $I_d \cap I_{d'} = I_d$ **then**
8:         split c'_c along dimension d' into the part c'_i that is overlapping with c in dimension d'
        and the remaining parts c'_{o1} and c'_{o2};
9:         enqueue(Q'_c, c'_{o1}); enqueue(Q'_c, c'_{o2}); $c'_c \leftarrow c'_i$;
10:     **else**
11:         /* I_d and $I_{d'}$ overlap */
12:         split c'_c along dimension d' into the part c'_i that is overlapping with c in dimension d'
        and the remaining part c'_o;
13:         enqueue(Q'_c, c'_o); $c'_c \leftarrow c'_i$;
14:     **end if**
15: **end for**
16: **return** Q'_c;

Algorithm F.5 Exact Matching with Breadth-First Split Strategy (EM-BFS)

Input: Stream predicate p and query predicate p'.

Output: (true, p), if $p' \Rightarrow p$; $(\text{false}, \bar{p})$, where $\bar{p}$ is a relaxed version of p such that $p' \Rightarrow \bar{p}$, otherwise.

1: $\bar{p} \leftarrow p$; *match* $\leftarrow$ true;
2: **for all** conjunctive subpredicates c' in p' **do**
3:      **if** quick check is activated $\wedge \text{QC}(\bar{p}, c') = 1$ **then**
4:          **continue**;
5:      **else if** quick check is activated $\wedge \text{QC}(\bar{p}, c') = -1$ **then**
6:          *match* $\leftarrow$ false;
7:          $\bar{p} \leftarrow \bar{p} \vee c'$;
8:          **continue**;
9:      **else**
10:         /* quick check is deactivated or returns 0 */
11:         $Q'_1 \leftarrow \emptyset$; $Q'_2 \leftarrow \emptyset$; enqueue$(Q'_1, c')$;
12:         **for all** conjunctive subpredicates c in $\bar{p}$ **do**
13:             $Q'_2 \leftarrow Q'_1$; $Q'_1 \leftarrow \emptyset$;
14:             **while** $Q'_2 \neq \emptyset$ **do**
15:                 $c'_c \leftarrow$ dequeue(Q'_2);
16:                 /* compare dimensions using Algorithm F.4 */
17:                 $Q'_c \leftarrow \text{CD}(c, c'_c)$;
18:                 $append(Q'_1, Q'_c)$;
19:             **end while**
20:             **if** $Q'_1 = \emptyset$ **then**
21:                 **break**;
22:             **end if**
23:         **end for**
24:         **if** $Q'_1 \neq \emptyset$ **then**
25:             *match* $\leftarrow$ false;
26:             $\bar{p} \leftarrow \bar{p} \vee c'$;
27:         **end if**
28:     **end if**
29: **end for**
30: **return** $(match, \bar{p})$;

Algorithm F.6 Exact Matching with Depth-First Split Strategy (EM-DFS)

Input: Stream predicate p and query predicate p'.
Output: (true, p), if $p' \Rightarrow p$; $(\text{false}, \bar{p})$, where $\bar{p}$ is a relaxed version of p such that $p' \Rightarrow \bar{p}$, otherwise.

1: $\bar{p} \leftarrow p$; $match \leftarrow \text{true}$;
2: **for all** conjunctive subpredicates c' in p' **do**
3:    **if** quick check is activated $\wedge \, \text{QC}(\bar{p}, c') = 1$ **then**
4:       **continue;**
5:    **else if** quick check is activated $\wedge \, \text{QC}(\bar{p}, c') = -1$ **then**
6:       $match \leftarrow \text{false}$;
7:       $\bar{p} \leftarrow \bar{p} \vee c'$;
8:       **continue;**
9:    **else**
10:       /* quick check is deactivated or returns 0 */
11:       $Q_{\text{init}} \leftarrow \emptyset$; $Q^{\text{LIFO}} \leftarrow \emptyset$; $Q_p^{\text{LIFO}} \leftarrow \emptyset$;
12:       $\text{enqueue}(Q_{\text{init}}, c')$; $\text{enqueue}(Q^{\text{LIFO}}, Q_{\text{init}})$; $\text{enqueue}(Q_p^{\text{LIFO}}, \bar{p})$;
13:       **while** $Q^{\text{LIFO}} \neq \emptyset$ **do**
14:          $Q_{\text{next}} \leftarrow \text{dequeue}(Q^{\text{LIFO}})$; $c'_c \leftarrow \text{dequeue}(Q_{\text{next}})$; $p^- \leftarrow \text{dequeue}(Q_p^{\text{LIFO}})$;
15:          **if** $Q_{\text{next}} \neq \emptyset$ **then**
16:             $\text{enqueue}(Q^{\text{LIFO}}, Q_{\text{next}})$; $\text{enqueue}(Q_p^{\text{LIFO}}, p^-)$;
17:          **end if**
18:          let c be the first conjunctive subpredicate in p^-; remove c from p^-;
19:          /* compare dimensions using Algorithm F.4 */
20:          $Q'_c \leftarrow \text{CD}(c, c'_c)$;
21:          **if** $Q'_c \neq \emptyset$ **then**
22:             **if** p^- is not the empty predicate **then**
23:                $\text{enqueue}(Q^{\text{LIFO}}, Q'_c)$; $\text{enqueue}(Q_p^{\text{LIFO}}, p^-)$;
24:             **else**
25:                $match \leftarrow \text{false}$;
26:                $\bar{p} \leftarrow \bar{p} \vee c'$;
27:                **break;**
28:             **end if**
29:          **end if**
30:       **end while**
31:    **end if**
32: **end for**
33: **return** $(match, \bar{p})$;

Algorithm F.7 Exact Matching with Mixed Split Strategy (EM-MIX)

Input: Stream predicate p and query predicate p'.

Output: (true, p), if $p' \Rightarrow p$; $(\text{false}, \bar{p})$, where $\bar{p}$ is a relaxed version of p such that $p' \Rightarrow \bar{p}$, otherwise.

1: $\bar{p} \leftarrow p$; *match* $\leftarrow$ true;
2: **for all** conjunctive subpredicates c' in p' **do**
3:      **if** quick check is activated $\wedge\, \text{QC}(\bar{p}, c') = 1$ **then**
4:          **continue**;
5:      **else if** quick check is activated $\wedge\, \text{QC}(\bar{p}, c') = -1$ **then**
6:          *match* $\leftarrow$ false;
7:          $\bar{p} \leftarrow \bar{p} \vee c'$;
8:          **continue**;
9:      **else**
10:         /* quick check is deactivated or returns 0 */
11:         $Q_{\text{init}} \leftarrow \emptyset$; $Q^{\text{LIFO}} \leftarrow \emptyset$; $Q_p^{\text{LIFO}} \leftarrow \emptyset$;
12:         enqueue(Q_{init}, c'); enqueue($Q^{\text{LIFO}}, Q_{\text{init}}$); enqueue($Q_p^{\text{LIFO}}, \bar{p}$); $m \leftarrow$ true;
13:         **while** $Q^{\text{LIFO}} \neq \emptyset$ **do**
14:             $Q_{\text{next}} \leftarrow$ dequeue(Q^{LIFO}); $p^- \leftarrow$ dequeue(Q_p^{LIFO});
15:             let c be the first conjunctive subpredicate in p^-; remove c from p^-;
16:             **while** $Q_{\text{next}} \neq \emptyset$ **do**
17:                 $c_c' \leftarrow$ dequeue(Q_{next});
18:                 /* compare dimensions using Algorithm F.4 */
19:                 $Q_c' \leftarrow \text{CD}(c, c_c')$;
20:                 **if** $Q_c' \neq \emptyset$ **then**
21:                     **if** p^- is not the empty predicate **then**
22:                         enqueue(Q^{LIFO}, Q_c'); enqueue(Q_p^{LIFO}, p^-);
23:                     **else**
24:                         $m \leftarrow$ false;
25:                         *match* $\leftarrow$ false;
26:                         $\bar{p} \leftarrow \bar{p} \vee c'$;
27:                         **break**;
28:                     **end if**
29:                 **end if**
30:             **end while**
31:             **if** $m =$ false **then**
32:                 **break**;
33:             **end if**
34:         **end while**
35:     **end if**
36: **end for**
37: **return** $(match, \bar{p})$;

F.5   Standard Evaluation (SE)

Algorithm F.8 Standard Evaluation (SE)

Input: Predicate p and data item i.
Output: true, if i satisfies p; false, otherwise.

1: **for all** conjunctive subpredicates c in p **do**
2:     $match \leftarrow$ true;
3:     **for all** pairs of corresponding dimensions d_c, d_i in c, i with $d_c = d_i$ **do**
4:         **if** the interval defined for d_c in c does not contain the value for d_i in i **then**
5:             $match \leftarrow$ false;
6:             **break**;
7:         **end if**
8:     **end for**
9:     **if** $match =$ true **then**
10:         **return** true;
11:     **end if**
12: **end for**
13: **return** false;

Bibliography

ABADI, D. J., AHMAD, Y., BALAZINSKA, M., ÇETINTEMEL, U., CHERNIACK, M., HWANG, J.-H., LINDNER, W., MASKEY, A. S., RASIN, A., RYVKINA, E., TATBUL, N., XING, Y., AND ZDONIK, S.: The Design of the Borealis Stream Processing Engine. In: *Proc. of the Conf. on Innovative Data Systems Research (CIDR)*, pp. 277–289, Asilomar, CA, USA, January 2005.

ABERER, K., CUDRÉ-MAUROUX, P., DATTA, A., DESPOTOVIC, Z., HAUSWIRTH, M., PUNCEVA, M., AND SCHMIDT, R.: P-Grid: A Self-organizing Structured P2P System. *ACM SIGMOD Record*, 32(3):29–33, September 2003a.

ABERER, K., CUDRÉ-MAUROUX, P., AND HAUSWIRTH, M.: The Chatty Web: Emergent Semantics Through Gossiping. In: *Proc. of the Int'l World Wide Web Conf. (WWW)*, pp. 197–206, Budapest, Hungary, May 2003b.

ABITEBOUL, S.: On Views and XML. In: *Proc. of the ACM SIGACT–SIGMOD–SIGART Symp. on Principles of Database Systems (PODS)*, pp. 1–9, Philadelphia, PA, USA, May 1999.

ABITEBOUL, S., SEGOUFIN, L., AND VIANU, V.: Representing and Querying XML with Incomplete Information. In: *Proc. of the ACM SIGACT–SIGMOD–SIGART Symp. on Principles of Database Systems (PODS)*, pp. 150–161, Santa Barbara, CA, USA, May 2001.

ABITEBOUL, S., SEGOUFIN, L., AND VIANU, V.: Representing and Querying XML with Incomplete Information. *ACM Trans. on Database Systems (TODS)*, 31(1):208–254, March 2006.

ADORF, H.-M., KERBER, F., LEMSON, G., MICOL, A., MIGNANI, R., RAUCH, T., AND VOGES, W.: Assembly and Classification of Spectral Energy Distributions – A new VO Web Service. In: *Proc. of the Conf. on Astronomical Data Analysis Software & Systems (ADASS)*, pp. 365–369, Pasadena, CA, USA, October 2004.

ADORF, H.-M., LEMSON, G., AND VOGES, W.: The GAVO Cross-Matcher Application. In: *Proc. of the Conf. on Astronomical Data Analysis Software & Systems (ADASS)*, pp. 695–698, San Lorenzo de El Escorial, Spain, October 2005.

AHMAD, Y. AND ÇETINTEMEL, U.: Network-Aware Query Processing for Stream-based Applications. In: *Proc. of the Int'l Conf. on Very Large Data Bases (VLDB)*, pp. 456–467, Toronto, Canada, August 2004.

ALTINEL, M. AND FRANKLIN, M. J.: Efficient Filtering of XML Documents for Selective Dissemination of Information. In: *Proc. of the Int'l Conf. on Very Large Data Bases (VLDB)*, pp. 53–64, Cairo, Egypt, September 2000.

ARASU, A., BABCOCK, B., BABU, S., DATAR, M., ITO, K., MOTWANI, R., NISHIZAWA, I., SRIVASTAVA, U., THOMAS, D., VARMA, R., AND WIDOM, J.: STREAM: The Stanford Stream Data Manager. *IEEE Data Engineering Bulletin*, 26(1):19–26, March 2003a.

ARASU, A., BABU, S., AND WIDOM, J.: An Abstract Semantics and Concrete Language for Continuous Queries over Streams and Relations. Technical Report 2002-57, Stanford University, November 2002.

ARASU, A., BABU, S., AND WIDOM, J.: CQL: A Language for Continuous Queries over Streams and Relations. In: *Proc. of the Int'l Workshop on Database Programming Languages (DBPL)*, pp. 1–19, Potsdam, Germany, September 2003b.

ARASU, A., BABU, S., AND WIDOM, J.: The CQL Continuous Query Language: Semantic Foundations and Query Execution. Technical Report 2003-67, Stanford University, October 2003c.

ARASU, A., BABU, S., AND WIDOM, J.: The CQL continuous query language: semantic foundations and query execution. *The VLDB Journal*, 15(2):121–142, June 2006.

ARASU, A. AND WIDOM, J.: A Denotational Semantics for Continuous Queries over Streams and Relations. *ACM SIGMOD Record*, 33(3):6–12, September 2004a.

ARASU, A. AND WIDOM, J.: A Denotational Semantics for Continuous Queries over Streams and Relations. Technical Report 2004-19, Stanford University, March 2004b.

ARASU, A. AND WIDOM, J.: Resource Sharing in Continuous Sliding-Window Aggregates. In: *Proc. of the Int'l Conf. on Very Large Data Bases (VLDB)*, pp. 336–347, Toronto, Canada, August 2004c.

ASCHENBACH, B.: Discovery of a young nearby supernova remnant. *Nature*, 396(6707):141–142, November 1998.

AVNUR, R. AND HELLERSTEIN, J. M.: Eddies: Continuously Adaptive Query Processing. In: *Proc. of the ACM SIGMOD Int'l Conf. on Management of Data*, pp. 261–272, Dallas, TX, USA, May 2000.

AYAD, A. M. AND NAUGHTON, J. F.: Static Optimization of Conjunctive Queries with Sliding Windows Over Infinite Streams. In: *Proc. of the ACM SIGMOD Int'l Conf. on Management of Data*, pp. 419–430, Paris, France, June 2004.

BABCOCK, B., BABU, S., DATAR, M., MOTWANI, R., AND WIDOM, J.: Models and Issues in Data Stream Systems. In: *Proc. of the ACM SIGACT–SIGMOD–SIGART Symp. on Principles of Database Systems (PODS)*, pp. 1–16, Madison, WI, USA, June 2002.

BABCOCK, B., DATAR, M., AND MOTWANI, R.: Load Shedding for Aggregation Queries over Data Streams. In: *Proc. of the IEEE Int'l Conf. on Data Engineering (ICDE)*, pp. 350–361, Boston, MA, USA, March 2004.

BABU, S., MUNAGALA, K., WIDOM, J., AND MOTWANI, R.: Adaptive Caching for Continuous Queries. In: *Proc. of the IEEE Int'l Conf. on Data Engineering (ICDE)*, pp. 118–129, Tokyo, Japan, April 2005.

BABU, S. AND WIDOM, J.: Continuous Queries over Data Streams. *ACM SIGMOD Record*, 30(3):109–120, September 2001.

BALMIN, A., ÖZCAN, F., BEYER, K. S., COCHRANE, R. J., AND PIRAHESH, H.: A Framework for Using Materialized XPath Views in XML Query Processing. In: *Proc. of the Int'l Conf. on Very Large Data Bases (VLDB)*, pp. 60–71, Toronto, Canada, August 2004.

BECKMANN, N., KRIEGEL, H.-P., SCHNEIDER, R., AND SEEGER, B.: The R*-tree: An Efficient and Robust Access Method for Points and Rectangles. In: *Proc. of the ACM SIGMOD Int'l Conf. on Management of Data*, pp. 322–331, Atlantic City, NJ, USA, May 1990.

BONNET, P., GEHRKE, J., AND SESHADRI, P.: Towards Sensor Database Systems. In: *Proc. of the IEEE Int'l Conf. on Mobile Data Management (MDM)*, pp. 3–14, Hong Kong, China, January 2001.

BORNHÖVD, C., LIN, T., HALLER, S., AND SCHAPER, J.: Integrating Smart Items with Business Processes – An Experience Report. In: *Proc. of the Hawaii Int'l Conf. on System Sciences (HICSS)*, p. 227.3, Waikoloa, HI, USA, January 2005.

BOTAN, I., FISCHER, P. M., FLORESCU, D., KOSSMANN, D., KRASKA, T., AND TAMOSEVICIUS, R.: Extending XQuery with Window Functions. In: *Proc. of the Int'l Conf. on Very Large Data Bases (VLDB)*, pp. 75–86, Vienna, Austria, September 2007.

BRAUMANDL, R., KEIDL, M., KEMPER, A., KOSSMANN, D., KREUTZ, A., SELTZSAM, S., AND STOCKER, K.: ObjectGlobe: Ubiquitous query processing on the Internet. *The VLDB Journal*, 10(1):48–71, August 2001.

BRETTLECKER, G. AND SCHULDT, H.: The OSIRIS-SE (Stream-Enabled) Infrastructure for Reliable Data Stream Management on Mobile Devices. In: *Proc. of the ACM SIGMOD Int'l Conf. on Management of Data*, pp. 1097–1099, Beijing, China, June 2007.

BRETTLECKER, G., SCHULDT, H., AND SCHATZ, R.: Hyperdatabases for Peer-to-Peer Data Stream Processing. In: *Proc. of the IEEE Int'l Conf. on Web Services (ICWS)*, pp. 358–366, San Diego, CA, USA, June 2004.

BRETTLECKER, G., SCHULDT, H., AND SCHEK, H.-J.: Towards Reliable Data Stream Processing with OSIRIS-SE. In: *Proc. of the Conf. on Database Systems for Business, Technology, and Web (BTW)*, pp. 405–414, Karlsruhe, Germany, March 2005.

BRUNKHORST, I., DHRAIEF, H., KEMPER, A., NEJDL, W., AND WIESNER, C.: Distributed Queries and Query Optimization in Schema-Based P2P-Systems. In: *Proc. of the Int'l Workshop on Databases, Information Systems and Peer-to-Peer Computing (DBISP2P)*, pp. 184–199, Berlin, Germany, September 2003.

BRY, F.: Towards an Efficient Evaluation of General Queries: Quantifier and Disjunction Processing Revisited. In: *Proc. of the ACM SIGMOD Int'l Conf. on Management of Data*, pp. 193–204, Portland, OR, USA, May 1989.

BUDAVÁRI, T., MALIK, T., SZALAY, A., THAKAR, A., AND GRAY, J.: SkyQuery – A Prototype Distributed Query Web Service for the Virtual Observatory. In: *Proc. of the Conf. on Astronomical Data Analysis Software & Systems (ADASS)*, pp. 31–34, Baltimore, MD, USA, October 2002.

BUDAVÁRI, T., SZALAY, A., MALIK, T., THAKAR, A., O'MULLANE, W., WILLIAMS, R., GRAY, J., MANN, B., AND YASUDA, N.: Open SkyQuery – VO Compliant Dynamic Federation of Astronomical Archives. In: *Proc. of the Conf. on Astronomical Data Analysis Software & Systems (ADASS)*, pp. 177–180, Strasbourg, France, October 2003.

CAMMERT, M., HEINZ, C., KRÄMER, J., SEEGER, B., VAUPEL, S., AND WOLSKE, U.: Flexible Multi-Threaded Scheduling for Continuous Queries over Data Streams. In: *Proc. of the Int'l Workshop on Scalable Stream Processing Systems (SSPS)*, Istanbul, Turkey, April 2007a.

CAMMERT, M., KRÄMER, J., AND SEEGER, B.: Dynamic Metadata Management for Scalable Stream Processing Systems. In: *Proc. of the Int'l Workshop on Scalable Stream Processing Systems (SSPS)*, Istanbul, Turkey, April 2007b.

CAMMERT, M., KRÄMER, J., SEEGER, B., AND VAUPEL, S.: An Approach to Adaptive Memory Management in Data Stream Systems. In: *Proc. of the IEEE Int'l Conf. on Data Engineering (ICDE)*, p. 137, Atlanta, GA, USA, April 2006.

CARNEY, D., ÇETINTEMEL, U., CHERNIACK, M., CONVEY, C., LEE, S., SEIDMAN, G., STONEBRAKER, M., TATBUL, N., AND ZDONIK, S.: Monitoring Streams – A New Class of Data Management Applications. In: *Proc. of the Int'l Conf. on Very Large Data Bases (VLDB)*, pp. 215–226, Hong Kong, China, August 2002.

CASTRO, M., DRUSCHEL, P., KERMARREC, A.-M., AND ROWSTRON, A.: Scribe: A Large-Scale and Decentralized Application-Level Multicast Infrastructure. *IEEE Journal on Selected Areas in Communications (JSAC)*, 20(8):1489–1499, October 2002.

CHAN, C.-Y., FELBER, P., GAROFALAKIS, M., AND RASTOGI, R.: Efficient filtering of XML documents with XPath expressions. *The VLDB Journal*, 11(4):354–379, December 2002a.

CHAN, C.-Y., FELBER, P., GAROFALAKIS, M., AND RASTOGI, R.: Efficient Filtering of XML Documents with XPath Expressions. In: *Proc. of the IEEE Int'l Conf. on Data Engineering (ICDE)*, pp. 235–244, San José, CA, USA, February 2002b.

CHANDRASEKARAN, S., COOPER, O., DESHPANDE, A., FRANKLIN, M. J., HELLERSTEIN, J. M., HONG, W., KRISHNAMURTHY, S., MADDEN, S., RAMAN, V., REISS, F., AND SHAH, M.: TelegraphCQ: Continuous Dataflow Processing for an Uncertain World. In: *Proc. of the Conf. on Innovative Data Systems Research (CIDR)*, Asilomar, CA, USA, January 2003.

CHANDRASEKARAN, S. AND FRANKLIN, M. J.: Streaming Queries over Streaming Data. In: *Proc. of the Int'l Conf. on Very Large Data Bases (VLDB)*, pp. 203–214, Hong Kong, China, August 2002.

CHANG, J.-Y. AND LEE, S.-G.: An Optimization of Disjunctive Queries: Union-Pushdown. In: *Proc. of the Int'l Computer Software and Applications Conf. (COMPSAC)*, pp. 356–361, Washington, DC, USA, August 1997.

CHEN, J., DEWITT, D. J., TIAN, F., AND WANG, Y.: NiagaraCQ: A Scalable Continuous Query System for Internet Databases. In: *Proc. of the ACM SIGMOD Int'l Conf. on Management of Data*, pp. 379–390, Dallas, TX, USA, May 2000.

CHEN, L., REDDY, K., AND AGRAWAL, G.: GATES: A Grid-Based Middleware for Processing Distributed Data Streams. In: *Proc. of the IEEE Int'l Symp. on High-Performance Distributed Computing (HPDC)*, pp. 192–201, Honolulu, HI, USA, June 2004.

CHEN, L. AND RUNDENSTEINER, E. A.: ACE-XQ: A CachE-aware XQuery Answering System. In: *Proc. of the Int'l Workshop on the Web and Databases (WebDB)*, pp. 31–36, Madison, WI, USA, June 2002.

CHERNIACK, M., BALAKRISHNAN, H., BALAZINSKA, M., CARNEY, D., ÇETINTEMEL, U., XING, Y., AND ZDONIK, S.: Scalable Distributed Stream Processing. In: *Proc. of the Conf. on Innovative Data Systems Research (CIDR)*, Asilomar, CA, USA, January 2003.

CLAUSSEN, J., KEMPER, A., MOERKOTTE, G., PEITHNER, K., AND STEINBRUNN, M.: Optimization and Evaluation of Disjunctive Queries. *IEEE Trans. on Knowledge and Data Engineering (TKDE)*, 12(2):238–260, March 2000.

CRANOR, C., GAO, Y., JOHNSON, T., SHKAPENYUK, V., AND SPATSCHECK, O.: Gigascope: High Performance Network Monitoring with an SQL Interface. In: *Proc. of the ACM SIGMOD Int'l Conf. on Management of Data*, p. 623, Madison, WI, USA, June 2002.

CRANOR, C., JOHNSON, T., SPATSCHECK, O., AND SHKAPENYUK, V.: Gigascope: A Stream Database for Network Applications. In: *Proc. of the ACM SIGMOD Int'l Conf. on Management of Data*, pp. 647–651, San Diego, CA, USA, June 2003a.

CRANOR, C., JOHNSON, T., SPATSCHECK, O., AND SHKAPENYUK, V.: The Gigascope Stream Database. *IEEE Data Engineering Bulletin*, 26(1):27–32, March 2003b.

CZAJKOWSKI, K., FERGUSON, D. F., FOSTER, I., FREY, J., GRAHAM, S., SEDUKHIN, I., SNELLING, D., TUECKE, S., AND VAMBENEPE, W.: The WS-Resource Framework, Version 1.0. March 2004, http://www.globus.org/wsrf/specs/ws-wsrf.pdf.

DAR, S., FRANKLIN, M. J., JÓNSSON, B. T., SRIVASTAVA, D., AND TAN, M.: Semantic Data Caching and Replacement. In: *Proc. of the Int'l Conf. on Very Large Data Bases (VLDB)*, pp. 330–341, Mumbai (Bombay), India, September 1996.

DEERING, S. E. AND CHERITON, D. R.: Multicast Routing in Datagram Internetworks and Extended LANs. *ACM Trans. on Computer Systems (TOCS)*, 8(2):85–110, May 1990.

DEMERS, A., GEHRKE, J., HONG, M., RIEDEWALD, M., AND WHITE, W.: Towards Expressive Publish/Subscribe Systems. In: *Proc. of the Int'l Conf. on Extending Database Technology (EDBT)*, pp. 627–644, Munich, Germany, March 2006.

DEMERS, A., GEHRKE, J., RAJARAMAN, R., TRIGONI, N., AND YAO, Y.: The Cougar Project: A Work-In-Progress Report. *ACM SIGMOD Record*, 32(4):53–59, December 2003.

DENNY, M. AND FRANKLIN, M. J.: Predicate Result Range Caching for Continuous Queries. In: *Proc. of the ACM SIGMOD Int'l Conf. on Management of Data*, pp. 646–657, Baltimore, MD, USA, June 2005.

DHAMANKAR, R., LEE, Y., DOAN, A., HALEVY, A., AND DOMINGOS, P.: iMAP: Discovering Complex Semantic Matches between Database Schemas. In: *Proc. of the ACM SIGMOD Int'l Conf. on Management of Data*, pp. 383–394, Paris, France, June 2004.

DIAO, Y., ALTINEL, M., FRANKLIN, M. J., ZHANG, H., AND FISCHER, P.: Path Sharing and Predicate Evaluation for High-Performance XML Filtering. *ACM Trans. on Database Systems (TODS)*, 28(4):467–516, December 2003.

DIAO, Y., FISCHER, P., FRANKLIN, M. J., AND TO, R.: YFilter: Efficient and Scalable Filtering of XML Documents. In: *Proc. of the IEEE Int'l Conf. on Data Engineering (ICDE)*, pp. 341–342, San José, CA, USA, February 2002.

DIAO, Y. AND FRANKLIN, M.: Query Processing for High-Volume XML Message Brokering. In: *Proc. of the Int'l Conf. on Very Large Data Bases (VLDB)*, pp. 261–272, Berlin, Germany, September 2003a.

DIAO, Y. AND FRANKLIN, M. J.: High-Performance XML Filtering: An Overview of YFilter. *IEEE Data Engineering Bulletin*, 26(1):41–48, March 2003b.

DIAO, Y., RIZVI, S., AND FRANKLIN, M. J.: Towards an Internet-Scale XML Dissemination Service. In: *Proc. of the Int'l Conf. on Very Large Data Bases (VLDB)*, pp. 612–623, Toronto, Canada, August 2004.

DOAN, A., DOMINGOS, P., AND HALEVY, A.: Reconciling Schemas of Disparate Data Sources: A Machine-Learning Approach. In: *Proc. of the ACM SIGMOD Int'l Conf. on Management of Data*, pp. 509–520, Santa Barbara, CA, USA, May 2001.

DOAN, A., DOMINGOS, P., AND LEVY, A.: Learning Source Descriptions for Data Integration. In: *Proc. of the Int'l Workshop on the Web and Databases (WebDB)*, pp. 81–86, Dallas, TX, USA, May 2000.

DOBRA, A., GAROFALAKIS, M., GEHRKE, J., AND RASTOGI, R.: Processing Complex Aggregate Queries over Data Streams. In: *Proc. of the ACM SIGMOD Int'l Conf. on Management of Data*, pp. 61–72, Madison, WI, USA, June 2002.

DOBRA, A., GAROFALAKIS, M., GEHRKE, J., AND RASTOGI, R.: Sketch-Based Multi-query Processing over Data Streams. In: *Proc. of the Int'l Conf. on Extending Database Technology (EDBT)*, pp. 551–568, Heraklion, Crete, Greece, March 2004.

DONG, X., HALEVY, A. Y., AND TATARINOV, I.: Containment of Nested XML Queries. In: *Proc. of the Int'l Conf. on Very Large Data Bases (VLDB)*, pp. 132–143, Toronto, Canada, August 2004.

ENDERLE, J., SCHNEIDER, N., AND SEIDL, T.: Efficiently Processing Queries on Interval-and-Value Tuples in Relational Databases. In: *Proc. of the Int'l Conf. on Very Large Data Bases (VLDB)*, pp. 385–396, Trondheim, Norway, August 2005.

FABRET, F., JACOBSEN, H. A., LLIRBAT, F., PEREIRA, J., ROSS, K. A., AND SHASHA, D.: Filtering Algorithms and Implementation for Very Fast Publish/Subscribe Systems. In: *Proc. of the ACM SIGMOD Int'l Conf. on Management of Data*, pp. 115–126, Santa Barbara, CA, USA, May 2001.

FISCHER, P. M., KOSSMANN, D., KRASKA, T., AND TAMOSEVICIUS, R.: Windows for XQuery – Use Cases. Technical Report, ETH Zurich, November 2006.

FLORESCU, D., HILLERY, C., KOSSMANN, D., LUCAS, P., RICCARDI, F., WESTMANN, T., CAREY, M. J., AND SUNDARARAJAN, A.: The BEA streaming XQuery processor. *The VLDB Journal*, 13(3):294–315, September 2004.

FLORESCU, D., HILLERY, C., KOSSMANN, D., LUCAS, P., RICCARDI, F., WESTMANN, T., CAREY, M. J., SUNDARARAJAN, A., AND AGRAWAL, G.: The BEA/XQRL Streaming XQuery Processor. In: *Proc. of the Int'l Conf. on Very Large Data Bases (VLDB)*, pp. 997–1008, Berlin, Germany, September 2003.

FOSTER, I. AND KESSELMAN, C. (eds.): *The Grid: Blueprint for a New Computing Infrastructure*. Morgan Kaufmann Publishers, 2nd edition, 2004.

FOSTER, I., KISHIMOTO, H., SAVVA, A., BERRY, D., DJAOUI, A., GRIMSHAW, A., HORN, B., MACIEL, F., SIEBENLIST, F., SUBRAMANIAM, R., TREADWELL, J., AND VON REICH, J.: The Open Grid Services Architecture, Version 1.0. January 2005, http://www.gridforum.org/documents/GWD-I-E/GFD-I.030.pdf.

FRANKLIN, M. J., JEFFERY, S. R., KRISHNAMURTHY, S., REISS, F., RIZVI, S., WU, E., COOPER, O., EDAKKUNNI, A., AND HONG, W.: Design Considerations for High Fan-in Systems: The HiFi Approach. In: *Proc. of the Conf. on Innovative Data Systems Research (CIDR)*, pp. 290–304, Asilomar, CA, USA, January 2005.

FREIRE, J., HARITSA, J. R., RAMANATH, M., ROY, P., AND SIMÉON, J.: StatiX: Making XML Count. In: *Proc. of the ACM SIGMOD Int'l Conf. on Management of Data*, pp. 181–191, Madison, WI, USA, June 2002.

FUNG, W. F., SUN, D., AND GEHRKE, J.: COUGAR: The Network is the Database. In: *Proc. of the ACM SIGMOD Int'l Conf. on Management of Data*, p. 621, Madison, WI, USA, June 2002.

GAEDE, V. AND GÜNTHER, O.: Multidimensional Access Methods. *ACM Computing Surveys*, 30(2):170–231, June 1998.

GANGULY, S., GAROFALAKIS, M., AND RASTOGI, R.: Processing Data-Stream Join Aggregates Using Skimmed Sketches. In: *Proc. of the Int'l Conf. on Extending Database Technology (EDBT)*, pp. 569–586, Heraklion, Crete, Greece, March 2004.

GEDIK, B. AND LIU, L.: Quality-Aware Distributed Data Delivery for Continuous Query Services. In: *Proc. of the ACM SIGMOD Int'l Conf. on Management of Data*, pp. 419–430, Chicago, IL, USA, June 2006.

GOLAB, L., BIJAY, K. G., AND ÖZSU, M. T.: Multi-Query Optimization of Sliding Window Aggregates by Schedule Synchronization. In: *Proc. of the ACM Int'l Conf. on Information and Knowledge Management (CIKM)*, pp. 844–845, Arlington, VA, USA, November 2006a.

GOLAB, L., BIJAY, K. G., AND ÖZSU, M. T.: Multi-Query Optimization of Sliding Window Aggregates by Schedule Synchronization. Technical Report CS-2006-26, University of Waterloo, August 2006b.

GOLAB, L. AND ÖZSU, M. T.: Data Stream Management Issues – A Survey. Technical Report CS-2003-08, University of Waterloo, April 2003a.

GOLAB, L. AND ÖZSU, M. T.: Issues in Data Stream Management. *ACM SIGMOD Record*, 32(2):5–14, June 2003b.

GOLAB, L. AND ÖZSU, M. T.: Processing Sliding Window Multi-Joins in Continuous Queries over Data Streams. In: *Proc. of the Int'l Conf. on Very Large Data Bases (VLDB)*, pp. 500–511, Berlin, Germany, September 2003c.

GRAY, J., BOSWORTH, A., LAYMAN, A., AND PIRAHESH, H.: Data Cube: A Relational Aggregation Operator Generalizing Group-By, Cross-Tab, and Sub-Totals. In: *Proc. of the IEEE Int'l Conf. on Data Engineering (ICDE)*, pp. 152–159, New Orleans, LA, USA, February 1996.

GUO, S., SUN, W., AND WEISS, M. A.: Solving Satisfiability and Implication Problems in Database Systems. *ACM Trans. on Database Systems (TODS)*, 21(2):270–293, June 1996.

GUPTA, A. K., HALEVY, A. Y., AND SUCIU, D.: View Selection for Stream Processing. In: *Proc. of the Int'l Workshop on the Web and Databases (WebDB)*, pp. 83–88, Madison, WI, USA, June 2002.

GUPTA, A. K., SUCIU, D., AND HALEVY, A. Y.: The View Selection Problem for XML Content Based Routing. In: *Proc. of the ACM SIGACT–SIGMOD–SIGART Symp. on Principles of Database Systems (PODS)*, pp. 68–77, San Diego, CA, USA, June 2003.

GUTTMAN, A.: R-Trees: A Dynamic Index Structure for Spatial Searching. In: *Proc. of the ACM SIGMOD Int'l Conf. on Management of Data*, pp. 47–57, Boston, MA, USA, June 1984.

HAAS, P. J. AND HELLERSTEIN, J. M.: Ripple Joins for Online Aggregation. In: *Proc. of the ACM SIGMOD Int'l Conf. on Management of Data*, pp. 287–298, Philadelphia, PA, USA, June 1999.

HALEVY, A. Y., IVES, Z. G., MORK, P., AND TATARINOV, I.: Piazza: Data Management Infrastructure for Semantic Web Applications. In: *Proc. of the Int'l World Wide Web Conf. (WWW)*, pp. 556–567, Budapest, Hungary, May 2003.

HAMMAD, M. A., AREF, W. G., AND ELMAGARMID, A. K.: Stream Window Join: Tracking Moving Objects in Sensor-Network Databases. In: *Proc. of the Int'l Conf. on Scientific and Statistical Database Management (SSDBM)*, pp. 75–84, Cambridge, MA, USA, July 2003a.

HAMMAD, M. A., FRANKLIN, M. J., AREF, W. G., AND ELMAGARMID, A. K.: Scheduling for shared window joins over data streams. In: *Proc. of the Int'l Conf. on Very Large Data Bases (VLDB)*, pp. 297–308, Berlin, Germany, September 2003b.

HANSON, E. N., CHAABOUNI, M., KIM, C.-H., AND WANG, Y.-W.: A Predicate Matching Algorithm for Database Rule Systems. In: *Proc. of the ACM SIGMOD Int'l Conf. on Management of Data*, pp. 271–280, Atlantic City, NJ, USA, May 1990.

HANSON, E. N. AND JOHNSON, T.: Selection Predicate Indexing for Active Databases Using Interval Skip Lists. *Information Systems*, 21(3):269–298, May 1996.

HEINRICH, C.: *RFID and Beyond: Growing Your Business through Real World Awareness*. Wiley & Sons, 2005.

HEINZ, C. AND SEEGER, B.: Towards Kernel Density Estimation over Streaming Data. In: *Proc. of the Int'l Conf. on Management of Data (COMAD)*, pp. 91–102, Delhi, India, December 2006.

HEINZ, C. AND SEEGER, B.: Adaptive Wavelet Density Estimators over Data Streams. In: *Proc. of the Int'l Conf. on Scientific and Statistical Database Management (SSDBM)*, p. 35, Banff, Canada, July 2007.

HELLERSTEIN, J. M. AND STONEBRAKER, M.: Predicate Migration: Optimizing Queries with Expensive Predicates. In: *Proc. of the ACM SIGMOD Int'l Conf. on Management of Data*, pp. 267–276, Washington, D.C., USA, May 1993.

HONG, M., DEMERS, A., GEHRKE, J., KOCH, C., RIEDEWALD, M., AND WHITE, W.: Massively Multi-Query Join Processing in Publish/Subscribe Systems. In: *Proc. of the ACM SIGMOD Int'l Conf. on Management of Data*, pp. 761–772, Beijing, China, June 2007.

HRISTIDIS, V. AND PETROPOULOS, M.: Semantic Caching of XML Databases. In: *Proc. of the Int'l Workshop on the Web and Databases (WebDB)*, pp. 25–30, Madison, WI, USA, June 2002.

HUANG, Q., LU, C., AND ROMAN, G.-C.: Spatiotemporal Multicast in Sensor Networks. In: *Proc. of the Int'l Conf. on Embedded Networked Sensor Systems (SenSys)*, pp. 205–217, Los Angeles, CA, USA, November 2003.

HUEBSCH, R., CHUN, B., HELLERSTEIN, J. M., LOO, B. T., MANIATIS, P., ROSCOE, T., SHENKER, S., STOICA, I., AND YUMEREFENDI, A. R.: The Architecture of PIER: an Internet-Scale Query Processor. In: *Proc. of the Conf. on Innovative Data Systems Research (CIDR)*, pp. 28–43, Asilomar, CA, USA, January 2005.

HUEBSCH, R., GAROFALAKIS, M., HELLERSTEIN, J. M., AND STOICA, I.: Sharing Aggregate Computation for Distributed Queries. In: *Proc. of the ACM SIGMOD Int'l Conf. on Management of Data*, pp. 485–496, Beijing, China, June 2007.

HUEBSCH, R., HELLERSTEIN, J. M., LANHAM, N., LOO, B. T., SHENKER, S., AND STOICA, I.: Querying the Internet with PIER. In: *Proc. of the Int'l Conf. on Very Large Data Bases (VLDB)*, pp. 321–332, Berlin, Germany, September 2003.

IVOA: VOTable Format Definition, Version 1.1 (IVOA Recommendation, August 11th, 2004). August 2004, http://www.ivoa.net/Documents/latest/VOT.html.

IVOA: IVOA Astronomical Data Query Language, Version 1.01 (IVOA Working Draft, June 24th, 2005). June 2005, http://www.ivoa.net/Documents/latest/ADQL.html.

JOHNSON, T., MUTHUKRISHNAN, S., SHKAPENYUK, V., AND SPATSCHECK, O.: A Heartbeat Mechanism and its Application in Gigascope. In: *Proc. of the Int'l Conf. on Very Large Data Bases (VLDB)*, pp. 1079–1088, Trondheim, Norway, August 2005.

KANG, J., NAUGHTON, J. F., AND VIGLAS, S. D.: Evaluating Window Joins over Unbounded Streams. In: *Proc. of the IEEE Int'l Conf. on Data Engineering (ICDE)*, pp. 341–352, Bangalore, India, March 2003.

KEIDL, M., KREUTZ, A., KEMPER, A., AND KOSSMANN, D.: A Publish & Subscribe Architecture for Distributed Metadata Management. In: *Proc. of the IEEE Int'l Conf. on Data Engineering (ICDE)*, pp. 309–320, San José, CA, USA, February 2002.

KEMPER, A., MOERKOTTE, G., PEITHNER, K., AND STEINBRUNN, M.: Optimizing Disjunctive Queries with Expensive Predicates. In: *Proc. of the ACM SIGMOD Int'l Conf. on Management of Data*, pp. 336–347, Minneapolis, MN, USA, May 1994.

KOCH, C., SCHERZINGER, S., SCHWEIKARDT, N., AND STEGMAIER, B.: FluXQuery: An Optimizing XQuery Processor for Streaming XML Data. In: *Proc. of the Int'l Conf. on Very Large Data Bases (VLDB)*, pp. 1309–1312, Toronto, Canada, August 2004a.

KOCH, C., SCHERZINGER, S., SCHWEIKARDT, N., AND STEGMAIER, B.: Schema-based Scheduling of Event Processors and Buffer Minimization for Queries on Structured Data Streams. In: *Proc. of the Int'l Conf. on Very Large Data Bases (VLDB)*, pp. 228–239, Toronto, Canada, August 2004b.

KOSSMANN, D.: The State of the Art in Distributed Query Processing. *ACM Computing Surveys*, 32(4):422–469, December 2000.

KOSSMANN, D., FRANKLIN, M. J., AND DRASCH, G.: Cache Investment: Integrating Query Optimization and Distributed Data Placement. *ACM Trans. on Database Systems (TODS)*, 25(4):517–558, December 2000.

KRÄMER, J. AND SEEGER, B.: PIPES – A Public Infrastructure for Processing and Exploring Streams. In: *Proc. of the ACM SIGMOD Int'l Conf. on Management of Data*, pp. 925–926, Paris, France, June 2004.

KRÄMER, J. AND SEEGER, B.: A Temporal Foundation for Continuous Queries over Data Streams. In: *Proc. of the Int'l Conf. on Management of Data (COMAD)*, pp. 70–82, Goa, India, January 2005.

KRÄMER, J., YANG, Y., CAMMERT, M., SEEGER, B., AND PAPADIAS, D.: Dynamic Plan Migration for Snapshot-Equivalent Continuous Queries in Data Stream Systems. In: *Proc. of the Int'l Conf. on Semantics of a Networked World (ICSNW)*, pp. 497–516, Munich, Germany, March 2006.

KRISHNAMURTHY, S., CHANDRASEKARAN, S., COOPER, O., DESHPANDE, A., FRANKLIN, M. J., HELLERSTEIN, J. M., HONG, W., MADDEN, S. R., REISS, F., AND SHAH, M. A.: TelegraphCQ: An Architectural Status Report. *IEEE Data Engineering Bulletin*, 26(1):11–18, March 2003.

KRISHNAMURTHY, S., FRANKLIN, M. J., HELLERSTEIN, J. M., AND JACOBSON, G.: The Case for Precision Sharing. In: *Proc. of the Int'l Conf. on Very Large Data Bases (VLDB)*, pp. 972–983, Toronto, Canada, August 2004.

KRISHNAMURTHY, S., WU, C., AND FRANKLIN, M. J.: On-the-Fly Sharing for Streamed Aggregation. In: *Proc. of the ACM SIGMOD Int'l Conf. on Management of Data*, pp. 623–634, Chicago, IL, USA, June 2006.

KUNTSCHKE, R. AND KEMPER, A.: Data Stream Sharing. In: *Proc. of the Int'l Workshop on Pervasive Information Management (PIM)*, pp. 45–56, Munich, Germany, March 2006a.

KUNTSCHKE, R. AND KEMPER, A.: Data Stream Sharing. In: *Current Trends in Database Technology – EDBT 2006, EDBT 2006 Workshop PhD, DataX, IIDB, IIHA, ICSNW, QLQP, PIM, PaRMa, and Reactivity on the Web, Munich, Germany, March 26-31, 2006, Revised Selected Papers, Lecture Notes in Computer Science (LNCS)*, vol. 4254, pp. 769–788, Springer Verlag, March 2006b.

KUNTSCHKE, R. AND KEMPER, A.: Matching and Evaluation of Disjunctive Predicates for Data Stream Sharing. In: *Proc. of the ACM Int'l Conf. on Information and Knowledge Management (CIKM)*, pp. 832–833, Arlington, VA, USA, November 2006c.

KUNTSCHKE, R. AND KEMPER, A.: Matching and Evaluation of Disjunctive Predicates for Data Stream Sharing. Technical Report TUM-I0615, Technische Universität München, August 2006d.

KUNTSCHKE, R., SCHOLL, T., HUBER, S., KEMPER, A., REISER, A., ADORF, H.-M., LEMSON, G., AND VOGES, W.: Grid-based Data Stream Processing in e-Science. In: *Proc. of the IEEE Int'l Conf. on e-Science and Grid Computing (eScience)*, p. 30, Amsterdam, The Netherlands, December 2006.

KUNTSCHKE, R., STEGMAIER, B., HÄUSLSCHMID, F., REISER, A., KEMPER, A., ADORF, H.-M., ENKE, H., LEMSON, G., AND VOGES, W.: Datenstrom-Management für e-Science mit StreamGlobe. *Datenbank-Spektrum*, 4(11):14–22, November 2004.

KUNTSCHKE, R., STEGMAIER, B., AND KEMPER, A.: Data Stream Sharing. Technical Report TUM-I0504, Technische Universität München, April 2005a.

KUNTSCHKE, R., STEGMAIER, B., KEMPER, A., AND REISER, A.: StreamGlobe: Processing and Sharing Data Streams in Grid-Based P2P Infrastructures. In: *Proc. of the Int'l Conf. on Very Large Data Bases (VLDB)*, pp. 1259–1262, Trondheim, Norway, August 2005b.

LERNER, A. AND SHASHA, D.: AQuery: Query Language for Ordered Data, Optimization Techniques, and Experiments. In: *Proc. of the Int'l Conf. on Very Large Data Bases (VLDB)*, pp. 345–356, Berlin, Germany, September 2003.

LEVY, A. Y., MENDELZON, A. O., SAGIV, Y., AND SRIVASTAVA, D.: Answering Queries Using Views. In: *Proc. of the ACM SIGACT–SIGMOD–SIGART Symp. on Principles of Database Systems (PODS)*, pp. 95–104, San José, CA, USA, May 1995.

LI, J., MAIER, D., TUFTE, K., PAPADIMOS, V., AND TUCKER, P. A.: No Pane, No Gain: Efficient Evaluation of Sliding-Window Aggregates over Data Streams. *ACM SIGMOD Record*, 34(1):39–44, March 2005a.

LI, J., MAIER, D., TUFTE, K., PAPADIMOS, V., AND TUCKER, P. A.: Semantics and Evaluation Techniques for Window Aggregates in Data Streams. In: *Proc. of the ACM SIGMOD Int'l Conf. on Management of Data*, pp. 311–322, Baltimore, MD, USA, June 2005b.

LI, X. AND AGRAWAL, G.: Efficient Evaluation of XQuery over Streaming Data. In: *Proc. of the Int'l Conf. on Very Large Data Bases (VLDB)*, pp. 265–276, Trondheim, Norway, August 2005.

LIM, H.-S., LEE, J.-G., LEE, M.-J., WHANG, K.-Y., AND SONG, I.-Y.: Continuous Query Processing in Data Streams Using Duality of Data and Queries. In: *Proc. of the ACM SIGMOD Int'l Conf. on Management of Data*, pp. 313–324, Chicago, IL, USA, June 2006.

LIN, K.-I., JAGADISH, H. V., AND FALOUTSOS, C.: The TV-Tree: An Index Structure for High-Dimensional Data. *The VLDB Journal*, 3(4):517–542, October 1994.

LIU, D. T. AND FRANKLIN, M. J.: GridDB: A Data-Centric Overlay for Scientific Grids. In: *Proc. of the Int'l Conf. on Very Large Data Bases (VLDB)*, pp. 600–611, Toronto, Canada, August 2004.

MADDEN, S. AND FRANKLIN, M. J.: Fjording the Stream: An Architecture for Queries Over Streaming Sensor Data. In: *Proc. of the IEEE Int'l Conf. on Data Engineering (ICDE)*, pp. 555–566, San José, CA, USA, February 2002.

MADDEN, S., FRANKLIN, M. J., HELLERSTEIN, J. M., AND HONG, W.: TAG: a Tiny AGgregation Service for Ad-Hoc Sensor Networks. In: *Proc. of the Symp. on Operating System Design and Implementation (OSDI)*, Boston, MA, USA, December 2002a.

MADDEN, S., SHAH, M., HELLERSTEIN, J. M., AND RAMAN, V.: Continuously Adaptive Continuous Queries over Streams. In: *Proc. of the ACM SIGMOD Int'l Conf. on Management of Data*, pp. 49–60, Madison, WI, USA, June 2002b.

MADDEN, S. R., FRANKLIN, M. J., HELLERSTEIN, J. M., AND HONG, W.: TinyDB: An Acquisitional Query Processing System for Sensor Networks. *ACM Trans. on Database Systems (TODS)*, 30(1):122–173, March 2005.

MALIK, T., SZALAY, A. S., BUDAVÁRI, T., AND THAKAR, A. R.: SkyQuery: A Web Service Approach to Federate Databases. In: *Proc. of the Conf. on Innovative Data Systems Research (CIDR)*, Asilomar, CA, USA, January 2003.

MANDHANI, B. AND SUCIU, D.: Query Caching and View Selection for XML Databases. In: *Proc. of the Int'l Conf. on Very Large Data Bases (VLDB)*, pp. 469–480, Trondheim, Norway, August 2005.

MANJHI, A., NATH, S., AND GIBBONS, P. B.: Tributaries and Deltas: Efficient and Robust Aggregation in Sensor Network Streams. In: *Proc. of the ACM SIGMOD Int'l Conf. on Management of Data*, pp. 287–298, Baltimore, MD, USA, June 2005.

MARIAN, A. AND SIMÉON, J.: Projecting XML Documents. In: *Proc. of the Int'l Conf. on Very Large Data Bases (VLDB)*, pp. 213–224, Berlin, Germany, September 2003a.

MARIAN, A. AND SIMÉON, J.: Projecting XML Documents. Technical Report, Columbia University, February 2003b.

MELTON, J. AND SIMON, A. R.: *SQL:1999 – Understanding Relational Language Components*. Morgan Kaufmann Publishers, 2002.

MISTRY, H., ROY, P., SUDARSHAN, S., AND RAMAMRITHAM, K.: Materialized View Selection and Maintenance Using Multi-Query Optimization. In: *Proc. of the ACM SIGMOD Int'l Conf. on Management of Data*, pp. 307–318, Santa Barbara, CA, USA, May 2001.

MOTWANI, R., WIDOM, J., ARASU, A., BABCOCK, B., BABU, S., DATAR, M., MANKU, G., OLSTON, C., ROSENSTEIN, J., AND VARMA, R.: Query Processing, Resource Management, and Approximation in a Data Stream Management System. In: *Proc. of the Conf. on Innovative Data Systems Research (CIDR)*, Asilomar, CA, USA, January 2003.

MURALIKRISHNA, M. AND DEWITT, D. J.: Optimization of Multiple-Relation Multiple-Disjunct Queries. In: *Proc. of the ACM SIGACT–SIGMOD–SIGART Symp. on Principles of Database Systems (PODS)*, pp. 263–275, Austin, TX, USA, March 1988.

NIETO-SANTISTEBAN, M. A., GRAY, J., SZALAY, A. S., ANNIS, J., THAKAR, A. R., AND O'MULLANE, W. J.: When Database Systems Meet the Grid. In: *Proc. of the Conf. on Innovative Data Systems Research (CIDR)*, pp. 154–161, Asilomar, CA, USA, January 2005.

O'MULLANE, W., BUDAVÁRI, T., LI, N., MALIK, T., NIETO-SANTISTEBAN, M. A., SZALAY, A. S., AND THAKAR, A. R.: OpenSkyQuery and OpenSkyNode – the VO Framework to Federate Astronomy Archives. In: *Proc. of the Conf. on Astronomical Data Analysis Software & Systems (ADASS)*, pp. 341–345, Pasadena, CA, USA, October 2004.

ONOSE, N., DEUTSCH, A., PAPAKONSTANTINOU, Y., AND CURTMOLA, E.: Rewriting Nested XML Queries Using Nested Views. In: *Proc. of the ACM SIGMOD Int'l Conf. on Management of Data*, pp. 443–454, Chicago, IL, USA, June 2006.

PAPADIMOS, V., MAIER, D., AND TUFTE, K.: Distributed Query Processing and Catalogs for Peer-to-Peer Systems. In: *Proc. of the Conf. on Innovative Data Systems Research (CIDR)*, Asilomar, CA, USA, January 2003.

PATROUMPAS, K. AND SELLIS, T.: Window Specification over Data Streams. In: *Proc. of the Int'l Conf. on Semantics of a Networked World (ICSNW)*, pp. 445–464, Munich, Germany, March 2006.

PIETZUCH, P., LEDLIE, J., SHNEIDMAN, J., ROUSSOPOULOS, M., WELSH, M., AND SELTZER, M.: Network-Aware Operator Placement for Stream-Processing Systems. In: *Proc. of the IEEE Int'l Conf. on Data Engineering (ICDE)*, p. 49, Atlanta, GA, USA, April 2006.

RAHM, E. AND BERNSTEIN, P. A.: A survey of approaches to automatic schema matching. *The VLDB Journal*, 10(4):334–350, December 2001.

RATNASAMY, S., FRANCIS, P., HANDLEY, M., KARP, R., AND SHENKER, S.: A Scalable Content-Addressable Network. In: *Proc. of the ACM SIGCOMM Conf. on Applications, Technologies, Architectures, and Protocols for Computer Communication*, pp. 161–172, San Diego, CA, USA, August 2001.

RATNASAMY, S., HANDLEY, M., KARP, R., AND SHENKER, S.: Topologically-Aware Overlay Construction and Server Selection. In: *Proc. of the IEEE Conf. on Computer Communications (INFOCOM)*, pp. 1190–1199, New York, NY, USA, June 2002.

ROSENKRANTZ, D. J. AND HUNT, H. B.: Processing Conjunctive Predicates and Queries. In: *Proc. of the Int'l Conf. on Very Large Data Bases (VLDB)*, pp. 64–72, Montreal, Canada, October 1980.

ROWSTRON, A. AND DRUSCHEL, P.: Pastry: Scalable, Decentralized Object Location, and Routing for Large-Scale Peer-to-Peer Systems. In: *IFIP/ACM Int'l Conf. on Distributed Systems Platforms (Middleware)*, pp. 329–350, Heidelberg, Germany, November 2001.

ROY, P., SESHADRI, S., SUDARSHAN, S., AND BHOBE, S.: Efficient and Extensible Algorithms for Multi Query Optimization. In: *Proc. of the ACM SIGMOD Int'l Conf. on Management of Data*, pp. 249–260, Dallas, TX, USA, May 2000.

SCHEK, H.-J., SCHULDT, H., AND WEBER, R.: Hyperdatabases: Infrastructure for the Information Space. In: *Proc. of the Working Conf. on Visual Database Systems (VDB)*, pp. 1–15, Brisbane, Australia, May 2002.

SCHLOSSER, M., SINTEK, M., DECKER, S., AND NEJDL, W.: HyperCuP – Hypercubes, Ontologies, and Efficient Search on Peer-to-Peer Networks. In: *Proc. of the Int'l Workshop on Agents and Peer-to-Peer Computing (AP2PC)*, pp. 112–124, Bologna, Italy, July 2002.

SCHOLL, T., BAUER, B., GUFLER, B., KUNTSCHKE, R., REISER, A., AND KEMPER, A.: HiSbase: Histogram-based P2P Main Memory Data Management. In: *Proc. of the Int'l Conf. on Very Large Data Bases (VLDB)*, pp. 1394–1397, Vienna, Austria, September 2007.

SCHULER, C., WEBER, R., SCHULDT, H., AND SCHEK, H.-J.: Peer-to-Peer Process Execution with OSIRIS. In: *Proc. of the Int'l Conf. on Service-Oriented Computing (ICSOC)*, pp. 483–498, Trento, Italy, December 2003.

SCHULER, C., WEBER, R., SCHULDT, H., AND SCHEK, H.-J.: Scalable Peer-to-Peer Process Management – The OSIRIS Approach. In: *Proc. of the IEEE Int'l Conf. on Web Services (ICWS)*, pp. 26–34, San Diego, CA, USA, June 2004.

SCHWENTICK, T.: XPath Query Containment. *ACM SIGMOD Record*, 33(1):101–109, March 2004.

SELLIS, T., ROUSSOPOULOS, N., AND FALOUTSOS, C.: The R^+-Tree: A Dynamic Index for Multi-Dimensional Objects. In: *Proc. of the Int'l Conf. on Very Large Data Bases (VLDB)*, pp. 507–518, Brighton, England, September 1987.

SELLIS, T. K.: Multiple-Query Optimization. *ACM Trans. on Database Systems (TODS)*, 13(1):23–52, March 1988.

SESHADRI, S., KUMAR, V., COOPER, B. F., AND LIU, L.: Optimizing Multiple Distributed Stream Queries Using Hierarchical Network Partitions. In: *Proc. of the IEEE Int'l Parallel and Distributed Processing Symp. (IPDPS)*, Long Beach, CA, USA, March 2007.

SHAH, A. AND CHIRKOVA, R.: Improving Query Performance Using Materialized XML Views: A Learning-Based Approach. In: *Proc. of the Int'l Workshop on XML Schema and Data Management (XSDM)*, pp. 297–310, Chicago, IL, USA, October 2003.

SHAH, M. A., HELLERSTEIN, J. M., AND BREWER, E.: Highly Available, Fault-Tolerant, Parallel Dataflows. In: *Proc. of the ACM SIGMOD Int'l Conf. on Management of Data*, pp. 827–838, Paris, France, June 2004.

SHAH, M. A., HELLERSTEIN, J. M., CHANDRASEKARAN, S., AND FRANKLIN, M. J.: Flux: An Adaptive Partitioning Operator for Continuous Query Systems. In: *Proc. of the IEEE Int'l Conf. on Data Engineering (ICDE)*, pp. 353–364, Bangalore, India, March 2003.

SHANMUGASUNDARAM, J., KIERNAN, J., SHEKITA, E., FAN, C., AND FUNDERBURK, J.: Querying XML Views of Relational Data. In: *Proc. of the Int'l Conf. on Very Large Data Bases (VLDB)*, pp. 261–270, Roma, Italy, September 2001.

SRIVASTAVA, U., MUNAGALA, K., AND WIDOM, J.: Operator Placement for In-Network Stream Query Processing. In: *Proc. of the ACM SIGACT–SIGMOD–SIGART Symp. on Principles of Database Systems (PODS)*, pp. 250–258, Baltimore, MD, USA, June 2005.

STEGMAIER, B.: *Query Processing on Data Streams*. Ph.D. Thesis, Technische Universität München, June 2006.

STEGMAIER, B. AND KUNTSCHKE, R.: StreamGlobe: Adaptive Anfragebearbeitung und Optimierung auf Datenströmen. In: *GI Workshop Dynamische Informationsfusion*, pp. 367–372, Ulm, Germany, September 2004.

STEGMAIER, B., KUNTSCHKE, R., AND KEMPER, A.: StreamGlobe: Adaptive Query Processing and Optimization in Streaming P2P Environments. In: *Proc. of the Int'l Workshop on Data Management for Sensor Networks (DMSN)*, pp. 88–97, Toronto, Canada, August 2004.

STOICA, I., MORRIS, R., KARGER, D., KAASHOEK, M. F., AND BALAKRISHNAN, H.: Chord: A Scalable Peer-to-peer Lookup Service for Internet Applications. In: *Proc. of the ACM SIGCOMM Conf. on Applications, Technologies, Architectures, and Protocols for Computer Communication*, pp. 149–160, San Diego, CA, USA, August 2001.

STOICA, I., MORRIS, R., LIBEN-NOWELL, D., KARGER, D. R., KAASHOECK, M. F., DABEK, F., AND BALAKRISHNAN, H.: Chord: A Scalable Peer-to-Peer Lookup Protocol for Internet Applications. *IEEE/ACM Trans. on Networking (TON)*, 11(1):17–32, February 2003.

SU, H., JIAN, J., AND RUNDENSTEINER, E. A.: Raindrop: A Uniform and Layered Algebraic Framework for XQueries on XML Streams. In: *Proc. of the ACM Int'l Conf. on Information and Knowledge Management (CIKM)*, pp. 279–286, New Orleans, LA, USA, November 2003.

SULLIVAN, M. AND HEYBEY, A.: Tribeca: A System for Managing Large Databases of Network Traffic. In: *Proc. of the USENIX Annual Technical Conference*, pp. 13–24, New Orleans, LA, USA, June 1998.

SUN, X.-H., KAMEL, N., AND NI, L. M.: Solving Implication Problems in Database Applications. In: *Proc. of the ACM SIGMOD Int'l Conf. on Management of Data*, pp. 185–192, Portland, OR, USA, May 1989.

SZALAY, A. S., KUNSZT, P. Z., THAKAR, A., GRAY, J., SLUTZ, D., AND BRUNNER, R. J.: Designing and Mining Multi-Terabyte Astronomy Archives: The Sloan Digital Sky Survey. In: *Proc. of the ACM SIGMOD Int'l Conf. on Management of Data*, pp. 451–462, Dallas, TX, USA, May 2000.

TAO, Y., YIU, M. L., PAPADIAS, D., HADJIELEFTHERIOU, M., AND MAMOULIS, N.: RPJ: Producing Fast Join Results on Streams through Rate-based Optimization. In: *Proc. of the ACM SIGMOD Int'l Conf. on Management of Data*, pp. 371–382, Baltimore, MD, USA, June 2005.

TATARINOV, I. AND HALEVY, A.: Efficient Query Reformulation in Peer Data Management Systems. In: *Proc. of the ACM SIGMOD Int'l Conf. on Management of Data*, pp. 539–550, Paris, France, June 2004.

TATARINOV, I., IVES, Z., MADHAVAN, J., HALEVY, A., SUCIU, D., DALVI, N., DONG, X., KADIYSKA, Y., MIKLAU, G., AND MORK, P.: The Piazza Peer Data Management Project. *ACM SIGMOD Record*, 32(3):47–52, September 2003.

TERRY, D., GOLDBERG, D., NICHOLS, D., AND OKI, B.: Continuous Queries over Append-Only Databases. In: *Proc. of the ACM SIGMOD Int'l Conf. on Management of Data*, pp. 321–330, San Diego, CA, USA, June 1992.

THEODORATOS, D. AND SELLIS, T.: Data Warehouse Configuration. In: *Proc. of the Int'l Conf. on Very Large Data Bases (VLDB)*, pp. 126–135, Athens, Greece, August 1997.

THEODORATOS, D. AND SELLIS, T.: Dynamic Data Warehouse Design. In: *Proc. of the Int'l Conf. on Data Warehousing and Knowledge Discovery (DaWaK)*, pp. 1–10, Florence, Italy, August 1999.

TUECKE, S., CZAJKOWSKI, K., FOSTER, I., FREY, J., GRAHAM, S., KESSELMAN, C., MAGUIRE, T., SANDHOLM, T., SNELLING, D., AND VANDERBILT, P.: Open Grid Services Infrastructure (OGSI) Version 1.0. June 2003, http://www.globus.org/alliance/publications/papers/Final_OGSI_Specification_V1.0.pdf.

URHAN, T. AND FRANKLIN, M. J.: XJoin: A Reactively-Scheduled Pipelined Join Operator. *IEEE Data Engineering Bulletin*, 23(2):27–33, June 2000.

VAN DEN BERCKEN, J., BLOHSFELD, B., DITTRICH, J.-P., KRÄMER, J., SCHÄFER, T., SCHNEIDER, M., AND SEEGER, B.: XXL – A Library Approach to Supporting Efficient Implementations of Advanced Database Queries. In: *Proc. of the Int'l Conf. on Very Large Data Bases (VLDB)*, pp. 39–48, Roma, Italy, September 2001.

VIGLAS, S. D. AND NAUGHTON, J. F.: Rate-Based Query Optimization for Streaming Information Sources. In: *Proc. of the ACM SIGMOD Int'l Conf. on Management of Data*, pp. 37–48, Madison, WI, USA, June 2002.

VIGLAS, S. D., NAUGHTON, J. F., AND BURGER, J.: Maximizing the Output Rate of Multi-Way Join Queries over Streaming Information Sources. In: *Proc. of the Int'l Conf. on Very Large Data Bases (VLDB)*, pp. 285–296, Berlin, Germany, September 2003.

VOGES, W., ASCHENBACH, B., BOLLER, T., BRÄUNINGER, H., BRIEL, U., BURKERT, W., DENNERL, K., ENGLHAUSER, J., GRUBER, R., HABERL, F., HARTNER, G., HASINGER, G., KÜRSTER, M., PFEFFERMANN, E., PIETSCH, W., PREDEHL, P., ROSSO, C., SCHMITT, J. H. M. M., TRÜMPER, J., AND ZIMMERMANN, H. U.: The ROSAT All-Sky Survey Bright Source Catalogue. *Astronomy and Astrophysics*, 349(2):389–405, July 1999.

VÖLK, H.: Gamma-Astronomie mit abbildenden Cherenkov-Teleskopen – Erste Ergebnisse und Pläne für die Zukunft. *Sterne und Weltraum*, pp. 1064–1070, December 1999.

W3C: Extensible Markup Language (XML) 1.0 (Fourth Edition) (W3C Recommendation, August 16th, 2006, edited in place September 29th, 2006). September 2006a, http://www.w3.org/TR/xml/.

W3C: Extensible Markup Language (XML) 1.1 (Second Edition) (W3C Recommendation, August 16th, 2006, edited in place September 29th, 2006). September 2006b, http://www.w3.org/TR/xml11/.

W3C: SOAP Version 1.2 Part 1: Messaging Framework (Second Edition) (W3C Recommendation, April 27th, 2007). April 2007a, http://www.w3.org/TR/soap12-part1/.

W3C: XML Path Language (XPath) 2.0 (W3C Recommendation, January 23rd, 2007). January 2007b, http://www.w3.org/TR/xpath20/.

W3C: XML Syntax for XQuery 1.0 (XQueryX) (W3C Recommendation, January 23rd, 2007). January 2007c, http://www.w3.org/TR/xqueryx/.

W3C: XQuery 1.0: An XML Query Language (W3C Recommendation, January 23rd, 2007). January 2007d, http://www.w3.org/TR/xquery/.

W3C: XQuery 1.0 and XPath 2.0 Formal Semantics (W3C Recommendation, January 23rd, 2007). January 2007e, http://www.w3.org/TR/xquery-semantics/.

WANG, B., ZHANG, W., AND KITSUREGAWA, M.: UB-tree Based Efficient Predicate Index with Dimension Transform for Pub/Sub System. In: *Proc. of the Int'l Conf. on Database Systems for Advanced Applications (DASFAA)*, pp. 63–74, Jeju Island, Korea, March 2004.

WANG, S., RUNDENSTEINER, E., GANGULY, S., AND BHATNAGAR, S.: State-Slice: New Paradigm of Multi-query Optimization of Window-based Stream Queries. In: *Proc. of the Int'l Conf. on Very Large Data Bases (VLDB)*, pp. 619–630, Seoul, Korea, September 2006.

WIDOM, J. AND CERI, S. (eds.): *Active Database Systems – Triggers and Rules for Advanced Database Processing*. Morgan Kaufmann Publishers, 1996.

WILSCHUT, A. N. AND APERS, P. M. G.: Dataflow Query Execution in a Parallel Main-Memory Environment. In: *Proc. of the Int'l Conf. on Parallel and Distributed Information Systems (PDIS)*, pp. 68–77, Miami Beach, FL, USA, December 1991.

WU, E., DIAO, Y., AND RIZVI, S.: High-Performance Complex Event Processing over Streams. In: *Proc. of the ACM SIGMOD Int'l Conf. on Management of Data*, pp. 407–418, Chicago, IL, USA, June 2006.

WU, K.-L., CHEN, S.-K., AND YU, P. S.: VCR Indexing for Fast Event Matching for Highly-Overlapping Range Predicates. In: *ACM Symp. on Applied Computing (SAC)*, pp. 740–747, Nicosia, Cyprus, March 2004a.

WU, K.-L., CHEN, S.-K., YU, P. S., AND MEI, M.: Efficient Interval Indexing for Content-Based Subscription E-Commerce and E-Service. In: *Proc. of the IEEE Int'l Conf. on E-Commerce Technology for Dynamic E-Business (CEC)*, pp. 22–29, Beijing, China, September 2004b.

XU, W.: The Framework of an XML Semantic Caching System. In: *Proc. of the Int'l Workshop on the Web and Databases (WebDB)*, pp. 127–132, Baltimore, MD, USA, June 2005.

YANG, B. AND GARCIA-MOLINA, H.: Designing a Super-Peer Network. In: *Proc. of the IEEE Int'l Conf. on Data Engineering (ICDE)*, pp. 49–60, Bangalore, India, March 2003.

YANG, Y., KRÄMER, J., PAPADIAS, D., AND SEEGER, B.: HybMig: A Hybrid Approach to Dynamic Plan Migration for Continuous Queries. *IEEE Trans. on Knowledge and Data Engineering (TKDE)*, 19(3):398–411, March 2007.

YAO, Y. AND GEHRKE, J.: The Cougar Approach to In-Network Query Processing in Sensor Networks. *ACM SIGMOD Record*, 31(3):9–18, September 2002.

YAO, Y. AND GEHRKE, J.: Query Processing for Sensor Networks. In: *Proc. of the Conf. on Innovative Data Systems Research (CIDR)*, Asilomar, CA, USA, January 2003.

ZHANG, D., GUNOPULOS, D., TSOTRAS, V. J., AND SEEGER, B.: Temporal and spatio-temporal aggregations over data streams using multiple time granularities. *Information Systems*, 28(1–2):61–84, March 2003a.

ZHANG, R., KOUDAS, N., OOI, B. C., AND SRIVASTAVA, D.: Multiple Aggregations Over Data Streams. In: *Proc. of the ACM SIGMOD Int'l Conf. on Management of Data*, pp. 299–310, Baltimore, MD, USA, June 2005.

ZHANG, X., DIMITROVA, K., WANG, L., EL SAYED, M., MURPHY, B., PIELECH, B., MULCHANDANI, M., DING, L., AND RUNDENSTEINER, E. A.: Rainbow: Multi-XQuery Optimization Using Materialized XML Views. In: *Proc. of the ACM SIGMOD Int'l Conf. on Management of Data*, p. 671, San Diego, CA, USA, June 2003b.

ZHAO, B. Y., HUANG, L., STRIBLING, J., RHEA, S. C., JOSEPH, A. D., AND KUBIA-TOWICZ, J. D.: Tapestry: A Resilient Global-Scale Overlay for Service Deployment. *IEEE Journal on Selected Areas in Communications (JSAC)*, 22(1):41–53, January 2004.

ZHOU, J., LARSON, P.-A., FREYTAG, J.-C., AND LEHNER, W.: Efficient Exploitation of Similar Subexpressions for Query Processing. In: *Proc. of the ACM SIGMOD Int'l Conf. on Management of Data*, pp. 533–544, Beijing, China, June 2007.

ZHU, Y., RUNDENSTEINER, E. A., AND HEINEMAN, G. T.: Dynamic Plan Migration for Continuous Queries Over Data Streams. In: *Proc. of the ACM SIGMOD Int'l Conf. on Management of Data*, pp. 431–442, Paris, France, June 2004.

VDM

Verlag
Dr. Müller

Wissenschaftlicher Buchverlag bietet

kostenfreie

Publikation

von

wissenschaftlichen Arbeiten

Diplomarbeiten, Magisterarbeiten, Master und Bachelor Theses
sowie Dissertationen, Habilitationen und wissenschaftliche Monographien

Sie verfügen über eine wissenschaftliche Abschlußarbeit zu aktuellen oder zeitlosen
Fragestellungen, die hohen inhaltlichen und formalen Ansprüchen genügt,
und haben **Interesse an einer honorarvergüteten Publikation**?

Dann senden Sie bitte erste Informationen über Ihre Arbeit per Email
an info@vdm-verlag.de. Unser Außenlektorat meldet sich umgehend bei Ihnen.

VDM Verlag Dr. Müller Aktiengesellschaft & Co. KG
Dudweiler Landstraße 125a
D - 66123 Saarbrücken

www.vdm-verlag.de